WOODY ON RYE

BRANDEIS SERIES IN AMERICAN JEWISH HISTORY, CULTURE, AND LIFE
Jonathan D. Sarna, Editor ~ Sylvia Barack Fishman, Associate Editor

For a complete list of books that are available in the series, visit www.upne.com

Vincent Brook and
Marat Grinberg, editors
Woody on Rye: Jewishness in the Films and Plays of Woody Allen

Mark Cohen
Overweight Sensation: The Life and Comedy of Allan Sherman

David E. Kaufman
Jewhooing the Sixties: American Celebrity and Jewish Identity — Sandy Koufax, Lenny Bruce, Bob Dylan, and Barbra Streisand

Jack Wertheimer, editor
The New Jewish Leaders: Reshaping the American Jewish Landscape

Eitan P. Fishbane and
Jonathan D. Sarna, editors
Jewish Renaissance and Revival in America

Jonathan B. Krasner
The Benderly Boys and American Jewish Education

Derek Rubin, editor
Promised Lands: New Jewish American Fiction on Longing and Belonging

Susan G. Solomon
Louis I. Kahn's Jewish Architecture: Mikveh Israel and the Midcentury American Synagogue

Amy Neustein, editor
Tempest in the Temple: Jewish Communities and Child Sex Scandals

Jack Wertheimer, editor
Learning and Community: Jewish Supplementary Schools in the Twenty-first Century

Carole S. Kessner
Marie Syrkin: Values Beyond the Self

Leonard Saxe and Barry Chazan
Ten Days of Birthright Israel: A Journey in Young Adult Identity

Jack Wertheimer, editor
Imagining the American Jewish Community

Murray Zimiles
Gilded Lions and Jeweled Horses: The Synagogue to the Carousel

Marianne R. Sanua
Be of Good Courage: The American Jewish Committee, 1945–2006

Hollace Ava Weiner and Kenneth D. Roseman, editors
Lone Stars of David: The Jews of Texas

Jack Wertheimer, editor
Jewish Education in an Age of Choice

Edward S. Shapiro
Crown Heights: Blacks, Jews, and the 1991 Brooklyn Riot

EDITED BY

VINCENT BROOK AND

MARAT GRINBERG

Brandeis University Press—Waltham, Massachusetts

Woody on Rye

JEWISHNESS
IN THE FILMS
AND PLAYS
OF WOODY ALLEN

Brandeis University Press
An imprint of University Press of New England
www.upne.com
© 2014 Brandeis University
All rights reserved
Manufactured in the United States of America
Designed and typeset by Mindy Basinger Hill
Typeset in Arno Pro

University Press of New England is a member of the
Green Press Initiative. The paper used in this book meets their
minimum requirement for recycled paper.

For permission to reproduce any of the material in this book,
contact Permissions, University Press of New England, One Court
Street, Suite 250, Lebanon NH 03766; or visit www.upne.com.

Library of Congress Cataloging-in-Publication Data

Woody on rye : Jewishness in the films and plays of Woody Allen /
edited by Vincent Brook and Marat Grinberg.
       pages   cm. — (Brandeis series in American Jewish history, culture, and life)
ISBN 978–1–61168–479–7 (cloth : alk. paper) —
ISBN 978–1–61168–480–3 (pbk. : alk. paper) —
ISBN 978–1–61168–481–0 (ebook)
1. Allen, Woody—Criticism and interpretation.
2. Jews in popular culture—United States.
3. Popular culture—Religious aspects—Judaism.
I. Brook, Vincent, 1946– editor of compilation.
II. Grinberg, Marat, 1977– editor of compilation.

PN1998.3. A45W76 2013
791.43092—dc23   2013017426

5   4   3   2   1

CONTENTS

Introduction— *Vincent Brook and Marat Grinberg*   ix

OVERVIEW

The Gospel According to Woody: From *Annie Hall* through *To Rome with Love*— *Vincent Brook*   3

COMPARATIVE ANALYSIS

The Birth of a Hebrew Tragedy: *Cassandra's Dream* as a Morality Play in the Context of *Crimes and Misdemeanors* and *Match Point*— *Marat Grinberg*   37

A Jew Leaves New York: Woody Allen's Gloomy British Angst— *Curtis Maloley*   58

SCHLEMIEL THEORY

Woody Allen's Schlemiel: From Humble Beginnings to an Abrupt End— *Menachem Feuer*   79

"Woody the Gentile": Christian-Jewish Interplay in Allen's Films from *What's New Pussycat?* to *Midnight in Paris*— *Joshua Louis Moss*   100

"Now You See Him, Now You Don't": Woody Allen's Vanishing Act in *Scoop*— *Peter J. Bailey*   122

WOMEN'S ISSUES

Woody's Women: Jewish Domesticity and the Unredeemed Ghost of Hanukkah to Come— *Giovanna P. Del Negro*   143

Reconstructing Woody: Representations of Religious Jewish Women in *Deconstructing Harry*— *Shaina Hammerman*   171

"Toot, Toot, Tootsie! (Goodbye)": Disposable Women in the Films of Woody Allen— *Elliot Shapiro*   190

CULTURAL STUDIES

Digesting Woody: Food and Foodways in the Movies of Woody Allen— *Nathan Abrams*   215

Schlemiel on Broadway: Woody Allen's Jewish Identity in His Stage Plays from *Don't Drink the Water* to *Honeymoon Motel*— *James Fisher*   235

Woody Allen: Filmography   259
Woody Allen: Play List   261
List of Contributors   263
Index   267

Woody Allen Retires [along with the Pope].
Two World Religions Now Leaderless!
—*Jewish Journal*, 2013 Purim issue headline[1]

VINCENT BROOK

AND MARAT GRINBERG

Introduction

"You don't have to be Jewish to appreciate Woody Allen, but it helps." Thus quipped Foster Hirsch in the "Jewish Connection" chapter of his 1981 study of Allen's films, *Love, Sex, Death, and the Meaning of Life*.[2] As the title of this book proposes, Hirsch's one-liner — if expanded to the Jewish*ness* of Allen's oeuvre and extended to the present — still holds. Curiously, however, few scholars have taken up the "Jewish question" in the three decades since Hirsch first broached it, even fewer since the major fissure in Allen's career caused by the Mia Farrow/Soon-Yi Previn scandal of 1992/93. Jeffrey Rubin-Dorsky's article "Woody Allen after the Fall: Literary Gold from Amoral Alchemy" (2003), which touches on Jewish issues and whose title foregrounds the scandal's significance, is a notable exception.[3] Yet Rubin-Dorsky's analysis ends with *Deconstructing Harry* (1997), thus leaving Jewishness in Allen's overall body of work, especially his more recent efforts, still largely unexplored.

Hirsch himself, in subsequent updates of *Love, Sex, Death, and the Meaning of Life* in 1990 and 2001, has left his original "Jewish Connection" chapter unchanged. Mashey Bernstein's 1996 essay "My Worst Fears Realized: Woody Allen and the Holocaust," in an exhaustive list of Holocaust references in Allen's films, similarly stops at 1992's *Shadows and Fog*.[4] Ruth B. Johnston's "Joke Work: The Construction of Postmodern Jewish Identity in Contemporary Theory and American Film" (2003) retreats to *Annie Hall* (1977) as the fulcrum for her psychoanalytic study of Allen's Jewish-inflected humor.[5] Charles L. P. Silet's 2006 anthology, *The Films of Woody Allen: Critical Essays*, contains three entries (out of twenty-four) dealing with Allen's Jewishness: Sanford Pinsker's "Woody Allen's Lovable Anxious

Schlemiels," Mark Bleiweiss's "Self-Deprecation and the Jewish Humor of Woody Allen," and Iris Bruce's "Mysterious Illnesses of Human Commodities in Woody Allen and Franz Kafka: *Zelig*." Yet all three fail to expand the discussion into the postscandal period; indeed, no mention is made of the scandal in the entire anthology, much less of its possible impact on Allen's work.[6] Even the latest entry in the fray, a 2012 issue of *Post Script* devoted exclusively to Allen's post-1990 output, has only one Jewish-themed article — Toni-Lynn Frederick's "Eleventh Jew: Humor and the Holocaust in Woody Allen's *Anything Else*" — that tiptoes into the post-2000 period.[7] The curious reluctance to more fully examine Jewishness in Allen's "complete works" is highlighted in Vittorio Hösle's *Woody Allen: An Essay on the Nature of the Comical* (2007). In an eighty-seven-page disquisition that manages to tie Allen to Aristophanes, Hegel, Schopenhauer, Bergson, Cervantes, Dostoevsky, and Tolstoy, among others, Hösle waits for the final paragraph to submit that "Allen's comic universe" owes something to his "Jewish form of intellectuality."[8]

This puts serious investigation of Jewishness in Allen's pre- and postscandal output about where it was in 1993. In addition to Hirsch's chapter and the aforementioned essays, this includes the following: Gerald Mast's "Woody Allen: The Neurotic Jew as American Clown" (1987); Richard Feldstein's "Displaced Feminine Representation in Woody Allen's Cinema" (1989); Richard Freadman's "Love among the Stereotypes, or Why Woody's Women Leave" (1993); Sam B. Girgus's "Philip Roth and Woody Allen: Freud and the Humor of the Repressed" (1993); the lengthy Allen section in David Desser and Lester Friedman's *American-Jewish Filmmakers* (1993); and Thomas Kinne's German dissertation *Elemente jüdischer Tradition im Werk Woody Allens* (Traditional Jewish elements in Woody Allen's work; also 1993).

The lack of a more all-inclusive discussion of Jewishness in Allen's work has not gone unnoticed. Danielle Berrin, in a review of a 2011 PBS documentary on Allen's career, found it curious that for all the "Jewish men involved with the project [director Robert Weide, executive producer Bret Ratner, and financier Fisher Williams], there is little in the film that deals with Allen's Jewish identity. And given that it's a recurrent theme in his work, both in subtle and not-so-subtle ways, the disregard feels like a gap."[9] One gap, in particular, that pleads to be filled, from a postscandal perspective especially, is Allen's "treatment" of women — Jewish and non-Jewish, on-screen and off. One section of *Woody on Rye* is thus devoted to women's issues in Allen's body of work. And on the "women's question," as on the Jewish question, Hirsch provides a lead-in.

"What, again?" a friend questioned his updated coverage of Allen's films in 2001. "Why do you want to write about that pathetic creep?" another friend complained, while a third "made an unprintable comment." All three anti-Allenites were women, from which a male friend extrapolated, "Women can't forgive him [for the Previn affair], guys can."[10] A 2012 *Newsweek* article concurred: "Most shocked of all [about the scandal] were Allen's legions of female fans," who felt betrayed by the quasi-incestuous action and insulted by the mangled Pascalian excuse: "The heart wants what it wants."[11] Allen apologists include documentary director Weide, who, in the PBS film on Allen, glossed over the scandal, showing himself, in Berrin's words, "to be a fan, his film 'a public thank you' to an artist he has long admired."[12] Hirsch himself, beyond his book's introductory disclaimer, eschews probing the postscandal gendered skew, admitting instead to a "strong identification" with Allen as a Jewish Manhattanite and to continuing admiration of "his wit and wisdom."[13]

Talking Points

Allen's sexual problematic in general — his "most popular theme" — Hirsch deconstructs at length.[14] The "conflict between Jew and gentile ... between the aspirations of the intellect and the desires of the body" culminates in a "shiksa complex."[15] With the exception of Julie Kavner's Treva in Allen's short film "Oedipus Wrecks" (one-third of the 1989 anthology feature *New York Stories*), his self-portrayed protagonists are invariably drawn to WASP goddesses, "whose pretty blond blandness represents both forbidden fruit and the incarnation of the American dream."[16] The relationships inevitably run aground, not due to ethnocultural incompatibility, however, but because of a "strong adolescent streak" that, on the one hand, "turns women into objects and appendages, and on the other ... tends to attract women of the smothering kind."[17] A Jewish element is thus reintroduced, compensating for the "straying from the fold" by transferring traits of the Jewish "(m)Other" onto the gentile object of desire, and by a form of *tik-*

kun olam (repairing the world) whereby the learned, cultured Jewish male "upgrade[s] the inarticulate, intellectually raw shiksa."[18] Ultimately, Allen's "troubles with women," Hirsch concludes, "are all attributes then of his inveterate Jewishness."[19]

Richard Freadman adds a "Pygmalion-like twist" to Allen's shiksa complex.[20] Allen's stand-ins may desire the non-Jewish female because her cultural Otherness "promises release from Jewish stereotypes of woman, be they maternal or matrimonial"; because she "symbolizes assimilation in mainstream American culture"; or because she "represents a kind of 'conquest' of the dominant culture that has kept the Jews at the margins." However, his alienation from and resentment toward the very "characteristics that constitute the Otherness of the Beloved" ultimately subvert her "shiks appeal."[21] Moreover, his attempt to resolve the conflict by "raising" the provincial WASP to his Jewish intellectual's standards only makes matters worse. By remaking the gentile into the Jew, the Woody character undoes, on the one hand, the very basis of her attraction; on the other hand, her newly endowed cultivation and sophistication makes him, from both her lofty Galatean and his "Jewish auto-antipathetic" perspective, inadequate.[22]

A corollary of the shiksa complex and, for Hirsch, the "central link" to Jewishness in Allen's (prescandal) work is Ruth Wisse's concept of "the schlemiel as [modern] hero."[23] This figure, along with "an ironic sense of self and the world" and "a joy in language," derives, in its twentieth-century guise from the Jewish American literary and comic tradition.[24] I. B. Singer's Gimpel the Fool, Saul Bellow's Herzog, Bernard Malamud's Fidelman, Philip Roth's Alexander Portnoy, and Joseph Heller's Yossarian provided a modern-day template for the "outsider and victim, the butt of jokes both local and cosmic, . . . who turn[s] out to have wisdom and endurance" — to which Allen contributed unique identification of the neo-schlemiel with his own neurotic Jew York persona.[25] From the borscht belt stand-ups (Milton Berle, Shecky Green, Mort Sahl, et al.) came a predilection for protagonists who are "wonderful performers who treat their lives as theater," and a narrative propensity for "comic sketches," "extended monologues," and "bawdy, revved-up, self-consciously clever outpourings."[26] Drawing on both the writers and comics, Allen's "divided, contradictory hero" is torn between Old World and New, between "the religious and social tradition in which he has been raised."[27] The ghost of European Jewish mysticism and the supernatural, à la "the paintings of Chagall and the parables of Kafka," hovers as well. From the dialectical "distrust of faith on the one hand and of 'pure' intellect on the other" arises a quest for "some acceptable way for modern neurotic man to mingle with Chagall's angels."[28] As for Allen's alleged (by some Jewish critics) Jewish self-hatred, Hirsch sees his "ethnic hostility" (the barbs at bearded rabbis and religious observance, not to mention public criticism of Israel) not "as a flight from Jewish tradition" but rather "as a passionate engagement" and "ongoing dialogue with Jewishness as a state of mind and a way of life."[29] Allen's own Kafkaesque rejoinder, "while it's true I am Jewish and I don't like myself very much, it's not because of my persuasion," affirms Hirsch's dialogical interpretation.[30]

Bleiweiss, as his essay title indicates, grounds Allen's Jewish humor in its self-deprecatory aspect. As outlined in Freud's *Jokes and Their Relation to the Unconscious*, and variously reinterpreted by subsequent theorists, self-deprecation can be deployed as a defense mechanism: laughing to keep from crying.[31] It can serve a preemptive function: Jews pointing out their flaws before others have the chance to do so. It can offer "escape from the tragic realities of Jewish life rather than as a justification for retaining flaws."[32] Its masochistic aspect arguably "has been essential to Jewish survival in the Diaspora over the last two millennia."[33] And "without being threatening or humiliating," it has permitted Jews "to deal honestly and openly with problems."[34] In two contradictory views especially pertinent to Allen, Dan Ben-Amos believes that Jewish comics, through a fictive persona, manage to distance themselves from the object of their denigration; while Stanley Brandes and Kurt Schlesinger claim that, to be effective, the Jewish comic cannot wholly deny affiliation with the mocked group. Heda Jason argues that self-mockery did not exist "until after Jews left the sheltered ghetto community," that it emerged from a "feeling of cultural ambiguity," and that the drive toward assimilation yet residual guilt associated with it nudges self-deprecation toward self-hatred — a charge consistently leveled at Jewish comedians, including Allen.[35] Not to worry, Salcia Landmann predicts, positing in Jews' increased assimilation, an end to Jewish humor altogether, "because Jewish humorists will soon have nothing new to mock."[36] Not so fast, Bernard Rosenberg and Gilbert Shapiro strenuously counter, perceiving a new Jewish humor in a "new dilemma for second- and third-generation American Jews. 'Where we previously hated ourselves for being Jews, we now frequently hate ourselves for not being Jews.'"[37]

Gerald Mast makes the historical case for Allen as "the first great American film-clown for whom being Jewish was not simply a hereditary accident but a way of life."[38] The Marx Brothers' anarchic irrationality and personae, Mast grants, "grew from Jewish roots in burlesque — in the turn-of-the-century 'Dutch' acts of Joe Weber and Lew Fields or the Howard Brothers, when 'Dutch' was a euphemism for *Deutsch*, and *Deutsch* was a euphemism for Yiddish."[39] Mel Brooks's 1970s film parodies, which emerged concurrently with Allen's early film successes, "represent a second generation disguise that sprang from the same [Marx Brothers/Weber and Fields] roots."[40] And Jerry Lewis, who might otherwise have superseded Allen's primacy as an explicitly Jewish clown, as he "rose from Borscht Belt nightclubs" to teaming with the "smooth *goy*" Dean Martin and starring in his own comedies, "came more and more to embody the unspecified genus of *shleppus Americanus*."[41]

Such de-Judaization had become commonplace, if not obligatory, ever since Hollywood's so-called Great Retreat from Jewish representation, in the face of rising anti-Semitism, in the 1930s.[42] Eddie Cantor's once strongly marked cinematic Jewishness declined in the 1930s, until by *Strike Me Pink* (1936) he "is still small, weak, cowardly, and clumsy, but not at all Jewish."[43] The 1940s Jewish comedy star Danny Kaye (ne Daniel Kaminsky) would never make the transition, cast from the start as a comic klutz "without any suggestion that the klutz might be Jewish."[44] George Burns (ne Nathan Birnbaum) and Jack Benny (ne Benjamin Kubelsky) remained similarly ethnically dissimulate throughout their careers. Allen, though he also changed his name (from Allan Stewart Konigsberg), broke the mold of the goyface Jewish comic; moreover, his persona, contrary to Cantor's and Lewis's, grew increasingly Jewish over time. From characters in *Take the Money and Run* (1969), *Bananas* (1971), and *Love and Death* (1975) "whose traits and names were clearly parodic but not particularly Jewish," his Miles Monroe in *Sleeper* (1973) and Alvy Singer in *Annie Hall* (1977) are Jewish beyond a reasonable doubt. The films as well develop from burlesque parody to "psychocomedy," set in Jew York City, featuring a neurotic, liberal intellectual "incapable of action, of *doing* anything," and "exploring the differences between the Jewish Allen characters and the *goyim* who become his lovers and friends."[45]

Desser and Friedman expand the conceptualization of Jewishness in Allen's work, identifying "three major traditions of Jewish art and expression . . . humor, social justice, and life-style changes," all subsumed, in governing structure or formal pattern, in the bildungsroman (educational novel).[46] Derived, as its German etymology suggests, from European high culture, the bildungsroman, in its Jewish American incarnation, thematically emphasizes "an urban setting and a marginal identity" and historically divides into three phases.[47] The first, stemming from the Eastern European immigrant waves of the late nineteenth and early twentieth centuries, confronted the wrenching adjustment from insular shtetl life to that of the bustling American metropolis. In the second, post–World War II phase, assimilated American interests came to outweigh residual Jewish concerns; artists and intellectuals of this generation, per literary critic Ted Solotoroff, stood at the end of "the Diaspora mentality," seeming "less marginally American than marginally Jewish."[48] The third phase, beginning in the mid-1960s, when Allen was starting his filmmaking career, was marked by a revived orientation toward Jewish (rather than American) issues, such as Israel and the Holocaust. This phase, however, while gaining sustenance from the ethnic pride and identity politics movements, was also undermined by Jews' increased absorption into the American mainstream. In problematizing the "comfortable concept of marginality," assimilation hampered access to the multiculture and generated new internal tensions: "between spiritual and secular being," in "relations to Israel," and in identification as both Americans and Jews. For Jewish American artists, these tensions bore creative fruit in reconnecting them "once again to the Diaspora and to the condition of radical doubt" — aspects that, however couched in universalist terms, are patently evident in Allen's work.[49]

Kinne's dissertation, befitting a study devoted exclusively to Jewish elements in Allen's oeuvre, offers the most extensive treatment to date of the writer-director-actor's Jewish influences. Starting with the Judaic ur-texts, Kinne counters the Talmudic injunction "All that is not levity is Torah" with Dov Lang's assessment of the Scriptures as possessing "a humor of irony," of "another way of telling the truth, of putting matters right."[50] More specifically in relation to Allen, Kinne cites Theodor Reik, who sees in Allen's Jewish jokes "a continuation of the ancient Wisdom-literature of Judaism," and Alan Spiegel, who regards Allen's persona in *Annie Hall* and

Stardust Memories (1980) as resembling the biblical Joseph, who "is perhaps the most porous and elusive of the traditional prototypes ... of the artist figure or the Jewish intellectual encircled by hostile opponents," and who in his modern guise succumbs to neurosis, paranoia, and narcissism.[51] The Talmud's privileging of discussion, rumination, and verbal dispute over action clearly fits Allen's Jewish protagonists to a tee. Taken to an extreme, as in the Chelm Fools — "those harebrained sages so consumed with their wrongheaded thought processes that they totally lost touch with mundane reality" — Jewish hyperintellectualizing provides meta-Talmudic fodder for Allen's satirical humor.[52] As Boris (Allen) states in *Love and Death*, "The trouble with intellectuals is, they always see both sides of every issue — when it comes to action they're impotent."

Jumping to the postemancipation era, Kinne preempts Allen's Jewish American antecedents, as cited by Hirsch (and others), with their European precursors — Heinrich Heine in particular. The first German author of humor and jokes, Heine can also be considered, per Stephen Whitfield, a proto-stand-up comic, through his invention (along with nineteenth-century physician and journalist Ludwig Börne) of the feuilleton: "the casual humorous monologue, in which a few Jews have excelled down through the Viennese café wits to Perelman and Allen."[53] Heine was also a pioneer of "city humor" and of another of Allen's staples, the "contrast joke," or the juxtaposition of the sacred and profane.[54] Like Allen, he was opposed to blind faith and organized religion, including Judaism but, despite his "conversion of convenience," remained proudly Jewish conscious. Art, for Heine as for Allen, was the closest thing to religion, and the artist was a quasi-transcendent being.[55] Most resonant with Allen's work, according to Salomon Seigbert Prawer, "Heine's writings ... convey the full gamut of responses to the Jewish situation: ... opposition to anti-Jewish attitudes, attempts at synthesis of traditional Jewish culture and the culture of the Gentile groups and societies, ... neurotic over-reactions of various kinds, living in 'masks' and camouflage, interiorization of the enemy's charges, ... making up and telling 'Jewish jokes.'"[56]

Prefiguring Kafka, whose strong influence Hirsch (among others) emphasizes and Allen openly cites in his work, Heine posited the "emancipated" Jewish predicament, with its sense of alienation, loneliness, and restlessness, as symbolic of society in general; and the Diasporic

Jew, with his fears and inability to fit in, as the modern-day Everyman.[57] As for Kafka specifically, Allen, by way of parodic homage, cribbed Kafka's collected works in *Shadows and Fog* (1992) — his "most Jewish movie" — and analogized Kafka's conformism neurosis in *Zelig* (1983), whose "Chameleon Man" additionally draws on Kafka's use of animals "as images for aspects of humanity."[58]

The other major European literary figure Kinne connects to Allen is Austrian playwright Arthur Schnitzler. The connection here is mainly psychoanalytic, via Schnitzler's Viennese Jewish compatriot Sigmund Freud's emphasis on drives and desire, dreams and the unconscious, and the death wish — for which, per Allen, we need look no further than *Love and Death*. Also like Allen, Schnitzler saw the artist as a (Jewish) doppelganger, a middleman between reality and illusion, a liaison between death and the joy of life.[59] Schnitzler's rejection of the movies for their crass commercialism, yet recognition of their potential for mining the dialectic of dreams and reality, likewise corresponds, mutatis mutandis, to Marvin Mudrick's view of Allen's cultural project as "like setting up a wailing wall in a supermarket."[60]

Among Allen's creative American kin, Kinne singles out Saul Bellow, whose Old/New World dialectic, especially in the figure of Herzog, aligns him most closely to Allen. The chief Bellow/Herzog intersections with Allen include a rejection of Orthodox Judaism but not of shtetl culture's *Menschlichkeit* (Heine's *Vernunft*, or decency) and *rachmones* (compassion); reverence for European high culture and aversion to American philistinism; ambivalent yet resigned acknowledgment of being a Jewish *American* rather than an American *Jew*; "animosity toward the Gentile along with envy of the Wasp"; and persistent, if not overdetermined, identification with the Holocaust and survival guilt.[61] The recurring role of the Holocaust in Allen's work has frequently been cited. Mashey Bernstein deems it his "most consistent, ongoing referent," "the defining moment of his identity," and the greatest "spur to his discontent."[62] Kinne adds Bruno Bettelheim's notion of the Shoah as a metaphor for the "extreme situation," in which "immediate death is possible and likely, although we feel our time is not yet ripe."[63] Indeed, Allen has Bettelheim, in a talking-head cameo as "himself," refer to the eponymous Zelig (Allen), who in one of his uncanny transformations "becomes" a Nazi, as "the ultimate conformist" suffering from "a minor malady almost every one suffers from — carried to an extreme."

Bellow and Allen similarly grapple with the Jewish scriptural and existential challenge of reconciling head and heart, and fear of death with the urge to joy. Just as Bellow has been called "a secular hasid, whether he knows it or not," Allen's writer Harry Block, in *Deconstructing Harry*, is told that he's really happy but just doesn't know it.[64] They both also pointedly reject Hemingway's tough-guy ethos, and no character, except perhaps Judah in *Crimes and Misdemeanors*, is "radically existentialist" in the atheistic sense of Camus.[65] Nor do existentialism's Christian forerunners Schopenhauer, Kierkegaard, or Nietzsche curry Bellow's or Allen's favor. Bellow castigates Kierkegaard for his sense of doom, "that we are waiting for the end," and Nietzsche for his "Christian view of history, seeing the present always as some crisis, some fall from classical greatness, some corruption or evil to be saved from."[66] Allen, somewhat more ambivalently, chooses a gentile psychotic, for whom he retains an erotic attraction, as a Schopenhauer speed-reader in *Stardust Memories*.

Duly acknowledging, and denouncing, life's absurdities and horrors, the Torah's "chose life, so that ye shall live" is Bellow's and Allen's motto — though Talmudic caveats remain. "Total explanations are a delusion, the desire to see everything in terms of simple antitheses a sign of paranoia," Bellow writes. "Reality eludes the visions we make of it . . . and transcends them. . . . We must accept the mixture [of life] as we find it — the impurity of it, the tragedy of it, the hope of it."[67] Or as Allen has Gertrude Stein pithily remark in *Midnight in Paris* (2011), "The job of art is not to succumb to despair but to find an antidote for the emptiness of existence." Last not least, in their writing *styles*, Bellow and Allen (as many of their Jewish American compatriots) were "deeply influenced by Yiddish," from its rhythms and intonations to "the very specific qualities of repetition, question, inversion, allusion, and inflection — giving to a populace starved by the dry Hemingway manner a strongly human voice."[68]

Philip Roth's voice, most definitively in the character of Alexander Portnoy, echoes Herzog's intonations while putting a heavier accent on the Jewish mother and shiksa complexes. Whereas Bellow, Roth, and Allen all ascribe to Arthur Hertzberg's notion that the "religion of the father was destroyed in America, but it was replaced by the religion of the mother," for Roth and Allen especially, the nurturing *Yiddishe momme* has been replaced, post–World War II, by the devouring Jewish mother and Jewish American princess, as well as the Talmud and existentialism by Freud.[69] Yiddish speech patterns, meanwhile, as Portnoy points out, though perhaps of benefit to the Jewish American *writer*, pose a problem for the Jewish American parvenu: "They will hear the *oy* at the end, and the jig will be up."[70] Nor will name changing do the trick. When Allen's Howard Prince in *The Front* (Martin Ritt, 1976) tells blacklisted comic Hecky Brown (played by the actually ex-blacklisted Zero Mostel), "There's nothing wrong with changing your name — it's not a crime," this may provide momentary emotional comfort. But the House Un-American Activities Committee (HUAC) knows better, later demanding of Prince (following Brown's suicide): "Did you know Hecky Brown, also known as Herschell *Brownstein*?!"

Roth's fictive psychiatrist sessions rhyme with Allen's in their resemblance to comedy routines, and both artists admit to being students of the Jewish vaudeville and Catskill comics. Allen's *Broadway Danny Rose* (1984) is a love letter to the borscht belt stand-ups, while Roth resurrects Kafka in his riff on the Jewish comedy tradition: "I would say I was more strongly influenced by a sit-down comic named Franz Kafka and a very funny bit he does called 'The Metamorphosis.' Interestingly, the only time Lenny Bruce and I ever met . . . it occurred to me that he was just about ripe for the role of Joseph K."[71]

Freud rather than Kafka, however, is Roth's and Allen's strongest comedic bond, achieving "its most exuberant expression" in the shiksa complex. "Humor operates in their works as a means for structuring latent meaning," Sam Girgus psychoanalyzes, particularly in defining ethnicity, sexuality, and gender. "In Roth and Allen, women exist on a sea of latent anxiety as targets of fear, aggression, and hostility; but women also serve as vehicles for learning, growth, and humanization." Adding another layer of ambivalence to Freadman's Pygmalion-like twist, Roth's and Allen's gentile love interests, while forcing their Jewish suitors "to face themselves and to grow . . . are even better pupils of how to live, leaving their male mentors behind in a morass of confused emotions."[72]

In their conflations of creator and character — Roth via his Zuckerman alter ego and Allen via his various Jew York schlemiels — both artists have emphasized their understanding of "self" in relation to their fictionalized worlds.[73] Roth's and Allen's resemblance to *each other* is hinted at in *Husbands and Wives* (in which Allen's writer character is called Gabe Roth) and highlighted in *Deconstructing Harry* (for whose eponymous, "Jewishly challenged writer," played by Allen, Roth purportedly provided the model).[74] Roth-Allen rhyming verges on outright imitation, on Allen's part, in the uncanny matches between *Portnoy's Complaint* (1969) and the shooting script of *Annie Hall*. Girgus indicated as much: "*Portnoy* anticipates Woody Allen's major films, especially the so-called breakthrough movie, *Annie Hall*"; "it is hard to imagine the triumphant popular reception of Woody Allen's movies without the success of Roth's initial assault and landing"; and "Portnoy's visit to the Campbells [his beloved Mary Jane's family] perfectly predicts Alvy's reaction to ... Annie Hall's family."[75] Kinne connects the dots:

> Alex Portnoy: "I ... beg forgiveness for my sin (which is what again?)."
> Annie Hall's mother: "What sins? I don't understand"; Alvy Singer's (Allen) father: "Neither do we."
> Alex defends the black cleaning lady against his mother. Alvy's father defends the black cleaning lady against his wife.
> Alex orders a list of books for Mary Jane to read. Alvy buys books for Annie to read.
> Mary Jane calls Alex "Max." Rob (a friend) calls Alvy "Max."
> Alex compares the Campbells to a Norman Rockwell painting. Alvy compares the Halls to a Norman Rockwell painting.
> Alex is invited to Thanksgiving dinner at the Campbells in Iowa. Alvy is invited to Easter dinner (Thanksgiving, in an earlier version of the script) at the Halls in Wisconsin.[76]

Among Allen's (admitted) Jewish American stage- and screenwriting mentors, Kinne highlights George S. Kaufman, for his witty repartee and wisecracks, and preeminently, S. J. Perelman and Robert Benchley.[77] *New Yorker* editor Roger Angell, for example, found Perelman's imprint in Allen's submissions to the magazine "recognizable in almost everything he wrote for us in the early years. I told him, 'Look, we already have one Perelman.'"[78] Allen's notorious antipathy toward Los Angeles and Hollywood, though hardly uncommon among New York intellectuals, hews to Perelman's deeming LA "the most barbarous of all [cities]" and Tinseltown "an unalloyed horror; ... viewed in full sunlight, its tawdriness is unspeakable."[79] Perelman and Benchley's combined influence extended beyond their comic writing style to the characters they created: Benchley's schlemielish Little Man "who doggedly fights the real world in spite of unrelieved failure," and Perelman's Walter Mitty-ish protagonist who is "propelled into his world of fantasy."[80]

Kinne's unqualified comparison of Allen with Arthur Miller — in regard to their alleged shared sense of personal integrity and social responsibility — is of course highly ironic, and pardonable, in light of the dissertation's prescandal publication. Pauline Kael's calling Allen, in a 1989 review of *Crimes and Misdemeanors*, "a clone of Arthur Miller" must also be taken with a prescandal pinch of salt.[81] The Allen-Miller analogies are also telling, however, in regard to the radical shift in Allen's personal and creative reputation in the wake of the Farrow/Previn scandal. "Allen's films from the late seventies through the eighties were acclaimed," Rubin-Dorsky avers, precisely for their "morality."[82] Allen's postscandal "denial that his actions created any moral dilemma at all" only highlighted the disconnect, coming as it did from someone, Samuel Dresner complained, "whose purpose was never just to entertain but to pass judgment, to moralize, to instruct the present angst-ridden generation that has revered him as a guru."[83] Allen's subsequent fall from grace, in other words, can be attributed as much to his prescandal esteem as to the ethical implications of his affair with his nineteen-year-old (and thirty-seven-year younger) de facto stepdaughter.[84]

Not that everyone, even prescandal, was enamored of Allen's "treatment" of women. Richard Feldstein, in a scathing feminist analysis of Allen's films in 1989, gave clear signs of the firestorm to come. Countering then still common celebrations of Allen as a "man who loves and understands women" and "who is sensitive to the needs and desires of women," Feldstein found that women, as a rule in Allen's work, "became specular icons in a circuit of desire that repeatedly shifted its focus to the modern-day schlemiel.... Then as now, Allen's female protagonists have been staged as scopophilic objects-to-be-looked-at while the schlemiel/protagonist has remained the visual, aural, and narrative center of attention." Allen only "grudgingly allows women agency in the narrative production," Feldstein charged. "Narcissistic recuperation invariably displaces feminine representation." In *Zelig*, for example, Allen's chronic shape-shifter becomes like all the people with whom he comes in contact, except women. And even in his first "serious," woman-centered film, *Interiors* (1978), the female characters are but "thinly veiled replicas of Allen." Most tellingly, from a postscandal perspective, the "misogynistic depictions" in a scene in *What's Up, Tiger Lily?* (1966) — in which Allen eats an apple while Asian American *Playboy* centerfold China Lee strips — exemplify "a gastronomical equation between food and sexuality" that couples "oral needs" with "sexual aggression" toward the "fetishized object of desire."[85]

So Why Still Write About "That Pathetic Creep"?

Although the interest on Allen's cultural capital may have dipped in the postscandal period, the value of his overall creative output has more than held its own. Indeed, it has gone through a major critical and popular revival in his latest, post–New York phase. For Desser, "the resurrection" of Allen's career "after the hit-and-miss and occasionally disastrous films of the period 1990–2004 is one of the great stories of film history. To become culturally relevant again . . . at his age and after such a precipitous fall is unique and exciting."[86] Certainly Desser and Friedman's 1993 placement of Allen on equal footing with a trio of other Jewish American directors — Mel Brooks, Paul Mazursky, and Sidney Lumet — requires readjustment. While Allen has maintained his prolific film-a-year pace in the interim, Brooks's last directorial credit was for the forgettable *Dracula: Dead and Loving It* (1995); and Mazursky's, for the similarly inconsequential *Faithful* (1996). Lumet (who died in 2011), although he has directed the greatest number of explicitly Jewish films (*The Pawnbroker* [1964], *Bye Bye Braverman* [1968], *Just Tell Me What You Want* [1980], *Daniel* [1983], and *A Stranger Among Us* [1992]), the last of these was released two decades ago. Nor has another Jewish American filmmaker emerged since the 1990s (including Judd Apatow and his "Jew Tang Clan") to challenge Allen's preeminence as a writer, director, and (if increasingly infrequent) star.

Jewishness aside, critic Vincent Canby has consistently hailed Allen as "our most important comedic director." Rubin-Dorsky removes the qualifier, calling Allen's imagination "perhaps the richest and most fertile of any contemporary director."[87] Girgus believes his work "should be studied with the same close attention given to serious artists and writers."[88] Meanwhile, *Jewish Journal* editor Rob Eshman pulls out all the stops: "He is the Chaplin of our time, the greatest living filmmaker in the world."[89] The critical assessment is not (as it rarely is) unanimous: Kael, already in the 1990s, assailed Allen "as predictable and self-indulgent"; and his work since the early 1990s has come in for special opprobrium. Kenneth Turan is not alone in regarding *Deconstructing Harry*, at least before the award-winning and box-office smash *Midnight in Paris*, as his "last significant film."[90]

Well before *Midnight in Paris* turned Turan around, however, and scored a "sky-high" ninety-three rating on the critical website *Rotten Tomatoes*, Rubin-Dorsky, in his "Woody Allen after the Fall" article, echoed Desser and Girgus in challenging the "irreversible decline" thesis. "Over the past ten years," he wrote in 2003, "Woody Allen has responded to exigency and circumstance — some, of course, of his own making — by replenishing and renewing his fundamental commitment to his art." The "radical changes in his private life," Rubin-Dorsky proposed, rather than stunting Allen's creativity, as others surmised, "have served as a trigger for his growth as a director."[91] Testing this counterthesis and judging whether Allen's "growth as a director" has continued in the nine years since Rubin-Dorsky's pronouncement are only two of the concerns of this volume. Given that seven of Allen's last ten films have severed him from his Siamese twin, New York City, and a like number have eliminated Allen's definitive on-screen persona altogether, another phase in the writer-director's post-"fall" period has clearly begun. Reexamining the Jewish aspects of this latest phase in the context of the larger period and Allen's career as a whole is *Woody on Rye*'s raison d'être.

The Menu

The chapters presented here offer multiple and at times contradictory approaches to the films, plays, and writings of Woody Allen. Approaches range from the philosophical to the intertextual, the biographical, the feminist, and the concerns of cultural studies, but the chapters all agree that Jewishness is pivotal for an understanding of Allen's art. The longevity of any serious artist's work lies in its openness to new cycles of interpretation, and Woody Allen's offers a powerful case in point. While no definitive account of his oeuvre can be produced, these chapters collectively showcase the interconnectedness of his creative output and the richness of his probing of culturally specific but also universal themes of human relations, good and evil, and identity. The chapters are organized thematically and concentrate on the films and plays since the Farrow/Previn scandal, but it is the dialogue among these films and Allen's work as a whole that serves as the true organizing principle of the anthology, whose ultimate hope is to illuminate the layers of Jewishness in Allen's entire film and theater career.

Vincent Brook's "Gospel According to Woody: From *Annie Hall* through *To Rome with Love*" serves as hors d'oeuvre for the volume. As the subtitle suggests, it provides a broad survey of Allen's oeuvre from the film that marked "his coming of age as a filmmaker and the coming together of his on- and off-screen selves" to a European period that found his neo-schlemiel character not only cut off from his New York City roots but also increasingly marginalized or absented altogether. In charting the various chronological phases and thematic shifts over this thirty-five-year span, Brook isolates Jewish tropes such as Allen's shiksa and chameleon complexes, the former shared with most Jewish male comics of his generation (and beyond), the latter resonating with practices and mythologies of Jewish adaptability. Building on Rubin-Dorsky's "after the fall" notion, Brook reads the postscandal films as employing four strategies for dealing with the incident's external and internal fallout: *struggling, escapist, defiant,* and *accepting.* Following no consistent pattern or trajectory and often overlapping in the same film, these strategies nonetheless offer insight into the moral and ethical issues the scandal engendered and Allen's means of grappling with them.

Marat Grinberg's and Curtis Maloley's chapters establish two models of interpreting representations of Jewishness in Allen's more recent phase and throughout his career. They offer different, yet complementary, readings of three of his more serious films — *Crimes and Misdemeanors* (1989), arguably Allen's most significant Jewish work; *Match Point* (2005); and *Cassandra's Dream* (2007) — what Grinberg calls a "moral trilogy." The methodological and conceptual thrust of Grinberg's "The Birth of a Hebrew Tragedy: *Cassandra's Dream* as a Morality Play in the Context of *Crimes and Misdemeanors* and *Match Point*" is to marry comparative Jewish literary studies and film studies. Grinberg identifies Allen as a serious moral thinker — a parabolist and a "nuanced moralist" — who places the issues of good, evil, and love into a Judaic framework, evocative of modern Jewish poetry, thought, and literature, while also polemicizing with Western works (Dostoevsky and Greek tragedy) from a Jewish position. The chapter reveals that the Jewish layers in Allen's oeuvre and thinking run deep, contrary to his own pronouncements on the matter, and that they shine through even in the absence of outward Jewish thematic, sociological, or biographical signs. For Grinberg, *Cassandra's Dream* is Allen's most provocative Jewish piece that transforms the explicit Jewish material of *Crimes and Misdemeanors* (in turn predicated on a subversive reading of Dostoevsky) into an idiosyncratic parable: a crossover between Greek tragedy and the Hebrew Bible. The chapter's "discovery" is the illuminating link between the film *Cassandra's Dream* and Jewish American modernist poet Edouard Roditi's narrative poem "Cassandra's Dream."

Maloley's "A Jew Leaves New York: Woody Allen's Gloomy British Angst" tackles the three films from another angle and casts his cinematic net wider: he is interested in what the shift in primary setting from New York to London, and Europe in general, means for Allen's art. He suggests that the absence of explicit Jewish material in the recent films signifies not so much, or not only, Allen's leaving Jewishness behind but also his disillusionment with the more hopeful take on existential issues represented by the earlier New York period. If for Grinberg, Allen is artistically solipsistic, always telling and retelling the same story, Maloley's Allen is much more attuned to what happens outside his window. Thus, his non–New York films are more pessimistic (or realistic) regarding the possibility of finding order in the universe because of how he sees the early twenty-first century: cold and driven by materialism and "social class anxieties." Even regarding the warmhearted and explicitly Jewish *Scoop* (2006), Maloley concludes, "Allen's Jewish persona is not adaptable to the British context [and] signifies a clear break with his previous work," and this is even truer of *Match Point*, *Cassandra's Dream*, and his last London-based film, *You Will Meet a Tall Dark Stranger* (2010).

The chapters by Menachem Feuer, Joshua Moss, and Peter Bailey provocatively reexamine what has become the staple of writings on Allen's Jewishness: his engagement with the Yiddish schlemiel tradition and creation of the New York schlemiel type. Feuer's "Woody Allen's Schlemiel: From Humble Beginnings to an Abrupt End" places Allen's work in a number of new contexts, most predominantly through the discussion on the role of art and humor in the post-Holocaust world by Theodor Adorno and Hannah Arendt's prominent concept of Jew as pariah, and asks how Allen's art incorporates the Holocaust and deals with its ongoing ethical implications. Feuer argues that, while in a number of his earlier writings, his stand-up routines, and some of his films Allen does not shy away from addressing history through the marginalized figure of the schlemiel, even if in an ironic manner, in his later films, especially *Hollywood Ending* (2002), *Whatever Works* (2009), and *Midnight in Paris* (2011), his protagonist strives to "normalize" the schlemiel and leave the burden of his heritage behind.

In contrast to Feuer's take on the schlemiel in terms of Jewish literary and philosophical traditions, Moss's "'Woody the Gentile': Christian-Jewish Interplay in Allen's Films from *What's New, Pussycat* to *Midnight in Paris*" views Allen's schlemiel character as a response to Christian norms of masculinity in contemporary American media and society. Moss identifies how Allen's earlier films, for instance *Sleeper* (1973), subversively engaged with various fin de siècle notions of Jewish masculinity. He suggests that in the aftermath of the Farrow/Previn scandal, Allen desired to distance himself from his own filmic persona and turned toward casting non-Jews in the "Woody" role, culminating in the schlemiel-like yet clearly goyish character of Gil Pender in *Midnight in Paris* (2011), played by Owen Wilson. If Feuer sees in Gil the normalization of the schlemiel, Moss recognizes in him the schlemiel's dialogical interplay with the gentile other.

Peter Bailey's "'Now You See Him, Now You Don't': Woody Allen's Vanishing Act in *Scoop*" mourns the death of the schlemiel altogether in the later Woody Allen. Especially interested in the schlemiel's proclivity toward magic in many of the films, Bailey locates in *Scoop* — whose portrayal of the ill-fated magician Sid Waterman he sees as Allen's symbolic swan-song role — a break with the schlemiel character, whose delusions can no longer be masked as illusions. Thus, Feuer and Bailey throw different lights on the dynamic between this Jewish type and the wider world. While for Feuer, Allen's ex-schlemiel marches on, happy to be embraced by the world, Bailey's ex-schlemiel is despondent, breaking away from it. How the three schlemiel chapters stack up against Allen's latest effort (as of this writing), *To Rome with Love*, is a question readers may wish to ponder. In his Roman postcard, not only did Allen return to playing a schlemiel type, a paradoxical down-to-earth hopeful dreamer, but also Jesse Eisenberg as another of the film's multiple protagonists, played an unmistakably Jewish character, who hardly strives for "normalization."

The relation between Allen's constructions of Jewishness and his films' attitudes toward women is the concern of the chapters by Giovanna Del Negro, Shaina Hammerman, and Elliot Shapiro. In her broad overview of this aspect in Allen's oeuvre, Del Negro's "Woody's Women: Jewish Domesticity and the Unredeemed Ghost of Hanukkah to Come" posits his films as permeated with "anxieties about Jewish domesticity," which may explain why Jewish women are at times ridiculed in his work and at times absented altogether. She locates in *Interiors* a rare exception of a Jewish woman, Pearl (Maureen Stapleton), presented as a vital and redeeming force, but points out that her Jewishness is suggested rather than made explicit in the film. Similarly, in *Scoop*, in which Scarlett Johansson's Jewish character usurps Allen's characters' erstwhile dominant position in the narrative, her figure is allowed to upstage his only because the aging Allen persona no longer poses a romantic threat, nor therefore she, a domestic one.

Hammerman's "Reconstructing Woody: Representations of Religious Jewish Women in *Deconstructing Harry*" is also concerned with the "problem" of Jewish domesticity and zeroes in on the eponymous 1997 film. While other chapters, notably Moss's, scrutinized the link between Jewishness and masculinity, Hammerman wonders what happens when Jewish femininity enters the equation. Surprisingly, she finds in *Deconstructing Harry*, the film most replete with unsavory depictions of Jews, a quite nuanced portrayal of religious Jewish women, whose voice is not silenced. She convincingly shows that while the donning of religious Jewish garb in *Annie Hall* reduced Alvy Singer (Woody Allen) to a demeaning stereotype, Doris's (Caroline Aaron) "born again" religiosity in *Deconstructing Harry* made her character more appealing, complex, and freer.

The target of Elliot Shapiro's "'Toot, Toot, Tootsie! (Goodbye)': Disposable Jewish Women in the Films of Woody Allen" is the significant number of female characters who end up dead in Allen's films. If in *Annie Hall* women who are no longer desired are dumped, and in *Manhattan* (1979) threats toward women are metaphoric, in *Crimes and Misdemeanors* lethal violence becomes all too real. Shapiro links the phalanx of disappearing women (as well as a plethora of prostitutes) in Allen's oeuvre with his intertextual engagement with classical Hollywood cinema, wherein Jews were often de-Judaized or presented in "coded terms." The chapter's underlying question is, does the vanishing woman symbolize the vanishing Jew? And paradoxically, does the fact that in *Scoop* the Jewish woman survives while the Jewish male dies point to femininity as the locus of Allen's more positive take on Jewishness in his post–New York phase?

Nathan Abrams's "Digesting Woody: Food and Foodways in the Movies of Woody Allen" provides an additional valuable account of Allen's films, now from a cultural studies perspective, choosing as its focus their link between Jewishness and food. Though the importance of gastronomy for Allen's philosophy has been noticed earlier,[92] Abrams compellingly demonstrates how food imagery is used by Allen as a commentary on "the Jewish American condition ... in the contemporary world." The chapter analyzes the significance of locales (restaurants), etiquette, and mannerisms (the contrast between Jewish and WASP [in]civility), religious meals (Seders), Jewish versus gentile foods (pastrami sandwich versus Wonder Bread), American versions of Jewish foods (pork dishes at Chinese restaurants), and the conflation of food and sex (seafood as sex organs). Abrams concludes that Allen's jokes about food always carry a serious meaning that often speaks to his attachment to Yiddishkeit and to Jews' struggles to preserve their ways and cultural practices even while assimilating.

James Fisher's "Schlemiel on Broadway: Woody Allen's Jewish Identity in His Stage Plays from *Don't Drink the Water* to *Honeymoon Motel*" provides a fitting conclusion to the volume. His concentrating on Allen's plays, a largely unexplored subject, enriches Woody Allen studies as a whole and points to future directions in the field. It also revisits the schlemiel persona and the impact the Farrow/Previn scandal has had on his stage work, particularly in regard to depictions of women and romantic relationships. Fisher locates in Allen's plays the roots of both his attachment to Jewish humor and his own life as the foundational material for his work. Case in point is his most recent theater piece, the one-act *Honeymoon Motel* (2011), both hailed by critics and seen by Fisher as following in the footsteps of the borscht belt comedy of the 1950s and 1960s, as well as resonating with the circumstances of the scandal. Fisher ultimately sees Allen the artist as striving for "something more universal and all encompassing" despite being an heir to the traditions of Yiddish theater and Jewish American culture.

Woody on Rye aims to accomplish something conceptually akin. Taking its cue from Allen's films, plays, stand-up routines, prose pieces, and indelibly Jewish persona, this anthology hopes to deepen understanding of his oeuvre from a broad-based yet specifically Jewish perspective, and to bring these aspects up to date (for now). At the very least, we hope to set the table for further examination (Jewish and otherwise) of this major American artist's life's work.

Notes

1. Allen has not retired. That's part of the joke.
2. Foster Hirsch, *Love, Sex, Death, and the Meaning of Life: The Films of Woody Allen* (Cambridge, MA: Da Capo, 1981), 131.
3. Jeffrey Rubin-Dorsky, "Woody Allen after the Fall: Literary Gold from Amoral Alchemy," *Shofar* 22 (2003): 5–28.
4. Mashey Bernstein, "My Worst Fears Realized: Woody Allen and the Holocaust," in *Perspectives on Woody Allen*, ed. Renée R. Curry, 218–52 (New York: G. K. Hall, 1996).
5. Ruth B. Johnston, "Joke Work: The Construction of Postmodern Jewish Identity in Contemporary Theory and American Film," in *You Should See Yourself: Jewish Identity in Postmodern American Culture*, ed. Vincent Brook, 207–29 (New Brunswick, NJ: Rutgers University Press, 2003).
6. Charles L. P. Silet, ed., *The Films of Woody Allen: Critical Essays* (Lanham, MD: Scarecrow, 2006).
7. Toni-Lynn Frederick, "The Eleventh Jew: Humor and the Holocaust in Woody Allen's *Anything Else*," *Post Script* 31, no. 2 (Winter/Spring 2012): 92–100.
8. Vittorio Hösle, *Woody Allen: An Essay on the Nature of the Comical* (Notre Dame, IN: University of Notre Dame Press, 2007), 86–87.
9. Danielle Berrin, "Who Is Woody Allen?" *Jewish Journal*, November 18–24, 2011, 38–39, 45.
10. Hirsch, *Love, Sex, Death*, ix.
11. "Sam Tanenhaus on Woody Allen's Black Magic," *Newsweek*, June 18, 2012, http://www.thedailybeast.com.
12. Berrin, "Who Is Woody Allen?" 38.
13. Hirsch, *Love, Sex, Death*, x.
14. Ibid., 141.

15. Ibid., 137.

16. Ibid., 141.

17. Ibid., 138.

18. Ibid., 144. The neologist notion of "(m)Other" is from Richard Feldstein, "Displaced Feminine Representation in Woody Allen's Cinema," in *Discontented Discourses: Feminism/Textual Intervention/Psychoanalysis*, ed. Marleen S. Barr and Richard Feldstein, 69–86 (Urbana: University of Illinois Press, 1989), 71.

19. Hirsch, *Love, Sex, Death*, 150.

20. Richard Freadman, "Love among the Stereotypes, or Why Woody's Women Leave," in *Semites and Stereotypes: Characteristics of Jewish Humor*, ed. Avner Ziv and Anat Zajdman, 107–20 (Westport, CT: Greenwood, 1993), 114.

21. Ibid., 110. The term "shiks appeal" was coined in the "Serenity Now" episode (season 9, episode 3) of the TV sitcom *Seinfeld* (1992–1998).

22. Freadman, "Love among the Stereotypes," 114.

23. Ruth Wisse, *The Schlemiel as Modern Hero* (Chicago: University of Chicago Press, 1971).

24. Hirsch, *Love, Sex, Death*, 131.

25. Ibid., 132, 133.

26. Ibid., 134, 135.

27. Ibid., 136.

28. Ibid., 137.

29. Ibid., 138.

30. Quoted in Lawrence J. Epstein, *The Haunted Smile: The Story of Jewish Comedians in America* (New York: Public Affairs, 2001), 196. Kafka, in a January 8, 1914, diary entry, wrote, "What have I in common with Jews? I have hardly anything in common with myself and should stand very quietly in a corner, content that I can breathe" (in *The Diaries of Franz Kafka*, ed. Max Brod [New York: Schocken, 1948–49]).

31. Sigmund Freud, *Jokes and Their Relation to the Unconscious* (1905; repr., New York: Norton, 1960); Avner Ziv, in Mark E. Bleiweiss, "Self-Deprecation and the Jewish Humor of Woody Allen," in Silet, *Films of Woody Allen*, 58–77; 59.

32. Martin Grotjahn and Maurice Samuel, in Bleiweiss, "Self-Deprecation," 59.

33. Theodor Reik, in ibid.

34. Joseph Dorinson, in ibid., 64.

35. Ibid., 60, 61, 62.

36. Ibid., 64.

37. Quoted in ibid.

38. Gerald Mast, "Woody Allen: The Neurotic Jew as American Clown," in *Jewish Wry: Essays on Jewish Humor*, ed. Sarah Blacher Cohen, 125–40 (Detroit: Wayne State University Press, 1987), 126.

39. Ibid., 126–27.

40. Ibid.

41. Ibid., 127.

42. Henry Popkin, "The Vanishing Jew in Our Popular Culture: The Little Man Who Is No Longer There," *Commentary* 14, no. 1 (July 1952): 46–55.

43. Mast, "Woody Allen," 129.

44. Ibid., 130.

45. Ibid., 130, 132, 134.

46. David Desser and Lester D. Friedman, *American-Jewish Filmmakers: Traditions and Trends* (Urbana: University of Illinois Press, 1993), 5–6.

47. Ibid., 6.

48. Ted Solotoroff, "American-Jewish Writers: On Edge Once More," *New York Times Book Review*, December 18, 1988, 31 (cited in Desser and Friedman, *American-Jewish Filmmakers*, 8).

49. Solotoroff, "American-Jewish Writers," 33; Desser and Friedman, *American-Jewish Filmmakers*, 8.

50. Quoted in Sarah Blacher Cohen, "Introduction: The Varieties of Jewish Humor," in Blacher Cohen, *Jewish Wry*, 1–15; 2; Dov Lang, "On the Biblical Comic," *Judaism* 11 (1962): 249.

51. Theodor Reik, *Jewish Wit* (New York: Gamut, 1962), 18; Alan Spiegel, "The Vanishing Act: A Typology of the Jew in Contemporary American Film," in *From Hester Street to Hollywood: The Jewish-American Stage and Screen*, ed. Sarah Blacher Cohen, 257–75 (Bloomington: Indiana University Press, 1983), 273.

52. Blacher Cohen, "Introduction," 2.

53. George Eliot, "German Wit: Heinrich Heine," *Westminster and Quarterly Review* 9 (January 1, 1856): 1–33; Stephen Whitfield, *Voices of Jacob, Hands of Esau: Jews in American Life and Thought* (Hamden, CT: Archon, 1984), 120.

54. Thomas J. Kinne, *Elemente jüdischer Tradition im Werk Woody Allens* (PhD diss., Johannes-Gutenberg-Universität Mainz, Germany, 1993; Frankfurt am Main, Germany: Peter Lang, 1996), 285, 291.

55. Ibid., 217, 267, 273–74, 281.

56. Salomon Seigbert Prawer, *Heine's Jewish Comedy: A Study of His Portraits of Jews and Judaism* (Oxford, UK: Clarendon, 1983), 759.

57. Max Brod, *Heinrich Heine* (Amsterdam: de Lange, 1935), 270–71.

58. Ritchie Robertson, *Kafka: Judaism, Politics, Literature* (Oxford, UK: Clarendon, 1985), 82; Kinne, *Elemente*, 304; Bernstein, "My Worst Fears Realized," 224. For more on Allen's Kafka complex, see also Iris Bruce, "Mysterious Illnesses of Human Commodities in Woody Allen and Franz Kafka: *Zelig*," in Silet, *Films of Woody Allen*, 171–97.

59. Kinne, *Elemente*, 316–18, 327, 329.

60. Marvin Mudrick, *On Culture and Literature* (New York: Horizon, 1970), 200.

61. L. H. Goldman, *Saul Bellow's Moral Vision: A Critical Study of the Jewish Experience* (New York: Irvington, 1987), 129; Kinne, *Elemente*, 354, 379–80 (translation by Vincent Brook).

62. Bernstein, "My Worst Fears Realized," 218, 223.

63. Kinne, *Elemente*, 201; Bruno Bettelheim, *Surviving, and Other Essays* (New York: Knopf, 1979), 11.

64. Chester Eisinger, *Fiction of the Forties* (Chicago: University of Chicago Press, 1968), 347.

65. Kinne, *Elemente*, 362, 364.

66. Saul Bellow, *Herzog* (Harmondsworth, UK: Penguin, 1964), 54, 316.

67. Bellow, *Herzog*, 77; Ihab Hassan, *Radical Innocence: Studies in the Contemporary American Novel* (Princeton, NJ: Princeton University Press, 1961), 291; Kinne, *Elemente*, 369.

68. Keith M. Opdahl, "The 'Mental' Comedies of Saul Bellow," in Blacher Cohen, *From Hester Street to Hollywood*, 183–96; 186.

69. Arthur Hertzberg, *The Jews in America: Four Centuries of an Uneasy Encounter* (New York: Touchstone-Simon, 1990), 196.

70. Philip Roth, *Portnoy's Complaint* (Harmondsworth, UK: Penguin, 1969), 137.

71. Philip Roth, *Reading Myself and Others* (New York: Bantam, 1977), 18, 75; on Broadway Danny Rose, see Jeffrey Rubin-Dorsky, "The Catskills Reinvented (and Redeemed): Woody Allen's *Broadway Danny Rose*," *Kenyon Review* 25 (Summer/Fall 2003): 264–81.

72. Sam B. Girgus, "Philip Roth and Woody Allen: Freud and the Humor of the Repressed," in Ziv and Zajdman, *Semites and Stereotypes*, 121–30; 122, 124, 130.

73. Rubin-Dorsky, "Woody Allen," 25.

74. Ibid.; John Baxter, *Woody Allen: A Biography* (New York: Carroll & Graf, 1998), 436.

75. Quoted in Kinne, *Elemente*, 409.

76. Kinne, *Elemente*, 409.

77. Ibid., 427, 441, 447.

78. Quoted in Gerald McKnight, *Woody Allen: Joking Aside* (London: W H Allen, 1982), 111.

79. Quoted in Israel Shenker, "S.J. Perelman," *Publishers Weekly* 19 (May 1975): 90; quoted in Joe Adamson, *Groucho, Harpo, Chico, and Sometimes Zeppo* (New York: Simon and Schuster, 1973), 126.

80. Walter Blair and Hamlin Hill, *America's Humor: From Poor Richard to Doonesbury* (New York: Oxford University Press, 1978), 435.

81. Pauline Kael, review of *Crimes and Misdemeanors*, *New Yorker*, October 30, 1989, 76 (quoted in Kinne, *Elemente*, 437). Kael's own already-shaky ethical

reputation has taken a severe hit since the 2011 publication of Lawrence Levi's scathing biography, *Pauline Kael: A Life in the Dark* (New York: Viking, 2011).

82. Rubin-Dorsky, "Woody Allen," 18.

83. Samuel H. Dresner, "Woody Allen and the Jews" (1992), in Curry, *Perspectives on Woody Allen*, 188–98; 191.

84. Allen and Soon-Yi were married in 1997 and have adopted two daughters, Bechet Dumaine in 1998 and Manzie Tio in 1999.

85. Feldstein, "Displaced Feminine Representation," 69, 71, 76, 78.

86. David M. Desser, e-mail to Phyllis D. Deutsch (relayed to the editors), October 22, 2012.

87. Rubin-Dorsky, "Woody Allen," 26.

88. Sam B. Girgus, *The Films of Woody Allen*, 2nd ed. (Cambridge: Cambridge University Press, 2002), 20.

89. Rob Eshman, "Send Woody on Birthright," *Jewish Journal*, June 27–29, 2012, 4.

90. Kael, quoted in Girgus, *Films of Woody Allen*, 20; Kenneth Turan, "*Whatever* Doesn't Work," *Los Angeles Times*, June 19, 2009, D4.

91. Rubin-Dorsky, "Woody Allen," 15.

92. See, for instance, Ronald D. LeBlanc, "*Love and Death* and Food: Woody Allen's Comic Use of Gastronomy," in Silet, *Films of Woody Allen*, 100–111.

OVERVIEW

VINCENT BROOK

The Gospel According to Woody *&* From *Annie Hall* through *To Rome with Love*

Annie Hall (1977) was the first of Woody Allen's films to proclaim both his coming of age as a filmmaker and the coming together of his on- and off-screen selves. It also marks a move beyond the social and sexual constraints of the classic schlemiel. Two earlier films in which Allen starred but did not direct, *Play It Again, Sam* (Herbert Ross, 1972) and *The Front* (Martin Ritt, 1976), had shifted the schlemiel's center of gravity (and levity) from the shtetl to New York City and turned the caricature of Yiddish folklore into a recognizable human being.[1] *Annie Hall* made the connection between the neurotic New York Jew and Woody Allen explicit. Not only is the film's protagonist, Alvy Singer, a successful professional comedian who has no trouble attaining, if still trouble retaining, a desirable (read gentile) woman, but also the eponymous shiksa he wins and loses was played by the woman with whom Allen had just concluded a lengthy affair, Diane Keaton. Henceforth, at least in the films in which he appears as prime or coprotagonist, the "fictionalized versions of Allen's own manufactured identity as Woody Allen" became an essential ingredient of his conjurer's art.[2]

As for Allen's films' aesthetic and thematic concerns, these had largely congealed by 1980, from *Annie Hall* through the three films that followed: *Interiors* (1978), *Manhattan* (1979), and *Stardust Memories* (1980). The self-reflexive aesthetic orientation derived unabashedly from the European art cinemas, most specifically Ingmar Bergman and Federico Fellini. The thematics, tilting heavily toward Bergman, centered on existential angst distilled through (Jewish) humor, the redemptive power but also problematic of art (particularly cinema) and relationships (largely of the shiksa variety), and the uniquely Jewish insider/outsider complex. The inability to fully reconcile the tension between Strindbergian psychodrama and borscht belt stand-up expressed itself, initially, in a gyration between *Annie Hall*–like satirical comedy (*Manhattan*) and deadly serious drama (*Interiors*).

Form and content have converged most compellingly — and originally — in Allen's exploration of the relation between documentary and fiction. While present in his work as early as *Take the Money and Run* (1969), the reality/illusion dialectic resonated anew in the 1980s, as an objective correlative of the Woody/Allen question. Given the semblance (however illusory) between Allen and his film persona, and both of these with neurotic New York Jewishness, those films in which Allen plays a prominent role are his most distinctly Jewish — the distinctiveness heightened by his characters' occupations or special talents that combine noted Jewish and Allenesque tropes. In the 1980s, these include Allen's "famed" filmmaker Sandy Bates in *Stardust Memories*; his Wall Street broker-cum-inventor Andrew in *A Midsummer Night's Sex Comedy* (1982); the eponymous human chameleon *Zelig* (1983) and borscht belt booking agent *Broadway Danny Rose* (1984); television producer Mickey Sachs in *Hannah and Her Sisters* (1986); and documentarian Cliff Stern in *Crimes and Misdemeanors* (1989).

Stardust Memories, on one level a comedic homage to Fellini's solipsistic *8½* (1963), about the creative conflict in the making of the very film we are watching, significantly extends the autobiographical conjunction of Allen's life and corpus. The dilemma that acclaimed director Bates confronts in *Stardust Memories* mirrors that which Allen experienced at the time: between making comedies like the financially and critically successful *Annie Hall* and *Manhattan* or dramas like the box-office flop and roundly panned *Interiors*. An added Jewish element is that the fans and critics at the Atlantic City retrospective of Bates's work, which serves as *Stardust Memories*' microcosmic setting, are almost all Jews, and played by Jewish actors. As Patricia Erens observed, "The rolling credits probably contain the longest list of Jewish names in film history, apart from the Yiddish cinema of the 1930s."[3] The ethnoreligious tribute is undermined, however, by the unsympathetic portrayal of fans and critics alike, leading to accusations — not the first or last — of Jewish self-hatred on Allen's part. What such criticism fails to recognize is *Stardust Memories*' grounding in Felliniesque grotesquerie and that, as David Desser and Lester Friedman point out, "Allen's clearest target is himself. His most vicious barbs are directed inward."[4]

The personal nature of the self-hatred is reinforced by the match between Allen's writer character's (Harry Block) assertion in the later *Deconstructing Harry* (1997) "I may hate myself, but not because I'm Jewish" and Allen's avowal in an interview that "while it's true I am Jewish and I don't like myself very much, it's not because of my persuasion."[5] Both disclaimers derive from Kafka's famous diary entry "What have I in common with Jews? I have hardly anything in common with myself and should stand very quietly in a corner, content that I can breathe," which Allen paraphrases in his farcically Kafkaesque *Shadows and Fog* (1991).[6] Allen's Hyman Kleinman, stuck "schlemielishly" in 1920s Austria-Hungary, when derided for not making the leap of faith necessary to believe in God, retorts, "Listen, I can't make the leap of faith necessary to believe in myself."

If *Stardust Memories* was an attempt to resolve the conflict between Allen's comedic and tragic impulses, it failed — but not to the detriment of his work. To the contrary, his films in the remainder of the decade, arguably the richest of his career, up the ante on the comedy/tragedy dialectic and provide a useful frame for the films' analysis from a Jewish standpoint. The comedic thesis proposed in *A Midsummer Night's Sex Comedy*, *Zelig*, *Broadway Danny Rose*, *The Purple Rose of Cairo* (1985), *Radio Days* (1987), and the "Oedipus Wrecks" segment of *New York Stories* (1989) confronts its dramatic antithesis in *September* (1987) and *Another Woman* (1988) and is seriocomically synthesized in *Hannah and Her Sisters* and *Crimes and Misdemeanors*.

By definition, and design, Jewish aspects recede in the 1980s films in which Allen himself does not appear. Sig Altman's observation that, by the 1960s, "the very word 'Jewish'" had become "laden with humorous overtones," combined with Allen's identification as a comic figure, further dictated that Allen recuse himself from the dramas.[7] Even minus his physical presence, however, palimpsestic Jewish traces are decipherable, as Desser and Friedman's description of the dramas (including the earlier *Interiors*) as "the WASP Women trilogy" indicates.[8] In *Interiors*, Jewishness returns from the repressed in the earthy, sensual, Jewish-*coded* character of Pearl (played by the Catholic Maureen Stapleton), who breathes color (literally) and life (belatedly) into an austere and morose, upper-crust Protestant household.[9] In the trilogy as a whole, Jewishness bleeds through the Bergmanesque thematics and mise-en-scène in the distinctive, and apparently inextinguishable, Allenesque dialogue.[10]

Chameleon Complex

Allen's voice comes through loudest and clearest, of course, in his self-starring comedies. In the mockumentary *Zelig*, borrowing another chapter from Kafka (and a few from Orson Welles and Warren Beatty), Allen plays the fictional historical figure Leonard Zelig. Though he doesn't wake up as a giant arthropod, Zelig is examined like a bug under glass for his miraculous ability to take on the physical and character traits of any person with whom he comes in contact, including Asians and blacks.

Bruno Bettelheim's talking-head linkage of Zelig's conformity compulsion to Kafka's was cited in this volume's introduction. Irving Howe, another of the real-life interviewees who appears to take Zelig's character seriously, similarly sees his condition as a reflection of "the Jewish experience in America: the great urge to push in, and to find one's place and then to assimilate into the culture." Susan Sontag joins the roster of Jew York intellectuals asked to take swings at the "historical" Zelig, while Anna Freud is indirectly referenced when Zelig morphs remorselessly into a member of the Nazi party. Besides literalizing "identification with the enemy," Desser and Friedman suggest, Zelig's turn(coat)ing into a Nazi demonstrates "the mechanism of self-hatred revealed by Allen himself, particularly as an artist who simultaneously makes fun of Jewish culture and religion while he reveals the tragic consequences of anti-Semitism."[11]

Zelig's pathological need to "be liked" also clearly echoes Sandy Bates's dilemma in *Stardust Memories* between making safer, popular comedies and riskier, more challenging dramas. Most self-reflexively, and self-critically, Chameleon Man's ersatz personality rhymes with Allen's cinematic proclivity toward parody and pastiche. Indeed, *Zelig*'s plumbing of the documentary/fiction divide, though it builds on Allen's previous work, is itself derivative — in this case less of Fellini and Bergman and more of Welles's faux documentary opening in *Citizen Kane* (1941) and Warren Beatty's real-people interview insertions in the John Reed biopic *Reds* (1981). To many critics, however, this reliance on outside sources — especially the art cinema ones — rather than a sign of sophistication, has been labeled pretentious at best, plagiaristic at worst. "For skeptics of Allen's originality," Sam Girgus summarizes, "all of the presumably fresh elements and concepts that are said to comprise his work are largely derivative, 'Xeroxed' borrowings. To his detractors, Allen repackages and markets the breakthroughs of his many predecessors from Welles to Bergman whom Allen himself recognizes and acknowledges."[12]

What the objections to Allen's "imitations" fail to acknowledge, however, is their own duplication of the centuries-old canard of Jewish imposture. Since the Jewish emancipation period of the late 1700s, German-speaking Jews especially confronted a creative double bind: while encouraged to assimilate into European culture on the one hand, they were regarded as inherently unassimilable on the other. As early as 1814, German playwright Alexander Sessa satirized "the absurdity (and implied impossibility) of Jewish assimilation" due to Jews' perceived "spinelessness, hopeless *mimicry*, lack of respect and character."[13] Sessa's critique was leveled mainly at the desperate attempts at social refinement of upwardly aspiring Jews who, despite their ardent efforts, ever (allegedly) remained philistines and arrivistes.[14]

Richard Wagner, in his infamous anti-Semitic tract *Judaism in Music* (1850), extended the parvenu argument into the cultural realm. Wagner found a "fundamental deficiency" in the Jewish artist due to his "inalienable status as outsider" that left him incapable of creating "true art."[15] As "scientific" racism became the vogue in the 1880s, Eugen Dühring, one of its main theoreticians, condemned Jewish cultural aspiration in terms most consonant with those of Allen's critics: "The Jew is lacking any free and selfless activity of the spirit"; Jewish language is "merely parody"; and their seemingly "deep" emotions are "borrowed."[16] Even some Jewish commentators decried the lack of seriousness in their coreligionists' creative efforts, which instead, according to Ludwig Börne, were limited to "wit" and "satire."[17] Notorious self-hating Jewish philosopher Otto Weininger went further, writing in 1903 (the same year he committed suicide) that Jews were "addicted to mockery."[18] It was "the Jew's mimicry of a world which he could never truly enter," Sander Gilman summarizes the received wisdom, "which produced works which were felt to be creative but, in fact, were mere copies of the products of *truly* creative individuals."[19]

What this anti-Semitic discourse obfuscated, of course, was the fact that

Jews' insider/outsider status, their living "at the margins between cultures," and the split or double consciousness this condition engendered, rather than hampering "true creativity," gave Jews an "epistemological advantage" that spurred some of the boldest thought of the modern age.[20] This liminal perspective found expression not only in the social and physical sciences — Marx, Freud, and Einstein — but also in all the arts from Schoenberg's atonal music to Toller's expressionist theater, Kafka's angst-driven literature, and a form of humor, combining the comic and the cosmic, whose tradition Allen clearly absorbed yet also expanded.

This co(s)mic orientation derived from an additional cultural bifurcation of Eastern European Jews in particular, an "internal bilingualism," in Max Weinreich's term, which placed *Ostjuden* "imaginatively, in sharply opposed worlds, the one reverential, austere, bound by duty, ritual, and awe, the other ironic, playful, mischievous."[21] The American translation of Ashkenazi bilingualism is marked, in Irving Howe's description, by a "yoking of opposites, gutter vividness with university refinement, street energy with high-cultural rhetoric . . . a deliberate play with the phrasings of plebian speech, but often, also, the kind that vibrates with cultural ambition, seeking to zoom into regions of higher thought."[22] The result, which Heinrich Heine pioneered and Allen Americanized and made his trademark, is the "comic double-take," the "ironic deflation," the "lofty perspective laid low by the common desire," the "encounter of learning and business in the same culture," or in stand-up terms, the "self-conscious byplay of *Kunst* and candy store."[23]

As for Allen's shoplifting from Bergman and Fellini specifically, this allegation also must be qualified. From the (anti-)religious standpoint, what Lutheranism is to Bergman and Catholicism is to Fellini, Judaism is to Allen. Stylistically, Allen's uses of pre-1950s popular music, plan sequence shooting, and off-screen interior space bear no one's signature but his own. And when it comes to alter egos, Allen goes Bergman's Max von Sydow/Erland Josephson and Fellini's Marcello Mastroianni one better, playing, until the "semi-retirement" of his screen image with 2006's *Scoop*, "his own man."[24] In the figure of Zelig moreover, Allen's "own man" is subject to, and an object of, an endless number of "selves," whose fabrication/fragmentation extends backward to the Jewish assimilationist discourse and forward to the postmodern historical moment.

From *Menschlekhayt* to Seriocomedy

Broadway Danny Rose conjures another, if more narrowly focused, "alternate autobiography," by way of the Jewish-dominated 1950s comedy-club circuit to which Allen himself, but for fortune, might have been consigned.[25] As the eponymous failed-comic-turned-two-bit-talent-agent, he also plays the schlemiel at his most (to that point) demonstrably, and sympathetically, Jewish: Danny (his name conjuring the put-upon biblical prophet) wears a *chai* pendant and on several occasions spouts the Yiddish expression "*Emmis* [truth], my hand to God." The "search for *menschlekhayt*," or "the desire for an honest life free from duplicity and prevarication," Jeffrey Rubin-Dorsky avers, are *Broadway Danny Rose*'s hallmarks.[26] This is not to say that the film is bereft of the more conflicted Jewish aspects of Allen's oeuvre. Danny demeans his relatives (as in *Take the Money and Run*, *Annie Hall*, and *Radio Days*). He says he doesn't believe in God but feels guilty about it (as in *Annie Hall*, *Hannah and Her Sisters*, *Crimes and Misdemeanors*, and *Husbands and Wives*). And in teaching his girlfriend Tina (Mia Farrow) "about the darker side of life, about guilt, and the need for love in a harsh world," he reproduces the recurring bildungsroman motif "of the shiksa's education by the Jewish man" (as in *Sleeper*, *Annie Hall*, *Manhattan*, and *Hannah and Her Sisters*).[27]

Menschlekhayt and ethnic ambivalence vie in *Radio Days* as well. A lighthearted, nostalgic tribute to the golden age of radio, the film's setting among an extended, working-class Jewish family in 1940s Brooklyn modulates "between genuine autobiography . . . and another of the thinly disguised fictions in his film canon."[28] But the film also pokes fun at Jewish pettiness, tribalism, and superficial religiosity. Meanwhile, in "Oedipus Wrecks," Allen literally sends up the Jewish mother complex by having his character's overbearing mother (the spitting image of Allen's own), momentarily banished by a magician's spell, reappear as a vengeful giant apparition above the Manhattan skyline for all to see.

In *Hannah and Her Sisters* and *Crimes and Misdemeanors*, Allen's character is the one that undergoes the transformation — a reduction rather than magnification, not of his Jew York disposition but rather of his positioning within the narrative. As much an observer as an active participant, his character is decentered — or rather relegated to one of two centers within the seriocomic dialectic, whose tonal poles intertwine in these two films as never before. Despite the valiant "attempt to mediate the binary conflicts between Jew and WASP, neurosis and psychosis, and self-hate and self-respect," Desser and Friedman suggest, Allen's indelible schlemiel "splits the film along the lines of WASP drama/Jew comedy."[29] Each of these modalities, moreover, contains an additional, ethnically inflected split. The WASP internal split is *physical*, through the three sisters' various marital and extramarital couplings: Hannah's (Mia Farrow) with her husband Elliot (Michael Caine); Lee's (Barbara Hershey) with the artist Frederick (Max von Sydow) and with Elliot; Holly's (Dianne Wiest) with David (Sam Waterston) and with TV producer Mickey Sachs (Allen). The Jewish split is metaphysical, through Mickey and his "bloodline's" irrepressible co(s)mic humor: "the sudden thrusting downward from sacred to mundane."[30] When, for example, Mickey asks his father to explain the existence of evil, more specifically how God could have countenanced the Nazis, his father snaps, "How the hell do I know why there were Nazis. I don't know how the can opener works!"

It takes more than a throwaway one-liner to banish Mickey's existential angst. Rather, as in most Allen's films since the *Casablanca* love letter *Play It Again, Sam*, redemption in *Hannah* comes from neither on high nor down low but rather cinema itself: in this instance, a revival-house offering through which the despairing Mickey experiences a life-affirming epiphany and the informed viewer, an intertextual revelation of exponential proportions. It is not just any old movie that resurrects Mickey's spirits but a Marx Brothers comedy, *Duck Soup* (1932), which resonates on both the auteurist and generic levels. The auteurist connection springs from the Marx Brothers' Jewish legacy generally, as exponents of a collective brand of "internal bilingualism," and from Groucho's link to Allen specifically, as one of Allen's comedic idols.[31] The generic tie-in begins with the scene's obvious evocation of Preston Sturges's *Sullivan's Travels* (1941), in which a successful comedic (wannabe dramatic) film director grasps, in witnessing the cathartic laughter a Disney cartoon provokes in a downtrodden prison audience, the importance of being "dis-earnest." It's a short leap from Sullivan's comedy-drama dilemma to Allen's own, as deconstructed in *Stardust Memories* and left hanging in his subsequent string of comparatively light fare, yet hopefully (in both senses of the word) resolved in the seriocomic conflation of *Hannah* itself.

Sam Girgus found the resolution successful: "*Hannah and Her Sisters* realizes the creative potential of all [Allen's] important films as well as the fulfillment of a promise about his artistic values and objectives that he has made throughout his mature years."[32] A sticking point for Desser and Friedman remained the WASP drama/Jew comedy divide. Rubin-Dorsky, and Allen himself, demurred more forcefully, considering *Hannah*'s "satisfying conclusion" to a "fundamentally bleak narrative" a cop-out.[33] Allen demonstrated his self-dissatisfaction by diverging from Sturges's (and Sullivan's) rediscovery that his "true calling" lay in making funny pictures. Allen did just the opposite, following up *Hannah* with the second and third of his dramatic "WASP Women" trilogy, *September* (a Chekovian reworking of Lana Turner's daughter's shooting of her gangster boyfriend Johnny Stompanato) and *Another Woman* (a *Persona*-like study of two women's psychotherapeutic entanglements).

Whether both films' critical and financial drubbing provided the motivation, Allen once again shelved serious drama and returned to the seriocomic mode for his next film, *Crimes and Misdemeanors*. A more successful fusion of dramatic and comedic elements than *Hannah*, Allen's Jewish take on Dostoyevsky's classic has come to signal for a consensus of critics the apex of his film career (from which subsequent efforts would be seen as spiraling — with intermittent rebounds — downward). To begin with, *Crimes and Misdemeanors* also manages to eliminate the WASP-Jew dichotomy that hounded *Hannah* — achieved, curiously but not coincidentally, by absorbing WASPness into Jewishness. Allen's documentary filmmaker Cliff, as in *Hannah*, serves as the film's comic foil. Atypically, however, the central dramatic character, ophthalmologist Judah Rosenthal (Martin Landau), combines traits generally associated with gentiles in Allen's previous films ("well-to-do and serious, well-behaved and thoughtful") with those of Allen's alter egos ("a compelling existential angst ... a profound sense of guilt").[34] Most significantly, Judah is also a murderer, but unlike the homicidal mother in *September* — and lethal literary figures from the Bible and Greek tragedy through Shakespeare, Dostoevsky, and disciples — Judah "gets away with it," both legally and psychologically.

This is the crux of the film's moral conundrum, and one not so easily transcended, as in Allen's other films, by art or love relationships. Indeed, relationships present their own conundrum in *Crimes and Misdemeanors*, one that returns the film's repressed (male) WASPness through the ineluctable figure of the shiksa. Judah, for example, contracts to have his gentile mistress Dolores (Anjelica Huston) killed, while Cliff's gentile girlfriend Halley (Mia Farrow) "kills [his] beliefs" by choosing in his stead the "worst kind of show business Jew," Lester (Alan Alda).[35] The film careens toward abject despair when the subject of Cliff's work in progress, Holocaust survivor/philosopher Louis Levy (an obvious stand-in for Primo Levi), commits suicide. The moral that God does not exist, or at best is blind to human suffering, is reinforced through the flipside motifs of vision and blindness: Judah's ophthalmology and Cliff's filmmaking professions; the blindness of justice (and his own conscience) to Judah's crime; and the actual blindness that befalls Judah's patient, the righteous rabbi Ben (Sam Waterston). The most cinema can hope to accomplish under such Job-like tribulation, as Levy's voice-over in Cliff's film (heard over a montage from Allen's) suggests, is to teach us to "take our joy only in moments and believe in love despite overwhelming evidence to the contrary." A far less "'happy' coda" than *Hannah*'s certainly, but one ephemerally realized in the film's final image of the blind rabbi joyfully dancing with his daughter at her wedding.[36]

(Fore)*Shadows and Fog*

The issue of guilt, probed philosophically in *Crimes and Misdemeanors*, would penetrate and encumber Allen's personal life in the early 1990s. The fifty-six year-old filmmaker's liaison with nineteen-year-old Soon-Yi Previn — adopted daughter, from a previous marriage, of his decadelong romantic partner/leading lady Mia Farrow (with additional accusations of sexual abuse of an adopted daughter of Allen and Farrow's, Dylan) — fueled a tabloid scandal that lasted from 1992 through 1995 and reverberates to the present. Allen was cleared of the abuse charges but was denied visitation rights with Dylan; their adopted son Moses refused to have anything to do with him; and he could only see hereditary son Satchel under supervision.

The scandal naturally (or perversely) enhanced the popular and critical tendency to connect Allen's work with his life, which *Husbands and Wives* (1992), made as the scandal was unfolding, further reinforced. The film features the breakup of a marriage between Allen's and Farrow's characters and his professor character's affair with a young college student (another shiksa, played by Juliette Lewis), about which Allen's professor Gabriel "Gabe" Roth confides to a faux documentary interviewer: "Everything about it was wrong, I know, but that did not deter me. If anything, maybe, as usual, there was something interesting." One was even tempted to rifle Allen's previous work for evidence of his Lolita — and Asian — complexes, which his character's affair with a high school student (another blond-haired shiksa, played by Mariel Hemingway) in *Manhattan* and the Asian American *Playboy* bunny China Lee featured in *What's Up, Tiger Lily?* readily provided. Nor was a 1986 interview reassuring, in which Allen chastised critics for taking his jailbait affair in *Manhattan* seriously ("They were completely convinced I wanted to marry a 17-year-old girl"), which in retrospect indicated either that he was fooling himself or, as his wife (played by Judy Davis) claims about his opera-director character in *To Rome with Love* (2012), "You were ahead of your time."[37]

Rabbi and scholar Samuel Dresner even found incriminating "evidence" in one of Allen's short stories, "Retribution" (1980), in which protagonist Harold Cohen finds himself "in love with two women. Not a terribly uncommon problem. That they happen to be mother and child? All the more challenging."[38] Nor was it easy to decouple the Semitism from the sordidness, as Allen's friend and former collaborator Marshall Brickman proffered in relation to the real-life custody battle: "So here were these two stereotypes: the neurotic Jew — self-obsessed, intellectual, weird — and suddenly he's hooked up with this saintly, sort of virginal yet highly fecund mother. Who's going to lose in that kind of a contest? . . . The whole thing was wildly ironic if you know even a little bit of it. It was a coming home to roost of the public images, and they really clashed."[39]

The wild irony that Brickman hints at but was glossed over at the time is the glaring disconnect between Farrow's "saintly, virginal" image and her own checkered past. The daughter of director John Farrow and actor Maureen O'Sullivan (who swung to fame playing Tarzan's Jane), the Catholic Farrow married the fifty-year-old Frank Sinatra at twenty-one and divorced him two years later. She became a star at twenty-three in (later scandal-plagued) Roman Polanski's *Rosemary's Baby* (1968), in which she gave eponymous birth to a new age Satan. Polanski's own actress wife, Sharon Tate, was brutally murdered the following year, along with their unborn child, by the Manson family, while Farrow herself would be accused of diabolical machinations by songwriter Dory Previn. Twenty years Dory's junior, the twenty-four-year-old Farrow had an affair with Dory's husband Andre Previn, became pregnant by him before their marriage, and adopted another child, Soon-Yi, shortly after. Dory, who suffered a breakdown over the episode, got a measure of revenge in her most famous song, "Beware of Young Girls (who come to your door wistful and pale)."

Allen's own rhetorical disconnect stemmed from the perceived postscandal "morality gap" between the lofty tone of his films and the turpitude of his personal life — exacerbated by his steadfast denial of any guilt for his actions. His two films prior to *Husbands and Wives*, *Alice* (1990) and *Shadows and Fog* (1991), also played into the scandal: the first, in highlighting the image clash Brickman alluded to; the second, in foreshadowing the scandal to come. In *Alice*, Farrow is cast as an upper-class Catholic schlemiel — virginal yet fecund on the one hand, a lovable yet unintellectual loser on the other. Her allegorical, semiautobiographical Alice, with the drug-induced boost of a White Rabbit–like Chinese healer (played by Keye Luke), grows both personally and politically, rejecting her shallow, materialistic trappings and loveless marriage in favor of a modest but fulfilling life dedicated to her two children and social service. *Shadows and Fog*, a period-piece mash-up of Kafka's *The Trial*, Brecht-Weill's *The Three Penny Opera*, and Bergman's *Stardust and Tinsel* (1953) and *The Magician* (1958), is set entirely at night in a nightmarish world. Allen's pathetic bookkeeper Hyman Kleinman is sent out from his cramped hovel on an "assignment" he never understands, into the *Caligari*-esque alleyways of a Germanic city choked by expressionist mist, impenetrable darkness, and a Mackie Messer/Cesare–like serial strangler. Eventually suspected himself as the killer, Kleinman finds sanctuary with a traveling Romani circus troupe and employ as the magician's assistant.[40]

Although Allen fails to bridge the seriocomic gap as successfully as he did in *Crimes and Misdemeanors* (or even *Hannah and Her Sisters*), from a Jewish perspective *Shadows and Fog* is one of his richest films. The Jewish self-hatred that Allen, following Kafka, has perhaps too strongly protested, returns from the repressed in *Shadows and Fog*. While the haughty university student Jack (John Cusack), with his existential self-loathing, is not explicitly coded as Jewish, the Joseph K–like Jewishness of Kleinman is spelled out in his name and reinforced through dialogue exchange: when asked whether he prays, he responds, "No, because my people pray in a different language, so I could never understand what they were saying. For all I know, they were requesting their own troubles."

Self-hatred's imbrication with the Holocaust is echoed in several references to Kleinman's (the name meaning "little man," in German) inadequacies, which further evince how self-hatred is internalized through contact with a hostile environment: "You cringe, like a worm"; "You're a coward, a worm, a yellow-belly," he is told. "I have the strength of a small boy, with polio"; "I'm a clerk, an ink-stained wretch is what I am," he says of himself. Meanwhile, his boss, whom he calls "Your majesty," sees him "as a cringing, slimy vermin more suited to extermination than life on the planet." Associations with the Final Solution are expanded into the larger Jewish community when Kleinman's neighbors, the Mintzes, are rounded up as "social undesirables," even though (or because) Herr Mintz "does quality circumcisions." Nor, finally, can the irony of Kleinman's "rescue" by the Romani troupe go unnoted, given Romanies' tragic associations with the Holocaust.

An additional Jewish element in *Shadows and Fog* of which Allen and most critics were possibly unaware is the Jack the Ripper–like figure — who, in the film as in real life, was never apprehended. Besides the Ripper's cultural association with *The Three Penny Opera*, whose theme music by the Jewish composer Kurt Weill is a major leitmotif in Allen's film, the perpetrator of the brutal murders and disembowelments in the Whitechapel district of London in 1888 was widely believed at the time, and even controversially to the present, to be a Jew. As late as 2006, handwritten notes newly acquired by Scotland Yard's Black Museum appeared to confirm what had long been suspected: that an eyewitness's identification pointed to the Polish Jew Aaron Kosminski as the killer.[41] The murderer in *Shadows and Fog*'s other clear association, with the somnambulistic strangler Cesare in *The Cabinet of Dr. Caligari* (1920), has multiple Jewish associations also. Besides the seminal expressionist film's predominantly Jewish creators — scenarists Hans Janowitz and Carl Mayer, director Robert Wiene, and producer Erich Pommer — the story of a mad psychiatrist and his monstrous killing machine was famously interpreted, in Siegfried Kracauer's canonical Weimar-cinema study *From Caligari to Hitler* (1959), as a prophetic metaphor for the Nazi horror to come.

16 *Overview*

In the end, Kleinman's description of his dire predicament, prior to his being taken in by the Romanies, offers an aptly tragicomic summary of the film's (conscious and unconscious) historical associations, as well as a prescient forecast of Allen's own problems in the post–Mia Farrow era. "I should be all right," he tells Farrow's circus sword swallower. "Apart from the fact that I'm wanted by a lynch mob, and the police are after me, and a homicidal maniac is on the loose, and I'm unemployed — everything is fine."

Reconstructing Harry

Allen would not remain unemployed for long, either as a metaphorical filmmaker in *Shadows and Fog* or as an actual one during and after the Farrow/Previn scandal. He would remain as prolific as ever. Besides churning out at least one film a year, he would write, direct, and star in the TV remake of his 1966 play and 1969 film *Don't Drink the Water* (1994); pen a one-act play, *Old Saybrook* (1995); star in the TV version of Neil Simon's *The Sunshine Boys* (1996); voice the lead insect in the animated feature *Antz* (1998); star in Alfonso Arau's *Picking Up the Pieces* (2000); and play himself (and his clarinet) in Barbara Kopple's documentary about his European Dixie-band tour, *Wild Man Blues* (1997). Due to fallout from the scandal, however, not everything was fine, with fans and critics alike, on the filmmaking front.

The negative repercussions (critically and at the box office) were greater on Allen than they might have been for another director for two reasons: the lofty, philosophical tone and "morality" of much of his previous work and the unique link between his on-screen and off-screen selves.[42] The "correspondence between Mr. Allen's work and Mr. Allen's life that made him so popular," *New York Times* columnist Maureen Dowd opined at the time, "still obtained, if not intensified, after the scandal."[43] Like the Thackeray hero brought down by the very traits that spurred his success, Allen became a prisoner of his "aura," in Girgus's sense, of "the complex merging of iconic image, indexical associations, and symbolic interpretations that [had] defined him for years."[44] Moreover, Allen's attempts to refashion his image by fraying the connection between private and public personae or by denying his guilt only further infuriated critics such as Dowd: "He still insists that he never behaved badly. . . . Where have you gone, Woody Allen? . . . . That likeable non-hero is gone forever." Early postscandal movies such as *Mighty Aphrodite* (1995), meanwhile, amounted to "a propaganda film, a sentimental exercise in self-promotion."[45] It certainly didn't help when characters played by Allen continued to be romantically involved with much younger shiksas played by the likes of Mira Sorvino in *Mighty Aphrodite*, Julia Roberts in *Everyone Says I Love You* (1996), and Elisabeth Shue in *Deconstructing Harry* (1997). The latter film at least had the virtue of critiquing its Allenish character's propensities, in the romantic arena and elsewhere; indeed, *Deconstructing Harry*'s confessional tone went a long way in rehabilitating Allen's auteurist stature despite his disingenuous protestations that "I'm nothing like Harry."[46]

It's hard to take this disclaimer as anything but a self-mocking one-liner, as the film, which John Baxter calls Allen's most "revealing" and for David Shumway affirmed that his films "are about his life and nothing else," for Girgus absolutely "compels identifying Allen with Harry Block."[47] Although allusions to Philip Roth were also intended by Allen, and duly noted by critics, the multiple overlaps with Allen's life and work are undeniable.[48] Block (played by Allen) is an acclaimed Jewish writer of sex farces who compulsively merges his life and art. His success in the public sphere — he's receiving an honorary doctorate from the college from which he was suspended as a student (Allen had been "bounced from NYU"[49]) — is countered by abject failure in the private sphere. He has had multiple failed marriages and affairs, undergone extensive psychotherapy, lost custody of a beloved son, been attacked for "taking everyone's misery and turning it into gold," and accused of Jewish self-hatred for his demeaning portrayals of Jews in his work. The cinematic illustrations of Block's writing, moreover, play like a retrospective of Allen's film oeuvre. Combined with the emphasis on the critical discourse (relating to personal life and career arc) and the mega mash-up of *8½* (self-reflexive premise and ending) and *Wild Strawberries* (honorary award-motivated journey of self-discovery), *Deconstructing Harry* could well be subtitled *Stardust Memories II*.[50]

The perennial Kafka connection is amply present as well, on both the creative and character levels. "Harry Block," Baxter declares, given his internal and external persecutions "is a writer the way Joseph K is a clerk."[51] But he is also a writer the way Kafka was a writer, as Block's professional and romantic rival, Larry (Billy Crystal), remarks (with mutual extratextual resonance): "We both started out wanting to be Kafka, and you wound up getting slightly closer than I did." Several other explicitly, generally demeaning, Jewish references are strewn throughout the film. Block calls one of his justifiably enraged ex-lovers, Lucy (Judy Davis), a "world-class *meshugenah* cunt." Block's fictional character Helen (Demi Moore), based on Block's half-sister Doris (Caroline Aaron), becomes "Jewish with a vengeance" and marries an Israeli. "Jews," Block tells his shrink (Robert Harper), "fearing a wrathful and vengeful God, give prayer and thanks for everything." Block's father (Gene Saks), in an imagined scene in hell, doesn't want to go to heaven because Jews don't believe in it (he'd rather go to a Chinese restaurant). And in the same scene, the Fallen Angel (Crystal again) claims that his downfall was running a studio for two years: "But you can't trust *those people*." In terms of casting, *Stardust Memories II* may actually trump its forebear in the sheer number of Jewish characters and actors it employs.

The film's most expansive disquisition on the pros and cons of Jewishness, arguably the most expansive and probing of Allen's career, comes in a confrontation between Block and the "born again" Doris that begs to be taken as a debate between Allen and critics of his alleged Jewish self-hatred. "You caricatured my religious dedication — I'm *too* Jewish, *professionally* Jewish," Doris complains of Block's offensive transpositions of her in his books, which she attributes to his resentment over her returning "to her roots." He counters that her Israeli zealot of a husband, Burt (Eric Bogosian), has filled her full of superstition — "*Tradition*," she corrects, to which he retorts, "Tradition is the illusion of permanence." Doris says, "You have no values — your whole life, it's nihilism, cynicism, and *orgasm*." Block, in a rejoinder that blends sexual politics with Allen's cinematic adoration by the French, responds, "You know, I could run on that slogan in France and win."

Block then widens the conceptual frame: "If our parents had converted before we were born, we'd be Catholics. They're clubs, they're exclusionary, all of 'em. They foisted on us the concept of the other so you know clearly who you should hate. If a Jew gets massacred, does it bother you more than ———?" "Yes," Doris interrupts, "they're my *people*." "They're *all* your people," he says. When he trots out the Kafka defense against her Jewish self-hatred charge ("I may hate myself but not because I'm Jewish"), she has a ready rebuttal: his short story about Max Pincus (played in the re-creation by Hy Anzell), a fat, old, ugly Jewish man with an even more revolting secret. Unbeknownst to his loyal wife Dolly (Shifra Lerer), first, Max had been married once before; second, he had butchered his first wife, their two children, and a neighbor with an ax; and third, he had eaten them. When Dolly learns of the skeletons in his stomach and throws them at him at the dinner table, he doesn't skip a bite: "Some bury, some burn, I ate."

Burt, the über-Jew, takes up the attack: "The Jews haven't suffered enough to be depicted by *this one* as homicidal cannibals." "He has no spiritual center," Doris adds, ironically encapsulating Block's philosophy in a way that would do Allen, and his alter egos, proud: "He's betting on physics and pussy." "Does he even believe in the Holocaust?" Burt delivers what he believes is the coup de grace but that only allows Block to riff on a topic Allen had expounded on in *Hannah and Her Sisters*. In that film, Frederick, the ponderously misanthropic artist, contended that the endless puzzlement about how the Holocaust could have happened contains "the wrong questions. Given how people are, what's surprising is not how it happened but why it doesn't happen more often," adding that "it does happen, of course, but in smaller ways." Block's response to Burt's rhetorical question is a one-liner: "Not only do I know that six million people died, but the scary thing is that records are meant to be broken."

Burt's humorless rejoinder — "He creates offensive stereotypes like in *Der Stürmer*" — may be the scene's final word but decidedly not its verdict. Ultimately, as in all of Allen's best work, it is precisely Jewish humor's ability to mediate between high and low, to confront some of life's profound questions while also bringing pleasure, that is the film's saving grace. As an admiring student of Block's says at the Bergman/Fellini-esque honorary doctorate ceremony, with all his real-life and fictional characters gathered in a carnivalesque chorus, "I've deconstructed your work, and I find that... underneath, your books are happy — but you just don't know it."

Given its confessional tone and self-lacerating humor that gets as much as it gives, *Deconstructing Harry* must be taken as at least a partial "apologia" for the Farrow/Previn scandal. "Not an outright apology for misdeeds and appropriations," Rubin-Dorsky explains, "but rather a deeper understanding of a life and career devoted to, indeed subsumed by, creative endeavor.... Harry may not be redeemed (he is delivered from neither sin nor guilt), but he is saved (his psychological life is intact)."[52] "Only his writing was calm," Harry says of his fictional writer-character Rifkin — paraphrasing

Allen's own remarks during the Farrow/Previn scandal — "it saved his life."[53] It also proved Allen's salvation for sympathetic critics harboring postscandal ethical doubts, enabling them to adopt a stance toward the director similar to Florence Barrett's (Andrea Marcovicci) toward Allen's crassly opportunistic character in the aforementioned blacklist satire *The Front*: "I've made this mistake before, confusing the artist and the man. I just want you to know, I still admire the artist."

The Four Strategies

The critical (if not popular) success of *Deconstructing Harry* would prove a double-edged sword for Allen, the auteur. For though the film was hailed by many pundits as a welcome return to form for the filmmaker, it subsequently would come to be seen, at least until *Midnight in Paris*, as more of a last hurrah than renaissance.[54] Regardless of its cinematic shortcomings, however, Allen's work would continue to deal, directly or indirectly, with Jewish issues and to reflect lingering tensions of the Farrow/Previn scandal. Indeed, while few films made in the scandal's wake confront the controversy as baldly as his farcical one-act play *Honeymoon Motel* (2011; see James Fisher's chapter for a detailed discussion), I would argue that all of Allen's postscandal films employ one or more strategies for dealing with the incident's external and internal aftereffects. As a heuristic for analyzing the strategies, I have divided them into four main (sometimes overlapping) categories: *struggling, escapist, defiant,* and *accepting*. *Struggling* films grapple seriously with issues of guilt and morality. *Escapist* films concertedly avoid them. *Defiant* films justify problematic affairs or privilege art over moral sensibilities. And *accepting* films evoke a chastened appreciation of human frailty.

Match Point (2005) and *Cassandra's Dream* (2007), in their overarching concern with guilt and morality, are the "struggling" films par excellence. As Marat Grinberg's and Curtis Maloley's chapters concentrate heavily on these two films, I will defer to their more in-depth discussions.[55] Suffice it to say that the films' "struggling" aspect lies not merely in the stricken consciences (or lack thereof) of the murderous main characters but also in the larger, and largely unresolved, question of the nature of good and evil with which the films (similar to *Crimes and Misdemeanors*) leaves the viewer.

Small Time Crooks (2000), the most "escapist" (and "small time") of the postscandal films, plays like a revamped *Take the Money and Run* (1969), except that Allen's bungling thief Ray Winkler has Jewish partners in crime — certainly Jon Lovitz's Benny Goldberg is Jewish, and Michael Rapaport's Denny as well as Ray's nasal-voiced wife Frenchy (Tracey Ullman) seem Jewish. *Midnight in Paris* (2011) foregrounds escapism intra-, inter-, and extratextually. Frustrated Hollywood screenwriter Gil Pender's (Owen Wilson) surrealistic retreat to the American expatriate circle in 1920s Paris matches Allen's attempt (and success) at revivifying his career in Europe. It also realizes the dream of hitting cinematic pay dirt in France that was prophesied for his filmmaker character in *Hollywood Ending* (2002), and takes place in the country where Allen the filmmaker (like Harry Block the writer) could run for office and win. As most often occurs when actor Allen is absent, Jewish aspects are peripheral but not excised. Gil Pender plays a schlemiel who has only ever hunted for bargains, he tells Ernest Hemingway (Corey Stoll); and Gertrude Stein (Kathy Bates) acts as muse and mentor for Pender's aspiring novelist. (Maloley's and Joshua Moss's chapters expand further on the film's Jewishness.)

The Curse of the Jade Scorpion (2001), a film-noir parody set in the early 1940s, combines "escapism" with "defiance." The film's period, genre, and parodic aspects highlight the escapism; defiance is apparent in two ways. First, not only does Allen's insurance investigator, C. W. Briggs, win the beautiful, blonde, comparatively young shiksa, Betty (played by half-Jewish, thirty-eight-year-old Helen Hunt; Allen was sixty-six), but also, according to reviewer A. O. Scott, all of the film's hot young numbers "seem to be on hand to pay tribute to Mr. Allen's — I mean Briggs's — sexual potency."[56] Second, despite his unavoidable identification with Allen (as Scott's review evinces), Briggs either denies his Jewishness or has converted somewhere along the way (first, the name; second, his statement midway through that "my clergyman will vouch for me").

Mighty Aphrodite (1995) and *Sweet and Lowdown* (1999) marry "defiance" with "acceptance." In the former, veiled allusions to the scandal emerge through the married Lenny's (Allen) liaison with Linda (Mira Sorvino), a prostitute thirty years his junior; and through the inspiration of the main story line — Lenny's search for his adopted son's birth mother — that matches Allen's concern about the "legally indeterminable heredity" of Mia Farrow's adopted daughter Dylan.[57] The liaison, as Dowd's above-cited critique indicates, was clearly defiant. Lenny's altruistic attempts to "upgrade" Linda's profession, however, and his playing *shadchen* (matchmaker) for her, move in the accepting direction. The film's comical Greek-chorus asides get it both ways. While the chorus's judgmental commentary evokes public critique of Allen's role in the scandal, their farcical portrayal (they do Broadway-style musical numbers, among other incongruities) undercuts their moral authority. *Sweet and Lowdown* operates in similarly bifurcated fashion, only the other way around. Django Reinhardt–like jazz guitarist Emmett Ray (Sean Penn), whose passion for his music dooms his love life, clearly serves as a brief for Allen's singular devotion to his art. Ray's sideline as a pimp, his sadistic shooting of rats, his abusive treatment of women in general, and his failure to seize true love when it smacks him in the face preempt *Mighty Aphrodite*–like charges of the film's "propaganda" or "self-promotion" aspect.

Celebrity's (1998) wedding of "defiance" and "acceptance" takes *Sweet and Lowdown*'s self-flagellation aspect to a satirical extreme. Playing like "*Manhattan* with a migraine," in Peter Bailey's diagnostic phrase, *Celebrity* gets it three ways by holding women, show business, and frustrated writer Lee Simon (Kenneth Branagh) mutually culpable for Simon's lugubrious love life and the "corruptions of the world."[58] Simon's "punishment" is the gravest, however, "for pursuing his novels' plots in the streets of Manhattan." Allen's "downfall" is further allegorized in Simon's "confounding of art and life." Unlike the comedic redemption provided by the Marx Brothers in *Hannah and Her Sisters*, the lack of any is *Celebrity*'s glass-half-empty epiphany. The film opens and closes on a scene from an avant-garde film titled *The Liquidator*: a Monica Vitti–like Melanie Griffith runs Antonioni-esquely through a barren urban landscape as the word "HELP" is skywritten above her, altogether underscoring Simon's and her (but also Allen's and our) "condition."[59]

All-out defiance was incipiently evident in Allen's second film "after the fall," *Bullets Over Broadway* (1994). Hack playwright David Shayne (John Cusack), for starters, is here only a partial Allen surrogate, sharing the stage (literally) with gangster/ghostwriter Cheech (Chazz Palminteri), the true, if unrecognized, artist. Allen himself, of course, has been considered a hack by some, a great artist by others, and during and after the scandal, a criminal. More significantly, for Rubin-Dorsky (in his "after the fall" article), Cheech's determination to sacrifice everything for his art, including the people closest to him (even by having them killed), matched Allen's postscandal "vision of the artist/writer as a carnivorous creator of beauty and form, completely indifferent to offering moral sensitivities or violating the personal sensibilities of those whose lives nurture and sustain him."[60]

The more forthrightly (if ambivalently) defiant *Deconstructing Harry* would seem to have left little autobiographical blood to spill. Five years later in *Hollywood Ending*, however, Allen returned to the theme of an artist's creative and personal ordeals, with even more direct scandal-tinged associations. His Val Waxman, a once critically acclaimed and financially successful director who is now lucky to do deodorant commercials, is handed a last chance at redemption through the intercession of his (yet again) beautiful, blonde, comparatively young shiksa ex-wife, Ellie (thirty-six-year-old Tea Leoni; Allen was sixty-seven), a high-powered producer engaged to studio mogul Hal (Treat Williams). Ellie convinces her skeptical fiancé to give Waxman the reins on a $60 million remake of the 1953 noir *The City Never Sleeps* (obviously recalling *Jade Scorpion*), based largely on the film's New York setting, which was one of Waxman's trademarks. Another obvious tie-in to Allen, given Zhao Fei's work on *Sweet and Lowdown* and *Small Time Crooks*, is Waxman's insistence, despite the resultant communication problems on the set, on using a Chinese cinematographer.

Things go from bad to impossible when Waxman, taking the "losing focus" motif in *Deconstructing Harry* to its ocular conclusion, goes completely blind at the start of production, a condition psychosomatically triggered by his troubled relationship with his estranged son Tony (Mark Webber) from a pre-Ellie marriage. That Tony, despite the estrangement, has inherited his father's Jewish sense of humor is revealed in his stand-up response to Waxman's plea that he "came to hold out an olive branch": "What is this, the Israeli parliament?!" Jewishness is most conspicuously displayed through Waxman's faithful agent Al (Mark Rydell), who is dragged, still wearing his *kipah*, from a Passover Seder to assist his blind client. Nothing can keep the blindly directed film from becoming an unmitigated disaster, however, except a Hollywood ending — to Allen's film, not Waxman's. Whereas *The City Never Sleeps* bombs at the box office and is savaged by American critics, it is hailed in France not merely as another Waxman masterpiece but as "the greatest U.S. film in fifty years!" "Here I'm a bum, but there I'm a genius.

Thank God for the French," Waxman trumpets — to which Al wistfully adds, "And France always sets the tone for the rest of Europe." But any good Hollywood ending, especially of the Francophone variety, requires romantic fulfillment. And what better way to have *la vie* imitate *l'art* than for the amorously rejuvenated Ellie to join Waxman in Paris, where they both had always dreamt of growing old together.

After his London trilogy (*Match Point, Cassandra's Dream,* and *Scoop*), Allen revisited Manhattan and returned with a vengeance to the defiant mode in *Whatever Works* (2009). In the biggest age differential of a romantic couple in his career, Allen has sixty-two-year-old Larry David, as the Allenish genius-curmudgeon, Boris Yellnikoff, hooking up with and marrying twenty-two-year-old Evan Rachel Wood's Southern naïf, Melody. The lone redeeming feature in this decidedly lackluster film is a rare, if all-too-brief, appearance in an Allen film of a gay character, Howard (Christopher Evan Welch), whose portrayal is winning both in Howard's charming, nonstereotypical personality and his "getting the guy" in the end.

Allen's second London-set film after *Match Point, Scoop* (2006), while not his most explicitly Jewish film, does add a Semitic and personal twist first explored in the New York–based *Anything Else* (2003). Fitting squarely in the "accepting" mode, both *Scoop* and *Anything Else* express this conciliatory gesture through a paradigm shift in Allen's character: unprecedentedly, he appears not in the central, romantic-hero role but rather as a desexualized mentor-schlemiel sidekick to a younger Allenish type. In *Scoop*, Scarlett Johansson's Sondra Pransky is an American journalism student who is handed the scoop of a lifetime by a recently deceased British investigative reporter, Joe Strombel (Ian McShane), whose ghost returns from the dead during one of the Great Splendini's (Allen) magic tricks. Splendini (born Sid Waterman), a two-bit trickster (akin to Allen's Tex Cowley in Arau's earlier *Picking Up the Pieces*), is also given to performing at bar mitzvahs, playing a Jew's harp (or "Jaw's harp," as he politically correctly calls it), and tossing off one-liners.[61] At a party of upper-crust Britishers, for example, he claims to have bought his first Reubens with his poker earnings — "a Reuben sandwich, that is," and quips, when asked about his religion, "I was born into the Hebrew persuasion, but when I got older I converted to narcissism."

Splendini makes his ethnic kinship with fellow Brooklynite Pransky clear from the get-go. In introducing her as an audience participant in one of his magic shows, he confuses her name with Mandelbaum: "Mandelbaum, Pransky, what's the difference? They celebrate the same holidays."[62] This particular show is also where the ghost of Joe Strombel, having jumped ship from the River Styx, informs Pransky (onstage, in the vanishing box) that Peter Lyman (Hugh Jackman), prominent son of a British lord, is the likely serial killer of a string of *dark*-haired prostitutes. Pransky and Splendini embark on a Sherlock Holmesky/Dr. Watsonberg quest to unmask Lyman, with the beautiful, *blond*-haired Pransky starting an affair with the tall, dark, and handsome Lyman, while Splendini digs up additional clues behind the scenes. Their adventures nearly get Pransky killed when Lyman catches wind of the double-dealing, and Splendini *is* killed in a car crash on his way to deliver the incriminating evidence. But in the end Lyman is caught, Pransky gets her scoop, and all is not lost for Splendini, who is last seen entertaining fellow boat mates on the River Styx.

Scoop can be seen partly as Allen's attempt, and a quite successful one, at an Ealing-style British comedy-thriller, a la *Kind Hearts and Coronets* (1951) and *The Ladykillers* (1955). It also can't help but conjure his own earlier (escapist) *Manhattan Murder Mystery* (1993), itself heavily indebted to Hitchcock's *Rear Window* (1954), Sturges's *Unfaithfully Yours* (1948), and Welles's *The Lady from Shanghai* (1947). The main similarity between *Scoop* and *Manhattan Murder Mystery*, the coed amateur detective team (in the latter case, Allen's and Diane Keaton's Larry and Carol Lipton), is also its main difference — from a Jewish and an Allen auteurist standpoint. First, Carol Lipton, one assumes from Keaton's casting, is a shiksa, while (the Jewish) Johansson's Pransky, we are told in no uncertain terms, is a New York Jew (and the first Jewish female protagonist in an Allen film; see Del Negro's chapter for more on this aspect). More significantly, the Liptons are married and their love is reaffirmed at film's end. Whereas Splendini dies at the end, and his relationship with Pransky, while affectionate, was unromantic and asexual on both sides; indeed, Splendini, for only the second time in Allen's career (*Anything Else* was the first), appears devoid of sexual desire altogether. Allen had frequently adopted mentor-pupil or master-apprentice stances with (generally younger, non-Jewish) women in other films but invariably with physical attraction (and its Oedipal implications) intact. Whether from enhanced fatherly instincts accruing with age (he turned seventy in 2005 and has two adopted children with Soon-Yi), or from a sense that his old man/younger woman romances were wearing thin (or for other scandal-ridden reasons), Allen has left his perpetual Lothario persona behind.

Full Circle

In *Anything Else*, the desexualizing of mentor-pupil relations between Allen's David Dobel and Jason Biggs's Jerry Falk are a given (at least for the invariably straight-playing Allen) but with a unique intertextual twist that allows Allen to partake of both positions. Allen's films from the outset have been in dialogue not only with his own filmmaking mentors (Bergman, Fellini, et al.) but also with one another — occasionally amounting, as in *Deconstructing Harry*'s conversation with *Stardust Memories*, to a quasi-remake. *Anything Else*, in relation to *Annie Hall*, takes the solipsistic conceit one step further, functioning as both remake and sequel. Allen's Alvy Singer in *Annie Hall* is a young, successful New York comic who romances, and enlightens, Diane Keaton's eponymous neurotic shiksa singer. Although he loses her in the end to another (non-Jewish) man (Warren Beatty was the real-life model) and a musical career in Hollywood, Singer transmutes the devastating experience into a hit play (just as Allen would turn it into a career-breakthrough film). In *Anything Else*, Allen's Dobel is an aging New York Jewish comic manqué who mentors fledgling Jewish comedy writer Falk. When Falk's relationship with neurotic shiksa actor Amanda Chase (Christina Ricci) crumbles when she takes up with a non-Jew, the break "frees" Falk to take the Hollywood writing job that Dobel has secured for him.

Although Falk's "Allen the Younger" is taller and more conventionally handsome than Allen ever was, he looks no less stereotypically Jewish than his model and cements the interpersonal connection through his eyeglasses and mimicry of Allen's stuttering speech, jerky hand movements, psychotherapeutic dependency, and pessimistic worldview. The novel Falk is writing, for example, is "about man's fate in an empty universe — no God, no hope, just human suffering." Amanda's birthday gift for him, Sartre's *No Exit*, was chosen in a close contest with Eugene O'Neil because "I couldn't decide whose nihilistic pessimism would make you happier." Stylistic similarities between *Annie Hall* and *Anything Else* include a flashback structure and Falk's recurrent Alvy-like direct-address asides to the audience. Narrative rhymes include the following: Falk's therapy sessions that, unlike Allen's more recent films in which shrinks are portrayed more sympathetically, revert to *Annie Hall*–like parody of the tight-lipped analyst whose advice, when he deigns to give any, is either esoteric or unhelpful; anti–Los Angeles jokes — in *Annie Hall*, Alvy's comment, that he "won't move some place where the only cultural advantage is that you can make a right turn on a red light," is converted in *Anything Else* to Amanda's applauding Falk's westward move because "idiots who are total losers in New York go to L.A. and become millionaires"; a coke-snorting scene where Falk doesn't naively blow the "blow" off the table, as Alvy did, but resists taking the drug because, "Call me a square Jewish boy, but I'm not putting anything up my nose"; and most hilariously — yet also telling of the changing times — Dobel's anti-Semitic paranoia, which turns an amusing throwaway in *Annie Hall* into a major plot point.

Alvy insisted to his Jewish friend Rob (Tony Roberts) that he was surrounded by anti-Semites, giving as examples a record store clerk's emphasizing the store's sale on "Wagner — get it?" and a TV producer's allegedly inviting him to lunch by asking, not "Did you eat?" but "*Jew* eat?" Dobel similarly tells Falk that he overheard two guys at a restaurant muttering, loud enough for others to hear, "Jews start all wars!" — upon which he takes Falk to buy a gun "so they don't put you in a box car" and you "wind up as black-and-white footage scored by a cello in a minor key."[63] When Falk brings a rifle home and Amanda wonders whom he needs protection from, Falk spouts the Dobel line: "Burglars, rapists, the Gestapo.... He's still not convinced that the slaughter of six million Jews is enough to satisfy the anti-Semitic impulses of the majority of the world." Dobel himself has an arsenal and a survival kit at his place and is given to binges of Jewish Defense League–like revenge when slighted. He justifies smashing the car of two rednecks who stole his parking space because, in Falk's words, "he wouldn't let the injustice rest. He resisted. There are always some people who will resist. As he says, 'The issue is always fascism.'" Resistance goes overboard in the end, however, when Dobel claims to have killed a state trooper who, after stopping him for speeding, "made remarks about my religion that I found in poor taste" (most infuriatingly, "that Auschwitz was basically just a theme park"). Although Dobel's having spent six months in an asylum lends both credibility and lunatic fantasy to his story, Falk, riffing on the reality/illusion motif in much of Allen's work, offers another interpretation: that the incident was "a piece of fiction" altruistically intended to wean Falk from his mentor and (similar to Pransky in *Scoop*) encourage him to make it on his own.

Although *Annie Hall* is clearly the overarching template for *Anything Else*, there are, as usual, winks to other Allen films as well. When Falk describes his nihilistic novel idea, Dobel advises him (per *Stardust Memories*) to "stick to the jokes — that's where the money is." And although Falk's Jewish agent Harvey Wexler (Danny DeVito) seconds the sentiment ("The dollars are in the jokes. I mean Funny is Money"), Dobel lumps Wexler with Alan Alda's "show business Jew" in *Crimes and Misdemeanors* (and himself with *Scoop*'s Splendini): "I am of the Hebrew persuasion, but the guy who handles you is a member of one of the Lost Tribes of Israel that should have remained lost." And like Kleinman in *Shadows and Fog*, whose walk through the city's streets at night gave him "an odd, free feeling — no stores, no civilization," Falk's nighttime New York City strolls, when he's unsure or troubled, clear his head and give him "a feeling of freedom and exhilaration."

The most exhilarating Jewish aspect of *Anything Else* is the tradition of Jewish humor Dobel passes on to Falk, and to the audience. "There's great wisdom in jokes, more insight into what I call the 'Giant So What' than in most philosophy books," Dobel tells his protégé in their first tutorial in Central Park. He then supports this assertion, as he does throughout the film, with a joke that cuts to the quick of Falk's specific, and life's more universal, predicament. It's the one about the mother who pleads with a priest to pray for her boxer son who's being beaten to a pulp in the ring (a la Falk's emotional pummeling by his neurotic girlfriend). "I'll pray for him," says the priest, "but it would help if he could punch." One particular joke comes back to haunt, yet also to strangely liberate, Falk at the end, while also bringing the film's narrative, and its Dobel/Falk, Falk/Alvy, and Alvy/Dobel interrelations, full circle. Falk triggers the joke (more like a Talmudic parable) when the limning of his novel's "empty universe" theme reminds Dobel of a cab ride he had taken years ago: "I was pouring my heart out to the cab driver about the stuff that you were prattling on about — life, death, the empty universe, the meaning of existence, human suffering — and the cab driver said to me [just as a cabbie tells Falk at the end, en route to catch the plane to Hollywood], 'Well you know, it's like anything else.'"

Three Parts Id

Allen's latest film, as of this writing, *To Rome with Love*, while a critical and financial step down from *Midnight in Paris*, took his defiant postscandal posture to new heights — or depths. After a five-film sabbatical, Allen returns to the screen along with the Repressed. His avant-garde opera director, Jerry, a parody of his hyperphobic New York Jew persona, has come to Rome with his psychiatrist wife Phyllis (Judy Davis) to see their daughter, her Italian fiancé, and his parents. Picking up where *Anything Else*'s Dobel and *Scoop*'s Waterman left off, Jerry is desexualized, if reasonably happily married. Allen's "heart wants what it wants" instincts haven't disappeared, however; they've been multiply displaced onto a series of ethically challenged affairs. Though all the errant couplings predictably run amok and send the infidels back to the fold chastened or sexually awakened, the justification for the peccadilloes is neither bildungsroman edification nor Rome's Eternal City logo. Phyllis hits the nail, and character motivation, on the head in one of her therapeutic stand-up routines with Jerry. When he counters her pop-Freudian analysis of his insecure behavior with a one-liner ("The id-ego-superego model doesn't work with me"), she has a ready capper: "No, you're three parts id."

The punch line's rehabilitative rub-off onto Allen's authorial presence and real-life experience is compromised by two other scenes: one mildly self-confessional, the other a stinging rebuke of Mia Farrow and, by association, of Soon-Yi Previn as well. The self-confession occurs, appropriately, with the "Italian Woody Allen," Roberto Benigni. Benigni's middle-class Mr. Nobody, Leopoldo, reverses Kafka's *Metamorphosis* by becoming an overnight media sensation precisely for being ordinary and nondescript. Hounded by paparazzi and swamped with sexy women, Leopoldo's (and the women's) adultery is justified by one of the bombshells: "Those rules don't apply when you're somebody special." This is not exactly news, except when laid alongside recent university studies of celebrity double standards. Researchers at Harvard and Duke, *New York Times Magazine* reported in 2011, "have found that creative thinkers are more likely to take unethical shortcuts for gain, possibly because their talents make them better at rationalizing bad behavior," or possibly because "they think they can win us back with a creative apology, a creative excuse or a creative defense in court." The bottom line, Francesca Gino summarizes, is that creativity "makes people more morally flexible."[64] The bottom line in the magazine article, titled "Creative Cheating," is a cartoonlike illustration of Woody Allen.

The rebuke occurs in the affair between young architecture student Jack (Jesse Eisenberg) and aspiring actress Monica (Ellen Page). Jaded architect John (Alec Baldwin) plays a combination *Play It Again, Sam* — like alter ego and *Anything Else* — like mentor to Jack, warning him of Monica's femme fatale wiles. When Monica predictably drops Jack for a role in a big-budget film in Los Angeles, his broken heart might have left us with bittersweet memories of Alvy Singer/Woody Allen's dumping by Annie Hall/Diane Keaton. Instead, the sweetness is spiked with strychnine. "Consider yourself lucky," John counsels; then, playing off Monica's past politicking against the Myanmar dictatorship, he supplies the coup de grace: "She would have you free-fall from a parachute and adopting Burmese orphans."

Whether we should take this barb as a sadomasochistic lapse (one of Farrow's orphan adoptees was the South Korean Soon-Yi and one of Allen and Soon-Yi's adopted daughters is Chinese) or as literary gold mined from amoral alchemy, only the three ids — or is it Yids? — of Woody know for sure.

Notes

1. Allen wrote the screenplay for *Play It Again, Sam*, based on his stage play; *The Front* was written by Walter Bernstein.

2. Sam B. Girgus, *The Films of Woody Allen*, 2nd ed. (Cambridge: Cambridge University Press, 2002), 1.

3. Quoted in ibid., 371.

4. David Desser and Lester D. Friedman, *American-Jewish Filmmakers: Traditions and Trends* (Urbana: University of Illinois Press, 1993), 57.

5. Lawrence J. Epstein, *The Haunted Smile: The Story of Jewish Comedians in America* (New York: Public Affairs, 2001), 196.

6. Franz Kafka, *The Diaries of Franz Kafka*, ed. Max Brod (New York: Schocken, 1948–49).

7. Sig Altman, *The Comic Image of the Jew: Explorations of a Pop Cultural Phenomenon* (Cranbury, NJ: Associated University Press, 1971), 11.

8. Desser and Friedman, *American-Jewish Filmmakers*, 53.

9. Pauline Kael veered from the critical consensus regarding Pearl's Jewish aspect (review of *Interiors*, *New Yorker*, September 25, 1978).

10. Bergman's longtime cinematographer Sven Nykvist filmed *Another Woman*, as he would the later *Crimes and Misdemeanors*.

11. Desser and Friedman, *American-Jewish Filmmakers*, 65.

12. Girgus, *Films*, 109.

13. Steven E. Aschheim, *Brothers and Strangers: The Eastern European Jew in German and German Jewish Consciousness, 1800–1923* (Madison: University of Wisconsin Press, 1982), 63 (emphasis added).

14. Ibid., 64.

15. Quoted in ibid., 65; Sander L. Gilman, *Jewish Self-Hatred: Anti-Semitism and the Hidden Language of the Jews* (Baltimore: Johns Hopkins University Press, 1986), 210.

16. Cited in Gilman, *Jewish Self-Hatred*, 212 (Eugen Dühring, *Die Judenfrage als Rassen-, Sitten-, und Culturfrage* [Karlsruhe, Germany: H. Reuther, 1881], 53).

17. Cited in Gilman, *Jewish Self-Hatred*, 151 (Ludwig Börne, *Sämtliche Schriften*, 5 vols. [Düsseldorf, Germany: Joseph Meltzer, 1964–68]).

18. Otto Weininger, *Sex and Character* (London: W. Heinemann, 1906), 319.

19. Sander Gilman, *The Jew's Body* (New York: Routledge, 1991), 129, 134.

20. Isaac Deutscher, "The Non-Jewish Jew," in *The Non-Jewish Jew and Other Essays*, ed. Tamara Deutscher, 25–41 (1958; repr. Oxford: Oxford University Press, 1968), 30; Thorstein Veblen, "The Intellectual Preeminence of Jews in Modern Europe," *Political Science Quarterly* 34 (March 1919): 33–42, reprinted in *The Writings of Thorstein Veblen*, ed. Leon Ardzrooni (New York: M. Kelley, 1964), 223–24.

21. Max Weinreich, "Internal Bilingualism in Ashkenaz," in *Voices from the Yiddish: Essays, Memoirs, Diaries*, ed. Irving Howe and Elezer Greenberg, 278–88 (Ann Arbor: University of Michigan Press, 1972). The quote's explication is from Mark Shechner, "Dear Mr. Einstein: Jewish Comedy and the Contradictions of Culture," in *Jewish Wry: Essays on Jewish Humor*, ed. Sarah Blacher Cohen, 141–57 (Detroit: Wayne State University Press, 1987), 145.

22. Irving Howe, "Introduction," in *Jewish-American Stories*, ed. Irving Howe (New York: New American Library, 1973), 47; see also Shechner, "Dear Mr. Einstein."

23. Shechner, "Dear Mr. Einstein," 147, 151, 153.

24. Allen's swan song as a protagonist was actually 2002's *Hollywood Ending*. In the three subsequent films in which he appears, he plays a sidekick/foil to the main characters in *Anything Else* (2003) and *Scoop*, and in *To Rome with Love* is the only nonromantic figure in a large ensemble-cast film otherwise obsessed with *amore*).

25. Desser and Friedman, *American-Jewish Filmmakers*, 69.

26. Jeffrey Rubin-Dorsky, "Woody Allen after the Fall: Literary Gold from Amoral Alchemy," *Shofar* 22 (2003): 5–28; 26.

27. Desser and Friedman, *American-Jewish Filmmakers*, 71.

28. Ibid., 78.

29. Ibid., 73.

30. Ibid., 74.

31. Eric Lax, *Woody Allen: A Biography* (New York: Knopf, 1991), 171; Girgus, *Films*. Allen's first cinematic homage to Groucho occurred in *Take the Money and Run*, via the Groucho disguises worn by Allen's character's father *and* mother in the film's faux-documentary interviews.

32. Girgus, *Films*, 108.

33. Rubin-Dorsky, "Woody Allen," 16; Woody Allen, *Woody Allen on Woody Allen: In Conversation with Stig Björkman* (New York: Grove, 1993), 156.

34. Desser and Friedman, *American-Jewish Filmmakers*, 92, 93.

35. Ibid., 95, 94.

36. Rubin-Dorsky, "Woody Allen," 16; Desser and Friedman, *American-Jewish Filmmakers*, 101.

37. Allen's quote is from "Sam Tanenhaus on Woody Allen's Black Magic," *Newsweek*, June 18, 2012, http://www.thedailybeast.com.

38. Quoted in Samuel H. Dresner, "Woody Allen and the Jews," in *Perspectives on Woody Allen*, ed. Renee R. Curry, 188–98 (New York: G. K. Hall, 1996), 189.

39. Quoted in Lax, *Woody Allen*, 384.

40. Besides the magician's metaphorical connection to Bergman, as Allen's cinematic mentor, Allen himself has had a lifelong fascination with magic and considerable ability in its practice. He auditioned as a child magician for two television shows at thirteen and performed in the Catskills at sixteen (Lax, *Woody Allen*, 49–50).

41. Stewart Tendler, "Official: Jack the Ripper Identified," *Times* (London), July 14, 2006, http://www.timesonline.co.uk. The eyewitness identification could not be used at the time because, according to the chief inspector's notes, the witness, also a Jew, refused to swear to it.

42. Rubin-Dorsky, "Woody Allen," 18.

43. Maureen Dowd, "Auteur as Spin Doctor," *New York Times*, October 1, 1995, Week in Review, 13; quoted in Girgus, *Films*, 149.

44. Girgus, *Films*, 149.

45. Dowd, "Auteur," 13; Girgus, *Films*, 149.

46. Quoted in Bernard Weintraub, "At the Movies," *New York Times*, January 2, 1998, B7.

47. John Baxter, *Woody Allen: A Biography* (New York: Carroll & Graf, 1998), 434; David R. Shumway, "Woody Allen, 'the Artist,' and 'the Little Girl,'" in *The End of Cinema as We Know It*, ed. Jon Lewis, 195–202 (New York: New York University Press, 2001), 202; Girgus, *Films*, 151.

48. See Rubin-Dorsky, "Woody Allen," 22.

49. Lax, *Woody Allen*, 79.

50. And these are only some of the links to Allen's work and life, much less to Fellini and Bergman; doing the connections justice would require a separate chapter.

51. Baxter, *Woody Allen*, 434.

52. Rubin-Dorsky, "Woody Allen," 20.

53. Ibid., 23–24.

54. Ibid.; see also Kenneth Turan, "*Whatever* Doesn't Work," *Los Angeles Times*, June 19, 2009, D4. One of the decidedly less brilliant results, and therefore relegated to an endnote here, is *Vicky Cristina Barcelona*, whose predictable narrative and clichéd characters somehow eluded Motion Picture Academy members who granted the film, and Allen, yet another Oscar nomination for best original screenplay.

55. *You Will Meet a Tall Dark Stranger* (2010) qualifies as a semi-"struggler," via Josh Brolin's frustrated writer, one of the ensemble film's multiple protagonists, who must cope with guilt, morality, and the likelihood of getting caught, after plagiarizing another writer's unpublished novel.

56. A. O. Scott, "Case of the Arch Gumshoe," *New York Times Magazine*, February 24, 1991, 74.

57. Peter J. Bailey, *The Reluctant Film Art of Woody Allen* (Lexington: University Press of Kentucky, 2001), 211.

58. Ibid., 262.

59. Ibid., 262, 263.

60. Rubin-Dorsky, "Woody Allen," 5.

61. Allen's magician character here, more literally than his magician's apprentice in *Shadows and Fog*, obviously draws on Allen's actual experiences as a performer (see note 40).

62. Another Jew-sy one-liner comes when Splendini hears from Pransky that Lyman is interested in marrying her: "You come from an Orthodox family — would they accept a serial killer?"

63. The cello-scored film is an obvious reference to Alain Resnais's classic Holocaust documentary *Night and Fog* (1955).

64. Quoted in Heather Havrilesky, "Creative Cheating," *New York Times Magazine*, December 18, 2011, 9.

COMPARATIVE
ANALYSIS

Don't turn this into one of your
big moral issues.—Yale to Isaac in *Manhattan*

MARAT GRINBERG

The Birth of a Hebrew Tragedy *or Cassandra's Dream* as a Morality Play in the Context of *Crimes and Misdemeanors* and *Match Point*

Sander Lee accurately points out that "throughout Allen's career, he has been frequently accused of narcissism and the advocacy of moral relativism, when in fact he has been, and continues to be, one of film's most forceful advocates of the importance that an awareness of moral values plays in any meaningful life."[1] Within his body of work, *Crimes and Misdemeanors* (1989), *Match Point* (2005), and *Cassandra's Dream* (2007) form the trilogy of good and evil. All three probe the question of justice and the director's obsessive concern: is there order to the universe, embodied in the divine moral directive, or does everything happen at the whim of chance, making any notion of absolute morality irrelevant? Jewishness and Judaism constitute the key aspect of the trilogy, whose artistry is carried out through diverse hermeneutic strategies, directed at various sources. Among the three films, *Crimes and Misdemeanors* is permeated with both the Jewish and Judaic thanks to its allusions and positions; *Match Point* functions as, what I would call, a translation film; and *Cassandra's Dream* should be seen as an almost unique example of Jewish hermeneutics and polemics on-screen, which become the movie's primary language.

The case study of these three films, and especially of the first and third, should engender a deeper understanding of the role of Jewish layers in

Woody Allen's tightly interwoven oeuvre as a whole. As the collective chapters in this volume make clear, various Jewish elements are central, for better or worse, to the director's body of work. Even when he, as some of the chapters claim, decides to leave them behind or conceal them (see Feuer, Moss, and Maloley), it is clear that he does so with the full and rich appreciation of what he is abandoning. What this chapter intends to show is that Woody Allen ought to be viewed as a serious Jewish artist and philosopher, whose Jewish or indeed Judaic thinking shines through even or especially in the absence of apparent Jewish markers, thematics, or identity. In contrast to Sam Girgus's assertion that "Allen's overall failure in the films since 1990 to create credible and workable moral drama has radically diminished the style and success of his art," I see *Cassandra's Dream* as a culmination of his moral thinking.[2] My analysis of *Cassandra's Dream* alongside of *Crimes and Misdemeanors* and *Match Point* will hopefully reveal how, through interpretive engagement with Jewish Scripture and modern Jewish texts, on the one hand, and Greek drama and modern Western classics, on the other, Woody Allen constructs Jewishness as a philosophical, religious, and artistic concept.

Crimes and Misdemeanors

Crimes and Misdemeanors develops through two parallel stories: of a doctor, Judah Rosenthal (Martin Landau), who decides to have his mistress killed after she threatens the security of his marriage; and of a schlemiel, director Cliff Stern (Allen), who fails in his attempts to find love or any meaning in life. The doctor, who initially possesses an acute sense of justice and morality, learns to live with the knowledge of the crime committed at his behest; furthermore, he puts any fear of God on the farthest backburner of his being. The film's interrogation of justice, while certainly in dialogue with Dostoevsky's novels, is framed in stark Jewish terms. It is the recollections of his father, a God-fearing observant Jew, and the debates at his parents' Passover Seder table that propel Judah's doubts and torments. It is also Judah's patient Ben, his rabbi, brilliantly played by Sam Waterston, who serves as the moral voice in the film, admonishing Judah in a dream, "But the Law, Judah. Without the Law it's all darkness." Allen's move is a daring one, considering that in the American imagination, both popular and literary, the question of morality is inextricably linked to Christianity, or at best to Judeo-Christian civilization, a strange concoction/child of American politics.

In Allen's oeuvre, Christianity serves as material for a joke, as in *Hannah and Her Sisters* (1986), or more interestingly, is inserted into a Jewish framework and, in the process, Judaized. As Jeffrey Rubin-Dorsky points out in his illuminating article on *Broadway Danny Rose* (1984), "Danny is a Jewish saint, and his Jewishness — outwardly signaled by his hand gestures, his use of Yiddish expressions and rhythms, his evocation of family ties, and (not least) by the *chai*, the Hebrew letter signaling good luck that he wears around his neck — provides the structure for his moral philosophy, the foundation of which is his abiding belief in the value of guilt."[3] Rubin-Dorsky notices that Danny's "sainthood" resembles that of St. Francis, who "shield[s] the weak." However, it's not just St. Francis but also the Christian heritage at large, including the figure of Christ, that is appropriated by Allen. Much like Yiddish and Hebrew modernist poets and writers, most notably Uri Zvi Greenberg, Itzik Manger, and Peretz Markish, he refashions Christ as a Jewish figure. The consequences of this polemical turn are of course profound, leading the Catholic Tina Vitale (Mia Farrow) in *Broadway Danny Rose* to embrace and be redeemed by a Jewish Christ, the Jewish comedian Danny.

In *Crimes and Misdemeanors*, Woody Allen operates within a self-sufficient Jewish intellectual and theological sphere. The film mirrors the classic Jewish debates of modernity: a traditionalist perspective, represented by Judah's father (David S. Howard) and Ben; a Jewish Marxist and violently atheist one, personified by Judah's Aunt May (Anna Berger); and finally the voice of Jewish existentialist, secular humanism (evocative of German Jewish heritage) that is represented in the film by philosopher Louis Levy, memorably played by psychoanalytic thinker Martin Bergmann, about whom Cliff is making a documentary. Similar to Martin Buber's philosophy of "I and Thou," Levy is trying to breach the chasm between God and humanity and reconcile the notions of a transcendent and an immanent God.[4] In one of the footages, used by Cliff for his film, Levy, in his thick German accent, paradigmatically states, "Now, the unique thing that happened to the early Israelites was that they conceive a God who cares. He cares, but at the same time, He also demands that you behave morally. But here comes the paradox. What's one of the first things that that God asks? That God asks Abraham to sacrifice his only son, his beloved son, to Him. In other words, in spite of millennia of efforts, we have not succeeded to create a really and entirely loving image of God. This was beyond our capacity to imagine." The secularism of Levy's position is unmistakable: he speaks of *conceiving* God, thus implying that God is a human creation; he also obliquely polemicizes with Christianity, which claims that it is through sacrifice that the divine love enters the world. Levy would have agreed with Harold Bloom, who points out that the idea of a God who carries through with the plan of killing his own son is inconceivable to Judaism.[5] As perhaps befits an existentialist, Levy commits suicide, leaving Cliff dumbfounded. In the last clip we see of him, Levy intones, "Human happiness doesn't seem to have been built into the universe.... It is only we, with our capacity to love, that give meaning to it."

With the character of Levy, Woody Allen writes his film into the canon of Jewish American writing.[6] The film bears interesting parallels with Saul Bellow's grand *Mr. Sammler's Planet*, whose protagonist, a one-eyed Jewish Tiresias, a Holocaust survivor, and an acutely moral conservative thinker, likely served as a prototype for Levy, also a survivor.[7] The concept of blindness and seeing connects the two works. Artur Sammler is blinded in one eye, yet he possesses an instinctive moral vision. Judah is an ophthalmologist, but his moral vision is corrupt. He treats Rabbi Ben, who loses his sight but who does not relinquish insight into the primacy of the Law. As in *Crimes and Misdemeanors*, in *Mr. Sammler's Planet* the question of justice wavers between the failing secular Jewish option, that of Sammler, and the traditionalist one, that of his cousin Elya Gruner, whom Sammler deeply respects.

Ultimately Allen, as does Bellow, leaves the question of good and evil in a Platonic state of aporia, or to use a Talmudic term, that of *kashya*, an insoluble issue. Is it that neither Levy's arguably absurdist and self-destructive quest for love nor the demands of the Law suffice? Indeed, Judah overcomes any sense of the impending punishment, yet there is no guarantee that retribution will not catch up with him after death, for once again, the possibility of God's existence remains on the table, potentially unshaken by Levy's talk of the construction of God's image. Inconsolable, Allen's character becomes the sign of the film's inconclusiveness, both lyrical and mesmerizing.

The sense of aporia is further complicated and arguably undermined by Allen's reading of Dostoevsky. As has been numerously commented on, *Crimes and Misdemeanors* is an especially rich and elusive film, not least due to its link to the Russian writer.[8] I would not dispute that but instead argue that Allen hermeneutically translates Dostoevsky's idiosyncratic Russian nationalist Christianity into his own Jewish terms. It is ideas and concepts rather than specific plot twists and character traits in Dostoevsky upon which he seizes. Attempts to see Judah Rosenthal as Raskolnikov or the direct mirror of one of the Karamazov brothers, for that matter, are misguided. Yet Michal Bobrowski is right in finding echoes of the so-called "mysterious visitor" episode in *The Brothers Karamazov* in *Crimes and Misdemeanors*.[9] In the novel, the mysterious visitor, Mikhail, confesses to the young father Zosima of the murder he committed in his youth, killing a young woman who did not return his love. Never convicted or even suspected of the crime, he lives the rest of his life as a virtuous family man. Ten years later, however, his guilt is reawakened and, after much soul-searching, he decides to turn himself in although doing so would damage the lives of those closest to him, his wife and children. This is exactly what transpires; furthermore, the confession results in his own death, the outcome of the sentence he receives.[10] At the core of the tale is the redemptive potential Dostoevsky finds within death, which, for him, is of course predicated on the purpose of Christ's crucifixion.[11]

Contemporary American readers of Dostoevsky should be reminded that, first and foremost, he is a Christian theological thinker. Woody Allen, I would claim, realizes that. Indeed, Judah's predicament is a response to Mikhail's. Like him, the Jewish ophthalmologist is able to move on with his life. If we were to imagine that some ten years later he would experience the need to confess, which is not at all improbable, as suggested by Mary Nichols,[12] the resolution of it one way or another would be very different from Dostoevsky's logic. In the film, Judah's father proclaims, "If necessary, I will always choose God over truth!" This is nothing but a direct rephrasing of Dostoevsky's famous dictum that he expressed first in a private letter and then in *Demons*: "If somebody were to prove to me that Christ is outside the truth, and indeed it would have been that the truth is outside of Christ, then it would have been better for me to remain with Christ than with the truth."[13] The Russian word Dostoevsky uses for "truth" is *istina*, which indicates its fundamental nature and theological meaning. By this usage, Dostoevsky means not some abstract concept but in fact the Truth — the God of the Old Testament.[14] Christ for him also resolutely signifies the Russian people, who in Dostoevsky's nationalist worldview embody the Savior and are the bearers of his mission in the world.

Allen "gets" Dostoevsky; his substitution of God for Christ, in the mouth of this old Jew, is a powerful retort to the writer's system of beliefs. Judah's father acknowledges the possibility of another truth — that there might be no God or that he might be unjust or indifferent — but, much like Job, opts for sticking with the Almighty instead of cursing him. In other words, while both the essential problem and answer for Dostoevsky are the nature and figure of Christ, for Allen the problem and the only answer, even if improbable, is the God of the Hebrew Bible. To recall *The Brothers Karamazov* again, Ivan, outraged at the injustices God allows to exist in the world, returns his ticket to the Creator and denounces him.[15] Sympathizing with Ivan's position, Alyosha reminds his brother that he forgot about Christ, whose death redeemed everyone's sins. Allen undoubtedly appreciates Ivan's anger as well, but Alyosha's response carries for him no weight.

What is significant is that in *Crimes and Misdemeanors* this Hebraic preoccupation with God and his justice conjoins with Allen's constant concern with the nature of love and relationships between men and women. It seems quite obvious that as the film's creator he is sympathetic to his character's predicament. Judah is caught up in his own lies and yet knows that his relationship with Dolores (Anjelica Huston) is bound to be fleeting and won't lead to a sustaining life. She is part of what Allen has identified, for better or worse, as a "kamikaze woman" type. Gabe Roth (Allen) wryly defines such women in *Husbands and Wives* (1992), saying, "I call them kamikazes because they, you know they crash their plane, they're self-destructive. But they crash into you, and you die along with them." Thus, in Judah's mind, his action is one of self-defense, which, to emphasize, should by no means excuse in the eyes of the viewer the severity of his crime or lessen Dolores's humanity, and the fact that it was gruesomely put to an end. The paradox is that the comfort Judah feels with his wife at the end of the film is genuine; Sander Lee provocatively but significantly misreads this aspect when he writes, "How could he find a joy in a relationship with a woman who bores him, whose idea of a birthday present is a treadmill? . . . How long will it be before he tires of the endless empty chatter of his home life and his wife's desire to entertain guests he finds shallow and frivolous?"[16] This description not only demeans the character of Judah's spouse (Claire Bloom) and what she has been put through but also misunderstands what Allen has been saying about the nature of marriage throughout his films.[17]

Allen the artist is a nuanced moralist whose work suggests that the institution of marriage or long-term commitment may be imperfect and requires constant reinvigoration, but it is also the only defense against the meaningless realities of life as well as the pitfalls of passion. The hope of marriage with the right person — or of sustaining relationships — triumphs, or at least is given a chance in practically all of his films, including the most recent: a tantalizing parable, *To Rome with Love* (2012). When things don't work out, as in, for instance, *Annie Hall* (1977), *Manhattan* (1979), and *The Purple Rose of Cairo* (1985), there is sadness, at times overwhelming, but again, much more than a hint of hope. Even in the parabolic *Whatever Works* (2009), where the very title seems to put a damper on the validity of long-term relationships, love comes out on top at the end, crucially fulfilled not just through heterosexual marriage or strict monogamy. The idea of "husbands and wives" becomes a broad existential and moral concept for Allen, with an ironic and comedic twist.

Similarly to Joyce's setup in *Ulysses*, Allen at times allows for the possibility that straying may rejuvenate marriage; *To Rome with Love* is again a case in point. Therefore, there is a great deal of rigidity to Judah's father's position that sees any crime or misdemeanor — any infidelity — as the Crime. Much like Dostoevsky's Ivan, however, this modern patriarch realizes that in the absence of the fear of God, boundaries would break, and in order to protect themselves, maintain the status quo, and find comfort, or conversely to ruin it, people will overcome moral inhibitions. Without God, the consolation Judah ultimately finds loses its redeeming potential and becomes the sign of the irreparable human condition, lacking in that fear of heavens. The two most central issues for Allen are the one of art and reality and the one of passion and reality. The question with both is how to learn to live in the world without sacrificing one's essence and destroying oneself, how to maintain love in the presence of routine and mortality. What makes *Crimes and Misdemeanors* so fascinating and crucial as a Jewish work is that the necessity of God's justice becomes paramount to the equation.

Allen's philosopher, Levy, seems to grasp that. His final words are more pragmatic and conservative than absurdist, which intensifies their debt to Bellow. He intones, "Most human beings seem to have the ability to keep trying, and even to find joy, from simple things like the family, their work, and from the hope that future generations might understand more." Levy confirms the horrific precariousness of Judah's situation but also the value of his attempts to save his marriage. For again if he were to confess now or later, he would damage those who are alive, those who imbue his life with meaning. For Levy, as was pointed out, God is a human invention. When he suddenly, at least in Cliff's eyes, commits suicide, he leaves a note that says, "I've gone out the window." Disturbed and puzzled, Cliff protests, "What the hell does that mean. . . . This guy was a role model, you'd think he'd leave a decent note!" With his mind of a schlemiel, Cliff knows that suicide is not an option for a Jew, hence his joke, "Listen, I don't know from suicide, you know, where I grew up, in Brooklyn, nobody committed suicide, you know, everyone was too unhappy!"[18] However, he is not trying hard enough to discern Levy's certainly "decent" note. It should be read in a rabbinic hermeneutic mode of *pshat* (plain literal meaning) and *drash* (figurative allegorical one). Literally, Levy means that he'd end his life by jumping out the window. Yet more profoundly he suggests that *he went out the window*. In other words, his ideas became null and void; they, which see God as a fantasy, have been found to be faulty.

This analysis of the film's radical translation of Dostoevsky and the meaning of Levy's suicide does not do away with the notion of aporia I suggested earlier, since the absence of God and his justice remains a very real possibility in the film; Aunt May might be the last one laughing after all. Yet at the end of the picture, we are left not with her but with the four other characters: the rabbi, Judah, Cliff, and Levy, modern incarnations of the four sons from the Passover Haggadah. All four seek to find meaning in "simple things." Judah's "success" is irrevocably tainted by having committed the worst of transgressions; Cliff, married to the wrong person, fails in his romantic pursuit of the right one; and Levy seems to denounce his own philosophy. It is only the rabbi, whom we see dancing with his daughter at her wedding, who remains intact and cherishes family life under the constant weight of the Law. A softer version of Judah's father, he is his alter ego. To suggest, as does Mary Nichols, that Allen "mocks the rabbi's moral vision by making him go blind" is to fail to appreciate the steadfastness of the rabbi's trust in God, which the film clearly upholds.[19]

A sentimental schlemiel, Cliff yearns for tragedy. He tells Judah about the hypothetical murderer, or rather Judah himself, "because in the absence of a God or something, he is forced to assume that responsibility himself," providing his tale with "tragic proportions." Judah, who knows that to remove God from this story is to falsify it, dismisses Cliff's suggestion as the stuff of movies. The development of this moral trilogy would provide an answer to Cliff's suggestion.

Match Point

A span of sixteen years separates *Crimes and Misdemeanors* from *Match Point*. While Allen's personal life was rocked by a scandal during this time, whose effect can perhaps be discerned in some of his work, Allen the artist and the thinker has not strayed from his main concerns. The rabbinic principle of reading Scripture — "There is no 'before' or 'after' in the Torah" — applies well to Allen's oeuvre and allows the critic to sidestep chronology in order to perceive his subject's body of work as a unified autonomous space. With this approach in mind, the two films are supremely joined. I view *Match Point* as a translation piece of another sort, an artistic and hermeneutic exercise for Allen who converted the Jewish play and terms of *Crimes and Misdemeanors* into a general parlance and in the process made the issues much less ambiguous. Jewishness is entirely absent from the new film precisely because Allen decided to turn "Saul" into "Paul" in order to put on an act of pure performance, utterly lacking in intricate theological or ethical referentiality. *Match Point*'s allusions are clear: either Western to Dostoevsky, or American to Dreiser; yet the nuanced polemical intertextual play so significant for *Crimes and Misdemeanors* is absent here despite the stark contrarian reading of the sources.

The film's protagonist commits an act almost identical to Judah's; Judah facilitates his mistress's murder, while Jonathan (Chris Wilton) commits the dirty deed himself. He and Judah, however, are polar opposites. Jonathan experiences a natural fear that he might be caught but carries none of

Judah's religious and family baggage. His crime is undiscovered due to pure chance and thus the film abandons the principle of aporia both artistically and philosophically; any assumption of a moral order in the universe, just or unjust, cancels itself out. It is of utmost significance that Allen does not translate the substantive Jewish allusions of *Crimes and Misdemeanors* into the serious Christian ones in *Match Point*, thus strongly suggesting that the two are not at all interchangeable. He clearly knows the difference between the two and is not thinking, as has been assumed, along vague religious or moral lines.[20] Indeed, the ingenuity of *Match Point* is that in adapting the Christian paradigm of universalizing the Jewish content, it does not substitute it with anything specifically Christian but produces a spectacle, almost absurdist in the extent to which its idea is carried. *Cassandra's Dream* returns obliquely to Jewishness and fully activates Allen's presentation of it as a concept.

Cassandra's Dream

Ostensibly, on its own *Cassandra's Dream* seems to be at best a minor crime flick, with a somewhat unexpected ending. However, when *read* as a conceptual work, both self-referential and commenting on Woody Allen's entire thought, it begins to shine. The film functions on at least two levels: hermeneutical, directed at interpreting the Hebrew Bible and modernist texts of Osip Mandelstam and Edouard Roditi; and polemical, pitting Allen's concept of justice and moral choice against the Aristotelian theory of drama. More specifically, he seizes upon Aristotle's fundamental element of catharsis, making it the centerpiece of the film's dramatic effect. Here Allen follows in the footsteps of Kafka, none of whose characters are distinctly Jewish; on the contrary, they are presented as decidedly non-Jewish.[21] At the same time, the Prague writer's texts are not only reflective of the predicaments of the assimilated Jews of his generation but also ultimately profound ruminations on the Judaic concepts of the Law, justice, and the people of Israel. Kafka's writings, as readers have long discovered, are deeply allegorical, on the one hand, and contrary to the very principle of allegory, detailed, specific, and inconclusive, on the other.

In *Cassandra's Dream*, Allen presents a biblical allegory, or even a parable, with elements of Greek tragedy, imbued with idiosyncratic Judaic content. Despite its schematic structure, necessarily symbolic and devoid of any pretense at psychology, as would be expected of classic tragedy, the film reaches the level of poignancy traditionally associated with the lyric. Its terrain is symbolic. Though we know that the events take place in today's England, it lacks, unlike the London of *Match Point*, any specificity.[22] The plot is centered on two brothers and their uncle, evocative of the evil Uncle Charlie from Hitchcock's *Shadow of a Doubt* (1943), one of Allen's favorite films.[23] The uncle, deftly played by Tom Wilkinson, promises to help the nephews with their troubles and aspirations, if they would agree to kill his business partner, who is intent on testifying against him in court on the matter of some shady dealings. The uncle's role is similar to that of *ha-satan* — the adversary — in the book of Job. He instigates and tempts but is not at all at the center of action. After much deliberation and soul-searching, the brothers do kill the man. The aftermath of the murder provides a blend of *Crimes and Misdemeanors* and *Match Point*. One brother, Terry (Colin Farrell), becomes the troubled Judah, while Ian (Ewan McGregor), resembles the amoral Jonathan. Finally, Terry, perhaps alluding to the character of Alberto in Juan Antonio Bardem's epic *Death of a Cyclist* (1955), decides to turn himself in. Having learned of this turn of events, the uncle convinces Ian to kill the brother; obedient and frightened, he resolves to poison Terry on an excursion on their boat, *Cassandra's Dream*. Something unexpected transpires there: Ian is unable to carry out the plan; the two brothers fight, and Terry accidentally kills Ian, exclaiming, "God, oh, God." In the next shot, we learn from the police that Terry killed himself by drowning immediately afterward. At first glance the brothers' characters bear no resemblance to Allen's other protagonists. They are not witty or original; they are not Jewish. The film's Jewish layer, however, opens up through a critical analysis.

Cassandra's Dream is linked to *Crimes and Misdemeanors* through not merely its subject matter but also the very figures of the brothers themselves. For it is, of course, Judah's brother Jack (Jerry Orbackl), who organizes the murder in *Crimes and Misdemeanors*. It is Jack who threatens to kill Judah if he were to reveal himself to the police. It is Jack, the wicked son from the Passover Haggadah's "four sons" tale (echoing the Seder theme that is central to the film), who foreshadows the lines to be spoken by Ian in *Cassandra's Dream*. Conversely, it is also Ian who begins to resemble Judah, with his final turn to reason and the embrace of postcrime survival. Ian emerges as the stark voice of anti-Judaic philosophy in Allen's oeuvre, yet again similar to Jack's in *Crimes and Misdemeanors*, telling Terry after the murder, "Then was then and now is now. We've done it and it's over. It's always now." The chilling power of these words, which echo Queen Clytemnestra's soliloquy after her murder of Agamemnon in Aeschylus's masterpiece,[24] resolutely contradicts the very premise of the Hebrew Bible. Its main injunction is "thou shalt remember," addressed to the Israelites and incumbent upon God himself, who swears to remember the people's misdeeds till the fourth generation and, of course, redeems the Israelites precisely because he recalls the promise made to their forefathers. Memory stands at the center of the biblical and consequently Judaic conception of the orderly universe. Ian, the specter of Jack, smashes it. While Terry invokes God's justice, admonishing Ian in no uncertain terms, "We broke God's law," Ian inveighs against it, whispering, "God? Terry, what God? What God, you idiot, God?" In this exchange, the word "God" is repeated five times, making it abundantly clear what concerns Allen the most.

The dichotomy of Terry and Ian runs in two directions. On the one hand, it is an interpretation of the Cain and Abel story as not only the saga of their brotherly rivalry but also an instance of the primordial murder. The notion of memory is central to the fourth chapter of Genesis as well, with God's eternal remembrance of Cain's sin and the prohibition against multiplying it. This scriptural context constitutes the film's allegorical and hermeneutic levels and is precisely why McGregor and Farrell play their roles as if they were wearing masks, for their characters are intently generic. Suggestively, the uncle is a famous plastic surgeon, a mass producer of masks. At the same time, Allen thwarts the allegorical structure by turning *Crimes and Misdemeanors*, whose characters are supremely psychological, into *Cassandra's Dream*'s main referent. This hermeneutic turn details the allegory and makes its Jewish biblical content plausible and tangible.[25]

The second direction of the Terry/Ian plotline is polemical and forms the core of the film's conceptual language. Allen ensures that the attentive viewer recognizes what constitutes his target. On the one hand, he replicates the devices of Greek tragedy in the film's very structure through an intricate set of allusions to a number of tragedies and, on the other, revisits Aristotle's theory of drama, paying particular attention to *catharsis*. Among the three dominant components of Aristotle's definition of tragedy — "imitation of serious and complete action," the necessity of it having a completion and a certain size, and it imitating action through "purgation of . . . emotions through pity and fear" — the latter, *catharsis*, looms largest. On a very general level, Allen's film does imitate action, a serious and complete one at that, and it certainly does have a neat structure. At the same time, these criteria are vague and can describe almost any Hollywood drama. In fact, Aristotle himself applies the same features of seriousness and completion to any work of art and especially epic poetry. While what Aristotle means by catharsis is quite murky, the term is absolutely specific to tragedy.[26] Recognizing both the concept's indeterminacy and its singular moral/aesthetic capabilities, Allen appropriates it for the film's goals and imbues in the process fresh meaning.

The turn to tragedy begins with an intertextual play. In a conversation between Ian, his actress girlfriend Angela, and her director, which immediately precedes the "God" exchange between Terry and Ian, the director (Richard Lintern) and Angela (Hayley Atwell) discuss which Greek tragedy they like the most. The director states that his is Euripides's *Medea*. Angela agrees, adding that for her Clytemnestra is the most powerful heroine. He overlooks her response, commenting that the best production of the play was done by Martha Graham, capturing beautifully "all the Aristotelian pity and fear." Ian, preoccupied with his thoughts, cannot quite understand what they are talking about; to the question of what his favorite play is, he confesses that he is "not all that familiar." Here Allen constructs an elaborate interplay of idiocy and blind spots, which, nevertheless, holds the key to his project. Medea, of course, has nothing to do with Clytemnestra, a character, most famously, in Aeschylus's *Agamemnon*, whose preliminary significance for the film was already established (see above). Thus at work is not a social satire, though indeed none of these characters — a bad actress; a bogus intellectual, evocative of Lester (Alan Alda) in *Crimes and Misdemeanors* who pontificates about the comedic aspects of *Oedipus*; and a lying murderer — know anything about Greek drama. Allen emphatically reproduces the very techniques of Greek tragedy, the most crucial of which is ironic foreshadowing. Most paradigmatically, *Oedipus Rex* functions through such a device. Indeed Terry, a character in a tragedy, is "not all that familiar" because his impeding "execution" will not be staved off. The audience recognizes this reality, while he, along with his backdrops, remains in the dark. In *Agamemnon*,

Cassandra formulates this trope of misunderstandings and misreadings, blindfolds and miscommunications: "You *are* lost, to every word I said."[27] Thus, the theme of blindness, central to both Greek drama and *Crimes and Misdemeanors*, enters the film. The director himself, a masterful puppeteer, takes on the role of an all-knowing Tiresias, a concoctor of a delicate network of concealed signs and allusions.

Ultimately, Allen reinterprets "all the Aristotelian pity and fear," turning it into his own concept of the Judaic justice. Throughout the film, Terry insists that one has a choice: to kill or not to kill. Once the killing is done, the mechanism of justice and punishment is set into motion. Thus, both Terry and Ian could have avoided the divine punishment had they made the right choice. This view directly contradicts the logic of Greek tragedy, where characters are marked by fate from the start, which they can neither control nor avoid: *Oedipus never has a choice*. Even in such tragedies as *Agamemnon*, obsessed with the notions of absolute justice, punishment, and suffering, at issue is not the human agent, confronting an ethical choice, but the preordained nature of a crime. "The one who acts must suffer / — that is law," states the chorus in *Agamemnon*.[28] Since to "act" here is to "live" as such, the notion of choice is taken out of the equation altogether.[29]

It is through the moment of catharsis that the spectators purge themselves of their own fears of suffering and the impending doom. Cognizant of the prevalent Western reading, or rather misreading, of Aristotle that perfectly suits his intent, Allen presents catharsis in moral terms, which produce, nevertheless, an exceptionally powerful aesthetic impact. What happens on the boat, when Terry accidentally kills Ian (who ironically just concluded that he is indeed his "brother's keeper" by choosing not to murder Terry) and subsequently drowns himself, is not the recognition of chance, as *Match Point* would have it, or of pills and booze, as the police seem to conjecture, but the enactment of the divine justice. A new choice not to kill does not cancel out the previous transgression. Unlike Cain's, in this Hebrew tragedy, Ian's or Terry's life, for that matter, would not be spared. Terry realizes this horror when he shouts, having killed Ian, "O God, God . . ." The audience does as well, having just experienced catharsis through this utterance. Thus, Woody Allen establishes an instance of primordial biblical justice, spelled out in the terms of Aristotelian pity and fear, which takes repentance here out of the equation due to the logic of the film's dramatic structure and also evokes Danny Rose's conviction that "we are all guilty in the eyes of God." The aporia of *Crimes and Misdemeanors* vanishes, and a new conceptual Jewish language is engendered.

Thus, what is especially striking about *Cassandra's Dream* is that Allen brings God back with vengeance. Levy might have been right in that the Hebrew God is not entirely loving, but it is precisely the God of justice that the director needs. The roots of the film's play with tragedy, as I pointed out, are in Cliff's final statement in *Crimes and Misdemeanors* — in the absence of God, the criminal himself must take responsibility for his actions and thus become a tragic character. In retrospect, we can say that much like Ian, Cliff is in the dark. Terry realizes that the yoke of responsibility comes not in the absence of divine justice but in the face of its paradoxically palpable and invisible power. Instead of secular tragedy, the result of God's nonexistence, Allen responds to his character (and perhaps himself) with Hebrew tragedy, the result of God's return or never having left the stage.

Osip Mandelstam and Edouard Roditi

Allen pits his radical reworking of Genesis and the Jewish net of allusions of *Crimes and Misdemeanors* against the Greek drama. The two are equalized, with the tragedy having the upper formalist hand, the poetics, and the conceptual Jewishness performed through it, maintaining the ideational and metaphysical end.

In 1926, major Russian modernist poet Osip Mandelstam (1891–1938), with whose poetry Allen may certainly be familiar,[30] wrote a review of a production of the Moscow Yiddish Theater, commenting on the performance of its legendary actor, Solomon Mikhoels:

> Mikhoels's face takes on the expression of world-weariness and mournful ecstasy in the course of his dance as if the mask of the Jewish people were drawing nearer to the mask of Classical antiquity, becoming [almost] indistinguishable from it.
>
> The dancing Jew now resembles the leader of the ancient Greek chorus. All the power of Judaism, all the rhythm of abstract ideas in dance, all the

pride of the dance whose single motive is, in the final analysis, compassion for the earth — all this extends into the trembling of the hands, into the vibration of the thinking fingers which are animated like articulated speech.[31]

One wonders why in such a meticulously constructed film as *Cassandra's Dream*, in the conversation with Angela, the director mentions the dance production of *Medea*, while dance plays no important role in the movie at all (Ian does dance with Angela once). A possible answer lies in the above quotation from Mandelstam.[32] Mikhoels is a Jewish actor whose dance is equal in greatness to the Dionysian frenzy of the Greeks. Allen's *Cassandra's Dream* emerges as this dance, painstakingly attentive to Greek energy, yet supremely concerned with pursuing its own independent vision. The film's enigmatic title adds another layer to this negotiation between Jewish and Greek poles.

At its most literal level, the title refers to the name of the brothers' fateful boat, which they purchase at the start of the film. Terry proposes that they call her *Cassandra's Dream*, the name of a winning horse that he has recently bet on at races. His winnings contribute to acquiring the boat. The boat is the film's master symbol: evocative of the brothers' happy days, she becomes the stage of their cathartic downfall. Inscribed into the very name of the tragic prophetess, their dream conceals the nightmare. As we know from *Seinfeld* (1990–1998), in life, or in art for that matter, "there are no big coincidences, or small coincidences, there are just coincidences," and even those turn out to be premeditated and deliberate.[33] Thus, the link between the film, *Cassandra's Dream*, and Edouard Roditi's poem, "Cassandra's Dream," cannot be coincidental.[34] On the contrary, Roditi's piece serves as a suggestive backdrop for Allen's conception.

Edouard Roditi (1910–1992), a fellow traveler of the French surrealist movement, a prolific translator, an art critic, and a significant American poet in his own right, wrote his long poem in 1939–1940 at Berkeley and then Kansas City. The piece, clearly modeled on T. S. Eliot's *The Waste Land*, is an amalgam of historical references, from the Crusades to the realities of prewar Central Europe; it is an impassioned philosophical rumination on the cyclical nature of history and the meaninglessness of any change in human existence. It is the poem of doom. Roditi commented on its composition, "I was then so intensely aware of doom, of the end of an era and of the impending Holocaust, that I suffered in quick succession some of the most violent seizures of my life and had to go into neuropsychiatric treatment, though with little positive effect."[35] Indeed, in his poetry, Roditi often presents himself as a visionary, whose ailment provides him with the gift of a prophetic insight. The poem proposes an Ecclesiastes-like worldview, with its pessimistic and almost cynical insistence on the interchangeability of epochs and human lives. "Yet beware of signs," the poet states, for "there is no end, / but an endless change from same to same."

In hindsight, the following lines bear an unmistakable allusion to Ian's statement on the "now" in the film:

> From the pain of the past and the pain
> Of the future, memory and foresight,
> Are lighter than pangs of the endless present
> In which we live, save in our sleep,
> In hopes, in fears, in poetry
> And in our death, those five sole doors
> Of escape (though one will open only
> Once from the present, allows no return
> To the present, if once we try this door).[36]

Hopes, fears, poetry, and death are, of course, the "stuff" of tragedy that breaks the comforting zone of the "now." It is, however, not the specific allusions to the text that link it most strongly to Allen's film but rather its "prehistory."[37] Roditi wrote regarding this aspect, "'Cassandra's Dream' is named after the long dramatic monologue composed in ancient Alexandria by the Greek poet Lycophron, whom Charles James Fox, in the eighteenth century, believed to have been the only Greek poet endowed with the same gift of prophecy as the Hebrew prophets."[38] Originally, "Cassandra's Dream" was published in a collection of Roditi's poems in 1949 and then republished in 1981 in a collection titled *Thrice Chosen*.[39] While the original 1949 edition is hard to come by, the 1981 one is readily available and contains Roditi's explanation quoted above. I would argue that it is precisely this link between the ancient Greek poet and the Hebrew prophets that attracted Allen's attention, substantiating his concept of the *Hebrew tragedy*.

Furthermore, in part 4 of the poem, the speaker, troubled by how his word would be understood in posterity, writes,

> I must know, as I write, what each word means
> Now to me and hereafter to all who read
> This and all that I write.
>   In spring, birds sing
> And the ear, turned to winter's dialectic,
> Hears sound without meaning, pauses to listen
> Like the bird that hears Old Homer's voice,
> The Song, but not the tale of Troy.[40]

These lines by this supposedly minor poet astound with both their precision and depth. Allen is their perceptive reader, for his *Cassandra's Dream* is both an homage/commentary and a reinterpretation of Roditi's masterwork. "The song, but not the tale of Troy": isn't this what his film is most profoundly about — a new Jewish content, where "the song" is the Aristotelian structure not "the tale of Troy"? While Roditi speaks to the disjunction between eras and the ultimate, surprising for a Western poet, "unsurvivability" of art, Woody Allen imbues this paradox with a positive impetus, pitting and yet equalizing "Athens and Jerusalem."

Roditi identified himself as a Jewish artist, perpetually attentive to Jewish traditions: biblical, mystical, and rabbinic alike. He wrote in the preface to *Thrice Chosen*, "Three of my grandparents were Jews, but the fourth, my maternal grandmother, was a Flemish Catholic, so that neither my mother nor I were born Jews according to traditional Jewish law. I chose, however, to be one of the Chosen people, a choice that already implies a kind of double election."[41] One can surmise that Woody Allen is doubly chosen as well, where the election of a Jewish artist is counterbalanced with "all the Aristotelian pity and fear." Unlike the unfortunate Ian from *Cassandra's Dream*, this Jew from New York is *all that familiar*.

Notes

This chapter is an expanded version of Marat Grinberg, "The Birth of a Hebrew Tragedy: Woody Allen's *Cassandra's Dream* as a Morality Play," *Journal of Religion and Film* 14, no. 1 (April 2010). http://www.unomaha.edu. The *Journal of Religion and Film* grants the permission to republish it here.

1. Sander H. Lee, "Existential Themes in Woody Allen's *Crimes and Misdemeanors* with Reference to *Annie Hall* and *Hannah and Her Sisters*," in *Woody Allen: A Casebook*, ed. Kimball King, 55–80 (New York: Routledge, 2001), 59.

2. Sam B. Girgus, "The Lost Transcendence of Woody Allen: From 'Divine Comedy' to *Celebrity*," *Post Script* 31, no. 2 (2012): 47.

3. It should be noted that "chai" is not a Hebrew letter but two Hebrew letters, *khet* and *yud*, which form the adjective "khai," meaning alive and symbolizing the survivability of Jews as a people. Jeffrey Rubin-Dorsky, "The Catskills Reinvented (and Redeemed): Woody Allen's *Broadway Danny Rose*," *Kenyon Review* 25 (Summer/Fall 2003): 264–81; 276.

4. Martin Buber, *I and Thou* (New York: Hesperides Press, 2006).

5. Harold Bloom, *Jesus and Yahweh: The Names Divine* (New York: Riverhead Books, 2005).

6. To an extent, Levy's philosophy replicates Martin Bergmann's own commentary on the Bible. See Martin S. Bergmann, *In the Shadow of Moloch: The Sacrifice of Children and Its Impact on Western Religions* (New York: Columbia University Press, 1992). I am thankful to Steven Wasserstrom for pointing me to Bergmann's writings.

7. Saul Bellow, *Mr. Sammler's Planet* (New York: Penguin, 2004). Bellow, of course, appeared as himself in *Zelig* (1983).

8. See, for instance, Ronald LeBlanc, "Deconstructing Dostoevsky: God, Guilt, and Morality in Woody Allen's *Crimes and Misdemeanors*," *Film and Philosophy* 7 (2000): 84–101; Olga Stuchebrukhov, "'Crimes without Any Punishment at All': Dostoevsky and Woody Allen in Light of Bakhtinian Theory," *Literature-Film Quarterly* 40, no. 2 (2012): 142–54.

9. Michal Bobrowski, "Disturbing the Balance — Woody Allen Reads Dostoevsky," *SCN* 4, no. 2 (2011): 82–93.

10. Fyodor Dostoevsky, *The Brothers Karamazov*, trans. Richard Pevear and Larissa Volokhonsky (New York: Farrar, Straus and Giroux, 1990), 301–12.

11. On the significance of the episode, see Caryl Emerson, "Zosima's 'Mysterious Visitor': Again Bakhtin on Dostoevsky and Dostoevsky on Heaven and Hell," in *A New Word on The Brothers Karamazov*, ed. Robert Louis Jackson, 155–79 (Evanston, IL: Northwestern University Press, 2004).

12. Mary P. Nichols, *Reconstructing Woody: Art, Love, and Life in the Films of Woody Allen* (Lanham, MD: Rowman & Littlefield, 1998), 158–59.

13. My translation. See Fyodor Dostoevsky, *Complete Collected Works* (Russian) (Leningrad: Nauka, 1985), v. 28, p. 176; Fyodor Dostoevsky, *The Demons*, trans. Richard Pevear and Larissa Volokhonsky (New York: Vintage Books, 1995), 249.

14. In the Hebrew Bible, God is at times referred to as the God of Truth (Emet). See, for instance, Psalm 31:5 and Isaiah 65:15.

15. Dostoevsky, *Brothers Karamazov*, 236–45.

16. Sander H. Lee, *Eighteen Woody Allen Films Analyzed: Anguish, God and Existentialism* (Jefferson, NC: McFarland, 2002), 162.

17. On the link between *Crimes and Misdemeanors* and Allen's philosophy of relationships, see Elliot Shapiro's chapter in this volume.

18. On Woody Allen and Jewish humor, see Menachem Feuer's chapter in this volume.

19. Nichols, *Reconstructing Woody*, 154.

20. Charles L. P. Silet, ed., *The Films of Woody Allen: Critical Essays* (Lanham, MD: Scarecrow, 2006), 34–49.

21. For an analysis of the link between Woody Allen and Kafka, see Silet, *Films of Woody Allen*, 171–97.

22. Allen acknowledges as much in an interview about the film. Cynthia Lucia, "Contemplating Status and Morality in *Cassandra's Dream*: An Interview with Woody Allen," *Cineaste* 33, nos. 1 and 2 (Winter 2007/Spring 2008), http://www.cineaste.com. It should be noted, of course, that there is a difference between Allen the creator of complex work, whose meaning is constantly refreshed through interpretation, and Allen the reader of his own work, whose presentation of its meaning is often deceptive and reductive.

23. Ibid. Linked to this is Elliot Shapiro's claim that *Match Point* alludes to Hitchcock's *Strangers on a Train* (1951).

24. "Here I stand and here I struck / and here my work is done. . . . Done is done." Aeschylus, *The Oresteia* (New York: Penguin, 1977), 161–62.

25. It is important to remember that as a text the Hebrew Bible is wary of any allegorizing. Its characters are singular in their predicaments. Imposing allegory on the Bible is part of a hermeneutic process itself. Much like the rabbis, Allen is especially interested in deriving moral if not didactic meanings from Scripture.

26. I find great Soviet classicist A. F. Losev's analysis of the history of interpretations of catharsis to be especially illuminating and comprehensive. See A. F. Losev, *Istoriia antichnoi estetiki: Aristotel' i pozdniia klassika* [History of Ancient Aesthetics: Aristotle and the Late Classics] (Moscow: Iskusstvo, 1975).

27. Aeschylus, *Oresteia*, 153.

28. Ibid., 167.

29. The value of suffering as part of Jewish historical experience, celebrated by Danny Rose, complicates the interplay between Greek and Hebrew paradigms in the film.

30. Mandelstam's name and work were of particular importance to American intellectuals at large, among which Allen can certainly be counted, during the Cold War thanks to the memoirs of Nadezhda Mandelstam, the poet's widow. See Nadezhda Mandelstam, *Hope Against Hope*, trans. Max Hayward (New York: HarperCollins, 1974).

31. Osip Mandelstam, *Sobranie sochinenii v chetyrekh tomakh* [Collected works in four volumes] (Moscow: Art-Buznis-Tsentr, 1990), 2:448; my translation.

32. For an analysis of Mandelstam's Jewishness, see Marat Grinberg, "In the Midst of Judaic Ruins: Osip Mandelstam and the Problematics of Russian Jewish Tradition," *Slovo/Word* 40 (2004): 116–28.

33. *Seinfeld*, "The Robbery," season 1, episode 4, 1990.

34. Edouard Roditi, *Thrice Chosen* (Santa Barbara, CA: Black Sparrow Press, 1981), 65–82.

35. Ibid., 17.

36. Ibid., 72.

37. Nevertheless, they are also revealing. The poem specifically tells of suicide, which becomes significant in light of Terry's drowning: "There is no other end but death: / between death and death, fast or slow, / no choice but self-inflicted. / Usurp time's powers, try to cheat / chance of its tricks, the end / is still the same: death by death's hand / or death by your own, guided by death's." I would argue that Allen replaces the notion of chance, central to *Match Point*, with that of divine and poetic justice.

38. Roditi, *Thrice Chosen*, 72.

39. Edouard Roditi, *Poems 1928–1948* (Norfolk, CT: New Directions, 1949), 79–95.

40. Ibid., 74.

41. Ibid., 17.

CURTIS MALOLEY

A Jew Leaves New York *in* Woody Allen's Gloomy British Angst

New York City has long been at the heart of Woody Allen's filmic oeuvre. Always more than just a setting or backdrop, Allen's New York is often framed as a central character in his films, as both an extension of his characters' neuroses, insecurities, and shortcomings, and as a space of possibility and transcendence that "comes as close as possible to a luminous 'city on the hill.'"[1] His on-screen and off-screen personas are inextricably tied to the city, as is the iconic representation of New York Jewishness that his films have cultivated since the late 1960s. As William Rothman has observed, "You can take Woody Allen out of New York, but you can't take New York out of Woody Allen."[2] In the last decade, however, Allen has left New York for Europe, and his films have taken a new, often gloomy (especially with regard to his London-based dramas) and overtly less Jewish turn. The distinctive Jewish humor and neurotic New York Jewishness that previously served to inflect the existential themes in Allen's most critically acclaimed efforts, like *Annie Hall* (1977), *Hannah and Her Sisters* (1986), and *Crimes and Misdemeanors* (1989), have all but vanished in his more recent European films like *Match Point* (2005), *Cassandra's Dream* (2007), *Vicky Cristina Barcelona* (2008), *You Will Meet a Tall Dark Stranger* (2010), *Midnight in Paris* (2011), and *To Rome with Love* (2012). And while many of these latest films certainly adhere to Allen's obsession with existential subjects as "the only subjects worth dealing with . . . the highest goal," they differ from his previous New York work in their typically rather overt exclusion of Jewish characters, traditions, and situations.[3]

Efforts like the London-based *Scoop* (2006) and *Whatever Works* (2009), Allen's only New York–based film since 2004, are two exceptions to the rule, but for the most part even the palimpsestian trace of Jewish signification that Vincent Brook identifies in Allen's earlier WASP dramas — *Interiors* (1978), *September* (1987), and *Another Woman* (1988) — is missing from his most recent engagement with questions of existential meaning and morality.[4] Allen's own atheistic authorial position was previously counterbalanced not only by (Jewish) humor but also by a skeptical (Jewish) respect for both life's mysteries and for the life-affirming power of meaningful illusions — love relationships, religious faith, and film spectatorship itself. However, I will argue that his recent phase of British films especially is characterized by a more despairing, humorless, and staunchly nihilistic worldview. In *Tall Dark Stranger*, the notion of meaningful illusion is recast unsympathetically as a meaningless delusion, while in *Match Point* and *Cassandra's Dream* it is twenty-first-century materialist social-class anxieties rather than either religious or secular Jewishness that inflect the representation of metaphysical angst.

The only London-based film that remains more or less faithful to Woody Allen's traditional comedic and Jewish filmic roots is *Scoop* (2006). Allen himself stars in the film (another recent rarity) as Sid Waterman, a second-rate vaudevillian magician who becomes embroiled in a whodunit (a la *Manhattan Murder Mystery* [1993]) with a young Jewish American journalism student named Sondra Pransky (Scarlett Johansson) who is searching for her first big scoop. It is the only European film of the first six shot outside of New York in which Allen actually appears, and it is a testament to Rothman's claim that "you can't take New York out of Woody Allen," as the Waterman character once again embodies Woody's conventional neurotic, New York Jewish persona. It differs, however, in a couple of important ways. First, as Brook notes, Allen's paradigmatic schlemiel persona is thoroughly desexualized in *Scoop*.[5] There is no hint of romance with the younger Pransky whatsoever. Second, Allen's own character actually dies in the film, a symbolically pregnant final curtain for an actor whose on-screen persona is famous for being morbidly solipsistic and terrified of death. Rushing to save an unsuspecting Pransky from her aristocratic serial-killer boyfriend, Waterman dies suddenly in a car accident because he "couldn't get used to driving on the goddamned wrong side of the street."

This apparently meaningless and unheroic death not only underscores the idea that Allen's Jewish persona is not adaptable to the British context but also signifies a clear break with his previous work.[6]

Scoop follows on the heels of *Match Point*, arguably his most serious and certainly his most critically acclaimed film since *Deconstructing Harry* (1997). For Allen, *Match Point* was a major achievement because it "could be serious, without jokes in it, without comedy in it, and it had a real audience — an audience like *Manhattan*, an audience like *Annie Hall*, that had a big audience.... That's why I'm so knocked out by *Match Point*, because despite the fact that I'm such a screw-up all the time, in *Match Point* I feel I didn't screw up."[7] Throughout his career Allen has frequently stated that he aspires to make "serious" films and wishes he had the talent to make the kinds of serious existential dramas mastered by Ingmar Bergman. For the most part, his more serious efforts before *Match Point* were deemed by both critics and Allen himself as failures. Films like *Interiors* (1978), *September* (1987), and *Another Woman* (1988) were box-office and critical flops. On the other hand, *Hannah and Her Sisters* and *Crimes and Misdemeanors*, which succeeded at bridging the comic and serious sides of Allen's oeuvre, both found large audiences and were critically successful but did not quite live up to Allen's own high standard for what he was trying to achieve. *Crimes* was "a little too mechanical,"[8] while in *Hannah* he "copped out a little.... I backed out a little at the end."[9]

Only with *Match Point* did Allen feel he finally hit the nail on the head: "I don't know if I can ever repeat it or make a film as good."[10] Relocating his production to London seems to have afforded Allen the opportunity to break with his Jewish New York persona and to articulate his starkest vision so far of his oft-cited belief "that the universe is godless and life is meaningless, often a terrible and brutal experience with no hope, and that love relationships are very, very hard, and that we still need to find a way to not only cope but lead a decent moral life."[11] In a recent volume of "Conversations" with Eric Lax, Allen emphasizes how many of his past efforts at addressing these darker themes were constricted by "the Woody Allen character" that he is forced to assume on-screen. After *Scoop*, he even vowed to stop "wasting [his] time" with "little" comedies: "I'm not going to be able to write *Cries and Whispers* or *The Bicycle Thief* and accommodate my character."[12]

The subsequent death, both symbolically and literally, of the Allen/Waterman character in *Scoop*, along with his new European financiers, have afforded Allen the opportunity to revisit the existential themes at the heart of his work with a new seriousness, and his specific references to Bergman and De Sica in this context are particularly instructive in unpacking the artistic intentions of his post–New York/post-Allen character films. The tragedy of *Cassandra's Dream*, for example, unlike so much of his past work, is organized around a (neorealist) depiction of contemporary working-class social reality, while in *Match Point* it is specifically social-class anxieties that are negotiated through a psychological (Bergmanesque) dramatic structure. In borrowing much of its content from both Theodor Dreiser's *An American Tragedy* (social-class drama) — and by extension its film adaptation *A Place in the Sun* (1951) — and Fyodor Dostoevsky's *Crime and Punishment* (psychological drama), *Match Point* lays a new foundation for Allen to readdress the wider existential themes in his work.[13]

Allen cues his audience to the particular importance of Dostoevsky in *Match Point* during an early scene when he frames his protagonist Chris Wilton (Jonathan Rhys-Meyers) in a close-up reading *Crime and Punishment* and, after a somewhat exasperated sigh, a copy of *The Cambridge Companion to Dostoevskii*. Chris has just succeeded in securing work as a tennis instructor at the very exclusive Queen's Club in West Kensington, London, and the scene serves to cue us both to his diegetic position as an outsider within his new "cultured" social milieu and to the extradiegetic significance of Dostoevsky's novel to the film's overarching themes. Allen previously paid homage to *Crime and Punishment* in *Crimes and Misdemeanors*, not only with its title but also with his protagonist Judah Rosenthal (Martin Landau), who is responsible for committing a murder and suffers from a similar sense of existential anguish and conflict over moral responsibility that Dostoevsky's antihero Raskolnikov suffers. Throughout the novel the nihilistic Raskolnikov is tormented by an involuntary inner anguish that eventually leads him to confess his crime and to experience a spiritual resurrection at the novel's end. Robert Belknap observes that in Dostoevsky's narrative, "the subconscious is deeply moral; Raskolnikov's dreams and impulsive actions struggle against his rational mind's rejection of moral values."[14] Raskolnikov comes to the realization that all along he had "sensed a profound lie in himself and his convictions," which would eventually "herald a future break in his life, his future resurrection, his future new vision of life."[15]

For Dostoevsky, human nature is implicitly religious (Christian), and morality is only possible through faith in God.[16] Allen's protagonist Judah, on the other hand, has his strong doubts about the existence of God and the relevance of Judaic morality confirmed when his crime goes unpunished. His own sense of anguish slowly disappears, leading him to the nihilistic position that God is simply "a luxury I can't afford." Leonard Storchevoy consequently reads *Crimes and Misdemeanors* as Allen's filmic rebuttal to Dostoevsky's novel, because "for each of the characters the underlying thesis evolves into its anti-thesis," and for Judah the moral conclusion is very clearly that "punishment and remorse belong in the world of fiction and movies; in real life, the wicked enjoy non-punishment and peace of mind."[17] The moral subconscious that caused so much of Raskolnikov's suffering and led to his eventual religious conversion has no such traction in the existentially amoral world of Woody Allen.

Match Point returns to the scene of *Crimes*, echoing its (a)moral in an even more pointed manner. In the second half of the film, Allen's protagonist Chris quite obviously treads another parallel path to Raskolnikov. He commits a double murder of an old woman and a young woman; he is very nearly compromised in the act of murder by a knock at the old woman's door; he makes off with the valuables of the old woman to make his crime look like a robbery; he is investigated by a savvy police detective who is convinced of his guilt; and he receives the unexpected luck of having someone else fingered for his crime. In Dostoevsky's telling, Raskolnikov decides not to throw his victim's possessions in the Neva River for fear that they may float and be discovered. Instead, he buries them under a heavy stone in a secluded courtyard, and were it not for the subconscious anguish that he could not so easily bury, Dostoevsky implies that Raskolnikov would certainly have gotten away with his crime.

In contrast, Allen's protagonist Chris experiences relatively little in the way of subconscious anguish or inner turmoil and doesn't think twice before tossing his victim's valuables into the already polluted Thames. When the last item he throws bounces up off a railing, the net-cord tennis metaphor that Allen introduces in the prologue of the film affirms the contingent role of luck as the determining factor in human fate. When a tennis ball hits the top of the net, it will bounce straight up in the air, lingering momentarily before it falls either forward or backward, resulting in either a winning point or a losing one, and only pure chance determines the outcome. In Chris's case, the old woman's ring does not fall forward into the river when it bounces up off the railing; instead, it lands safely back on the ledge as an incriminating piece of evidence. Allen offers the audience what seems like a conventional plot twist: fate conspires against Chris so that he will now have to face justice for committing murder. But, as chance would have it, the unlucky bounce of the ring turns out to be very lucky indeed, as the evidence is ultimately found in the pocket of a junkie who commits a parallel murder, providing Chris with the perfect alibi in the eyes of the law. The possibility of moral justice gives way to an absurd fate that is governed only by blind chance.

Chris later justifies his murders with a quasi-Nietzschean explanation that "the innocent are sometimes slain to make way for a grander scheme." In Dostoevsky's novel, Raskolnikov also initially measures his actions against the will of Napoleon himself — he wishes to "become a Napoleon" (or a superman, as Nietzsche would have it) — and explains to the inspector his philosophy that there are some "extraordinary" men who have the right "to step even over a dead body, over blood," if the idea is grand enough.[18] But while Raskolnikov eventually comes to the clear realization that he is not a Napoleon, Chris succeeds at asserting what Nietzsche would call his "will to power" — the aggressive, expansive human desire to be totally free and to be master of one's own life and moral actions.[19] As with Judah, Chris too abandons any concerns about moral responsibility, existential meaning, or the possibility of God's justice. He concedes that it would be fitting if he were apprehended and punished because "at least there would be some small sign of justice, some small hope for the possibility of meaning," but he sees no such moral forces at work in the world. Allen is once again clear as a bell on this particular "match point" with Dostoevsky: an implicit moral order is nowhere to be found.

While both *Crimes and Misdemeanors* and *Match Point* share a similar Dostoevskian theme, their respective paths to Allen's more despairing thesis differ in significant ways. Allen has always been very clear that even though his Jewish ethnic identity is obviously a central element in his larger oeuvre, Judaism has had little meaning for him; "it was a non-factor."[20] And while we must always be careful about giving an artist's own words too much authority, Allen's art has been quite consistent in its wider rejection of religious authority. Yet, with *Crimes and Misdemeanors* he nonetheless gives an articulate voice to the Judaic faith through both Judah's father Sol (David S. Howard) and his friend and rabbi Ben (Sam Waterston). The symbolism of Judah's profession as an ophthalmologist and of Ben's deteriorating eyesight and eventual blindness no doubt speak to Allen's rejection of religion as a viable solution to the problem of a meaningless universe: Judah can ultimately see the harsh truth about life to which Ben is blind. But the final image of the film tellingly lingers on a grateful and happy rabbi as he dances with his daughter at her wedding.[21] Allen uses a voice-over by Professor Louis Levy (Martin S. Bergmann), a Holocaust survivor and existential philosopher who serves as the film's true moral conscience, to articulate the concluding sentiment that "it is only we, through our capacity to love, that give meaning to the indifferent universe."

This idea, which has long been at the heart of Allen's most moral films — *Manhattan* (1979), *Broadway Danny Rose* (1984), and *Hannah and Her Sisters* — serves to comment obliquely on both Judah's murder of his mistress and Levy's own untimely suicide before Allen's character Cliff can finish his documentary on the man's life-affirming philosophy. Some might read this existentially shocking plot twist as further confirmation of Judah's pessimistic nihilism, but Levy himself underscores the point that "we need a great deal of love to persuade us to stay in life." Framed always as an isolated figure in Cliff's documentary footage, it is quite likely that Levy himself has succumbed to loneliness and a lack of the necessary love relationships that make life worth living. Allen's critique of religious faith and morality are nonetheless inflected, as Gary Commins observes, by an acknowledgment that an ethical life is still necessary and "the power of redemption, the power to liberate, comes . . . through the power of love that enters the world through vulnerability."[22] Our individual choice to give and receive love in spite of life's inherent meaninglessness is at the center of what Allen depicts as an ethical life. Despite their respective sufferings and differing beliefs about the ultimate meanings of religious faith, both Ben and Levy are testament to the importance of moral action. As Sander Lee argues, "The source of the dialectical opposition in [Allen's] films, and indeed the source of much of his greatness as a film artist, lies in his unwillingness to give in to his despair, his need to continue to fight for his values."[23] The absence of God, or any other universal moral authority in *Crimes and Misdemeanors*, is thus tempered by an existential ethics of individual moral responsibility and personal integrity. Consequently, Judah does not get the last word despite his position as the principle protagonist in the film. Unlike Dostoevsky who could see no morality without Christ, Allen seems to maintain that existential meaning comes only from the free *choice* to live a moral life in spite of the meaningless void that confronts us.

Match Point and Allen's other London-based films outside of *Scoop* seem to mark a break with his previous work in their relative negation of the kind of ethical ambiguity or dialectical opposition that is present in *Crimes*. The Judaic ideal of ethical struggle that Lee and others like Mark Bleiweiss identify as a central feature of Allen's past work has been more or less completely abandoned in his British phase.[24] Rather than negotiating moral action through the prism of faith or religion, Allen's latest films bring the debate into the era of late capitalism by focusing specifically on materialist social-class anxieties. His protagonists still adhere to an outsider status in his London-based films, but it is no longer of the Jewish-schlemiel variety. In *Match Point*, *Cassandra's Dream*, and *You Will Meet a Tall Dark Stranger*, moral choices and actions are inflected by much less ambiguous social-class pressures that are faced by each of Allen's male protagonists.

Chris Wilton's class ambitions in *Match Point* are born explicitly out of an impoverished upbringing in Ireland. He has come to London to work his way up the social ladder after a largely unsuccessful stint on the professional tennis tour. He is not a character of intellectual depth or sophistication; his interests in literature and art are depicted as largely superficial, despite his self-professed love of opera; and he fully understands that his future success is "all about who you know." When Chloe Hewett (Emily Mortimer), daughter of an aristocratic family that has "nothing but money," takes a shine to him, he is all too eager to pursue a relationship with her despite his obvious lack of romantic desire. He makes shrewd use of his personal Horatio Alger tennis narrative to win the affections of Chloe's father Alec Hewett (Brian Cox) and borrows insights from his quick study of *The Cambridge Companion to Dostoevskii* so as not to appear "trivial" when they discuss literature.

Allen nonetheless goes to great lengths to depict Chris's overall lack of cultural capital as he dates Chloe and begins spending time with her family. From his "old-fashioned" insistence on paying for gallery tickets on dates with Chloe or his awkward attempt to pick up the check after a drink with her brother Tom Hewett (Matthew Goode) at the tennis club to his ordering the roast chicken instead of the caviar blini when they all go to dinner at the posh Brasserie Max and his failed attempt at grouse shooting with Alec and Tom at the family's country home later in the film, Chris very clearly lacks what Pierre Bourdieu terms the "class habitus" of the aristocratic Hewett family.[25] The point is driven home comically at Brasserie Max when Tom ignores Chris's order, substituting the caviar blini, and Chloe excuses Chris by asking him if his father specialized in etiquette. Even Chloe's mother, Eleanor Hewett (Penelope Wilton), comments that she does not "understand what he is aiming for" when they first start dating. By emphasizing these class differences, Allen illustrates that the only avenue of real social mobility open to Chris is his romantic relationship with Chloe. Without her genuine affections, he has no shot at ever being anything more than the club tennis pro, a fate that he confesses would make him want to "cut his throat if he thought he'd have to do it forever."

Chris's subsequent marriage to Chloe succeeds at opening up his social-class ambitions. Alec finds him a job in "the company," enrolls him in "a business course at school" to help speed up his career advancement, and welcomes him into the family in order to make his daughter happy. Here, the common Allen trope of having his New York schlemiel-protagonist "improve" the shiksa love interest or the young schlemiel protégé like Jerry Falk (Jason Biggs) in *Anything Else* (2003) is reversed, so that it is the protagonist himself who must obtain an education in order to be successful in this WASPY British social world. In this sense, Chris's narrative evokes the historical experience of Jewish assimilation in general and of Allen and his generation's into American culture in particular, but the film's very specific British context and its emphasis on Chris's lust and self-interest motivates *Match Point* with more far-reaching twentieth-first-century material concerns. Chris is able to ascend the Hewett's social-class ladder quickly and relatively effortlessly, but his newfound privilege threatens to come crashing back down on him when his lust for Nola (Scarlett Johansson) — Tom's ex-girlfriend — becomes an obsession and he ends up getting her pregnant, an offense that is particularly egregious given that he has so far been unable to achieve the same goal with Chloe.

Nola's insistence on confronting Chloe with the news mirrors Judah's crisis with Dolores (Anjelica Huston) in *Crimes* and positions Chris in a parallel moral predicament. If he takes responsibility for his infidelity, then his "very comfortable life" will quickly come to an end. His consequent decision to murder his pregnant mistress (and her completely innocent elderly neighbor in the process) is thus a moral choice that is predicated on specifically material concerns; it is Chris's new social-class position that is the most valuable thing in his life, and he is willing to preserve it at all costs. That he suffers so little (Jewish) guilt compared to Judah despite the enormity of his crimes, and that *Match Point* offers no ethics of redemptive love or dialectical opposition to Chris's immoral actions, is a clear signal of the staunchly nihilistic position that is at the heart of Allen's British phase. In interviews, Allen has tried to soften the nihilism of the film by speculating that Chris's choices will ultimately lead to an unhappy life:

> I think he's in a situation that he's not delighted with. He's married to a woman he's not passionate about. He's a son-in-law who likes the easy life he's married into but is claustrophobic working in the office. His wife is already saying to him that she wants another child.... He's got what he's wanted and he's paid the price for that. It's a shame that that's what he wanted. I can see down the line that he won't be content in that marriage and maybe he'll be on such a good financial footing that he'll leave her.[26]

Allen's comments illustrate the point, however, that Chris's primary motivations have little to do with romantic love or existential meaning, and thus the so-called price he has had to pay is relatively minor in comparison to all that he has gained in his marriage with Chloe, especially if he is ever in a financially secure enough position to be able to leave her willingly. He may not be delighted with his situation, but it remains the best of all possible options. In Allen's construction of Chris's character and his actions, status and material comfort trump all else.

The link between materialism and morality is also present in *Match Point*'s sister film, *Cassandra's Dream*, Allen's third London-based film. Structured according to classic principles of Greek tragedy, the film tells the story of two working-class English brothers, Ian (Ewan McGregor) and Terry (Colin Farrell), whose material aspirations get them into serious financial troubles that eventually lead to murder and their tragic demise. Ian fancies himself a big-shot real estate investor and is desperate to secure both his financial future and his tenuous relationship with a beautiful young waitress named Angela (Hayley Atwell) by getting together enough capital for a hotel investment in California. Terry is a gambling addict whose middle-class desire to buy a house with his girlfriend Kate (Sally Hawkins) leads him to push his luck at a high-stakes poker game, landing him ninety thousand dollars in debt to a loan shark. When the boys turn to their rich Uncle Howard (Tom Wilkinson) for help, he agrees to secure both their financial futures on the condition that they "get rid" of a former business associate who is going to testify against him with regard to some high-risk business dealings that could land him in jail for the rest of his life. As was the case in *Match Point*, the protagonists are faced with a moral choice of either personal and financial ruin or committing a murder to secure their respective material well-being.

Allen's decision to frame the brother's moral predicament within a tragic narrative structure offers several different possibilities for understanding the predominant themes in *Cassandra's Dream*. The title of the film recalls the tragic female beauty of Greek mythology Cassandra, who was given the gift of prophecy but was cursed by Apollo so that "none would ever believe what she prophesied."[27] Drawing on insightful links between Allen's film and Edouard Roditi's poem "Cassandra's Dream," Marat Grinberg argues persuasively for a reading of the film that combines an Aristotelian narrative structure with a Judaic content to form a "Hebrew Tragedy."[28] Grinberg observes that unlike the logic of the Greek tragedy, Allen's characters are imbued with a *choice* not to commit the murder that their rich uncle asks of them. Indeed, Terry stresses this point in the latter half of the film when he reexamines their murderous deed and Ian states in unequivocal terms at the beginning of the film that he believes "we make our own fate." Consequently, when Terry accidentally kills Ian on their boat and then drowns himself at the end of the film, Grinberg reads this tragic demise as an enactment of a distinctly Judaic form of biblical justice.[29] Their choice to transgress "God's Law" does not go unpunished, in effect supporting the moral faith of Judah's father Sol in *Crimes and Misdemeanors* who argues that "whether it's the Bible or Shakespeare, murder will out!" In the later film's case, the figure of Cassandra is a metaphor for the young men's moral conscience, which they choose to ignore at their own ultimate peril. Yet, this particular reading also contradicts much of Allen's own commentary on the film, most notably that he does not believe in religious solutions and that "we must not forget that ... the uncle gets off scot free."[30] Uncle Howard, after all, was the agent and primary beneficiary of the murder, even if he did not commit it with his own hands, and he is certainly no less guilty of breaking God's law than is Terry or Ian. An alternative reading is to understand the brother's free choice to commit a murder within the Aristotelian structure of *Cassandra's Dream* as a specifically *existential* tragedy.

Terry and Ian's eventual demise is certainly a consequence of their antithetical abilities to deal with the guilt of having committed a murder, but the unfolding of tragedy does not begin with the murder. Rather, the boys turn to murder as the only solution they can conceive of for solving their significant financial problems (Terry) and desires for material wealth and status (Ian). It is materialist social-class anxieties that set the plot in motion, beginning with the brother's desire to own a sailboat they cannot afford. In concert with *Match Point*, Allen once again emphasizes the role of luck in human affairs as Terry ends up hitting a sixty-to-one long shot at the dog races, allowing the boys to buy their much-coveted boat outright. The winning dog's name is "Cassandra's Dream," which Terry suggests is "a lucky name" for their new boat. Ignorant of the name's mythological reference, Terry ignores not one but two distinct warnings that he is "pushing his luck": once while betting on dogs and once while playing poker, when he is almost completely wiped out while gambling. In both cases, he misinterprets his eventual luck as fate, explaining to his girlfriend that "sometimes you just get a lucky feeling, I can't even explain it." Treating luck as something more than blind chance, as a mysterious force he can harness, and as something meaningful rather than meaningless is the root cause of Terry's tragic fall. It is Woody Allen who is our Cassandra here, reminding us through the figure of Terry about the truth of contingency and the meaninglessness of the universe.

In both *Crimes and Misdemeanors* and *Match Point*, the protagonists get away with murder and return to their wealthy, privileged lives without having to account for their transgressions or suffer any form of biblical justice. In effect, the same would also have been true for both Terry and Ian, as it was for their Uncle Howard, had it not been for Terry's Raskolnikov-like conflict of moral conscience. *Cassandra's Dream* effectively synthesizes the antithetical relationship between Dostoevsky's conscience-stricken and Allen's existential protagonists through the figures of the two brothers. Like Judah and Chris, Ian is fully prepared to move on with his life after the murder. He pleads with Terry to get past the guilt and to acknowledge that the world is inherently cruel. But Terry, like Raskolnikov, is anguished by the meaning and justifications of his immoral actions, echoing what Northrop Frye refers to as the "mythos" of Greek tragedy when he tells Ian that their actions set things "off-kilter," that they had disrupted "the order of things," and that he had to confess his crime in order to set things right again.[31]

In the end, it is Terry and Ian's inability to reconcile these two binary moral positions that leads finally to their tragic deaths. Consequently, the film opens up two contradictory moral conclusions. If we follow Terry's conclusion that he and his brother have broken "God's Law," then their deaths certainly make sense as a form of biblical justice, a Hebrew tragedy. But if we follow Ian's position, which is morally consistent with Allen's past protagonists and reflects his oft-stated philosophy that the universe is godless and life is meaningless, then the tragedy in *Cassandra's Dream* is one of personal rather than biblical morality and justice. It is an existential tragedy in that Terry and Ian are responsible for their own demise, not because they have sinned, but because they could not get past Terry's internalized sense of moral anguish. Just as the boys were free to commit or not commit a murder for their uncle, they were also morally free to suffer or not suffer from the guilt associated with their crime. "If it doesn't bother you to commit a crime, then it doesn't bother you," Allen has commented, "And if you get away with it, you get away with it. It's not like a fairy tale; there is no penalty."[32]

Woody Allen's gloomy British angst culminates in his fourth London-based film, *You Will Meet a Tall Dark Stranger*, a dark, ironic comedy that once again depicts the melodramatic entanglements of an ensemble cast of privileged British characters. Rather than focus predominantly on materialist social-class anxieties as in *Match Point* and *Cassandra's Dream*, Allen returns to his more conventional fare of romantic love relationships and morbid anxieties less dominated by but still framed around a larger quest for existential meaning. But in contrast to his past engagement with these themes, *Tall Dark Stranger* reflects the gloomy nihilism of his two

British dramas in its depiction of the possibilities for human happiness, moral redemption, and meaningful experience. Once again there is nothing in the way of Jewish characters or situations, nor is there a larger Judaic thematics of ethical struggle at work in *Tall Dark Stranger*.

David Desser and Lester Friedman have argued that Judaism has been the "structuring absence of [Allen's] mature films; his cinema is a constant working out of this missing link, a continual search and substitute for Judaism."[33] They point, in particular, to the role of art and cinema (as well as love relationships, as discussed above) as substitutes for religious meaning in much of Allen's oeuvre. In *Manhattan*, it is both art and relationships that make life worth living for Isaac (Woody Allen). The same is true in *Hannah and Her Sisters*, only in this case it is specifically the film experience — the Marx Brothers' *Duck Soup* (1932) — that gives Mickey (Woody Allen) the will to keep living and begin a meaningful relationship with Holly (Dianne Wiest).[34] Another variation on the life-affirming role of movies is present in *Shadows and Fog* (1991), but in this case it is a conjurer's magic that stands in for the meaningful illusions provided by the movies. Allen's character Kleinman is a schlemiel who discovers existential meaning in his life when he works with the carnival magician Irmstedt (Kenneth Mars) to escape death at the hands of a serial killer, happily accepting a job as the man's apprentice at film's end. He comes to the final realization that nothing could be more gratifying than to give people the gift of illusions: "They need them," concludes Irmstedt, "like they need the air." Magic and the supernatural are also taken seriously as a redemptive elixir in *Alice* (1990) where "the mystical is as real as the mundane" at the diegetic level of the film.[35] In *Tall Dark Stranger*, however, the notion of meaningful illusion — art, love, and magic — has been drained of a similar redemptive power.

The double entendre in the title of Allen's *You Will Meet a Tall Dark Stranger* plays off both the clichéd prophesies of fortune-tellers who claim to know our fate and the one inescapable mortal fate that awaits us all. The film employs an omniscient voice-over narrator who frames the film with a quote from Shakespeare's *Macbeth*, stating that life is "full of sound and fury, signifying nothing." This narrative device serves to distance the audience from the film's characters, who are depicted with relatively little sympathy or room for spectatorial empathy. As Allen himself explains it, *Tall Dark Stranger* is a story about "people needing some kind of certainty in life, people deluding themselves into some sense that life has got some purpose or that there's some extra meaning to life when in fact it's a meaningless experience."[36] Alfie Shebritch (Anthony Hopkins), for instance, has left his wife of forty years, Helena (Gemma Jones), because, as he explains to the young prostitute/actress Charmaine (Lucy Punch) he ends up marrying, "she allowed herself to become old, and I wasn't prepared to accept that." Alfie is portrayed as pathetically afraid to acknowledge the fact of his mortality. He tries to buy back his youth through personal training, a new sports car, a bachelor pad, a fake suntan, a bottle of Viagra, and a relationship with Charmaine with whom he wants to have a son. She does eventually end up pregnant, but not apparently with his child, and not before he has thrown away untold sums of money in his deluded attempts to "start a life" with her.

Helena suffers a nervous breakdown following the breakup with Alfie and turns her fate over to a fortune-teller named Cristal (Pauline Collins), who she delusively believes "has the power of prophecy" to help her understand her fate and find meaning in life. Unfortunately for her daughter Sally (Naomi Watts), Cristal's prophetic insights ("the planets tell her that I must not enter into any financial transactions for the indefinite future") translate into Helena not being able to lend Sally the capital she desperately requires in order to start her own art gallery at the end of the film. Sally has also just gone through a breakup with her husband Roy (Josh Brolin) after deluding herself about the possibility of a romantic relationship with her very wealthy boss (Antonio Banderas). Her character is left miserably in flux at the close of the film.

Roy, for his part, is a struggling novelist who has failed to write a successful follow-up to his first book. After his most recent attempt is rejected by publishers, he resorts to breaking into the apartment of his writer-friend Henry Strangler (Ewen Bremner) to steal his first manuscript after he receives news that Henry has died in a car accident. With the help of Henry's brilliant novel, Roy gets a new book contract and even manages to convince his beautiful neighbor Dia (Frieda Pinto) to leave her fiancé for a relationship with him. Everything is falling into place until at film's end he discovers that Henry is not dead but in a coma and has a better than fifty–fifty chance of recovering from it. These tragicomic ironies abound. Art and literature offer no existential solace, romantic relationships are doomed from the start, and each of the main characters suffers from meaningless delusions and perpetual bad faith.

The omniscient narrator in *Tall Dark Stranger* returns at the end of the film to remind us once again that this has been a "little tale of sound and fury, signifying nothing," but he concedes that in light of all the pain and uncertainty in life, "sometimes the illusions work better than the medicine." In the final scene, Helena and her new boyfriend Jonathan (Roger Ashton-Griffiths), an occult bookshop owner, sit under an enormous elm tree, ruminating on their sudden discovery that Helena was almost certainly Joan of Arc in one of her past lives. This couple is the only exception to the gloomy British rule of *Match Point* and *Cassandra's Dream*: unlike Allen's other characters in this film and in the others discussed above, Helena and Jonathan find "true" happiness. Precisely how we should interpret their happiness, however, is another matter. There is little question that it is genuine and heartfelt, however deluded, and perhaps even illustrative of Levy's final voice-over in *Crimes*, whose moral underscores the point that "it is only we, through our capacity to love, that give meaning to an indifferent universe." Such a reading is also consistent with another of Allen's recent films, *Whatever Works*, where Boris (Larry David) comes to the grand existential conclusion that "whatever love you can get and give, whatever happiness you can filch or provide, every temporary measure of grace, whatever works." After all, if the world is inherently meaningless and ultimately absurd, then it doesn't much matter what moral or ethical meaning system you subscribe to as long as it gets you by and, if you are lucky, can foster a genuine sense of love in your life. And yet, at the same time, the ethical relativism of this position can also be understood rather cynically in contrast to the sorts of solutions Allen has attempted to offer in his past films.

While Helena and Jonathan's happiness in *You Will Meet a Tall Dark Stranger* may be sincere, it is only possible because it is so far removed from the actual realities that surround them. Informed by a narrator whose voice is inflected far more by irony than any kind of pathos, this portrait of two deluded old lovebirds on a park bench can certainly also be read as a rather patronizing image of happiness rather than a redemptive one. It seems to stand out in contrast to the meaningful depictions of Mickey and Holly in *Hannah and Her Sisters*, Ben and his daughter in *Crimes and Misdemeanors*, or Isaac and Tracy (Mariel Hemingway) in *Manhattan*. If Allen intends this final sentiment in *Tall Dark Stranger* as an earnest resolution, then it would seem that he has indeed given in to the despair and nihilism that his films have so long fought to resist, however fragile or tenuous their resolutions may have been. Even the meaningful illusions of Irmstedt the magician in *Shadows and Fog* are grounded in a mutual acceptance of suspended disbelief, rather than a total delusion of existential reality. While few of Allen's past characters have ever been able to fully resolve their existential anxieties, they have always done their best to achieve real solutions.

In eschewing both his New York persona and most traces of Jewishness, and in reassessing the existential and moral themes in his past work from a more staunchly nihilistic perspective, Woody Allen's British phase reveals a gloomier perspective on the godless and meaningless universe that has previously been so central to his work. But while his recent films lack much of the ethical and philosophical depth of his earlier pictures, they nonetheless offer a timely commentary on the cultural anxieties that have become predominant in late capitalist societies. *Match Point* and *Cassandra's Dream* both dramatize the impact of materialism on individual identity, desire, and morality, while *You Will Meet a Tall Dark Stranger* reveals how the struggle for moral integrity and existential meaning that was once at the heart of Allen's work no longer seems to register a beat in a postmodern world where themes of love, artistic meaning, and faith signify little more than their own lack of meaning. His next truly great film will be the one that breathes new hope into this empty void.

Notes

1. Leonard Quart, "Woody Allen's New York," in *The Films of Woody Allen: Critical Essays*, ed. Charles L. P. Silet (Lanham, MD: Scarecrow, 2006), 19–20.

2. William Rothman, "Woody Allen's New York," in *City That Never Sleeps: New York and the Filmic Imagination*, ed. Murray Pomerance, 65–76 (New Brunswick, NJ: Rutgers University Press, 2007), 75.

3. Woody Allen, *Woody Allen on Woody Allen: In Conversation with Stig Björkman* (New York: Grove, 1993), 211.

4. See Vincent Brook's chapter, "The Gospel According to Woody," in this volume.

5. Ibid.

6. See Peter Bailey's chapter, "Now You See Him, Now You Don't," in this volume.

7. Eric Lax, *Conversations with Woody Allen: His Films, the Movies, and Moviemaking* (New York: Knopf, 2007), 359.

8. Ibid., 123.

9. Allen, *Woody Allen*, 156.

10. Lax, *Conversations*, 98.

11. Ibid., 123–24.

12. Ibid., 184–85.

13. I am grateful to Vincent Brook for drawing my attention to Dreiser in this context.

14. Robert L. Belknap, "Dostoevskii and Psychology," in *The Cambridge Companion to Dostoevskii*, ed. W. J. Leatherbarrow, 131–47 (Cambridge: Cambridge University Press, 2002), 136.

15. Fyodor Dostoevsky, *Crime and Punishment*, trans. Richard Pevear and Larissa Volokhonsky (New York: Vintage Classics, 1992), 545.

16. Paul Ramsey, "No Morality without Immortality: Dostoevski and the Meaning of Atheism," *Journal of Religion* 36, no. 2 (April 1956): 90–108; 100. See also Stephen Bullivant, "A House Divided against Itself: Dostoevsky and the Psychology of Unbelief," *Literature and Theology* 22, no. 1 (March 2008): 22.

17. Leonard Storchevoy, "The Case of Woody Allen vs. Dostoevsky: Judeo-Cinematographic Philosophy of Crime and Non-Punishment," *Fine Arts International Journal* 14, no. 1 (2010): 58–64; 60–61.

18. Dostoevsky, *Crime and Punishment*, 261, 415.

19. Friedrich Nietzsche, *On the Genealogy of Morals and Ecce Homo*, trans. Walter Kaufmann and R. J. Hollingdale (New York: Vintage, 1989), 76–79.

20. Eric Lax, *Woody Allen: A Biography*, 2nd ed. (Cambridge, MA: Da Capo, 2000), 40.

21. David Desser and Lester D. Friedman, *American Jewish Filmmakers: Traditions and Trends*, 2nd ed. (Urbana: University of Illinois Press, 2004), 94.

22. Gary Commins, "Woody Allen's Theological Imagination," in Silet, *Films of Woody Allen*, 48.

23. Sander H. Lee, *Woody Allen's Angst: Philosophical Commentaries on His Serious Films* (Jefferson, NC: McFarland, 1997), 365.

24. Mark E. Bleiweiss, "Self-Deprecation and the Jewish Humor of Woody Allen," in Silet, *Films of Woody Allen*, 58–77; 73.

25. Pierre Bourdieu, *Distinction: A Social Critique of the Judgement of Taste*, trans. Richard Nice (Cambridge, MA: Harvard University Press, 1984), 65–80, 169–75.

26. Lax, *Conversations*, 125–26.

27. Robert Graves, *The Greek Myths: Volume Two* (New York: George Braziller, 1959), 264.

28. See Marat Grinberg's chapter "The Birth of a Hebrew Tragedy" in this volume.

29. Ibid.

30. Cynthia Lucia, "Contemplating Status and Morality in *Cassandra's Dream*: An Interview with Woody Allen," *Cineaste* 33, nos. 1 and 2 (Winter 2007/Spring 2008), http://www.cineaste.com.

31. Northrop Frye, *Anatomy of Criticism: Four Essays* (Princeton, NJ: Princeton University Press, 2000), 209.

32. Lucia, "Contemplating Status."

33. Desser and Friedman, *American Jewish Filmmakers*, 38–39.

34. Ibid., 72.

35. Lee, *Woody Allen's Angst*, 306.

36. Raffi Asdourian, "Woody Allen Discusses 'You Will Meet a Tall Dark Stranger,'" Film Stage, October 16, 2010, http://thefilmstage.com.

SCHLEMIEL THEORY

MENACHEM FEUER

Woody Allen's Schlemiel From Humble Beginnings to an Abrupt End

At the outset of *Annie Hall*, Alvy Singer (Woody Allen) retells a one-liner that he says could have been told by one of two modern Jews: Sigmund Freud or Groucho Marx. It may be the most often repeated Jewish joke in modern Jewish history: "I would never want to belong to a club that would have someone like me for a member." Singer explains to his viewing audience that this is "the key joke of my adult life in terms of my relationships with women." This explanation complicates matters. On the one hand, by retelling the joke, Singer is situating himself in a modern tradition of Diasporic Jews, what Jacob Golomb called Grenzjuden ("marginal Jews"), such as Sigmund Freud and Groucho Marx.[1] Like them, Singer is the odd one out. He doesn't identify with his own people and cannot be fully accepted into a wider society. On the other hand, this explanation seems to be displaced since Singer interprets the joke "in terms of my relationships with women," that is, sexuality and not his Jewishness ("me") or society ("the club"). Regardless of his reading, this characterization of Singer as a sexual schlemiel is, in a Freudian sense, a displacement of Jewishness. It is the tip of a larger comic iceberg that, while appearing deceptively common on the surface, is inseparable from a Jewish particularity that lurks below.

To be sure, Woody Allen's humor is often assumed to be synonymous with Jewish humor. But what makes this joke or any of Allen's jokes, in prose or film, Jewish? What does the Jewish joke accomplish? These questions are not by any means arbitrary. Jokes, in a postmodern sense, don't *mean*, they *do*. But what does a Jewish as opposed to a non-Jewish joke do? Does it make one the odd one out, or does it confirm that one already is?

To understand the paradigm of Jewish humor and see if it applies to Woody Allen's work, the case for non-Jewish humor must first be made. It can be made in modern terms, namely, with respect to the claim made by the nineteenth-century thinker Friedrich Schiller that "life is serious; art is lighthearted."[2] According to Theodor Adorno, what Schiller means by art is comedy. Following Adorno's lead, Schiller's expression should be translated as follows: life is serious; comedy is lighthearted. Thus, the goal of lighthearted comedy is freedom from the weight of necessity ("life").[3] Comedy, so to speak, takes the sting out of life (necessity) and grants its hearer and teller freedom from life. When he associates lightheartedness with "urban freedom," Adorno further suggests that this goal is modern. Søren Kierkegaard, who read and admired Schiller's work, also argued that the modern poet ("the master of irony") is truly free.[4] This association implies that Schiller's claim about comedy is not confined to the context of nineteenth-century German Romanticism; it is generally modern.[5] For Adorno, this claim to aesthetic freedom is quintessentially modern since it posits that comedy, like modernity, renounces everything (necessity, philosophy, theology, and even politics) in the name of freedom.

Jewish humor is entirely different. It doesn't look to negate necessity in the name of freedom so much as to disclose the tension between them. It has learned the lessons of history that, unfortunately, have often wounded many Jewish hopes and aspirations for freedom and redemption. Given its deep experience and memory of suffering and disappointment, Jewish humor, while lightening the load somewhat and looking to affirm Jewish survival despite it all, cannot pretend to be free of history and necessity. Its ironies retain the weight of wounded hope rather than the lightheartedness of freedom. Jewish irony remembers suffering and evil while at the same time remembering that the Jews are still here and, hopefully, are on the way to something better. It remembers that the world is, as they say in Yiddish, *tsebrokhener* (broken). Jewish irony also remembers that the world can be fixed and that justice will have its day, somehow. Both memories are in conflict. Jewish hope, while foolish, is wounded by reality, memory, and suffering.

The character that best exemplifies the wounded hope of Jewish humor is the schlemiel. The schlemiel (traditional male) foolishly thinks he is doing good and accomplishing something in the world while the viewer/reader sees that he is mistaken. The schlemiel's deeds, thoughts, or words, while well intentioned, are not affective. The schlemiel — often called a "man-child" — reminds the reader/viewer that, though it remains, the viewer/reader's naive hope is wounded. As long as the hope that suffering will someday end remains — alongside the deep knowledge that evil is relentless — the schlemiel will exist. But if one believes that evil can be eradicated by the affirmation of freedom and the negation of necessity, the schlemiel will cease to exist. For this reason, freedom from necessity is not the concern of a Jewish fool or the Jewish joke; it is the concern of a non-Jewish fool and the non-Jewish joke.

The schlemiel, as is well known, is Woody Allen's staple character. I would argue, however, that Allen's humor presents an interesting borderline case of the schlemiel. In his early work, we find schlemiels who have elements of Jewish humor and non-Jewish humor. From his early stand-up routines and prose work through his filmic oeuvre, we see sometimes a comic character whose goal is freedom, while at other times we see a character who cannot escape history and memory. At times, Allen's schlemiel is serious and lighthearted, while at other times he is unabashedly lighthearted.

Allen's approach to the schlemiel is often ambiguous in early films such as *Take the Money and Run* (1969), *Bananas* (1971), and *Love and Death* (1975), and in middle-period films such as *Annie Hall* (1977), *Zelig* (1983), and *Shadows and Fog* (1991). But this changes radically, I would argue, in his later films such as *Hollywood Ending* (2002), *Whatever Works* (2009), and *Midnight in Paris* (2011). In his later work, Allen has his schlemiels go from pursuing and achieving a lighthearted, aesthetic freedom to pursuing and achieving a type of freedom that lacks any form of irony. All of these films may begin with Jewish humor, but they end with non-Jewish humor and a happy ending in which the main character, who is no longer a schlemiel, is "truly" free. By the end of the film, the character is reconciled with what Hannah Arendt would call "the world." Although it is reconciled and unironic, one can still call this freedom lighthearted because it lightens something that has, for Allen, become a burden, namely, the unreconciled otherness of the schlemiel that, as we saw at the outset, leaves the Jew to be the odd one out.

While Allen saw the schlemiel as essential to lighthearted, ironic urban freedom in his early and middle work, I would argue that he later realized the only thing that stood between himself and the world was the schlemiel. The achievement of authentic freedom as opposed to the celebration of the alienated freedom of the schlemiel has, since 2002, become Allen's new goal. In Arendt's terms, to be discussed below, one can say that he was fed up with being a pariah, hence Allen's new approach to the schlemiel in his later films.

But in Allen's work there is more on the table than a conflict over the meaning and purpose of irony. The movement away from Jewish humor and the schlemiel prompts an urgent question about Allen's relationship to comedy "After Auschwitz." To be sure, there is a link since the modern humor Allen appeals to and utilizes in many of his films has been seriously challenged by the Holocaust.

Given Theodor Adorno's well-argued claim that lighthearted humor is "inconceivable After Auschwitz," how do we understand Allen's general embrace of lightheartedness throughout his career? What Adorno means by his claim about lightheartedness "After Auschwitz" is that Western history — the realm of necessity and suffering — is no longer something that can conceivably be lightened by comedy, let alone theology or philosophy. "After Auschwitz" humanity can no longer believe that aesthetic, philosophical, or theological claims to freedom could possibly transcend or redeem evil. To do so, for Adorno, would be unethical. In other words, the comic affirmation of radical freedom is unethical, while a humor that makes note of suffering — but doesn't negate it — is ethical. Irony remains, but its meaning and form change. Given this reading, how would Allen's films fare?

Adorno's claim regarding the end of lightheartedness "After Auschwitz" implies that all humor should, in a sense, go from being aesthetic to being Jewish and moral. With respect to Allen's work, we can say that humor, if it is to be moral and not aesthetic and if it is to remain "Jewish," should insist on the tension between freedom and necessity rather than negate or mitigate it. Once Allen's work (and humor) fails to do this, we have good reason to ask whether or not it is still "Jewish."

A Tale of Two Schlemiels: Between Wisse and Arendt

The first test of whether or not Allen's humor is Jewish can be found in the "one-liner." The structure of these jokes gives us our first clue. In *The*

Schlemiel as Modern Hero, Ruth Wisse informs us that the structure of the Jewish joke says much about the tension between hope and skepticism. In the first part of the joke, there is a sense of gravity and reality, while the second part makes light of the first. However, this making light of the first part is not lightheartedness, and the goal of this movement is not freedom. Wisse's example of this movement is a Yiddish joke about the election of the Jewish people. The first part is in Hebrew (which gives us the ideal of the Torah), while the second part, which parodies the first, is in Yiddish (the language of exile, history, and suffering): "You chose us from amongst the nations; why did you have to choose the Jews?" The second part of the joke introduces skepticism and creates a tension with the first part. What calls biblical election into question is suffering: historical reality. In this joke, belief and disbelief are held in check. The belief remains, but through a comic conceit it is wounded.[6]

Jewish humor, as Wisse points out, is a "balanced irony." But Jewish humor can become nihilistic and unbalanced. Wisse notes that sometimes the second part of the joke cancels the first. And this, Wisse tells us, is the meaning of sarcasm. More often than not, we find sarcasm in non-Jewish humor since it is a means of negating necessity and affirming radical freedom. The schlemiel, traditionally, is not sarcastic because his humor is often used to preserve some sense of hope, dignity, and humanity, even if this hope is wounded or hounded by the world, history, and suffering. When the schlemiel becomes sarcastic, however, he seems to have left the fold and turned, instead, to himself and his freedom to negate the world, history, and suffering through humor. Rather than maintain the tension between freedom and necessity or hope and skepticism, the sarcastic schlemiel either affirms skepticism while negating hope or negates both in the name of a highly self-conscious wittiness.[7]

When thought of in relation to Wisse's definition of schlemiel humor, Woody Allen's humor is revealing. Some of Allen's jokes are outright sarcastic and lighthearted, while others are not. The fact that they fluctuate indicates that Allen, in the spirit of the schlemiel, struggles with the meaning of Jewish identity.

The "Vodka Ad" joke, which Allen used in his stand-up routine in the early 1970s, is very telling in this regard. At the outset of the joke, Allen foregrounds his Jewishness when he says, as if he were beginning the Torah: "Let me start at the very beginning." But the second part of the joke profanes the first: "I did a vodka ad, that's the first important thing." The next part of the joke goes on to tell why he was selected to do the ad. It is intentionally sarcastic and freely negates the absurd arrogance of stardom: "They wanted to get Noël Coward originally for it. But he was not available, he had acquired the rights to *My Fair Lady*, and he was removing the music and lyrics, to make it back into Pygmalion." But when he comes to his punch line, and divulges how he was chosen, Allen tells us about the Holocaust: "They tried to get Laurence Olivier, and Howdy Lokey — they finally got me to do it. I'll tell you how they got my name, it was on a list in Eichmann's pocket, when they picked him up."

The second part of the joke doesn't simply negate the first part; it wounds it. And it also wounds the speaker. This is the joke of a schlemiel whose words allow him some sense of freedom, but this freedom, ultimately, is tempered by the Holocaust. As the punch line of the joke tells us, Allen's name was on Eichmann's list; he was slated, that is, chosen to die, and this is why he was "chosen" to do the vodka ad. This moment renders the vodka ad and the seriousness of doing such an ad absurd, not lighthearted. Moreover, it puts an interesting accent on the notion of chosenness.

Hannah Arendt would have an entirely different reading of the Jewish joke and its purpose. In contrast to Wisse, Arendt, in her essay "The Jew as Pariah: A Hidden Tradition," claims that the essence of the schlemiel's humor (and the Jewish joke, structurally) is freedom and not the tension between freedom and necessity. Instead of finding the root of the schlemiel in the Eastern European tradition, as does Wisse, Arendt claims that this character originates in the West and starts with Heinrich Heine. The German-Jewish poet teaches us that "innocence is the hallmark of the schlemiel" and it is out of the Jewish people's innocence that the "people's poet — its 'lord of dreams' — is born."[8]

Using oppositional terms, Arendt depicts Heine's schlemiel as a poet of the people who is "poles apart" from the "conception of" the Jewish people as parvenus, the "wealthy Jews of the upper classes."[9] For the parvenu, the schlemiel is an "impudent" pariah. He doesn't simply turn to the people; he turns to nature for humanistic insight. As a pariah, the schlemiel (and his audience) looks at civility — namely, at the Jew who acts as if he is not Jewish (the parvenu) — as foolish and smiles "to himself at the spectacle of human beings trying to compete with the divine realities of nature. The bare fact that the sun shines on all alike affords him daily proof that all men are essentially equal."[10]

However, the schlemiel remains a "lord of dreams" because these "divine realities" are not recognized by society. This identification grants the "lord of dreams" — the pariah — a kind of freedom because the source of its freedom is a denial of the harsh reality of the "social order."[11] The schlemiel is a challenge to the status quo. What emerges from Arendt is a schlemiel who is a poet of the people (Ferdinand Tönnies's *Gemeinschaft* — organic community — as opposed to *Gesellschaft* — artificial community[12]). The pariah as the "lord of dreams" goes against the status quo of the artificial community by bonding with the people and nature. But the bottom line is not simply that the pariah is the pariah because she or he goes against the grain of society and is the odd one out; rather, the "lord of dreams" is the pariah because she or he is essentially rooted in freedom, not faith or hope, as would be the case in the Eastern European counterpart.

For Arendt, the schlemiel's absentmindedness, the "aloofness of the pariah from all the works of man," his being the odd one out, is not simply a comic conceit or irony; it is what Heine deems "the essence of freedom."[13] Arendt calls this a "natural freedom" and asserts that Heine was the "first Jew to whom freedom meant more than the mere 'liberation from the house of bondage.'"[14] This new type of freedom, the freedom of a certain kind of schlemiel, is the domain of the modern artist. As Arendt suggests, it does not come from the Jewish tradition; it is modern.

And this is something with which Schiller and Kierkegaard would certainly agree. The only problem, however, is that this type of freedom, this natural freedom, comes, as we have pointed out, at the expense of Jewishness. Indeed, the freedom of Heine's schlemiel is not Jewish; it is closer to the freedom mentioned above, the one aspired to by Kierkegaard and Schiller. This schlemiel is different from the one we find in Yiddish humor, literature, and folklore. For Arendt, the goal of the schlemiel is freedom, while for the Jewish tradition, to which Wisse is attuned, the schlemiel stresses the tension between hope and skepticism. This tension can only be resolved through the eradication of evil.

The schlemiel, in traditional Yiddish stories, retains this tension by being good and acting "as if" good exists (the first part of the joke, so to speak) in a world that denies goodness (the second part). We see this in the joke on chosenness cited by Wisse and the "Vodka Ad" joke. We also see it in I. B. Singer's classic schlemiel tale, "Gimpel the Fool." Both Allen's and Singer's schlemiels are moral in the sense that while they cling to goodness, we, as an audience, see that they are wounded by suffering, history, and evil. In contrast to Arendt's schlemiel, which thrives on freedom, the schlemiel's goodness and its tension with evil are highlighted in the "Vodka Ad." Freedom is not.

Chain of Fools: From Abraham to the Hasidic Schlemiel

Although the "Vodka Ad" is an exception to the rule, in much of his early work Allen took the moralization of the schlemiel as his target. And by doing this, he also challenged the Jewish aspect of the schlemiel. In Arendt's sense, Allen made appeals to sarcasm and waged this battle in the name of freedom.

The most moral of schlemiels, as Allen and Wisse know quite well, is to be found in the Hasidic tradition. Wisse traces the secularized Yiddish schlemiel of I. L. Peretz, Mendele Mocher Sforim, Sholem Aleichem, and I. B. Singer back to the Hasidic tradition. It should be no surprise that the Hasidic Jew, who appears in both Yiddish and Hasidic literature as a simple, pious Jew, makes several crucial appearances in Allen's films and prose.

In a prose piece written in the early 1970s titled "Hassidic Tales, with a Guide to Their Interpretation by the Noted Scholar," Allen takes Martin Buber's pietistic classic *The Hasidic Tales* to task.[15] Allen's piece reduces the mysticism and morality of the Hasidic tale to the amoral and absurd schlemiel humor one might find in I. B. Singer's *Fools of Chelm* stories (but not in I. B. Singer's "Gimpel the Fool"). All the characters in Allen's tale — and even the narrator, the "Noted Scholar" himself — are schlemiels. But unlike their Hasidic precursors, they really don't know much about morality, religion, or faith. They don't act "as if" good will triumph over evil (and neither does their author). At the end of the prose piece, the Noted Scholar tells us what we can learn from these Hasidic tales. Instead of illustrating a moral way of life or the depths of mysticism, we find that the "small masterpiece amply illustrates the absurdity of mysticism."[16] But when he explains why this is the case, the Noted Scholar shows us something else, namely, the hidden treasure of modern schlemiel scholarship. The pious mystic is really just a simple Jew/schlemiel who wants to make a buck: "The Rabbi dreams three straight nights. The Five Books of Moses subtracted from the Ten Commandments leaves five. Minus the brothers Jacob and Esau leaves three. It was reasoning like this that led Rabbi Yitzchok Ben Levi, the great Jewish mystic, to hit the double Aqueduct fifty-two days running and still wind up on relief."[17]

In addition to using the schlemiel to revise the meaning of Hasidism, Allen sarcastically revises the meaning of God and piety in a prose piece titled "The Scrolls." In that piece, God expects the Jews to be lighthearted — not pious or desirous of truth and justice. Allen reenacts the sacrificial binding of Isaac (the Akeda) by his father Abraham: "'Never mind what I said,' the Lord spoke. 'Doth thou listen to every crazy idea that comes thy way?' And Abraham grew ashamed. 'Er — not really . . . no.' 'I jokingly suggest thou sacrifice Isaac and thou immediately runs out to do it.' And Abraham fell to his knees. 'See, I never know when you're kidding.' And the Lord thundered, 'No sense of humor. I can't believe it.'"[18]

In Allen's version Abraham is portrayed as a gullible moron while God is portrayed as chastising Abraham for "not having a sense of humor." Instead of reading the Akeda in terms of obedience and piety, as the Jewish tradition does, Allen reads it in terms of modern aesthetic irony or what Adorno above calls the "lightheartedness" of "urbanity." He doesn't mourn the passing away of religion from modern Jewish American life; instead, Allen lightheartedly rejects its greatest gift to Jews, which is embodied in the naive and simple schlemiel. In the most sarcastic manner, Allen is calling the simpleton (and remember that Abraham and Gimpel are simpletons) a twit. Unlike in Yiddish literature, in Allen's prose the tension between hope and skepticism is effaced. So much for the pious schlemiel.

Leaving the Schlemiel Behind

Even though most of Allen's schlemiels in his early and middle career are lighthearted and aesthetic rather than moral, they are not reconciled with the world. Regardless of their sarcasm and appeals to freedom, they are not totally free. They are often snagged. As in "The Scrolls" joke above, the voice of the teller in this and in many jokes is still the voice of someone who is the odd one out. And this is how their Jewishness is expressed. However,

Allen puts the schlemiel through a rehabilitative process in many (though not all) of his latest films. At the end of this process, Allen leaves the schlemiel — the odd one out, the outsider — for the insider, or what Arendt would call "normalization."[19] Like Arendt, Allen was ultimately not satisfied with aesthetic freedom and the freedom of the pariah. Like Arendt, Allen turned to reality and normalization as the true space of freedom. To be free is to be accepted by others — in a society of true equals — as normal.

This turn from the outsider to the insider reveals that in his more recent films Allen no longer has an ambiguous understanding of the schlemiel. His turn toward normalization is synonymous with his rejection of partial lightheartedness, on the one hand, and Jewish humor, on the other. Like Arendt, Allen is ultimately interested in freedom and reconciling his characters with the world.

Arendt's words on the matter are worthy of consideration before we examine the schlemiel in a few of Allen's later films. Arendt saw the schlemiel as a pariah, as Heine's lord of dreams. This figure's freedom was a challenge to the status quo. However, Arendt saw this freedom as necessary only in a time when human rights were not a reality and Jews were not accepted as equals, even after believing, like the parvenu, that they had successfully assimilated. Until that was the case, she insisted that the Jew remain a pariah. The freedom afforded by the pariah gave Jews a sense of dignity that they were lacking since they didn't have a "world" to live in.

However, this all changes after Charlie Chaplin, the last pariah. Although he wasn't Jewish, Arendt calls him the "little Yid." She argues that his challenge to the status quo was necessary but that, ultimately, Chaplin — a schlemiel-pariah — was replaced by Superman: "Men had stopped seeking release in laughter; the little man decided to be a big one. Today it is not Chaplin but Superman. When, in *The Great Dictator* (Charlie Chaplin, 1940), the comedian tried, by the ingenious device of doubling his role, to point out the contrast between the "little man" and the "big shot" ... he was barely understood."[20]

Furthermore, Arendt notes that Kafka, a significant character for Allen, wanted only one thing as a pariah: to be normal. "He speaks for the average small-time Jew who really wants no more than his rights as a human being: home, work, family, and citizenship."[21] This does not mean that Kafka wanted to affirm the status quo. Rather, it means that Kafka desired a world where the status quo, which regarded Jews as outsiders, would change. At that point, the pariah would no longer be necessary and the "little Yid" could become a normal member of the world and be truly free. At that point, there would be no distinction between a pariah and a parvenu.

Arendt clearly states that the schlemiel, whose life is odd and "exceptional," must be abandoned in the name of a normal life: "A true human life cannot be led by people who feel themselves detached from the simple basic laws and lives of humanity nor by those who elect to live in a vacuum, even if they are led to be in persecution. Men's lives must be normal, not exceptional."[22]

For Arendt, Heine, and Chaplin, freedom (lightheartedness), while exceptional, natural, and bound up with the minority, may have been right for their time but was still alienated. Now that Jews can live a "true human life," they no longer have to be "lords of dreams" or play the role of the "exceptional" pariah. The purpose of Arendt's essay on the schlemiel was to interpret this comic character in terms of freedom, but ultimately Arendt believes that the goal of freedom is not simply to negate necessity but also to be reconciled with a world in which Jews can live a normal life. This can happen only once the status quo — whether it was during the nineteenth century for Heine or during the American era of immigration for Chaplin — changes.

For Arendt, to be normal is to move from the schlemiel's alienated freedom, the freedom of an outsider who battles against the status quo, to the "authentic" freedom of an insider in a world that accepts the Jew as an equal: as an actor on the stage of politics and the world (an insider) instead of as an outsider. Given her vision, Heine's freedom, because it is aesthetic, was not authentic. The same goes for Chaplin, whom Allen emulates in many of his films (especially *Bananas*, which at the outset directly parodies Chaplin's *Modern Times* (1935). Heine and Chaplin's freedom, the freedom of the "lord of dreams" and the pariah, lacks a "world" in which to be truly free. Hence, Arendt's moral project — to fully embrace freedom and to end the plague of being the odd one out — begins where the schlemiel ends.

Along these lines, Allen's rejection of the schlemiel in his later films is cast in moral rather than aesthetic terms. The lightheartedness of Allen's newer schlemiels is tempered by a moral crisis in which, as part of the process, the schlemiel is forced to sacrifice sarcasm and lightheartedness (alienated freedom) for normality (authentic freedom). By moral I don't mean what was meant above with respect to acknowledging history; rather, morality here has to do with transforming the schlemiel into a "normal" human being who is reconciled with the world rather than being pitted against it.

As with Arendt, this kind of morality inheres not in acknowledging the tension between hope and skepticism so much as actually reconciling oneself with the social world. To be free, one must not be ironic, worldless, and "exceptional." Ironic freedom works only in a world where Jews are pariahs.

But Allen realizes that one cannot just stop being ironic. To go beyond irony and alienated freedom, the schlemiels in his later films must engage in a process whereby they go from outsiders to insiders, from worldless schlemiel-pariahs to worldly citizens. In his world, the world of New York or Paris, there isn't a status quo to be challenged by this or that schlemiel-pariah. To be sure, New York and Paris become, in his later films, worlds that are waiting to "authentically" embrace the artist who no longer has to be a pariah. In fact, if the world is there waiting to accept him, it is only up to the schlemiel-pariah to change his ways. We see this in three films: *Hollywood Ending*, *Whatever Works*, and *Midnight in Paris*.

In *Hollywood Ending*, the main character, Val, is a once-great filmmaker. When the film starts, we see him in one failed project after another. He is, without a doubt, a schlemiel, because his dreams are bigger than reality. He wants to make big things happen, but in each opportunity he has to follow through, he fails. He was so obsessed with his original success and thought so highly of himself and his work that he became impossible to work with and, in the process, lost his wife. In her place, he finds Laura (Debra Messing), a fellow-schlemiel girlfriend. As schlemiels, they both inhabit a world outside of the world. They are odd ones out.

To be sure, when we meet Val for the first time in the film, he is a "lord of dreams," a luftmensch. And his girlfriend is just as much of a dreamer as he is; but, unlike Val, she has no successes in her past to speak of. Their combined and excessive sense of dream-reality makes Val the odd one out. However, there is hope. When Val is provided with a movie project by his ex-wife Ellie (Téa Leoni), he is given an opportunity to get back into the movie business and change his life. He can go from a worldless schlemiel to a commercial success — once again — if and only if he produces a film that works within the parameters of the studio. The problem, of course, is the fear that Val's artistic excesses, his schlemiel excesses (so to speak), will ruin the film. These excesses are brought to the fore when, in the midst of his endeavors, Val is afflicted with blindness. Strangely enough, this blindness hits him, like a plague, on the night of Passover. When Val realizes he is blind, he calls Sal (Mark Rydell), his agent, who helped to get him this new film opportunity. Sal is in the middle of his Passover Seder when Val calls. The blindness remains a secret between them because Sal and Val want the film to be a success. Only Val and Sal know that Val is blind in a literal sense. But in a metaphorical sense everyone knows that Val is a blind schlemiel. Now the schlemiel's absentmindedness becomes a physical impediment. It turns into the comic conceit of a schlemiel.

As the movie rolls on, Allen acts "as if" he is a real director. What happens thereafter is a comic disaster. The ironies abound, and this part of the film is truly entrenched in the antics of the schlemiel who is literally disconnected from the world. He literally can't see it. This is much greater than simple schlemiel absentmindedness. And things get worse for this schlemiel. At a certain point, Sal must leave the set. In response, he decides, along with Val, that the only other person who can know the secret of his blindness, the only person who can be on set with him and help him along, is Val's ex-wife, Ellie. She, as we shall see, will help Val to dispel his schlemiel blindness. Ellie is a major conduit for Val to change from being grounded in dreams to being grounded in reality.

As she helps him to make out reality and direct the film, the film changes. Val becomes more self-conscious of his real problems. He slowly comes to terms with himself. As we learn from a scene between Val and his psychiatrist, Val's blindness is not a simple physical ailment; it is psychosomatic and can be cured. By way of his encounter with his psychiatrist, the viewer can understand that Val's ironic existence — his blindness — is informed by the fact that he is a narcissist. This is what leads Val to fail miserably. But his narcissism has a specific cause; it is not simply based on his successes. It is based on Val's failure to be a father and love his son.

The missing link is his relationship with his son (Mark Webber), and this, in turn, is related to his relationship with his ex-wife and the film he is blundering on because he is blind. Once Val takes the advice of his psychiatrist and, near the end of the film, mends his strained relationship with his son, he regains his eyesight, tries his best to salvage the film, and returns to his ex-wife. In the process of his normalization, Val goes from being viewed as a schlemiel and an outsider by others to being part of a world. Indeed, he is reconciled with a world that he shares with his ex-wife and his son who now both love him. He is no longer the "lord of dreams." He is no longer blind to the world; he can see.

Irony is not dispensed with altogether. At the end of the film we learn that the best world for Allen is not America: neither Hollywood nor Manhattan will suffice. It is the more aesthetically sophisticated Paris, which has been waiting for him all along. It is the world of the French, who think his film, though abstract and muddled, is a work of art. He decides to start again in Paris. To mark off this new symbolic spring, Allen has the final scene take place during the springtime in New York. It is a new beginning for Val, since he is now going to live life as a free and normal individual — not as a schlemiel or outsider, with his schlemiel-girlfriend Lori — but in Paris with his ex-wife Ellie. This is literally a "Hollywood ending" where all of the characters, in the end, are truly free and reconciled with the world. They can live happily ever after and live the lives they want to live — here, the artistic life — which is free of the machinations of the American studio system. Val, at the end of the film, is a new man, a normal man who can see who he is and what lies before him.

In *Whatever Works* we see a similar pattern. In this film, it is skepticism and sarcasm that are seen as the basis for the schlemiel's outsider status. Boris, played by Larry David, was, like Val in *Hollywood Ending*, once a success, but because of his skepticism, he is unable to adjust to reality. It would be fair to say that skepticism in this film also creates a kind of myopic blindness to the world around Boris. He is, as Arendt would say, exceptional and alienated.

Boris goes through a psychological transformation once he meets Melody (Evan Rachel Wood), a naive young girl from the South who grows up with a staunchly Christian family. At first, she and he — like Val and Lori in *Hollywood Ending* — are two schlemiels: one is naive and dreams too much (Melody); the other is cynical and too realistic (Boris). Regardless of their type of schlemiel-ness, both are not reconciled with the world. Both have an alienated form of freedom that has nothing to do with the world but more to do with their personal issues.

But this all changes by way of their relationship with each other. Unlike the relationship of two schlemiels in *Hollywood Ending*, these two schlemiels help each other to change. Through his love for her, she grows more and more independent and less naive, and he eventually goes from being a skeptical schlemiel to a normal person. As in *Hollywood Ending*, love in this film is the catalyst for true freedom and reconciliation with the world.

His initial freedom, gained through his skeptical and urban way of relating to the world, is ultimately worldless because, as Allen shows, this way of living lacks love and trust (two things that Arendt would see as essential to being-in-the-world). This skepticism and the freedom urbanity affords Boris (by being an outsider) is exchanged for an "authentic freedom" embodied at the end of the film when he finds a new loving relationship and becomes optimistic.

His optimism is won through discarding an inherent tendency toward cynicism and skepticism exacerbated by failed relationships and personal trauma. Early on in the film, we learn that his hidden ghost is a suicide attempt he made when he was with his first wife. In effect, Boris rejected the world by deciding it wasn't worth living in. His failed suicide attempt made him even more cynical and skeptical. But the real issue was that he didn't know what it meant to love and be loved. Once Boris rediscovers love through Melody, he slowly learns that he no longer needs to reject the world by being a cynical schlemiel. He can embrace and be embraced by it, as we see (after a brief relapse) at the end of the film. When Melody leaves him for a man closer to her age, Boris again attempts suicide by jumping out a window. But this time his fall is broken not by an awning but by a woman. And this time he doesn't relapse into his old cynicism. He has learned how to love and is now able to overcome and correct this negative character trait. To this end, he ends up falling in love with the woman, Helena (Jessica Hecht), upon whom he fell. And, in the final scene, on New Year's Eve, he and his new love, Melody and her new love, and their relatives and friends and new loves are all off to a new year and a new beginning. The ending is truly lighthearted. Everyone, including Boris, is happy and free in the best of all worlds: Manhattan — a world of open-minded, optimistic, and radically free New Yorkers.

Now, instead of the tension between hope and skepticism, we have the negation of this tension through a movement that is lighthearted but not ironic. This contrasts greatly to the irony that attends all of Allen's early forays into lightheartedness. This negation of tension is synonymous with Boris's reconciliation with the world. At the end of the film, he is not a schlemiel, the odd one out; he is an insider. Boris's freedom is that of a normal man, not the freedom of an alienated pariah-schlemiel.

In *Midnight in Paris*, we see the same structure. Gil, played by Owen Wilson, is a schlemiel. He is the classic "lord of dreams": he dreams of being a writer, but he can't seem to finish his novel. He dreams of having a better relationship, but he can't find anyone in reality. When we meet Gil for the first time, he is dwarfed by his future in-laws, his fiancée (Rachel McAdams), and his failure to be a successful writer. He can't seem to satisfy her, them, or his dreams. In other words, Gil is not a normal "man"; he is the odd one out.

Gil cannot stand up to his in-laws, love his fiancée, or write. Here, the world is not wrong, as it is in traditional schlemiel stories; Gil is wrong. The film suggests that Gil must change, not us. And while the people Gil surrounds himself with are difficult, the ideal world to which he ascribes is the world of the writer and artists. His world, that of the artist's salon, is the world of freedom. And if he changes himself and becomes a real artist, he can make this dream into a reality. He will no longer be a failure in reality; he will be a success.

When in Paris with his fiancée, Gil is given an opportunity to prove himself and go from being a schlemiel to being a man. But his opportunity comes from a magical reality, which opens up to him at midnight. After leaving his fiancée and his future in-laws for a walk, Gil stumbles upon his artistic dream of freedom through a time hole of sorts: Paris in the early twenties, but not any Paris; rather, a Paris that is populated by other American artist/ex-patriots whom, throughout his life, Gil has emulated. Here he has a chance to be a poet, but not in the ironic sense; he has a chance to be a "real" artist instead of a "lord of dreams" kind of artist.

In the film, Gil meets many artists such as Salvador Dali (Adrien Brody), F. Scott Fitzgerald (Tom Hiddleston), Picasso (Marcial Di Fonzo Bo), and Gertrude Stein (Kathy Bates), among other stars of the art scene in the early twentieth century, but the artist from whom he takes the most advice is Ernest Hemingway (Corey Stoll). He tells Gil that to be an artist one must first be a man. Here, in a nutshell, is the imperative that Allen uses to send Gil through the process of normalization. To stop being the odd one out, to stop being a "lord of dreams," Gil, and no one else, must make his dreams come true. To this end, Gil becomes enchanted with Picasso's mistress (Marion Cotillard), enchants her, wins her love, and because of his actions, he writes a book that satisfies a successful writer such as Gertrude Stein.

By the end of the film, Gil has become a man and a writer. As the film progresses, we can see a clear change in the way he interacts with people who, at the beginning of the film, made him look cowardly, naive, and aloof. His way of responding to them takes on more resolve and strength. By presenting this change, Allen is showing us what it looks like to go from being a schlemiel to being a man, from being an outsider of the world to being an insider, and from having an alienated (imaginary) freedom to having a real, tangible kind of freedom.

Gil is reconciled with the world; he is recognized as a normal human being. At the end of the film, he is not a schlemiel. There is nothing ironic about him at all. The film finishes on the most unironic note, in fact: Gil walks off into the rain with a woman (Léa Seydoux) he had bumped into earlier and exchanged words and glances. She is not the woman he saw and fell for in his magical reality and left for reality. No, she is a real girl who lives in the real world. Earlier in the film, he meets her accidentally, but he carefully courts her and "wins" her love. This is something a schlemiel, like Alvy Singer in *Annie Hall*, cannot do. Alvy is the odd one out; Gil, at the end of the film, clearly is not.

His love is there waiting for him at the end of the film and together they go off in the rain without complaining. After all, complaining is, as we saw in *Whatever Works*, too Jewish. At the end of the film Gil doesn't kvetch. He is normal and optimistic; he has no reason to complain. He is no longer a "lord of dreams"; he is the lord of reality. He is free. Like the previous two films, this is a Hollywood ending. But instead of being en route for Paris at the end of the film, as Val is in *Hollywood Ending*, the main character, no longer a schlemiel, is *in* Paris. This is a big difference. It's as if Allen has completed the journey away from the schlemiel and America (in *Hollywood Ending*) to Paris and true, "authentic" manhood (in *Midnight in Paris*). Owen Wilson, under Allen's direction, completes the journey and, so to speak, closes the schlemiel circle.

In all of these later films the joke is on the schlemiel, not on us. He and not Woody Allen is now the odd one out. The world doesn't have to change, the schlemiel does. As viewers, we, like all of these characters, get to leave the theater knowing that we, like Woody Allen, are somehow free of the burden of what Arendt called the "hidden tradition of the pariah." Like Val, Boris, and Gil, we are free of the schlemiel's psychological ailments. We are free of sarcasm and lighthearted irony. We are insiders and not outsiders. Like these characters, we feel that we can go from being schlemiels to being equals in an urban(e) world.

All of these films suggest that Allen has decided the schlemiel is not worth salvaging; nonetheless, he does decide to employ it for a moral project that is premised on becoming free, normal, and reconciled with the world. The schlemiel only persists in these films for the purposes of edification.

Allen's reformed schlemiels are at home in the world. They don't need irony or sarcasm to carve out their space. The lightheartedness of these later schlemiels is now translated into the happiness of the reality-adjusted ego, the self-actualized individual who can assert and experience his wholeness and authentic freedom. Indeed, each of Allen's later characters fixes their fragmented, worldless Jewishness by way of their own actions. They are moral. They love and are loved. But their goodness, their truth, is in healthy self-improvement; it is not about preserving the good in a world that no longer believes in it, as we saw above in the joke on chosenness, and in Allen's "Vodka Ad" joke.

Self-consciousness rather than absentmindedness is what turns the schlemiels in *Hollywood Ending*, *Whatever Works*, and *Midnight in Paris* into normal and free insiders. In each film, characters become conscious of their schlemiel flaws (so to speak) and they change. While these qualities may be sensible, Adorno tells us that "After Auschwitz," self-consciousness and freedom are a distraction from the real issue. They are indistinguishable from a lightheartedness that is blind to suffering: "It is in the lightheartedness of art that subjectivity first comes to know and become conscious of itself. Through lightheartedness it escapes entanglement and returns to itself."[23] Strangely enough, instead of being "entangled" in history, suffering, and evil, lightheartedness enables the self to untangle and return to itself with its world fully intact.

Adorno tells us that this self-consciousness, premised on lightheartedness, has become especially problematic "After Auschwitz" because, in its freedom from necessity, it fails to address the presence of evil and suffering.

Indeed, the core of Adorno's criticism is interested in putting the freedom afforded to the modern subject into question. His argument makes it clear that a self unaffected by the Holocaust's rupture of Enlightenment ideals — freedom and equality being the greatest — is problematic and even unethical.

For if the self survives — if, as in *Hollywood Ending*, *Whatever Works*, and *Midnight in Paris*, it is premised on overcoming that which keeps it from being whole — it preserves the ideal of freedom and autonomy espoused by nearly every Enlightenment thinker. This is what Arendt sought when she insisted that the schlemiel and his false self-consciousness be sacrificed for true self-consciousness and true freedom-in-the-world. The free and self-conscious man — as opposed to the schlemiel — is not wounded by history. He is free from it and therefore free from "necessity." From Allen's later films, we can see that this is a claim with which Allen is in full agreement.

But Adorno, I believe, would beg to differ with Arendt and Allen. "After Auschwitz," the schlemiel cannot simply be negated in the name of "authentic freedom" or normality; the schlemiel cannot be reconciled with the world. The schlemiel's exceptional and abnormal existence, however, is not his fault or problem. As the "Vodka Ad" joke points out, the historical event, the Holocaust, makes us all — not merely Jews — the odd ones out.

And the experience of being taken away from oneself, which we can hear in that joke, is the experience of mourning. It is the experience of loss. Jewish humor is acutely conscious of this experience, as we have shown. But Allen, it seems, doesn't think this experience has a place anymore, at least in his later comedy. History no longer makes us the odd ones out. Apparently, there is no need to mourn by way of humor.

Conclusion

Clearly the goal of Woody Allen's comedic project in regard to the schlemiel has changed over the years: from privileging the lightheartedness of the ironic schlemiel over the weight of the pious schlemiel earlier on, to rejecting the schlemiel altogether in his later work.

The schlemiel, in the most prophetic sense, is a troubling comic character. He reminds us that suffering still exists: freedom and normality cannot transcend history. To lose this aspect of the schlemiel would be to lose a legacy that is at once comic and Jewish in the most ethical sense. Once the schlemiel is used in a process of disavowal, we become passive spectators and relinquish our ethical relation to this comic character and his Jewishness.

Paraphrasing Elie Wiesel, we cannot forget, especially in Jewish humor, that the tension between freedom and necessity remains unresolved — whether through comedy, politics, religion, or philosophy.[24] Our world is and remains broken. Thus, if Allen in his later work is engaged in what Nietzsche would call "active forgetfulness" of evil and history, Jewish humor is engaged in the opposite: mourning.[25] This type of comedy and this type of schlemiel, while not new for the Jewish tradition, are new for modern art; they emerge "After Auschwitz." And from this vantage point, perhaps all humor "After Auschwitz" should become Jewish if it is to remain ethical.

However, as I have shown, Allen is not that interested in Adorno's challenge. Nor, I would argue, is he interested in the challenge of Jewish humor. As I have shown, Allen's humor has oscillated between Jewish and non-Jewish humor. But over the last twelve years, it has evoked and rejected Jewish humor by way of rejecting the schlemiel in the name of freedom, lightheartedness, modernity, and a world that once regarded Jews as outsiders but now, somehow devoid of evil, accepts Jews as insiders. For Allen this world no longer has a use for a schlemiel, save as an example of what not to be.

The joke that Allen told at the outset of *Annie Hall* is no longer true for him. "I would never want to belong to a club that would have someone like me for a member" could apply to what we see in the first part of a film like *Whatever Works*, for instance, but in the last part of the film it would not. To be sure, Allen and any of his characters in these later films — whether Val, Boris, or Gil — would join such a club because they are not schlemiels. They are normal.

Allen's movies over the last twelve years have written the obituary of the schlemiel. The title that stands on the cover of the June 1, 2009, *New York Magazine* — which includes a feature article on *Whatever Works* — says it all: "Last of the Schlemiels: Notes on the End of Jewish Humor (May It Rest in Peace) and the Beginning of Something Nu."[26] Based on what I have argued in this chapter, I would say that that "something *nu*" is not something Jewish. Although the schlemiel in the past retained the tension between freedom and necessity, hope and skepticism, this "something nu," which we see in *Hollywood Ending*, *Whatever Works*, and *Midnight in Paris*, does not.

Notes

1. See Jacob Golomb, "Nietzsche and the Marginal Jews," in *Nietzsche and Jewish Culture*, ed. Jacob Golomb (London: Routledge, 1997), 159–60.
2. Quoted in Theodor Adorno, *Notes to Literature: Volume II*, trans. Shierry Weber Nicholsen (New York: Columbia University Press, 1992), 247.
3. Ibid., 248.
4. Søren Kierkegaard, *The Concept of Irony*, ed. and trans. Howard V. Hong and Edna H. Hong (Princeton, NJ: Princeton University Press, 1989), 324.
5. Adorno, *Notes to Literature*, 250.
6. Ruth Wisse, *The Schlemiel as Modern Hero* (Chicago: University of Chicago Press, 1980), 47.
7. Ibid.
8. Hannah Arendt, "The Jew as Pariah: A Hidden Tradition," in *The Jewish Writings*, ed. Jerome Kohn and Ron H. Feldman, 275–97 (New York: Schocken, 2007), 278.
9. Ibid., 279.
10. Ibid.
11. Ibid., 280.
12. Ferdinand Tönnies, *Community and Society*, trans. Charles P. Loomis (Mineola, NY: Dover, 2011).
13. Arendt, "Jew as Pariah," 281.
14. Ibid., 280.
15. Woody Allen, *The Insanity Defense: The Complete Prose* (New York: Random House, 2007); Martin Buber, *The Tales of Rabbi Nachman*, trans. Maurice Friedman (Highland, NJ: Humanities Press International, 1988).
16. Allen, "Hassidic Tales, with a Guide to Their Interpretation by the Noted Scholar," in *Insanity Defense*, 42–47; 47.
17. Ibid., 47.
18. Woody Allen, "The Scrolls," in *Insanity Defense*, 135–40; 138.
19. Arendt, "Jew as Pariah," 295.
20. Ibid., 288.
21. Ibid., 291.
22. Ibid., 295.
23. Adorno, *Notes to Literature*, 280.
24. Elie Wiesel, *Night* (New York: Hill and Wang, 2006), 118.
25. Friedrich Nietzsche, *The Genealogy of Morals*, trans. Walter Kaufmann (New York: Random House, 1989), 57–58.
26. "Last of the Schlemiels: Notes on the End of Jewish Humor (May It Rest in Peace) and the Beginning of Something Nu" (cover title), *New York Magazine*, June 1, 2009.

And I think what we've got, what we're dealing with, basically, is a nose. —Miles Monroe (Woody Allen) in *Sleeper* (1973)

JOSHUA LOUIS MOSS

"Woody the Gentile"
Christian-Jewish Interplay in Allen's Films from *What's New Pussycat?* to *Midnight in Paris*

There is a joke in Woody Allen's *Midnight in Paris* (2011) that encapsulates the central character flaw of the film's protagonist, aspiring novelist and hack screenwriter Gil Pender (Owen Wilson). After traveling backward in time to visit his idealized Parisian bohemia of the 1920s, Gil self-deprecatingly describes himself to his French muse, Adriana (Marion Cotillard), with the following: "I'm jealous and I'm trusting. It's cognitive dissonance. F. Scott Fitzgerald talked about it." The joke operates on two levels. Within the diegesis, it reveals Gil's obliviousness regarding his own creative limitations. He has become so enamored with the great writers of the past that even his self-diagnosis cannot be validated unless it was once mentioned by Fitzgerald. But there is another reading strategy at work in the humor structure of the joke that locates entirely outside of the narrative. Gil is echoing the recognizable self-deprecating comedy style that audiences and critics have long associated with Woody Allen.

Examples of Allen-style comedy in Paris are most noticeable when Gil's masculinity is called into question. When Gil comes face-to-face with his literary hero, the hypermasculine Ernest Hemingway (Corey Stoll), Hemingway asks Gil what his greatest fear is. Gil replies, "dying." Hemingway asks Gil if, when he makes love to a beautiful woman, Gil is able to forget about his fear of death. Gil replies with an emphatic "No, that doesn't happen." In another sequence, Hemingway asks Gil if he has ever hunted. "Only for bargains," Gil replies. Gil's responses play up several classic Woody character traits such as an obsession with death to the point of creative paralysis and an inability to understand "conventional" masculine activities such as hunting.

As with most auteurs who also perform in their work, a reliance on spectatorial familiarity with the auteur's established persona is understood as central to the reading strategy of the text. Woody Allen comedies will invariably contain self-reflexive patterns and traces of Allen's long-familiar scenarios, characters, and jokes. But the specific conceptual ventriloquism of Gil-as-Woody also produces a paradox. As embodied and performed by non-Jewish actor Owen Wilson, Gil represents a complete inversion of both the physical and performative attributes that have long defined the Woody Allen persona. This is seen in Wilson's WASP physicality (blond hair, blue eyes, and boxer's nose) and his laconic, happy-go-lucky performance style.[1]

Consider how Gil experiences both the real and fantastical events of *Paris*. Unlike the typically hyperanxious and insecure Allen character, Gil is only marginally concerned that he might be marrying the wrong woman, his fiancée Inez (Rachel McAdams). He appears unfazed by the insults of his politically conservative future in-laws (Kurt Fuller and Mimi Kennedy). While experiencing his time-traveling adventure to the 1920s, Gil remains in a bemused, enchanted, and untroubled state of excitement and bliss. Once in Parisian bohemia, he is easily accepted by his artistic and literary idols as one of their own. Even in the area of sexual seduction, a foundational source of anxiety for numerous Allen characters, Gil remains cool, calm, and untroubled. When Wilson's performance is contrasted with the spasmodic, hysterical, slapstick destruction brought about by the Woody Allen characters from *Take the Money and Run* (1969), *Bananas* (1971), *Sleeper* (1973), and *Love and Death* (1975), the differences are striking.

At the 2011 Cannes Film Festival, Allen acknowledged this incongruence, observing that "it was great to see Owen do it because Owen is the opposite of me.... He gives the character an enormous dimension that I never could have given it."[2] By the time of the 2012 Academy Awards, it was this very incongruity between performer and auteur that seemed to encapsulate the film's unlikely box-office success. The host of the show, Billy Crystal, made this point clear during his opening-song montage by delivering the line, "Owen Wilson was so great as 'Woody the Gentile!'"[3]

Crystal's joke makes three important points. First, it links the "opposite" (as Allen put it) personas of Wilson and Allen to a distinct Jewish-Gentile (Christian) relationship. Second, it argues that audiences hold an implicit understanding that every protagonist of a Woody Allen comedy begins as an essentialist "Jewish" extension of Allen himself. Third, when the actor playing the Woody role is clearly not Jewish, as with Owen Wilson, a unique form of comedic alchemy is produced. In Crystal's understanding, the spectator is an active participant that must produce two simultaneous and paradoxical readings for the comedic protagonist's humor to succeed. The on-screen comedic, masculine binary produced between Gil Pender and his imagined Ernest Hemingway thus becomes a textual reflection of the auteur reinvention taking place between Woody Allen and Owen Wilson.

The seeming paradox of "Woody the Gentile" cannot be understood without first recognizing that similar cloaking substitutions have defined the schlemiel protagonist throughout Allen's six-decade career. Allen's film comedies, in a number of distinct iterations, produce the "Woody" as a destabilizing, and therefore comedic, signifier. Woody characters operate as hybrid representations caught between conflicting articulations of masculinity, gender, sexuality, and power. Allen's construction of normative power, defined in this chapter as "Christonormativity," serves as the dramatic fodder for the Woody protagonist's oppositional, and thus comedic, "Jewish" alterity. Woody is comedic because he represents both his "flawed" Jewish alterity *and* the normative Christian hero that he has usurped. There is the hero (comedic), but there is also the specter of what the hero is not (dramatic) but dreams of becoming.[4] In *Midnight in Paris*, Wilson-as-Woody both recalls and recalibrates this hybrid technique. But, as this chapter will argue, this binary configuration has been central to Allen's comedy since his hapless Jewish schlemiel first began appearing in films in the 1960s.

Christonormativity

Ruth D. Johnston, by way of Homi Bhabha and Sigmund Freud, argues that Allen's joke structure has always located a gentile spectator at the center of his cinematic address.[5] When Allen appears on camera as Woody, he is funny to the majority non-Jewish audience because they see him as immutably Jewish, despite how cosmopolitan, erudite, or disavowing of his Jewish lineage he tries to be. This containment, imposed on Woody by the spectator, becomes central to the Bergsonian paradox at the core of the Allen protagonist's inability to transform and transcend his own limitations.[6] No matter what Woody does to earn credibility, the presumed gentile (and Jewish) audience will always read him as Jewish and therefore flawed. Adding Freudian fuel to the fire, Allen transmutes this paranoia, generated in his characters by their unmasking, into psychosexual panic. This panic is overdetermined, but also subverted, by the actor-auteur's awareness that he is being watched on a metatextual level by primarily non-Jewish (and thus potentially anti-Semitic) audiences.

Vincent Brook, building on Sander Gilman, calls this the "damned if you do, damned if you don't" paradox of Jewish visibility.[7] Yet while Allen's schlemiel persona suffers from this dilemma throughout many of his films, Allen-the-auteur locates a solution to this diegetic paradox. When audiences receive Allen's flawed Jewish schlemiel in place of the gentile ideal, the paradox of Jewish visibility is self-reflexively satirized and therefore neutralized. Allen's schlemiel may face indignities or embarrassments that normative (dramatic) male protagonists do not. But, simply by being featured as the "hero" of a Hollywood film, he has already triumphed over the physiognomic expectations that define conventional (aka non-Jewish) masculinity.

A joke sold by Allen when he was eighteen years old, one of many he was selling to newspapers and working comics while he was still in high school, offers early insight into this formulation.[8] The simple one-liner "I am at two with nature" was intended as a parody of the pretentiousness of the back-to-nature movement of the early 1950s. But it also reveals Allen's realization of the comedic value of presenting a fractured, unresolvable "neurotic" identity. Whereas the normative male would presumably be at one with nature, Woody is at "two." Yet by succeeding in delivering a funny joke, Allen at least partially overcomes what Sander Gilman calls the "double bind" of Jewish identity.[9] The more Woody flailed in the text, the more Allen-the-comedic-auteur could succeed.

Once established as a director, Allen described his central filmmaking philosophy as exploring "the inherent contradiction that an intellectual rationalist is also an animal who lusts after women."[10] This rationality-carnality binary reflects an expansion of Allen's "two with nature" dichotomy into both the sexual and intellectual realms, but the underlying comedic principle of fragmentation remains the same. The dichotomy between intellect and animality is rendered humorous through contrast with either the desired female or the normative ("one with nature") male.[11] As a comedian who emerged during the destabilization of WASP archetypes by the counterculture in the 1960s, Allen intuited how recognizable character types offered an effective way to define his "two with nature" comedy. At least from Allen's perspective, this interplay between Christian power and Jewish alterity was a convenient culturally specific vehicle to express musings on life, art, eroticism, and the creative process. For Woody to be comedic, there had to be a dramatic other. Since Woody was self-reflexively playing up his "Jewish" lack, the normative other had to be the hypermasculine "Christian."

Historian Steve Cohan describes how the 1950s mass-media landscape had produced an "increased value for white Anglo-Saxon identity."[12] An abstract, Christian whiteness became recurrent throughout Hollywood film and in the increasingly dominant medium of television. This homogenously white, rigidly constructed landscape of the U.S. culture industry could be seen in everything from middle-class, suburban sitcoms such as *The Adventures of Ozzie and Harriett* (1952–66) and *Father Knows Best* (1954–60) to Doris Day and Rock Hudson's sanitized romantic couplings in *Pillow Talk* (1959), *Lover Come Back* (1961), and *Send Me No Flowers* (1964). With an emphasis on blonde (or straight dark) hair, blue eyes, small noses, chiseled features, and clearly delineated masculine and feminine body types, Nordic and British beauty standards replaced the far more ethnically diverse array of stars in the 1930s and 1940s. Besides Day and Hudson, golden boy and girl icons of the 1950s and early 1960s included the likes of William Holden, Tab Hunter, James Dean, Grace Kelly, and Marilyn Monroe. This paradigm of "whiteness" developed, Cohan argues, largely as a response to a Cold War America threatened by perceived political subversion, renewed ethnic awareness, and the emergent civil rights and women's movements.

This dichotomy is not meant to downplay the complexity of many of the performances and star personas of the 1950s. My point here is only that collectively these stars embodied a distinct formulation of physiognomy and postwar gender normativity. One of the central projects of the countercultural politics and aesthetics of the late 1960s was to challenge this hierarchy by exposing the artificiality of its construction. A seminal moment in this process occurred when Jewish director Mike Nichols cast the unknown Dustin Hoffman over Robert Redford in *The Graduate* (1967). The dissonance between the written-as-WASP character of Benjamin and Hoffman's Jewish identity corporeally thematized the notion of generational change taking place in the text.[13] Like Allen, who was emerging at the same time, Hoffman represented a direct physiognomic challenge to a 1950s-era white, Christian, movie-star body paradigm. Hoffman signified this destabilization of masculine iconography simply by being *not Redford*.

Allen and Hoffman were two of the first major figures to embody this new countercultural construction of "flawed" (Jewish) masculinity as new masculinity, what David Biale describes as the "little man with the big libido."[14] A slew of other identifiably (in name and looks) Jewish romantic lead actors soon followed, including Richard Benjamin, Barbra Streisand, Elliott Gould, George Segal, Charles Grodin, and Gene Wilder, helping to produce what J. Hoberman describes as the "Jewish New Wave."[15] Their collective inversions of the chaste 1950s era of blond-haired and blue-eyed Teutonic beauty challenged normative understandings of gender, beauty standards, and sexual mores. To compensate, many of these performers attempted to mask this destabilization through comedic self-denigration. This technique utilized comedic doubling as a solution to what David Desser calls the "masculinist bind" (and feminist bind, in the case of Streisand) imposed on Jews through mainstream images of normative "Christian" gender type.[16] What appeared to be performances of Jewish "self-hatred" were actually acts of empowerment. Allen's "two with nature" comedic structure wedded itself to these cultural determinants. But, as Desser observes, the more Allen satirized himself as flawed, cowardly, and feminized, the more he reclaimed his masculinity under an alternative, and therefore "Jewish," rubric.

This link between power, gender, physiognomy, and Christian identity in Allen's work exemplifies what I, building on the work of Jean-Luc Nancy and Michael Warner, term "Christonormativity."[17] It is a concept intended to highlight the inherent connections drawn between whiteness, Nordic physiognomy (blond hair and blue eyes), conventional gender roles, and an abstract, but clearly defined, ecumenical Christian identity of the 1950s and 1960s. It is defined not only in the Teutonic/Aryan bodies and gender stereotypes that Allen satirizes throughout his career but also in concepts such as sin, heaven and hell, sexual guilt, emotional repression, and representations of the family (perhaps most famously seen in the split-screen family dinner sequence in *Annie Hall* in 1977). By linking a normative power structure to "Christian" physiognomy, Allen positions Christonormativity as a default (and humorless) representational hegemony. Since comedy is inherently disruptive, Woody's Jewish identity becomes central to his role as an outsider/usurper of the normative power structure.

At the heart of Allen's interplay between "Christian" and "Jewish" archetypes lies Nancy's understanding of the relational nature of Christian doctrine. Nancy argues that Christianity contains an ongoing (and unresolvable) need to define what it is *not* (Jewish, Islamic, polytheism, etc.) as the means by which it is able to define what it is. Nancy describes this incomplete doctrine as a "subject in relationship to itself in the midst of a search for self."[18] Allen's Jewish schlemiel foregrounds this configuration by inverting it. The inversion is comedic simply by revealing the constructed artificiality supporting the seemingly "natural" and cohesive Christonormative order. Woody is funny because he is an essentialized Jewish other, the disruptive force at work within Christian hegemony, whether he likes it or not. But Woody is also a necessary precondition of its existence. Without the dramatic, there can be no comedic.

"America's Most Unlikely Hero"

In each of his scripted and directed films of the 1965–79 period, as well as acting-only roles in *Casino Royale* (1967) and *The Front* (1976), Allen highlighted his outsider schlemiel's masculine flaws through contrast with a dominant "Christian" counterpoint.[19] In these films, "Christian" physiognomy was embodied by a cartoonish Teutonic masculinity. "Jewish" physiognomy, as mostly (but not always) embodied by Allen, was its inverse. Where masculine Christian men were brave, Woody was cowardly. Where masculine Christian men were tall, broad shouldered, and square chinned, Woody was frail and wore glasses. Where masculine Christian men could seduce beautiful women with ease, Woody was in a perpetual state of sexual panic and hysteria.

Allen's first produced screenplay and film role, for *What's New Pussycat?* (1965), demonstrated this binary to the point of self-reflexive parody. The film ostensibly focuses on Michael (Peter O'Toole, in a role originally written for Warren Beatty), a young, handsome, well-to-do Londoner with numerous sexual partners. Michael represents a cartoonish caricature of the imagined lothario benefiting from the free-love movement in "Swinging London" of the 1960s. Counterpointing Michael are two figures embodying his opposite. As Victor, Michael's nebbishy crypto-Jewish sidekick, Allen's first screen performance introduced the staccato delivery, nerdy eyeglasses, and nervous sexual energy that would define the Woody character for decades. Similarly, Michael's psychiatrist, Dr. Fassbender (Peter Sellers) is a clichéd parody of an Austrian Freudian psychoanalyst. While neither Victor nor Fassbender is explicitly identified as Jewish, both embody Jewish stereotypes. Victor is a typical American schlemiel. Fassbender is a satire of the European Jewish intellectual using his intelligence to mask secret sexual perversions. Michael is their masculine inversion, a Teutonic Christian ideal.

The contrasting figures of Michael and Victor/Dr. Fassbender introduced Allen's career-long understanding of the comedic value of playing the tropes of the male protagonist against cinematic convention. Through the casting of O'Toole, the film represents normative masculine beauty as the tall, blonde, blue-eyed movie-star archetype of the early to mid-1960s. In counterpoint to Michael's suave confidence, both Victor and Dr. Fassbender are neurotic, sexually obsessed hysterics. Throughout the film's sex-farce bedroom mishaps, the two nebbishes are forced to lust after Michael's conquests and live vicariously through his sexual adventures. But it is precisely their failures, counterpointed against Michael's success, that underscore the transformation in archetype taking place in the 1960s. The debonair template of the Hugh Hefner 1950s/1960s was reaching the end of its cycle. This figure's replacement began to coalesce, with considerable assistance from Allen, as an alternate masculine construction: the libidinal, hyperverbal, cowardly Jewish schlemiel. But both "Jewish" and Christonormative figures, as opposites, were essential for Allen's sex-farce comedy to function.

Two years later, Allen's performance as Jimmy Bond, the cowering and traitorous nephew of James Bond in *Casino Royale* (1967), confirmed Woody as a challenge to the normative (WASP) masculine archetype. Allen's cowardice and pathological sexual compulsions are played as comical inversions of the masculinity inherent in the James Bond prototype. Jimmy

Bond's unsatisfied sexual desire inspires him to transform himself into an equally hapless villain, Dr. Noah. Dr. Noah's plan is to release a toxic chemical that, as Dr. Noah's recorded voice explains, "will make all women beautiful and destroy all men over four feet six inches." In this joke, Allen's persona establishes his twin compulsions: pathological sexual desire mixed with rage at the normative (Christian) alpha-male bodies standing in his way. Just as he had with the Victor-Michael friendship in *Pussycat*, Allen configures his hypersexual Dr. Noah as the raging Jewish id lurking beneath the facade of a 1950s/early 1960s Christian masculine caricature.

By the time of the film adaptation of Allen's Broadway play *Play It Again, Sam* (1972), Allen had fully realized the comic potential of his "flawed" Jewish schlemiel when contrasted with classic Hollywood masculinity. Alan Felix (Allen), like Victor and Jimmy Bond/Dr. Noah, contains the defining tropes of the Woody protagonist. Alan is compulsively libidinal yet terrified of women and is in the process of trying to betray his best friend, Dick (Tony Roberts), by seducing Dick's wife, Linda (Diane Keaton). Alan possesses none of the self-sacrificing noblesse oblige located in the classic Hollywood hero. To place these deficiencies into relief, the movie-obsessed Alan invokes the ghostlike presence of one of classical Hollywood's romantic male archetypes, Humphrey Bogart (Jerry Lacy). Promising that emotional repression is the key to sexual seduction, the spectral Bogart serves as Alan's mentor in controlling, rather than expressing, his inner desires.[20] The film's notion of Christian repression as a key to sexual success operates as a manifestation of Allen/Alan's paranoia. Alan assumes that he cannot seduce Linda until he drops his "Jewish" identity and performs a classic version of Hollywood masculinity.

In the imagined cinema world of *Play It Again, Sam*, the "flawed" Jewish schlemiel could rewrite his own identity and become the idealized Hollywood masculine archetype. He did this by invoking, and rewriting, the normative (Christian) specters that informed this insecurity. Just as Gil's 1920s artist phantoms are conjured up in *Midnight in Paris*, the ghost of Bogart was a product of Alan's (and Allen's) desire to reinvent his identity through the power of art. Alan might daydream of transforming into the classical Hollywood Christonormative model of masculinity. But he ultimately triumphs by accepting Jewish identity as a destabilizing comedic signifier that exposes the artificiality of normative (dramatic) construction.

"I Came to See the Nose"

In 1973's *Sleeper*, Allen's satirical play with the Christian-Jewish masculinity binary takes on a broader historical resonance. By relocating Woody out of his contemporary setting and dropping him into a dystopian future, the film links the changing mores of Hollywood masculinity to the legacies of early twentieth-century eugenics theory.[21] The historical and ethnoreligious connections are made palpable in the film's main structuring comedy motif, one of the central tropes of twentieth-century anti-Semitism: the contested landscape of the Jewish nose.[22]

Sleeper immediately establishes the essentialist notion of the male Jewish body via the introduction of the Woody protagonist, Miles Monroe (Allen).[23] When scientists in a futuristic lab unwrap the cryogenically frozen Miles, the first part of his body to be revealed is his nose.[24] From there his full face is uncovered, complete with unruly, long hair, eyeglasses, and a silly smile. Miles's/Allen's body is comical on two levels. As a sci-fi genre parody, Miles is the unlikely "hero" of a film in which he is completely ill equipped to be heroic. But as a political satire of future-shock fascism, his mock-essentialized Jewish body is presented as the ultimate threat to a fascist (and non-Jewish) world.

Nose jokes recur throughout the film in both dialogue and sight gags. In Miles's first attempt to seduce Luna (Diane Keaton), he brags that his girlfriend back in Greenwich Village has both blonde hair and "a great upturned nose, you know it was really dynamite." When Miles is taken to have a suit made by two robotic tailors, the robots are revealed to have bulbous wire noses, argue loudly with each other in Yiddish-inflected dialogue, and are named Ginsberg and Cohen. By the third act of the film, Christian and Jewish noses come into literal conflict when Miles and Luna discover that a terrorist attack has destroyed the Leader's entire body, leaving only his nose intact. The antiterrorist Aries Project hopes to secretly clone a new Leader from the residue of his nose.[25] Miles and Luna join up with the resistance fighters, who are on a mission to destroy the nose before it can be cloned.

Once Miles and Luna join the resistance, Christian-Jewish nose conflict moves into the area of sexual contestation. Miles's desire for Luna becomes challenged by Erno (John Beck), the leader of the revolution who is depicted as a prototypical muscular, square-jawed, Grecian-nosed hero. A love triangle emerges, allowing Miles's fits of jealousy (and Erno's indifference to it) to drive much of the comedy.[26] The personal rivalry between Teutonic hypermasculinity and Jewish comedy echoes *Sleeper*'s eugenics-driven dystopia. Miles rages at Erno's überconfident Aryan masculinity by focusing on Erno's body and referring to him as "Mr. White-Teeth" and "the rebel chieftain with the wall-to-wall muscles on his chest." When Luna teases Miles for being jealous, he responds self-deprecatingly, "With a body like mine, you don't have to be jealous."

The stereotypes are taken to a comic extreme when, late in the film, Erno and Luna are forced to perform as "Jewish" in an attempt to deprogram the brainwashed Miles. Miles has been somnambulated by the state into believing that he is a calm, happy, untroubled, Christian worker. He has begun speaking in calm, measured tones. He attends a robotic Catholic confessional where he confesses his sins calmly and rationally in a very un-Woody-Allen-like voice. When Erno and Luna attempt to shock Miles out of this trance, they must re-create a traumatic event from his past. This is revealed to be a Jewish Shabbat dinner in which Miles informs his parents that he is getting a divorce. The sequence begins with comedic Christian-Jewish inversion rooted in basic archetypes. The WASP figures of Erno and Luna perform as Miles's Jewish parents through the reading (and misreading) of phonetic translations of Yiddishisms and clichéd Jewish dialogue ("Oy gevalt!" "Let's eat!"). But the comedic reversal of types quickly shifts from religion to gender. Before returning to his Jewish state, the still-hypnotized Miles detours into a performance from Tennessee Williams's *A Streetcar Named Desire*. But rather than identifying with the feral and brutish Stanley Kowalski, Miles's subconscious instead casts him as the deluded female protagonist, Blanche DuBois.

Miles's selection of Blanche over Stanley fits directly into the "self-hating" framework of Jewish men understanding themselves as feminized and therefore deficient. But, as Desser argues, this self-deprecation technique actually signifies masculine reclamation under an alternative Jewish comedic paradigm.[27] By choosing Blanche, and not Stanley, Miles reclaims his Jewishness through the duplicitous nature of comedic paradox. The more Miles denigrates his masculinity under 1950s-era Christonormative standards (Miles cannot see himself as Marlon Brando, who famously starred as Stanley in the 1951 film adaptation of *Streetcar*), the more Allen produces an alternative masculine formulation as a response to what Erno represents.

After successfully capturing and destroying the Leader's nose (by throwing it under a steamroller that flattens it into a cartoonish pancake), *Sleeper*'s motif of Christian-Jewish body contestation is finally resolved in the act of sexual selection. Miles pleads with Luna to awaken to the cyclical and destructive nature of politics, stating, "Don't you realize? In six months, we'll be stealing Erno's nose!" Whether fascist or Marxist, all Aryan noses pose the same threat to Miles. However, Miles's Jewish paranoia is disarmed when Luna declares her love for him. The real "sleeper" of the film turns out not to be Miles but the unquestioning shiksa (non-Jewish) female of privilege, Luna. When Luna "awakens" politically as a resistance fighter, she is also awakened sexually to her desire for the nebbishy Miles. This act of sexual syncretism by Luna, the choosing of the Jewish nose over the Christian nose, represents the true destruction of *Sleeper*'s fascist state.[28] The role of the essentialized Jewish (and Christian) body in this configuration is affirmed when Miles delivers the biblically inspired joke "An eye for an eye, a tooth for a tooth, and a nose for a nose."

The physiological solution is essential to *Sleeper*'s connection between the individual sexual act and state resistance. The successful coupling of Miles and Luna neutralizes Miles's masculine/Jewish crisis at the same moment it also becomes an emancipatory political act.[29] The completion of Luna's awakening is signified by a shift from the Christonormative male beauty standards of the 1950s (Erno) to the alternative Jewish "unhero" of the late 1960s and early 1970s (Miles). By satirizing early twentieth-century European understandings of Jewish men as flawed, bookwormish "sissies," Allen reminded audiences of the shift in masculinity that had taken place.[30] It is Allen's Jewish schlemiel, with his Jewish nose, that ultimately triumphs over the fascist state.

In each of the previous examples, Allen's Jewish schlemiels were situated in opposition to a normative Christian power structure. Allen linked this power to a distinctly "Christian" identity through his use of Teutonic body types and clearly codified gender roles. In contrast, "Woody" was the disruptive Jewish challenge to normative (and unfunny) institutional power. As *Sleeper* made clear, Allen saw "Jewish" physiognomy as an essentialist part of his disruptive, and therefore comedic, role. By linking masculine hierarchy with protofascist, eugenics-inspired body politics, he drew an explicit connection between masculine lack and Jewish alterity. Allen's schlemiels, from Victor through Miles, were the proverbial fly in the (Christian) hegemonic ointment. But under Allen's authorial power (as well as the other artists of the "Jewish New Wave"), it was Jewish alterity that embodied a new construction of gender, sexuality, and heroism in the late 1960s and 1970s.

Fractured Woody

Allen's transformation from the Jewish-centric Woody to non-Jewish, happy-go-luckier Owen Wilson's Gil Pender in 2011 contained many intermediary steps. Two of Allen's films in the 1980s demonstrate a shift away from textual Christian-Jewish substitution binaries. In both *Hannah and Her Sisters* (1986) and *Crimes and Misdemeanors* (1989), Allen introduces a second protagonist of equal weight as a counterpoint to the Woody character. Allen had ventured into Bergmanesque melodrama with *Interiors* (1978), *September* (1987), and *Another Woman* (1988). He was also producing genre comedies during this period, such as *Broadway Danny Rose* (1984) and *The Purple Rose of Cairo* (1985). But *Hannah* and *Crimes* represented his first attempts to hybridize comedic and dramatic storytelling within a single text.

For most of Allen's career, comedy and drama had tended to break along Christian-Jewish lines—drama: Christian; comedy: Jewish.[31] In both *Hannah* and *Crimes*, the two generic modes become interconnected, and so does the Christian-Jewish interplay. In *Hannah*, two male protagonists, Mickey (Allen) and Elliot (Michael Caine), are given equal narrative weight among a number of other characters in the ensemble. Their ethnicities, however, remain generically distinct. The Jewish Mickey's death-obsessed panic and subsequent search for God is played for comedy. The gentile Elliot's affair with his sister-in-law (Barbara Hershey) unveils in a realist dramatic mode (even bringing in Bergman alter ego Max von Sydow, as a nihilistic artist, to confirm the gravitas). In *Crimes*, Allen similarly splits the narrative into comedic and dramatic plotlines of equal weight. Here, the ethnic orientations are intertwined. The romantic-comedy story line again features Allen's Woody character, Cliff, a Jewish documentary filmmaker who courts and loses the shiksa Halley (Mia Farrow) to the obnoxious Jewish television executive Lester (Alan Alda). This story line is counterpoised with a nearly completely unconnected second story involving the existential crisis experienced by the Jewish Judah (Martin Landau) after he has his gentile mistress (Anjelica Huston) murdered.

As Brook (drawing on Desser and Friedman) also discusses in his chapter, the split storytelling of *Hannah* and *Crimes*, and especially the bridging of the ethnically based comedy-drama divide, showcased a new development in Allen's increasingly complex subversion technique. Archetypal formulations of "Christian" and "Jewish" masculinity, presented in competition, remain in both films. But these representations were now being mobilized as challenges not only to normative gender roles and spectatorial assumption but also to the generic tropes of storytelling itself. In *Hannah*, Mickey's Jewish crisis of faith is played for laughs; Elliot's WASP crisis of fidelity is inherently dramatic. In *Crimes*, Allen further problematizes the overdetermined relationship between "Christian" drama and "Jewish" comedy. Both protagonists are now Jewish, *and* they operate on both sides of the comedy-drama divide. In both examples, Allen's Jewish-Christian binary continues as a signifier of Allen's authorial style. But it has relocated from interpersonal bodily rivalry toward a fracturing of the single-protagonist narrative structure.

The doubled nature of these narratives suggests creative exhaustion with reliance on obvious Christian-Jewish substitutions as a means of structuring the joke. They also represented an opening up of possibilities for Jewishness to inform drama. Whether purely comic, as in *Hannah*, or seriocomic, as in *Crimes*, the crisis of Jewish identity in a seemingly godless universe extended the Woody protagonist's obstacles beyond the power structure of Christonormative body hierarchy of the 1960s and 1970s. Yet Jewish alterity, presented in counterpoint to a Christonormative power, remained a central structuring motif for Allen's philosophical and creative explorations in both films.

Christian Woody

By the early 1990s, Allen introduced a new wrinkle in his configuration of the Woody protagonist. For arguably the first time (if one discounts Mia Farrow's female quasi-variations in the 1980s), Allen cast another actor in what was clearly written as the Woody role: the non-Jewish John Cusack as David Shayne in *Bullets Over Broadway* (1994). Lacking only physical resemblance, Shayne exhibits all of the tropes of the familiar Woody protagonist. He is a struggling playwright of little talent who ends up taking credit for the far more authentic, ghostwritten voice of the feral but clearly talented gangster, Cheech (Chazz Palminteri).[32] Shayne engages Allen's career-long meditation on how the artist takes inspiration from life to create (or not create) art. He is also—not insignificant after the Farrow-Previn scandal two years prior—a philanderer. Shayne cheats on his wife with the seductive theater star Helen Sinclair (Dianne Wiest), after being encouraged to live a libertine life by the only explicitly Jewish presence in the film, the loud, brash, opinioned, and sex-obsessed Marxist philosopher, Sheldon Flender (Rob Reiner). Flender is ultimately revealed (in another seeming reference to the scandal) to have used his antibourgeois ethics to justify his affair with Shayne's wife (Penelope Ann Miller).

Cusack-as-Woody introduced an important shift in Allen's narrative address. Before *Bullets*, Allen had relied on a presumed default Jewishness, regardless of the actor playing his comedic protagonist(s). When not played by Allen himself, Allen had cast exclusively Jewish actors in textually identified (or implied) Jewish roles. Gene Wilder as a sheep-fetishizing doctor in *Everything You Always Wanted to Know About Sex* (*But Were Afraid to Ask)* (1972), Martin Landau as Judah in *Crimes and Misdemeanors* (1989), Sydney Pollack as Jack in *Husbands and Wives* (1992), and even Reiner as Sheldon Flender in *Bullets Over Broadway* serve as reminders of the indexical nature of Jewish identity for the 1960s generation. Beginning with *Bullets*, however, Allen began to denature the Jewish specificity of his protagonists. This relocation perhaps reflected the exhaustion of the comedic assault on normative convention embodied by the Jewish New Wave. If the essentialized Jewish Woody of *Sleeper* had embodied an overturning of the normative (Christian) masculine "hero" tropes of the 1960s and 1970s, then Cusack signified a new step: a rewrite of the rewrite.

Following Cusack, nonexplicitly Jewish "Woodys" included Kenneth Branagh as a struggling screenwriter in *Celebrity* (1998), Will Ferrell as a struggling actor in *Melinda and Melinda* (2004), Josh Brolin as a struggling novelist in *You Will Meet a Tall Dark Stranger* (2010), and the gentile Woody par excellence, Owen Wilson in *Midnight in Paris* (2011). In each of these films, the actor performed the Woody role either as outright Allen mimicry, as with Branagh's widely derided portrayal in *Celebrity,* or as a tribute to Allen's mannerisms, as with Ferrell's performance as Hobie, a struggling actor, in *Melinda and Melinda*.[33] When Hobie delivers a series of overtly Allenesque cracks to the hypermasculine, safari-hunting millionaire, Greg Earlinger (Josh Brolin), his rival for Melinda's (Radha Mitchell) affections, Allen's comedic love triangle formulation is unmistakable.[34] Yet actor Josh Brolin himself would step into the Woody role a few years later in *Dark Stranger,* continuing the increasingly un-Jewish, yet quasi-Woody, performances of subsequent Allen protagonists in the 2000s. The challenge to Christonormative power by a "Jewish" comedic alterity remained in these films. But this binary shifted from physiognomic body contrast to the signifier of the comedic voice.

Allen, like his hero, Groucho Marx, has long resisted (and resented) any notion of a unifying Jewish element present in his comedic address.[35] As Jason Kalman points out, scholars and critics tend to read Allen's comedy within a framework of Jewish essentialism regardless of the distinctions of Allen's many disparate texts. Allen's comedy is understood as either anti-Semitic (Allen is self-hating) or classic Jewish humor hidden in a postmodernist framework. Implicit in either case is that Allen's humor and Woody characters can never be separated from an essentialist Jewish specificity.[36]

Deconstructing Harry (1997), in which Allen reprised his Woody role in its most base, carnal form, also provided the most blatant send-up of his awareness of the compartmentalizing tendency of his critics. Harry (Allen), the eponymous writer character, is once again prone to using his life as fodder for his acclaimed fiction. In one of several self-lacerating texts-within-the-text, a television show is being produced on Harry's life. Harry discovers, much to his dismay, that the producers have cast actor Richard Benjamin as the "screen" version of Harry. Benjamin had gained fame playing the alter ego of acclaimed Jewish novelist Philip Roth in the film adaptations of Roth's *Goodbye, Columbus* (1969) and *Portnoy's Complaint* (1972). Like Sydney Pollack, Rob Reiner, and Martin Landau in Allen's earlier films, Benjamin invoked the indexical and physiognomic function of 1960s-era Jewish identity. The casting of Benjamin as Harry, and Harry's subsequent anger over the reductive "Jewish" imposition on his work, pokes fun at

Allen's own awareness of how Woody will always be seen by others, no matter how many rewrites he attempts, as a Jewish body.

Over the next two decades, only Larry David in *Whatever Works* (2009) can be read as a notable Jewish actor occupying the Woody-like role.[37] Allen cast David off his hit HBO series *Curb Your Enthusiasm* (2000–), in which David's Jewish schlemiel had become an iconic next-generation Woody. The similarities between the two personas are unmistakable, and David has often been compared to Allen by the popular press.[38] Allen makes the lineage of Jewish entertainers explicit by beginning the film with a clip of Groucho Marx from *Animal Crackers* (1930). However, David's character, Boris Yellnikoff, a misanthropic professor of nuclear physics, is far closer to the hypersexual Woody character of the 1970s and 1980s. Boris's fixation on the barely legal, poor, unintelligent Southern runaway, Melody (Evan Rachel Wood) produces the same May–December romantic entanglement that Allen had explored in films such as *Manhattan* and *Husbands and Wives*.

Not all of Allen's films from *Bullets* onward engage the post-1990s authorial reinvention of the Woody character. Christian-Jewish interplay prevails, however, in a number of formulations. *Small Time Crooks* (2000), *The Curse of the Jade Scorpion* (2001), and *Hollywood Ending* (2002), which feature Allen in the lead role, hark back to vintage "Woody" and contrast Allen with conventionally masculine rivals. The serious films from his British phase—*Match Point* (2005) and *Cassandra's Dream* (2007)—perhaps also owing to their über-WASP setting, abide by the "drama: Christian" rule. Comedies such as *Anything Else* (2003), *Scoop* (2006), and *To Rome with Love* (2012) get it both ways, with an older, Allen-played Woody acting as mentor, sidekick, or a parody of himself to younger, implied-Jewish "Woodys" played by Jason Biggs, Scarlett Johansson, and Jesse Eisenberg, respectively. And in the critically and financially triumphant *Midnight in Paris*, "Woody the Gentile" returned in all his anti-Christonormative glory.

Two with Nature

As Jacques Lacan argues, the subject who dreams of the Other, in the act of desiring the Other, actually produces the self.[39] Woody has long been defined by his double-coded role as a Jewish schlemiel able to usurp Christonormative masculinity but also plagued by his inability to transform into the normative Other that he longs to be. Allen's use of Christian and Jewish archetypes, in either oppositional or erotic configuration, highlighted this Lacanian configuration through comedic binary. It was the means of Allen's philosophical framework for most of his career, if not always the ends.

The climax of this deconstructive process, at least to this point in Allen's prolific career, occurs in *Midnight in Paris*. Owen Wilson represents a next-generation reconfiguration of Allen's career-long "two with nature" technique. But Wilson produces Allen's Christian-Jewish masculine binary not through contrast, as in Allen's films of the 1960s and 1970s, or relocation in the comedy-drama divide, as in his films of the 1980s and 1990s, but by dialectically exploding and subsuming it in a hybridized gentile-Jew singularity. Gil is *both* at one with nature (as embodied by the unhysterical Wilson) and at two with nature (in delivering Allen's "neurotic" jokes). By echoing the Woody humor structure in his speech, but looking and performing as a Christian "un-Woody," Wilson's Gil Pender is both familiar and entirely new. Gil nostalgically recalls Allen's early Christian-Jewish archetypal binaries while relocating both identities within the very calm and cohesive WASP protagonist that Allen has long rebelled against. This is also a reflection of the central thematic idea of the film. Gil's nostalgic Paris is a depoliticized and cartoonish phantasm produced by an artist unable to become that which he desires. Just as Allen once summoned Bogart in *Play It Again, Sam*, "Woody the Gentile" extends nostalgia beyond the text and to the point of spectatorship. The presumed gentile spectator summons up an imagined and spectral Woody just as Gil conjures up a false Paris. In both cases, art is the means by which spectatorial projection takes place.

For Allen, no work of art can exist in a vacuum. As Gil's (mis)appropriation of F. Scott Fitzgerald's "cognitive dissonance" makes clear, each text is an amalgam of ideas that once inspired the author, now transformed by the author's lived experience. These themes are reflected in the spectator's long relationship with the Woody Allen persona. "Woody the Gentile" signifies this by ultimately reproducing the Jewish Woody as he has always been: a problematic and flawed construction located in the gap between (dramatic) Christonormative power and (comedic) Jewish alterity. Gil's melancholia, informed by his reliance on (and limited understanding of) the great literature of the past, recalls Woody's desire, and inability, to become the 1950s-era Christonormative hero. Gil's creative paralysis occurs not because Gil cannot write but because, like "Woody," Gil is *written*. He is a reinvented version of the hybridized Jewish-WASP interplay that constitutes one of the main philosophical dilemmas of Allen's career. In "Woody the Gentile," Allen simply finds a new modality to subvert, and relocate (outside of the text), the conjoined Christian-Jewish double address that was central to his persona from the start.

Notes

1. Wilson's star-making turn as Kevin Rawley, the virile, rich, successful WASP alternative to Ben Stiller's neurotic, middle-class, Jewish Gaylord Focker in *Meet the Parents* (2000), established Wilson as the antithesis of the Jewish schlemiel. Wilson and Stiller would continue to play up their WASP/Jewish alterity in the sequels, *Meet the Fockers* (2004) and *Little Fockers* (2010), as well as in films such as *Starsky and Hutch* (2004).

2. Gregg Kilday, "Woody Allen Never Felt He 'Had Depth' to Be an Artist," *Hollywood Reporter*, May 11, 2011, http://www.hollywoodreporter.com.

3. Academy Awards telecast, ABC, February 26, 2012.

4. As Andrew Stott observes, the foregrounding of a discrepancy between performer and character, especially in terms of gender masquerade, is one of the oldest comedic techniques in theater of antiquity and the middle ages. Andrew Stott, *Comedy: The New Critical Idiom* (New York: Routledge, 2005), 62–66.

5. Ruth D. Johnston, "Joke-Work: The Construction of Jewish Postmodern Identity in Contemporary Theory and American Film," in *You Should See Yourself: Jewish Identity in Postmodern Culture*, ed. Vincent Brook, 207–29 (New Brunswick, NJ: Rutgers University Press, 2006), 219.

6. Eli Rozik observes that Henri Bergson's seminal work on laughter argues that automatism occurs at the moment a character reveals to the audience the central flaw that he or she cannot, and will not, overcome. Eli Rozik, *Comedy: A Critical Introduction* (Eastbourne, UK: Sussex Academic Press, 2011), 109–10.

7. Vincent Brook, "'Y'all Killed Him, We Didn't!' Jewish Self-Hatred and *The Larry Sanders Show*," in Brook, *You Should See Yourself*, 298–318; 312.

8. Eric Lax, *Woody Allen: A Biography* (New York: Knopf, 1991), 39.

9. Sander L. Gilman, *Jewish Self-Hatred: Anti-Semitism and the Hidden Language of the Jews* (Baltimore: Johns Hopkins University Press, 1990), 2.

10. Roger Ebert, "The View from Woody Allen's Window," *Chicago Tribune*, July 16, 1982, http://rogerebert.suntimes.com.

11. Concurrently, in literature, Philip Roth's titular unhero in *Portnoy's Complaint* (1969) located the neurosis of the highly sexualized Jewish schlemiel as a product

of the discrepancy between the idealized Christonormative fantasy and the dysfunctional reality of the Jewish experience. Barry Gross describes how Portnoy's fixation on 1950s Aryan beauty culminates with his obsession with the "upturned nose" of actress Debbie Reynolds. Barry Gross, "Seduction of the Innocent: *Portnoy's Complaint* and Popular Culture," *MELUS* 8, no. 4 (Winter 1981): 82–85.

12. Steven Cohan, *Masked Men: Masculinity and the Movies in the Fifties* (Bloomington: Indiana University Press, 1997), 13.

13. As Nichols explained his casting choice, "My unconscious was making (*The Graduate*) . . . it took me years before I got what I was doing, that I was turning Benjamin into a Jew." Quoted in Mark Harris, *Pictures at a Revolution: Five Movies and the Birth of a New Hollywood* (New York: Penguin, 2008), 319.

14. David Biale, *Eros and the Jews: From Biblical Israel to Contemporary America* (Berkeley: University of California Press, 1997), 206.

15. J. Hoberman and Jeffrey Shandler, eds., *Entertaining America: Jews, Movies, and Broadcasting* (Princeton, NJ: Princeton University Press, 2003), 220. Matthew Frye Jacobson elaborates on the cultural shifts of the 1960s that led to a strong, ethnic awakening in terms of Jewish American identity (Matthew Frye Jacobson, *Roots Too: White Ethnic Revival in Post-Civil Rights America* [Cambridge, MA: Harvard University Press, 2006], 131).

16. David Desser, "Jews in Space: The 'Ordeal of Masculinity' in Contemporary American Film and Television," in *Ladies and Gentlemen, Boys and Girls: Gender in Film at the End of the Twentieth Century*, ed. Murray Pomerance, 267–82 (Albany: State University of New York Press, 2001), 270.

17. Michael Warner first introduced the concept of "heteronormativity" in the early 1990s to describe an embedded power structure that worked to sublimate and deny queer and oppositional gender and sexual perspectives. In introducing Christonormativity, I argue that hegemonic frameworks articulate a specific Christian-normative subset of heteronormativity that produces Judaism, Islam, Hinduism, atheism, and so forth, as structuring absences. Judaism, however, as the parent religion of Christianity, operates in a privileged position over other ethnic, racial, and religious configurations (both Christian and non-Christian) as the means of challenging the Christonormative framework. Michael Warner, "Introduction: Fear of a Queer Planet," *Social Text* 29, no. 4 (1991): 3–17. Jean-Luc Nancy, *Dis-Enclosure: The Deconstruction of Christianity* (New York: Fordham University Press, 2008).

18. Nancy, *Dis-Enclosure*, 38.

19. This subheading was a tagline on the poster for *The Front* (1976). The artwork featured a hand-drawn arrow pointing at Woody Allen and handwritten text reading "America's most unlikely hero."

20. Henry Bial argues that Allen uses the Bogie character as a familiar trope to make the Woody character's neurotic Jewish sexuality more palatable to the

non-Jewish segment of the mass audience. Henry Bial, *Acting Jewish: Negotiating Ethnicity on the American Stage and Screen* (Ann Arbor: University of Michigan Press, 2005), 93.

21. The Jewish-born Catholic convert Otto Weininger, in his notoriously anti-Semitic book *Sex and Character: An Investigation of Fundamental Principles* (New York: Putnam, 1906), claimed the Jewish body was sexually deficient and physically deviant, a feminized manifestation of anxieties of viral contagion inspired by the new sciences of the time.

22. Sander Gilman, *The Jew's Body* (New York: Routledge, 1991), 170–72.

23. The name "Miles Monroe" suggests both the black jazz artist Miles Davis (the film's Dixieland jazz score reinforces this) and the object of 1950s-era blonde female idealization, Marilyn Monroe, suggesting Miles's role as a Jewish proxy for both feminine and ethnic identification.

24. As Jay Geller has summarized, numerous scholars have shown the central physiognomic role that the Jewish nose played in early twentieth-century pseudo-science. Jay Geller, "(G)nos(e)ology: The Cultural Construction of the Other," in *People of the Body: Jews and Judaism from an Embodied Perspective*, ed. Howard Eilberg-Schwartz, 243–82 (New York: State University of New York Press, 1992), 250–52.

25. During Hitler's rise to power in the early 1930s, the ability of some Jews to "pass" as Aryan provoked German anxiety about not looking German enough, or possibly being mistaken for a Jew. Sander Gilman, *Making the Body Beautiful: A Cultural History of Aesthetic Surgery* (Princeton, NJ: Princeton University Press, 1999), 176.

26. Marjorie Garber describes how love triangles are a critical methodology for opening spaces of intersubjective interplay between normative and deviant sexual perspectives. Marjorie Garber, *Vice Versa: Bisexuality and the Eroticism of Everyday Life* (New York: Touchstone, 1995), 423.

27. Desser, "Jews in Space," 271–74.

28. Gilman argues that anxieties of Jewish noses played a central role in the development of the optional surgical procedure of rhinoplasty, first introduced in Weimar-era Germany of the 1920s and 1930s. Gilman, *Jew's Body*, 184–87.

29. As Foucault, Marcuse, and Bataille have argued, individual acts of sexual expression are a form of political resistance directed toward methods of ideological control imposed by the nation-state. Georges Bataille, *Eroticism: Death and Sensuality* (San Francisco: City Lights Books, 1986), 107–8; Herbert Marcuse, *Eros and Civilization: A Philosophical Inquiry into Freud* (New York: Vintage Books, 1962), 15–17; Michel Foucault, *The History of Sexuality: An Introduction*, vol. 1 (New York: Vintage Books, 1990).

30. Daniel Boyarin, *Unheroic Conduct: The Rise of Heterosexuality and the Invention of the Jewish Man* (Berkeley: University of California Press, 1997), xviii–xix.

31. Andrew Stott notes that early Christianity was explicitly hostile to laughter. Church doctrine viewed laughter as a "vulgar eruption of the body" (Stott, *Comedy*, 128).

32. Jeffrey Rubin-Dorsky describes this role as a substitution, a role Allen once would have "reserved for himself." Jeffrey Rubin-Dorsky, "Woody Allen after the Fall: Literary Gold from Amoral Alchemy," *Shofar* 22 (2003): 5–28; 13–14.

33. I have left out of the discussion the drama *Match Point* (2005) and the comedy *Vicky Cristina Barcelona* (2008). Allen himself does not appear in either film, and it would be difficult to argue that the non-Jewish male leads, played by Jonathan Rhys Meyers and Javier Bardem, respectively, are obvious Woody alter egos.

34. When Greg asks Hobie what he does for exercise, Hobie responds with the Allenesque, "Tiddlywinks. And an occasional anxiety attack."

35. Groucho Marx wrote in *The Groucho Phile*, "We Marx Brothers never denied our Jewishness. We simply never used it." Quoted in Simon Louvish, *Monkey Business: The Lives and Legends of the Marx Brothers* (New York: Thomas Dunne Books, 1999), 76.

36. Jason Kalman, "Heckling the Divine: Woody Allen, the Book of Job, and Jewish Theology after the Holocaust," in *Jews and Humor*, ed. Leonard J. Greenspoon, 175–94, Studies in Jewish Civilization 22 (West Lafayette, IN: Purdue University Press, 2010), 175–80.

37. The Italian American actor Jason Biggs as Jerry Falk in *Anything Else* (2003), Sean Penn as Emmitt Ray in *Sweet and Lowdown* (1999), and Jesse Eisenberg in *To Rome with Love* (2012) can also be plausibly read as Jewish characters.

38. A cover story in *New York Magazine* described the Allen-David collaboration as "Twilight of the Tummlers." Mark Harris, "Twilight of the Tummlers," *New York Magazine*, May 25, 2009, http://nymag.com.

39. Jacques Lacan, *Écrits*, trans. Bruce Fink (New York: Norton, 2006), 682–83.

PETER J. BAILEY

"Now You See Him, Now You Don't" in Woody Allen's Vanishing Act in *Scoop*

For a good while now, Woody Allen has been expressing reservations about appearing in the films he scripts. In 2005, he complained to Eric Lax that writing himself into scripts commits the film to a broad (and, after all these years, somewhat predictable) humor that overdetermines the rest of the film. "When I'm in comedies, they tend to be comic in the tradition I enjoy playing and feel comfortable in, which is light and frivolous," he told Lax. "But now I feel I'd be better off doing serious pictures without me in them."[1] Four months later, Allen talked even more critically about casting himself in his films: "It's hard to write good films and accommodate my character. It's always been a problem. That's why I'd just as soon keep out of my movies in the future and I won't burden myself and I won't burden the audience and I'm free to do any movie I want and not have to face the problem of creating a good story and one that also has a funny part for a limited actor — me."[2] *The Curse of the Jade Scorpion* (2001), he insisted, would have been a better film with another actor in insurance inspector C. W. Briggs's role; he played Harry Block in *Deconstructing Harry* (1997) only after Robert De Niro, Dustin Hoffman, Elliott Gould, and Albert Brooks declined the role,[3] and Allen has often regretted the Cliff subplot of *Crimes and Misdemeanors* (1989), insisting that it was much less compelling than the Judah/Dolores murder plot. Many viewers of the PBS American Masters series presentation *Woody Allen: A Documentary* (Robert B. Weide, 2011) suspected that Allen was involved in numerous decisions about his depiction, perhaps including which films would be excerpted and which would not: *Mighty Aphrodite* (1995), *Small Time Crooks* (2000), *Anything Else* (2003), *The Curse of the Jade Scorpion*, *Hollywood Ending* (2002), and *Scoop* (2006) — the last six films in which he appeared — were represented in the documentary only by interviews with other actors who appeared in them. Allen has often remarked that he never enjoys watching the films he has made; clearly, he enjoys even less watching the ones in which he appears.

My argument here, one slightly muddied by *To Rome with Love* (2012), in which he wrote himself a small role, is that *Scoop*, an otherwise unremarkable film of the Allen canon, is intriguing because it represents, somewhat self-consciously, Allen's farewell to portraying the protagonist in Allen-directed films.[4] Richard A. Blake was the first Allen critic to speculate that Sidney Waterman's death-by-driving-on-the-wrong-side-of-London-roads represented more than a comic-macabre ending for a lightweight film. Blake asked, "Could this be Allen's way of telling his audience that he is finally laying to rest the nebbish character he embodied in dozens of films over the last forty years?"[5] Given Allen's lifelong antipathy for any form of ceremony or occasion, however, his withdrawal of the "Woody" protagonist from his films must necessarily be muted, getting signaled — if at all — only by largely comic allusions to earlier Allen portrayals. Consequently, I'm contending that his enactment of Sidney in *Scoop* contains numerous echoes of other Allen roles (Jewish characters in particular) as a distinctly hedged acknowledgment of Allen's valedictory performance. Although we'll notice in *Scoop* echoes of a few other Allen movies in which he has screen time, the film most consistently alluded to throughout is *Broadway Danny Rose* (1984), a highly significant choice because Danny Rose was the role in which Allen invoked most emphatically his Catskills entertainment heritage and therefore drew most substantially (with affectionate satire) upon what Sidney Waterman characterizes as his "Hebrew persuasion." Although these two films could not be more different in terms of tone and sincerity of dramatic purpose, they evoke each other in the showbiz effusiveness of their protagonists' shared idiolect, one that, for Allen, recalls fondly his early years as a gag writer and stand-up comic. To recognize the significance of Waterman as Allen's farewell to acting in *Scoop*, however, we have to notice not only that he is emphatically Jewish in a way reminiscent of Danny Rose but also that he is a self-consciously Jewish magician — "Splendini," whose name derives, no doubt, from Harry Houdini, a Jewish Hungarian. And although his films' attitude toward magic is always somewhat equivocal, Allen's later movies generally cleave to the pattern established in *Stardust Memories* (1980) when Sandy Bates is interrogated by his fans:

> MAN: Do you believe in magic? I know, I've read all your interviews.
> SANDY: No. No, no, I don't. I used to do magic tricks when I was a kid, but, but no more.

Scoop, I'm contending here, contains a thoroughly tacit argument predicated upon Allen's increasing skepticism toward magic to vindicate Allen's personal withdrawal from acting. By invoking his previous films' preoccupation with magic, and then dramatizing how little credence he currently places in the existence of the magical, Allen slyly performs and offers the reason behind his "Woody" protagonist's vanishing act from the screen.

In his Allen biography, John Baxter explained how Danny Rose differed from Allen's earlier "Woody" roles: "Rose is the first 'Woody' character to suggest any strong attachment to Allen's Jewish roots," Baxter suggested. "He wears a chai religious emblem on a chain around his neck, makes repeated use of Yiddishisms — 'it's the *emess*'; 'my hand to God' — and delivers homilies like, 'As my uncle Sidney used to say, 'Acceptance, forgiveness, and love.'"[6] It was Julian Fox, however, who saw that Danny's Jewishness may have had more to do with the real-life model on whom he was based than it did with religion. In the mid-1950s, Harvey Meltzer, the older brother of one of Allen's Midwood High School classmates, offered to become the fledgling comedian's manager, and during the five years that he served Allen in that capacity, he pocketed from 30 to 35 percent of Allen's earnings.[7] (As we'll see, Danny Rose's willingness to sacrifice himself financially for his clients was apparently not modeled on Meltzer.) Fox explained, "Although the relationship was finally strained (Woody left Meltzer after five years for Rollins and Joffe), Meltzer is affectionately immortalized as the good-natured Danny, while the latter's ornamented Runyonesque patter ("Might I interject a concept at this juncture?") is also reputedly drawn from life. With his sub–Dale Carnegie catchphrases and a philosophy borrowed from his saintly Uncle Sidney, Danny begins to come across as a sort of "radical innocent" like Chaplin."[8]

At least in part, Danny Rose's "radical innocence" is a product of the comedians (all Jewish) who swap Danny Rose stories in the Carnegie Deli, their tale-telling providing the narrative frame of *Broadway Danny Rose*. Corbett Monica and Morty Gunty (the screenplay uses the comedians' actual names, making no attempt to fictionalize them) are bemoaning the state of comedy in the United States in the early 1980s — the fact that foolproof one-liners fail to provoke hilarity from audiences; that many of the Manhattan venues for comedy have closed; that they need to drive to Baltimore and Washington for work; and that, when they do, the audience sits "there like they were an oil painting."[9]

Sandy Baron, Howard Storm, and Jackie Gayle join the comics' confab, and the nostalgia for the good old days deepens as Baron recalls the clubs in New Jersey, where "they [the audience] never left. They never left at all." The Danny Rose narrative Baron subsequently renders for his colleagues and the film's audience emphasizes that Danny was a manager who "never left," who was unfailingly loyal to his clients, no matter how limited their talents. He manages a one-armed juggler, a one-legged tap dancer, a blind xylophone player, and other acts no other manager would touch — acts whose performances manifest primarily overcoming physical limitations. Danny's tacit agenda in supporting them is to demonstrate that "that's the beauty of this business. . . . Overnight, you can go from a b-bum to a hero," which is also the moral of this feel good movie.[10] Danny's triumph in the film is the result of his persuading former mob moll Tina Vitale (Mia Farrow) away from her "do it to the other guy first, or he'll do it to you" ethic toward his Uncle Sidney's credo of "acceptance, forgiveness and love." She evinces that conversion by appearing on Thanksgiving at Danny's apartment, where his clients have gathered for his annual holiday celebration of frozen turkey TV dinners. Tina seeks his forgiveness for the role she played in persuading Danny's biggest act, Lou Canova, to dump Danny and sign with a more prestigious manager. Initially rejecting her offer of friendship, Danny thinks better of it and follows her out onto Broadway. Catching up with her in front of the same Carnegie Deli where his story will be recounted, he leads her back toward his apartment. In apparent substantiation of the success of the Tina-Danny union, the comedians delight in the fact that the Danny Rose special that has been added to the Carnegie Deli menu is "cream cheese on a bagel with marinara," the honor all but confirming that Danny has "gone from a b-bum to a hero."

Sandy Baron's somewhat different agenda for the narrative seems to be to remind his colleagues of the existence of professional managerial loyalty, prompting Will Jordan to ask, "I mean, where you gonna find that kind of devotion today?" The purpose of Baron's "greatest Danny Rose story" is to lift the spirits of the comedians gathered around the table at the Carnegie Deli, to reassure them that the showbiz world that Danny favors — "Well, you know, they call me old-fashioned, but, but if it's old-fashioned to like Mr. Danny Kaye . . . Mr. Bob Hope, Mr. Milton Berle, you know what I mean, then all right, I'm old-fashioned" — has not vanished, that their shared profession isn't doomed by business disloyalty and American humorlessness. As if in testament to the story's intermediacy, Corbett Monica picks up the check for the table, explaining, when his colleagues express shock, "For these kinds of laughs, I figure it's worth the price." The telling of the "greatest Danny Rose story" has been efficacious in the most immediate and functional of terms.

Vincent Canby called *Broadway Danny Rose* Allen's "love letter not only to American comedy stars but to all those pushy hopefuls who never made it to the top in showbiz, but also to the kind of comedy that nourished the particular genius of Woody Allen."[11] That kind of comedy, obviously, is Jewish comedy, and what better way to celebrate it could he have devised than to put its actual practitioners — Milton Berle as well — into the film? Because there *is* no Danny Rose beyond Sandy Baron's narrative (he vanishes in the conclusion of his tale), it is impossible to distinguish fact from myth in the film; all we have is the "landlocked Hebrew" of their telling whose message is "acceptance, forgiveness and love" and who will arguably become more noble and self-sacrificing with every telling of his story by the comedians who ritualistically gather at the Carnegie Deli to cheer themselves with sentimental constructions of the superiority of yesterday to today.

Beyond the myth, however, who is the Danny Rose Allen portrays in the movie? When he's not being "the beard" with Tina for Lou Canova or fleeing mobsters, Danny is incessantly talking, endlessly taking interest in and providing pep talks to practically everyone he meets. In trying to sell his blind xylophone player to Phil Chomsky of Weinstein's Majestic Bungalow

Colony (young Allan Konigsberg — as Woody was known before becoming Woody — performed magic tricks there one summer in the 1950s), Danny emphasizes not his client's musicianship but his human virtues: "Philly, hear me out, will you please hear me out? The man is a beautiful man. He's a, he's a fantastic individual." "This is personal management I'm in," Danny insists, "You know, it's the key word, it's personal," though the Carnegie Deli comics agree that you go into it only after your own act has stiffed. In an intensely personal session with a couple that fabricates animals out of balloons, Danny counsels, "I don't see you just folding your balloons in joints, you know.... You're gonna fold your balloons at universities and colleges. You're gonna make your snail and your elephant at, at, at, on Broadway.... But the thing to remember, before you go out onstage, ... you gotta look in the mirror, and say your three S's: Star, Smile, Strong." Danny, clearly, is a walking Catskills self-help guide, a motivational mouthpiece who sentimentally embraces all the magic in the world of showbiz that magician Sidney Waterman has thoroughly abandoned.

Danny's most iconic moment is imaged up in response to Howard Storm's recollection of the Danny Rose act that breathed its last breath in the Catskills. Wielding his microphone, Danny approached an elderly woman in the audience: "Tell me, God bless you, sweetheart, ... let me, let me ask you a question. How old are you?" He marvels at her response: "Eighty-one years old! Isn't that fantastic? ... This is fantastic! ... I mean that. Unbelievable.... You don't look a day over eighty. No, I mean it. I'm just kidding, darling, really. I love you, sweetheart. You're really beautiful." In *Scoop*, Sidney Waterman has adopted the idiom, but in him Danny Rose's winning ingenuousness is gone.

When his personal management devotion to Lou Canova's appearance at the Copa on a Sunday night interferes with his attentions to his other clients, Danny apologizes to one of them: Herbie Jayson, whose bird-act performers have just been reduced by the predation of a cat. "You know, I've been very busy with another client," Danny explains. "After Sunday night, my hand to God, you have me, I'll be yours exclusively. I know how you feel." To Ralph, who doesn't want to pay because Herbie didn't perform, Danny pleads, "Pee Wee. Pee Wee was the son he never had, so it's, you know ..." Then back to Herbie: "Ah, I promise after Sunday night, really, I'm with you. [Raising his hand in a pledge] It's the *emess* [truth]."

Danny Rose's dialogue must be quoted at some length to make the point that he is certainly the most other-directed of Allen's characters, the one whose commitment to his profession and his clients is the most unequivocal. Lou Canova is a temperamental has-been who drinks too much, but, Baron affirms, "the only one who believes in him is Danny Rose.... Danny... has faith," and the one perhaps most resigned to his lack of faith in anything but his clients. He tells Lou Canova that "sooner or later... you're going to have to square yourself with the big guy," but when Tina asks whether he believes in God, Danny's response is, "No, no, but, uh, I'm guilty over it." In a very quiet, unassuming way ("But this thing is all like inside the mask, right?" Howard Storm asks at the outset of the comedians' tale swapping), Allen made one of his most sympathetic self-portrayals his most markedly Jewish in a movie whose closure is perhaps the most compellingly consonant in his oeuvre. As Jeffrey Rubin-Dorsky suggested in an article on the film, "In spite of its insularity and materialism, what Allen locates in the Jewish world of the Catskills, and what Danny recreates with his rag-tag band of odd 'acts,' is the sense of unforced community that existed among a people gathered together to share a culture that would inevitably disappear in the process of Americanization.... Allen, whose popular film personae often embody the torturous search for values and meaning amidst the egocentrism of contemporary American life, for one moment in *Broadway Danny Rose* finds a nurturing spiritual connection to the Jewish past, thus assuring the film of a special place in his body of work as well as in his viewers' affection."[12]

The other reason for quoting Danny at length is because Sid Waterman of *Scoop* so regularly echoes Danny Rose, though I'll be arguing that Danny's Runyonesque register and Waterman's differ because of the level of sincerity each of these protagonists projects. Before we move on to that contrast, however, we need to address the other highly significant aspect of Sidney Waterman, one to which numerous essays on Allen's films have been entirely devoted: magic. Waterman, I'm suggesting here, is a culmination of Allen's career-spanning, deepening skepticism about magic, a prestidigitator whose most impressive trick is his concealment from his audience of his contempt for their incredulity toward his act. On the other hand, Danny Rose's tomato juice concoction that transforms drunken Lou Canova to a performance-ready lounge act seems a genuine species of magical intercession, as do his conversions of Tina and the comedians gathered in the Carnegie Deli to his optimist's ethic. (For all his insistences that he's just a sports fan who happens to make movies,[13] it seems Allen intuits that only someone touched with at least a bit of genius could write and produce forty-two movies in forty-two years, and that he doles out a bit of that specialness to some of his protagonists: Andrew Hobbes in *A Midsummer Night's Sex Comedy*; Sandy Bates in *Stardust Memories*; Hyman Kleinman in *Shadows and Fog*; Alice of *Alice*; Sheldon Mills and his mother in "Oedipus Wrecks"; Harry Block, the "black magician" of *Deconstructing Harry*; Emmet Ray in *Sweet and Lowdown*; Val Waxman in *Hollywood Ending*; and Gil Pender in *Midnight in Paris* are a few of them.) Of course, magic so pervades Allen's work that it's not necessary to seek it where it must be cunningly inferred.

Characteristically phlegmatic when being interviewed, Allen was anything but that in expressing his childhood enthusiasm for magic to Eric Lax. Recalling the magic catalogs he pored over, Allen recalled that "everything looked so wondrous and fabulous. If you're hooked on it, you're hooked on it, and I was just completely, absolutely hooked. I had a big drawer and it was full of magic tricks and I had these books and that was almost all I cared about."[14] That fervor for magic is glimpsed in *Stardust Memories* (1980) when Sandy Bates projects his juvenile magician self into a show that he and Daisy (Jessica Harper) are watching. As "the Amazing Sandy" causes a glowing globe to levitate, the audience bursts into applause, and Judith Crist, host of the Sandy Bates film festival, effuses, "The boy's a natural. I've never seen anything like it. A born magician." (Crist wasn't always so unequivocally positive about the Woody Allen art that Sandy's magic symbolizes.) But Allen is seldom unequivocal about anything, most particularly in *Stardust Memories*, and Crist's "born magician" testimonial cuts to Sandy's mother, who responds, "Well, he should be. He sits in his room alone and practices for hours." An unidentified skeptic wonders if Sandy wasn't doing something else in there: "Oh, he does that, too," his mother responds, holding up photographs of half-nude women, "I found these pictures hidden in his drawer." Maurice Yacowar commented expansively on the relationship linking magic, art, and masturbation in *Stardust Memories*:

"When young Sandy strokes his rod, he produces a bouquet of false flowers. Making films is the adult's version of magic: 'You can't control life [Yacowar quotes Bates]: "It doesn't wind up perfectly. Only art you can control. Art and masturbation — two areas in which I am an absolute expert.'... Magic and art are associated with masturbation," Yacowar contends, "because they are solitary fantasies that do not improve the human condition. As the nurse reminds Sandy, "All those silly magic tricks you do couldn't help your friend Nat Bernstein' [who died of Lou Gehrig's disease].... Allen's point is that we use deluding art — the boy's magic, the man's films — to avoid facing our ephemerality."[15]

Magic proves equally ineffectual in Allen's 1981 play *The Floating Light Bulb*. The Pollack family lives in Brooklyn in "an apartment reeking of hopelessness and neglect.... It is not so much that the apartment is dirty; it is simply that it has been too difficult to keep pace with its rate of decay."[16] Mrs. Pollack's dream of deliverance from hopelessness and decay resides in her son, Paul, a boy whose stuttering and incapacitating shyness relegate him to his bedroom, where he incessantly rehearses magic tricks. Mrs. Pollack meets the brother of a neighbor, Jerry Wexler, who is in show-business management, and she arranges for him to come to the apartment to see Paul's magic act in the hope that Wexler will sign up the boy as a client. When she insists that Paul wear a turban for the performance, he balks, but she is adamant: "The idea is not to be a boy in a dark blue suit doing tricks. It's to create an illusion. The Great Paul Pollack. A miracle worker should not look like a CPA."[17] The miracle she would have him work is familial redemption, but because this play is so strongly inflected by Tennessee Williams's *The Glass Menagerie* (replete with the sudden defection of the "gentleman caller"), there's no magic and no miracles. Consumed by anxiety, Paul fumbles and stutters his way through the act and flees in humiliation to his bedroom halfway through it; out in the living room, Mrs. Pollack and Wexler warm to each other, but his exclamation, "Boy! This has turned out to be an evening of magic in its own way!"[18] is immediately followed by his confession that tomorrow he's moving with his mother to Arizona for her health. Wexler leaves, Mr. Pollack arrives, the family collapses into rancorous quarrels, and finally Mrs. Pollack asks what Paul is doing in his room. "I'm p-practicing," he replies, "... p-practicing."[19] The play offers little hope that Paul's practicing will improve anything in his family's dysfunctionality.

The resolutions of both *Midsummer Night's Sex Comedy* (1982) and *Alice* (1990) depend upon the intervention of magic, but in each film the magic seems more plot premise than anything Allen takes seriously. The "spirit ball" machine that Andrew Hobbes (Allen) invents emerges in *Midsummer Night's Sex Comedy* largely to refute the materialist assumptions of Professor Leopold Sturgis (Jose Ferrer), who intones, "Nothing is real but experience, that which can be touched, tasted, felt, or in some scientific fashion proved." Hobbes's gadget, however, proves itself capable only of rejuvenating the characters' human passions that already exist within them. The herbs of Dr. Yang (Keye Luke) in *Alice* create wonderful comedic scenes in which Alice (Mia Farrow) flies over Manhattan with her first love, becomes invisible, and compels all the men at a Christmas party to fall helplessly in love with her, but the major impact Dr. Yang has is to persuade Alice to terminate her marriage to a wealthy business tycoon and pursue her own more maternal, altruistic, and humanistic instincts. In both movies, magic is a remarkably unsupernatural means of restoring characters to themselves.

Magic is substantially more significant in *Shadows and Fog* (1991), where it gets configured as the only alternative to the political insidiousness of the town plotters whose efforts to capture "the killer" end up instead creating factions at war with each other. ("Soon we're going to do his killing for him,"[20] Kleinman [Allen] accurately predicts.) After Kleinman has escaped the mob that, believing he is the killer, wants to lynch him, he follows Irmy (Farrow) back to the circus that employs her as a sword swallower. Disproving his reputation as a cowering ink-stained wretch, Kleinman distracts the killer's attempt to make Irmy his next victim, but magic proves even more effectual in dealing with him. Whereas the townspeople's rival plans are either impotent before the threat the killer poses or contributory to it, the circus magician, Irmstedt (Kenneth Mars), is able to use his illusions to temporarily capture the killer. Irmstedt and Kleinman first hide in a trick mirror, transforming themselves into images unaffected by the killer's subsequent destruction of the prop; then Irmstedt entraps the killer in a circular cage before making him disappear and rematerialize ("He was here — and now he's there!"), chained hand and foot to a stool. "We have captured the beast!" Irmstedt exults, but by the time the other circus performers arrive to witness his triumph, the killer has slipped his bonds and fled. "No man could have escaped," Irmstedt complains, attesting to the notion that it wasn't a man he'd shackled, "those were the real locks. Even *I* could not have escaped." Taking up this cue, the circus roustabout replies, "Looks like he's a greater magician than you" — perhaps invoking death's ability to make people disappear forever.

"Meanwhile," the roustabout proceeds to goad Irmstedt: "Your tricks didn't stop the killer." "No," the magician admits, "but we checked his reins for a moment. Perhaps we even frightened him." Art's illusions can distract us briefly from the inexorability of death, in other words, convincing us that through the imposition of artistic permanence upon materiality, we have immobilized the passage of time, circumventing mortality. But Irmstedt's magic, by his own acknowledgment, allows him only to escape from trick locks not from the real ones that death easily evades. ("All those silly magic tricks" *still* can't help Nat Bernstein when it's his time to die.) As for Irmstedt's bravado in claiming to have frightened the killer with what the magician derisively calls his "paraphernalia," it's only necessary to recall Irmy's initial characterization of him after Kleinman has told her what a great artist he believes Irmstedt is: "He's a great artist when he's sober." Irmstedt is a drunk, Paul the clown (John Malkovich) is a womanizing philanderer, and the circus incarnating the redemptive power of human fantasy is, in Paul's estimation, "a completely mismanaged stupid traveling show." Art, Allen's films consistently maintain, is only as pure or perfect as the artist who creates it, and is, consequently, utterly incapable of achieving the triumph that Modernist aesthetics often ascribed to it: the transformation of temporal progression into humanly intelligible meaning. Allen's films' typical attitude toward the artistic process, instrumentally considered, is perhaps best summarized by Rain (Juliette Lewis), Gabe Roth's graduate writing student in *Husbands and Wives*, who disparages the mimetic achievement he lauds in her stories: "It's just a trick, you know," she replies. "When I was ten I wrote this whole story on Paris. It's just a trick — you don't have to know [Paris in order for the trick to work]." However ineffectual tricks and magic prove to be in reversing existential dilemmas, at the end of *Shadows and Fog*, Kleinman signs on as the magician's assistant nonetheless, asking Irmstedt rhetorically, "What better way to spend the rest of my life, than to help you with those wonderful illusions of yours?" The magician's tricks and illusions can't subdue the killer or defeat mortality, but Kleinman commits himself to them for the reason that Irmstedt offers in the film's closing line: "We need them — like we need the air."

Cut to Allen's 2006 interview with Richard Schickel, in which the need for magic remains but the likelihood of its intercession has not increased: "It's like we're all checkmated, and unless somebody can find a move that will relieve us, that will free us from the checkmate, then we ... we've had it. And I, I think if it's not magical, it's not going to happen. Because all the other solutions I see around me — religious solutions, scientific solutions, intellectual solutions — you know, everything is a little too late and not good enough, and all the things that are in the eyes of writers and poets are not redeemingly effective. They may well say, well, it's too bad, it's the best we can do, but it's not good enough, and what you really need is some kind of magic."[21]

In *Melinda and Melinda* (2004), Allen has musician Ellis Moonsong (Chiwetel Ejiofor) express less tentatively the same comment on magic that Allen offered in his interview with Schickel: "Well, I believe in magic; in the end, I think it's the only thing that can save us." In the comedic ending of *Curse of the Jade Scorpion*, it's difficult to tell how much the romantic union of C. W. Briggs (Allen) and Betty Fitzgerald (Helen Hunt) owes to their having been simultaneously entranced by magician Voltan Polgar (Donald Ogden Spiers); that is, perhaps "ordinary life" retained enough residue of magic for them not to have to suffer the "dropping of the curtain" of actuality or the surrendering of the "fabulous illusion" of erotic love. Polgar, the wielder of the "magical" jade scorpion, initially uses hypnotic suggestion to convince Briggs and Fitzgerald that they're deeply in love, so that each time he utters a specific word ("Constantinople" for him, "Madagascar" for her), they fall under his power, becoming helpless to resist his suggestions that they perform criminal acts and reexperiencing as well the affection he'd compelled them to feel for each other. (Add Polgar to the list of Allen magicians of dubious character: he uses his powers to transform ordinary citizens into thieves.) In the final scene of *Scorpion*, Briggs asks Fitzgerald, whom he believes — mistakenly — to be in her "Madagascar" trance, to rehearse his virtues, and once she has showered him with praises, he declares, "Someday, I'm gonna make you feel those things, just really feel them." "Anything's possible," she responds, "I made *you* feel that way, and I didn't even have to say 'Constantinople.'" Briggs does not know where he is once Fitzgerald has said this, but we've been here before: the only magic Woody Allen really believes in is romantic love, and he implies as well that even it may only be the detritus of a hypnotist's mental prestidigitations.

The kind of magic Sidney Waterman practices in *Scoop* isn't remotely that potent.

We first encounter Sidney on a London stage, where he is plying his trade — "the astonishing magic of Splendini!" — for an audience comprised largely of children and their parents. (He subsequently admits that Splendini isn't his name, acknowledging that "I go exotic to give the square haircuts some charisma now and then.") Their ages notwithstanding, he claims to love the audience: "Thank you, ladies and gentlemen, you're an incredible audience, and I say that from the bottom of my heart. Every time I come to London, I get a sincere sensation because you're a marvelous people, beautiful humans." When Sondra Pransky (Scarlett Johansson) volunteers to be the subject of one of his "experiments," she turns out to love him, too. Ascribing to himself a perfect ear for geographic accents, Sidney guesses she's from Alabama, and when she corrects him — it's Brooklyn — he exults, "God bless you, darling — I'm from Brooklyn, too. That is fantastic. I feel such love coming from this woman, I can't tell you," he assures the audience. "I say this with all sincerity from the bottom of my heart — you're an incredible human being and a credit to your race." If the lexicon is pure Danny Rose channeling Harvey Meltzer, Sidney soon begins sounding notes that Danny never does. Asking her to step inside his dematerializer box, he encourages the subject he addresses as "Mandelbaum" not to be afraid, and she reminds him that her name is Pransky. "Pransky, Mandelbaum," he responds. "What's the difference? They take off the same holidays." Sidney's subsequent references to Jews similarly construe them as an annoying cultural group rather than as adherents to a religion.

Whereas *Broadway Danny Rose* is tacitly commendatory of Jewish culture (or Jewish comedic culture, at any rate), *Scoop* is pervaded by Sidney's slighting asides about his religion/ethnicity. When Peter Lyman (Hugh Jackman) asks Sidney, whom, Sondra has convinced Peter, is her father, whether he plays a musical instrument, Sidney responds that he "plays blues harp. . . . It used to be called 'Jew's harp,' but you know how those people are. The slightest hint of anti-Semitism and they write letters." It's possible that Sidney is trying to persuade British nobility Peter Lyman that his "daughter" and he *aren't* Jewish, but at a subsequent party at the Lyman mansion, Sidney stakes claim to his heritage before disparaging it. A woman who identifies herself as Christian asks what he is: "Me? I, I was born into the Hebrew persuasion, but when I got older, I converted to narcissism."

Danny Rose, in the comedians' version of him, is sincere in his protestations of affection for others because, in their "greatest Danny Rose story," they're mythologizing him as faultlessly loyal and anything but narcissistic. Perhaps the culmination of his other-directed extroversion is dramatized best by the Thanksgiving celebration, where Danny is depicted as being sincerely happy to host his clients and excited to announce to his guests that "the twins" are telephoning to send their holiday greetings to everyone. Sidney's affirmations of affection, conversely, are all rhetoric. He tells another audience volunteer during his act, "I love you, Wendy, I really do. I love this woman from the bottom of my heart. You're an incredible woman and I say that with all due respect, Wendy." In a subsequent scene, Sidney describes Wendy to Sondra: "I don't know where they get these people, but she looked like Sitting Bull." In his interviews with Eric Lax, Allen commented, "I used to read about myself, but I completely stopped because talk about unhelpful distractions — the absurdity of reading that you're a comic genius or in bad faith. Who needs to ponder such outlandish nonsense?"[22] Sidney, at least, needs to ponder the issue of being in remarkably bad faith.

If Sidney professes no serious belief in Judaism, he believes even less in magic. Sondra encounters the ghost of recently departed journalist Joe Strombel (Ian McShane) while undergoing the "experiment," and she returns to the theater the following day in hopes of finding his spirit there again in Sidney's contraption. She doesn't understand why she remains alone in the dematerializer, while Sidney is outside, assuring her that he's beginning to "agitate the molecules" while checking his watch and yawning with boredom. Sidney isn't surprised when Strombel is a no-show. "What's to understand?" Sidney asks her. "I built [the dematerializer] out of plywood. What do you think? There's spirits and a world of departed people? Darling, I don't know what you've been smoking, but don't try to bring it through customs."

Sondra makes an effort, ultimately successful, to draw Sidney into her investigation of Lyman as the tarot-card killer, but he's initially reluctant, playing the role Allen played opposite Carol (Diane Keaton) of the incurious and pusillanimous partner in *Manhattan Murder Mystery* (1993).[23] (Sidney begs off one foray with Sondra sounding like *Floating Light Bulb*'s Paul Pollack with the excuse that he needs to "practice [his] magic tricks.") "This [investigation]," Sidney tells her, "is not for me, Sondra. I don't do this. I do occasional bar mitzvahs and kids' parties." For Sidney, there is no distinction between bar mitzvahs and kids' parties — they're both places where those gullible enough to believe in anything beyond the natural world can whoop and applaud over a bouquet appearing from an empty cylinder or a human being seeming to vanish in a dematerializer. In "Oedipus Wrecks" (1989), Treva Marx (Julie Kavner), a spiritualist who initially fails to help Sheldon Mills bring his mother down from the skies above Manhattan, bemoans the disappointments of her lifelong pursuit of the supernatural: "I always have hopes, I always think there's more to the world than meets your eye — hidden meanings, special mysteries. Nothing ever works, ever." Her love for Sheldon proves to be the magic needed to coerce Mrs. Millstein's return to earth, and it's often the case in Allen's films (see Wexler's comment about he and Mrs. Pollack having made some magic the night when Paul Pollack failed to) that human love is the only magic there is. (That Treva is Jewish also helps with Mom Millstein's return from the sky.) Danny Rose's Uncle Sidney affirms "acceptance, forgiveness and love"; Sidney Waterman's only comment about love in *Scoop* is to wonder whether it will result in Sondra becoming pregnant, and there's little of the magical underlying his deduction that in loving Peter Lyman, Sondra has been loving a murderer of two other women.

Although not as extreme as Dobel in *Anything Else*[24] or Boris Yellnikoff (Larry David) in *Whatever Works* (2009),[25] Sidney represents the skeptic in Allen, the one who would never even acknowledge the possibility of a redemptive magic. So hard-bitten is Sidney in his nihilist assumptions that even when he's confronted with proof that there is something beyond the natural — Strombel's ghost appears to him midway through the film — he doesn't ask any of the questions about death and what comes afterward that we'd thoroughly expect an Allen protagonist to ask. Nor is he particularly surprised at the fact that, upon suffering his own death-by-auto-accident, he finds himself in a boat captained by the grim reaper on its voyage to the afterworld — the same boat from which Strombel escaped briefly to waylay Sondra Pransky in Sidney's dematerializer. Sidney's response to surviving mortality is to treat the land of the dead as if it were the exact image of the realm of the living — a place full of dupes anxious to be taken in by card tricks.

In discussing his youthful enthusiasm for magic, Allen recalled when the catalogs of tricks that had so excited him gave way to a more self-reliant form of prestidigitation: "That's what you wanted to be," he told Lax. "Not an illusionist, not a stage magician, you wanted to be a sleight-of-hand-expert. Then you were complete. You showed up someplace, if there was a saltcellar, a thimble, some coins, some cards, whatever, you could work."[26] It is through performing this sort of magic that Allen makes his final appearance as the protagonist in his movies. Finding himself on the afterworld vessel, Sidney pulls out a deck of cards with which to entertain his fellow passengers and offers what could be Allen's last on-screen soliloquy, one evocative of the autobiographical Allen glimpses this chapter has been tracing: "I just want to say, from the bottom of my heart," Sidney affirms, "I mean this sincerely, I say this with all due respect; you are a wonderful and a fantastic group of people. I love you and I feel that coming back from you. You may be deceased, but you should not be discouraged. Don't think of being dead as a handicap. Because when I was a child, I stuttered, but with stick-to-itive-ness and perseverance, you know, you can never tell what could happen. All right — Now I want you to take a card, Alma, any card. I love you, this is fantastic." Being dead is "fantastic"? It is if it gives Sidney a new audience for sleight-of-hand and card tricks — an audience that seems particularly needful of a magician's prestidigitory distractions.

Allen, I'm arguing, views magic much in the way as did one of his contemporary Jewish American writers. In *The Dick Gibson Show*, Stanley Elkin had his eponymous protagonist, after thoroughly debunking a myth of resurrection on the island of Mauritius, deliver a soliloquy of his own repudiating the supernatural: "Well, ladies and gentlemen," Dick Gibson informs his radio audience, "there is no astrology, there's no black magic and no white, no ESP, no UFOS. Mars is uninhabited. The dead are dead and buried. Meat won't kill you and Krebiozen won't cure you and we'll all be out of the picture before the forests disappear and the water dries up. Your handwriting doesn't indicate your character and there is no God. All there is ... are the strange displacements of the ordinary."[27] Perhaps Jewish writers, comedians, and screenwriters are working at their most Jewish when they're skewering the values that gentile believers so desperately embrace.

Accordingly, Sidney makes no exalted Irmstedtian claims for his magic having "checked [death's] reins for a moment," nor does he pretend that "perhaps we even frightened him." Kleinman signs on as Irmstedt's magician's assistant at the close of *Shadows and Fog* expressly "to help you with those wonderful illusions" — illusions that, like all other circus acts, do nothing less — nor more — than to distract audiences from the grim facts of their lives. That's all Sidney Waterman finds in the afterlife, and it's plenty for him: the dead need to be entertained as much as do the living, and he's got the cards and the Harvey Meltzerian patter to keep them thoroughly entranced. In addition, his soliloquy is a stunning and personally revealing parting speech upon which Woody Allen bowed out of his films as protagonist by suggesting how he had translated his own (and Paul Pollack's) disfluency into a signature element of his stand-up comedy and his appearances in more than thirty of his films. We, the moviegoing audience, have our on-screen counterparts in the dead witnessing Sidney's card tricks, of course, and although Allen can't be accused of ever having referred to us as "a fantastic group of people," he values us in exactly the same way that Sidney values those on the ship of the dead: the artist needs an audience.

Broadway Danny Rose comes to its wonderfully consonant close as Danny catches up with Tina outside the Carnegie Deli in which his "greatest story" will be retold — or re-created — by Jewish comedians intent upon convincing themselves that the golden age of comedy isn't dead and that their careers aren't either. *Scoop* concludes on something more of a grim joke. Sidney prophesies his ending in telling Sondra, "I love London, don't get me wrong. I can't take the driving, you know, because it's on the wrong side, and every time I drive a car here, I'm sure I'm gonna die in a crash." Driving to rescue Sondra from Peter Lyman, Sidney crosses over into the wrong lane and collides with another car, perhaps taking with him all the "Woody Allen protagonists" — Alvy Singer, Danny Rose, and Lee Simon — for whom driving a car isn't a natural or comfortable act.

It's much too extreme to say that in Sidney Waterman, Danny Rose has reverted from being a hero to being a bum; fairer would be to suggest that when the magician no longer believes in the magic he's performing, it's well past time for him to let others create it for him.

Notes

1. Eric Lax, Conversations with Woody Allen: His Films, the Movies, and Moviemaking (New York: Knopf, 2007), 42.
2. Ibid., 55.
3. Ibid., 157.
4. Allen appears in John Turturro's film *Fading Gigolo* (2013), but I'm addressing only the films that he writes and directs.
5. Richard Blake provided the inspiration for this argument in his chapter "Allen's Random Universe in His European Cycle: Morality, Marriage, Magic," in *A Companion to Woody Allen*, ed. Peter J. Bailey and Sam B. Girgus (Malden, MA: Wiley-Blackwell, 2013).
6. John Baxter, *Woody Allen: A Biography* (New York: Carroll & Graf, 1998), 321.
7. Eric Lax, *Woody Allen: A Biography* (New York: Knopf, 1991), 90.
8. Julian Fox, *Woody: Movies from Manhattan* (Woodstock, NY: Overlook Press, 1996), 151. When Tim Carroll interviewed Meltzer in 1992 for *Woody and His Women* (London: Warner, 1993), 228, phrases like "may I interject one concept at this juncture?" punctuated Meltzer's side of their conversation.
9. Woody Allen, "Broadway Danny Rose," in *Three Films of Woody Allen* (New York: Vintage, 1987), 148.
10. In his interview with Robert Benayoun, Allen emphasized that "*Broadway Danny Rose* is a spontaneous film, the way I like them." Robert Benayoun, "Interview with Woody Allen," in *Woody Allen: Interviews*, ed. Robert E. Kapsis and Kathie Coblentz, 78–82 (Jackson: University Press of Mississippi, 2006), 80. Its "spontaneity," I'm assuming, does not conflict with the possibility that the comedians' frame suggests more than Allen has acknowledged.
11. Vincent Canby, "'Danny Rose': Runyonesque, but Pure Woody Allen" (review of *Broadway Danny Rose*), *New York Times*, January 29, 1984.
12. Jeffrey Rubin-Dorsky, "The Catskills Reinvented (and Redeemed): Woody Allen's *Broadway Danny Rose*," *Kenyon Review* 25 (Summer/Fall 2003): 264–81.
13. "I'm more the guy that's home with the beer in his undershirt watching the television set, watching the game on television, than I am, you know, poring over the Russian novelists." Richard Schickel, *Woody Allen: A Life in Film* (Chicago: Ivan R. Dee), 153.
14. Lax, *Woody Allen*, 49.
15. Maurice Yacowar, *Loser Take All: The Comic Art of Woody Allen* (New York: Continuum, 1991), 228–29.
16. Woody Allen, *The Floating Light Bulb* (New York: Random House, 1982), 3.
17. Ibid., 60.
18. Ibid., 95.

19. Ibid., 104.

20. For an excellent essay on *Shadows and Fog*, the Holocaust, and Franz Kafka, see Iris Bruce's "Lurking in the Shadows: Kleinman's Trial," in Bailey and Girgus, *Companion to Woody Allen*.

21. Schickel, *Woody Allen*, 143–44.

22. Lax, *Conversations*, 324.

23. *Scoop*'s comedic murder mystery plot seems separable enough from the issue of Sidney Waterman as Allen's final on-screen role that I'm largely ignoring its formulaic trajectory here.

24. Here is one of Dobel's diatribes to his mentee, Jerry Falk: "Since the beginning of time, people have been, you know, frightened and unhappy, scared of death and of getting old, and there have always been priests around, and shamans, and now shrinks, to tell 'em, I know that you're frightened, but I can help ya. Of course, it's gonna cost you a few bucks. . . . But they can't help you, Falk, because life is what it is."

25. Boris Yellnikoff importunes his fellow musicians: "In America, they have summer camps for everything — rich kids, basketball camp, magic camp, movie director camp. They should have a concentration camp: two weeks mandatory so that they would understand what the human race is capable of." "Who would send their kid to a concentration camp?" one of Boris's friends wonders. Boris responds, "A responsible parent who wants their child to grasp reality."

26. Lax, *Woody Allen*, 54.

27. Stanley Elkin, *The Dick Gibson Show* (New York: Random House, 1971), 229.

WOMEN'S ISSUES

GIOVANNA P. DEL NEGRO

Woody's Women ler Jewish Domesticity and the Unredeemed Ghost of Hanukkah to Come

From early slapstick comedies and parodies like *What's Up, Tiger Lily?* (1966) or *Bananas* (1971) to romantic comedies like *Annie Hall* (1977) and to more serious films like *Husbands and Wives* (1992) or *Deconstructing Harry* (1997), Woody Allen's films are remarkably uniform in their treatment of Jewish women. As Joyce Antler and others have observed, while the narratives often deal richly with the lives of Jewish men, Jewish women are often absent from Allen's fictive worlds, and when they do make an appearance, they are generally depicted in terms of shticky one-liners or comical exaggerations.[1] In those situations where the Jewish women aren't fervently intellectual or ambitious careerists, they tend to focus on the domestic milieu, nervously worrying over children and husbands, whom they suffocate with love. As for the ubiquitous, often anachronistic standby, the Jewish mother, she is also typically portrayed as an old-fashioned, overbearing housewife who is responsible for making her son angst ridden and neurotic, a nebbish protagonist that Allen has made a career playing.[2]

By psychological conditioning, Allen's schlemiel runs from the Jewish women, whom he finds threatening, to the less frightening arms of ethereal gentile beauties, who in turn leave him. While the characters that Allen plays are afraid of long-term relationships in general, they are even more afraid, specifically, of Jewish domesticity — a stifling marriage, a sexually disinterested wife, the burden of children and religion, and a placid home life that inexorably leads to the loss of male identity and lack of pleasure. Indeed, the problem of Jewish domesticity is key to unlocking the subtle logic by which Allen creates his social universe and is crucial for elucidating the hidden principles of gender and ethnicity by which Allen, the writer-director, decides what kinds of relationships are possible, or even imaginable. Exploring prominent films from all periods of his oeuvre, this chapter will show how such a logic even shapes the rare films, such as *Scoop* (2006), in which Jewish women take center stage, or where Jewish mothers are presented sympathetically, as in *Interiors* (1978). While Allen's world is one in which Jewish female characters are largely erased or ridiculed, his representations of their identity are more ambivalent and complex than this might suggest. Indeed, Jewish women are often portrayed as strong and independent by comparison to their more insecure and timid gentile counterparts to whom Allen's characters are invariably attracted and whom he finds less threatening. With these broader dynamics in mind, I will show how the treatment of Jewish women in Allen's films can be doubly read as expressing both the anxieties about and the promise of Jewish domesticity.

Two Jews Spell Disaster

The Jewish female characters in Allen's films are by and large smart, assertive, articulate, often politically engaged intellectuals, whose focus on career and motherhood sometimes comes at the expense of sex. Alongside these academics and professional women, one also finds devoted, family-oriented housewives who are usually too domesticating for the characters that Allen plays. However, whether attractive or ordinary, earthy or cerebral, and secular or religious, all of Woody's Jewish women can be as sharp and tenacious as they can be emotional and irrational. In *Annie Hall*, for example, Alvy Singer's (Allen) two former wives, who are both Jewish (as they were for Allen in real life), prove to be too erudite, political, or ambitious. The marriage to his first wife, Allison Porchnik (Carol Kane) — a pixie-like, pale blonde with curly hair and a small voice, whom Alvy admits in hindsight was beautiful, intelligent, and willing — inexplicably dissolves; while his fashionably dressed, left-leaning, social-climbing, darkly attractive second wife, Robin (Janet Margolin), is incapable of having an orgasm and loses her appeal. As it turns out, both these women are too involved with the life of the mind: Robin is alienated from her body, disengaged from the mundane world of everyday pleasures; Allison, though a pretty, idealistic literature scholar with a social conscience and a healthy libido, is just too bookish. Indeed, in the scene in which Allison accuses Alvy of using his obsession with the Kennedy assassination as a pretext for avoiding sex, the bedroom is filled with piles upon piles of books. Even though, in a flashback, Alvy confesses that he doesn't quite know why he left Allison, suggesting that perhaps there is a deeper unconscious force at play of which Alvy (and Allen) might not be fully aware, it is clear that his ex-wife's intellectual intensity and ardent commitment to social change is intimidating to him.

Though the characters that Allen (or his surrogates) plays are usually attracted to women who are dangerously beautiful but trouble, Grace (Julie Kavner) from *Deconstructing Harry* is of the plain-looking kind, a seemingly harmless Jewish housewife with an accommodating personality. When Mel (Robin Williams), her actor husband, is sent home from the set one day because he is literally out of focus and blurry, Grace is dutifully worried and concerned. Unable to identify the root of his problem, she works hard to adjust to the visual distortion that her husband has become, and in an act of self-sacrifice, she has the entire family wear glasses to see him more sharply. Later in the film, we discover that Mel is actually a fictional character from a story by Harry Block (Allen), a troubled author with writer's block, who eventually has a panic attack and becomes blurry as well. While the circumstances that lead to Harry's disorder are clear — his personal life is in shambles — Mel's condition appears unmotivated. He has all of the trappings of a happy Jewish home life, an adoring wife and cute children, but despite it all he is miserable, afflicted by an unnamed problem for which doctors have no cure. This story of cloying domesticity not only reveals Harry's ambivalent feelings toward the Jewish home, which he partly represents as a place of familial warmth and intimacy — the epitome of *haimishe* (cozy and homelike) ideals — but also expresses his deep-seated fears of marriage to Jewish women who presumably turn their husbands into confused, anxiety-stricken creatures who are unable to properly function in society.

In Harry's fictional world, Jewish domesticity proves to be so intellectually numbing and normalizing that it turns otherwise healthy, passionate individuals into mindless conformists, one-dimensional cartoon figures. In Mel's case, domesticity has made him soft, docile, ill defined, and insecure. Uncertain about his affliction, in the last scene we find him half-heartedly accepting his fate, literally and figuratively muddling through life, not knowing what ails him or what to do to change his situation. A projection of Harry's confused state of mind and his debilitating writer's block, Mel is unstable, conflicted, and overwhelmed, perhaps a work in progress, still in need of greater clarity and focus. Until then, however, the Mel of Harry's imagination is a weak, ineffectual, passive father whose authority has been usurped by a wife on whom he is completely dependent.[3] Ultimately, Mel's crisis of identity — gendered and ethnic — is never resolved but merely tolerated as part of the Jewish man's burden.

At the opposite pole of Grace, the dotingly happy Jewish homemaker, is Harry's wife Joan (Kirstie Alley), whose zeal for Judaism is only matched by the rage she feels for her philandering husband who turns the misery he causes into literary gold. In another of Harry's tales, Helen, a fictional character based partly on Joan, becomes a fanatical Jew and rediscovers the value of tradition, lights candles on the Sabbath, contemplates circumcising her older son, and in a slapstick moment, blesses her husband's genitalia during sex. Indignant, her husband (Stanley Tucci), a secular Jew, reminds his wife, a psychoanalyst (like Joan), that religion is a sham. But in a final act of betrayal, Helen leaves him for an Israeli client (Floyd Resnick) who embodies her newfound commitment to the Jewish state.

Later in the real-life portion of the film, Harry has an affair with a client from Joan's practice, but when his wife storms into his office to confront him, Harry responds with an Allenesque one-liner, meekly suggesting that perhaps his sexual transgression was a "disguised plea for closeness." Adding insult to injury, he cowardly accuses his wife of abandoning him after the birth of their son and, as a punch line, bashfully confesses that his affair with the "large-bosomed Jewish woman" from her practice met a need for "hot, meaningless, passionate sex" that their "solid, tranquil, peaceful marriage" lacked. Just as Harry cannot resist having an affair with his wife's client — a troubled young woman on the verge of a therapeutic breakthrough — Allen the filmmaker and comic cannot resist a joke about a Jewish woman's large breasts. Here, Woody's women are easy bait: either exploited for their mammary excess or rejected for their sexually stunted intellectualism.

In the disturbingly funny, yet tragically poignant office-confrontation scene, Joan is depicted as a frumpy, disheveled, observant Jew who wears somber-colored outfits that hide her body behind turtlenecks, long skirts, and loose-fitting sweaters; she looks more like the wife of a Hasidic Jew (without a wig) than a fashionably dressed, New York professional. This unhinged, modern-day Jewish shrew who in a fit of rage tries to strangle her husband, however, regains her professional demeanor almost as fast as she loses it, calmly escorting her client (the Allenish Wallace Shawn) into her office to begin her next session — then just as abruptly bolts out of her chair to resume castigating her husband. Finally, losing all composure, she runs into the hallway screaming invectives, sobbing inconsolably before falling to the floor emotionally spent and defeated. At the end of her hysterical outburst, the overly Jewish Joan has fallen victim not only to Harry's infidelity and narcissism but also to the "scornful gaze of Allen's camera," in Jeffrey Rubin-Dorsky's phrase, which makes her appear "bloated and apoplectic."[4]

The character of Doris (Caroline Aaron), Harry's estranged sister, like Joan and the fictional Helen, is a once-secular Jew whose faith in Judaism has been rekindled. Though also modestly dressed, the kindhearted sibling, who helped Harry survive his childhood, receives the most humane treatment of any of the other Jewish women (or Harry's other relatives) in the film. When Harry shows up to visit, Doris is still angry with her brother for using the details of her life to depict his now ex-wife with contempt. Appalled by his lack of sensitivity toward her religious conversion, she accuses her atheist brother of having no spiritual center and only believing in "nihilism, cynicism, sarcasm, and orgasms." When she adds, "You were always enraged by the fact that I returned to my roots," Harry responds sarcastically, "What roots, you were a wonderful, sweet kid. Then you go to Fort Lauderdale, meet this fanatic zealot [husband, a fervent Jewish nationalist] who fills you full of superstitions." However, what is perhaps more disturbing to Harry about Doris's return to religion is that by virtue of her gender, she is responsible for maintaining and preserving Jewish tradition, a tradition that finds its fullest expression in the rituals and foodways tied to the household. Here, the Jewish home is not only gendered female but also marked as insular, confining, and parochial, all the things the cosmopolitan, heavy-drinking, urbane Harry finds unenlightened and narrow-minded. It seems no accident that when Harry visits his sister, he enters upon a quaint domestic scene, with Doris sitting at the dinner table folding cloth napkins.

As with many of the Jewish women in Allen's world, especially those set in the domestic sphere, Doris is a plain, ordinary-looking, middle-aged woman with short hair. The viewer is not expected to linger on her form or made to remember anything distinctive about her appearance. What we do remember from Harry's interaction with his sister is her candor, intelligence, and kindness toward her troubled brother. She is an articulate, self-possessed woman who speaks her mind and is unphased by Harry's jokey banter and penchant for embellishing his recollections of past events. Like Joan, Doris calls Harry to account for his lapse in judgment — she is the ethical voice in the wilderness — but Harry is incapable of having an honest conversation without resorting to lies and sarcasm. However, Doris, like Harry, is well versed in the art of verbal sparring and occasionally raises Allen's comedic ante with jokes of her own. For example, when Harry tries to pass off Cookie (Hazelle Goodman), a prostitute accompanying him on his trip to accept an award, as his son's nanny, Doris sarcastically quips, "Did you get her at an agency or a massage parlor?"

Unlike the peevish responses of most Jewish women to Allen's character, the gentile women who fall for him in both *Annie Hall* and *Deconstructing Harry* enjoy his pithy remarks, verbal affectations, and quirky otherness. They are amused and smitten by the weirdly dark, peculiarly funny little man with glasses who wears chinos, sweaters, and tweedy jackets; they are not put off but rather take pleasure in his idiosyncrasies — laughing approvingly at his satirical jokes and listening admiringly. Allen's characters' "difference" holds far less charm or appeal for the Jewish women in his filmic universe, for whom his witty repartee, self-deprecating humor, and fatalistic worldview are old hat. Ex-wives Allison, Robin, and Joan, and sister Doris, all share Allen's characters' cultural and religious frames of references and draw on similar stocks of knowledge. Moreover, Allen's characters' brand of pessimism, which many of his gentile women characters, at least at first, find strange and oddly charming, is all too familiar to Jewish women whose experiences, like that of Jewish men, have been indelibly marked by a history of oppression and anti-Semitism.

These outspoken Jewish women with their arsenal of ready-made Catskill comebacks are not the insecure, inexperienced ingenues who defer to Allen or his alter egos and depend on them for mentoring and reassurance. They are, as Judith Stora-Sander reminds us, the strong-willed descendants of their shtetl grandmothers who ran businesses and helped their families survive the hostile world around them.[5] They do not need to be led on a journey of self-discovery like Allen's shiksas, who tag along with their Jewish tour guide to see the world as he does, and who may become a little Jewish in the process. The Jewish women are not in search of a Svengali; the projects they seek to realize are theirs, not another's. Thus when Alvy and Harry look into their eyes, rather than the shiksas' adoration and gratitude, what they see is disappointment and disapproval. And the "logical" conclusion they draw is that the romantic union of two independent-minded but similarly inclined Jews spells disaster.

While the exogamous relationships in Allen's films thrive on difference that weakens the power of culture while ostensibly allowing for individuality to flourish, endogamous relationships build a surplus of Jewishness. As we saw with Joan and Doris, the union of two Jews is ultimately "too Jewish" for Allen, producing an excess of ethnicity that, for his alter egos, is untenable, if not nightmarish. Making the point explicit in *Deconstructing Harry*, Joan and Doris are accused of being "professionally Jewish," or "Jewish with a vengeance." And while he didn't invent the demeaning stereotype, neither has Allen shied away from exploiting it. Moreover, if the obsession with status, disinterest in sex, and pride in one's appearance are the hallmarks of the Jewish American princess, *Annie Hall*'s Robin fits the bill to a tee. However, the career-minded, sarcastic, and verbally skilled Robin has more in common with Alvy than appears at first blush. For example, in the scene where Alvy escapes to the bedroom to watch a Knicks basketball game during a party, Robin, like Doris and other of Woody's Jewish women, gives as good as she gets, calling the players "pituitary cases trying to stuff a ball through the hoop."

Allen's contemptuous portrayal of Robin, however, must be understood in relation to his mockery of the Jewish mother and to the wider historical context in which these pejorative Jewish female images gained sway. Indeed, the generationally and culturally specific mindset that produced Allen's comic portrayal of the Jewish American mother (JAM) also produced the Jewish American princess (JAP), with both stereotypes acting as scapegoats for Jewish male anxieties about gender, assimilation, and identity. In the JAM construction, the son of the domineering, infantilizing Jewish mother, to whom he is nonetheless attached, finds his masculinity compromised. The modern-day, well-educated JAP, meanwhile, is seen as challenging the Jewish male's position in the social hierarchy by demanding and competing for the same material benefits and privileges. In the post–World War

II context in which Allen came of age, these newly emerging visions of Jewish womanhood, real or fabricated, were at odds with the idealized, middle-class gender roles of the dominant, gentile society, which celebrated self-effacing housewives who deferred to their breadwinning husbands. Allen, like Philip Roth and other Jewish artists of his generation, rebelled against both types but negotiated between them, by courting non-Jewish women who were attracted to Jewish sophistication and humor but who didn't look or sound like dowdy Jewish mothers or emasculating Jewish American princesses.[6]

Mommy Angst

While the comically overprotective, domineering, suffocating Jewish mother that we see in Allen's films provides a critique of the insularity and claustrophobia that he often associates with Jewish domesticity, it also helps explain the conditions under which the neurotic, angst-ridden schlemiel developed. A staple of Jewish stand-up comedy, jokes about Jewish mothers can be detected in Allen's films as early as the spoof *What's Up, Tiger Lily?* whose Japanese, James Bond–like character (from a low-budget Japanese film), upon inspection of a brothel on board an old submarine, discovers his mother seemingly working as a prostitute. When the surprised son, whose dialogue was rewritten and overdubbed by Allen, asks, "Ma, what are you doing here?" his Japanese mother replies with an overdubbed, whiny Yiddish voice: "You don't call. [You don't write.]" This one-liner reflexively pays homage to the jokes of the Catskill comics, but its additional humor derives from defying the viewer's expectations. First, we do not anticipate finding an older, maternal Jewish figure in a place of ill repute, scolding her son for failing to keep in touch. What's even funnier is the disparity between the overdubbed Yiddish voice and the beautiful Japanese actress who looks more like a femme fatale in a film noir than an archetypical Yiddishe mama. Indeed, the very idea of an attractive, youthful-looking older Jewish woman, who also happens to be a mother, appears ludicrously incongruous, especially given the stereotypical images of Jewish mothers as aggressive, self-sacrificing, postmenopausal nudges who by definition are sexually undesirable.[7]

Another of Allen's Jewish mother jokes that draws on surprise and incongruity is featured in the sketch with Ruth (Charlotte Rae) from *Bananas*, who performs complex surgery alongside her doctor husband (Stanley Ackerman), with whom she bickers while dispensing maternal advice to her son, the socially inept product tester, Fielding Mellish (Allen). In this absurd scenario, Fielding timidly interrupts his parents during the operation to tell them about his plans to go to South America to find his estranged, social-activist girlfriend with whom he hopes to be reunited. As the consummate Jewish mother, Ruth laments her son's lack of education and nudges him to go back to school. But when Fielding's father echoes the same sentiment and badgers his son for being a college dropout, Ruth rebukes her husband and tells him to "get off his [Fielding's] back." In a tender, if still absurd, moment of parental solidarity, both Ruth and her husband reaffirm their love and commitment to their son and proudly urge him to complete the medical procedure.

From a patriarchal perspective, the doting Jewish mother clearly appears miscast in the role of a trained medical practitioner who holds a position of power and respect typically associated with the WASP male establishment. Thus, at least on one level, the image challenges the gender assumptions on which the Jewish mother joke is based: the maternal domestic who slaves away in the kitchen, making sure she has prepared sufficient food to keep her hungry brood from starvation and totally devoted to the welfare of her family at the exclusion of her own personal fulfillment. Given the gains of the feminist movement during the period in which the film was released (early 1970s), it would not have been inconceivable for Allen, a third-generation American Jew who fancied himself an intellectual, to envision a Jewish mother as a competent doctor. The very idea of a Jewish mother in the role of a surgeon who beams with pride for her "nerd-o-well" son, however, appeared too irresistible, even for Allen, the auteur filmmaker. After all, Allen's humor is steeped in the years he spent writing jokes for Sid Caesar and other borscht belt comedians, who regularly mocked Jewish mothers in their routines.[8] The traditional repertoire of Jewish humor with its stock characters and Yiddishisms is an important part of Allen's comedy, as is his Jewish nebbish persona, a partial progeny itself of the overprotective and tyrannical Jewish mother. What is paradoxical about the scene with Ruth is that as it pokes fun at the overindulgent mother for egging on her offspring to complete a surgical procedure for which he is untrained, it inverts the standard joke in which the Jewish mother boasts about her son, the doctor. Here the doctor happens to be the mother, while Fielding is the *schmendrick* (loser), the unworthy recipient of maternal praise.

Annie Hall was released six years after *Bananas*, a time when second-wave feminism was in full swing, with many Jewish female writers and activists such as Betty Friedan and Gloria Steinem leading the charge. In spite or because of this phenomenon, besides Robin's Jewish American princess, the Jewish mother (Joan Newman) in *Annie Hall* is not only still overbearing but also has been thrust back into the kitchen as a nervously fretting, working-class housewife who tries to conform to the WASP, white-glove image of female respectability — but fails. At the outset of the film, we are introduced, via flashback, to Alvy Singer: a morose, red-headed schoolboy who refuses to do his homework because he has learned that the universe is expanding and threatens to annihilate us all. Troubled by her son's apathy and, to her, meaningless philosophical musings, Ally's mother turns for help to her dentist, who tries to reassure Alvy that Brooklyn won't be expanding for millions of years and that he should enjoy his life while he can. As the visibly depressed Alvy slouches in Dr. Flicker's (C. M. Gampel) waiting room, his mother tries bravely to conceal her anger and maintain her composure. Despite her efforts to effect the proper demeanor of a picture-perfect, pre–WWII housewife with her tailored outfit, pale-green blouse, coiffed brown hair, and hat, she loses her temper and, clinging to her handbag and white gloves, raises her voice and waives her hands about.

The scolding Jewish mother of Alvy's childhood is frantic with worry that her son lacks the focus and ambition to succeed in life, and she has no patience for his flights of fancy and broader existential ennui. What she most desires is to get her son's head out of the clouds, so that he can do his homework. Already at Alvy's young age we see the traces of despair, pessimism, and fatalism that will define his (and Allen's) worldview as an adult, but we also see early signs of a richly fertile imagination, which will offer a creative outlet for his ideas and the coping mechanisms he needs to survive the harshness of life. The chastising, judgmental, anxious Jewish mother, however, with all her ambitious desires and inherited fears of persecution and anti-Semitism, will always be there to call her son back to reality and remind him that all his intellectualizing and fanciful thinking won't keep him safe from harm.⁹ Ultimately, the paranoid, obsessively practical-minded Jewish mother of Alvy's flashback is a killjoy and a stifler of creativity.

Mrs. Singer's WASPish pretentions, meanwhile, are further ridiculed in the now famous split-screen scene that contrasts the polite, calm, and orderly Easter meal at the Halls with that of the Singers' loud, boisterous, and argumentative holiday gatherings. While Annie's patrician-looking mother (Colleen Dewhurst) is a graceful, modern, elegantly dressed, mature woman who spends more time sipping her drink and puffing her cigarette than she does eating, Alvy's Jewish matriarch is a zaftig, old-fashioned housewife who patiently presides over her ill-mannered clan, making sure no one goes hungry. Unlike members of the Hall family who compliment the cook and exchange pleasantries, the Singers whine, bicker, gossip, and lament the loss of the recently departed, while shoving food down their mouths as if it might be their last.

From a class standpoint, the Halls are marked as a modern, "healthy," middle-class family who could easily be featured in an old layout of *Life* magazine. The Singers look like immigrant, working-class folks from an earlier era. Allen's anachronistic vision of the Jewish family of his childhood features an elderly uncle wearing a suit and tie from the previous generation and a father whose slightly more modern outfit—plaid shirt and suede bomber jacket—fails to conceal the brittle edges of his lower-working-class Jewish identity. The stocky, older aunt with a drab floral dress and pinned-up braids appears to be out of the 1950s television show *The Goldbergs* (1949–56), while Alvy's mother, wearing a gray-colored dress with lace trimming and with another nicely coiffed mane of brown hair, dutifully stands by administering the obligatory second helping right out of Dan Greenburg's classic "training manual," *How to Be a Jewish Mother*.¹⁰ In Alvy's highly exaggerated rendition, the Jewish mother is out of touch; barely one generation removed from the shtetl and an observant Jew, she celebrates Yom Kippur but without fully comprehending why. Like the post-Haskalah (Jewish enlightenment) writers before him, Allen makes it his task to satirize what he believes to be the backward social mores of his group.

Indeed, like Tevye from *Fiddler on the Roof*, Alvy's Jewish relatives are equally baffled by their Byzantine traditions. When in Alvy's paranoid imagining, Annie's mother asks Mrs. Singer how she plans to spend the holidays, she replies in a whiny, Yiddish-inflected voice, "We fast." "You know, to atone for our sins," Mr. Singer adds with his mouth full. Mrs. Hall, on the other side of the screen, asks with a calm, collected, mildly inebriated demeanor, "What sins, I don't understand?" Mr. Singer replies as if delivering the punch line of a borscht belt joke: "To tell you the truth, we don't understand either." As Martha Ravits's work on the image of the Jewish mother argues, for many upwardly mobile, assimilating Jewish men of the post–WWII period, the domestic Jewish mother constitutes the realm of "Otherness, Old World [values], backwardness, loudness, and vulgarity, clannishness, and ignorance," from which they longed to distance themselves.[11] If Annie's non-Jewish mother represents the epitome of cool detachment and modern rationality, Alvy's mother, and the domestic milieu she is responsible for nurturing, represents the premodern past with all of its superstitions and outdated modes of thinking.

Double-Coded Jews

While the Jewish female characters in Allen's films are usually explicitly identified as Jewish, others can be read as implicitly Jewish, such as Pearl (Maureen Stapleton) in *Interiors* (1978). Interestingly, this crypto-Jew is no longer the butt of the joke, and the Jewish mother that Allen has mocked throughout his films is here a source of sympathy and admiration. When the rather ordinary-looking but colorfully dressed Pearl, the Jewish interloper whom Arthur (E. G. Marshall) plans to marry, enters the orderly, cultivated, repressed atmosphere of his Long Island beach home, everyone else in the family is taken by surprise. The earthy, spontaneous, uncomplicated Pearl is the antithesis of Arthur's wife Eve (Geraldine Page), a tall, striking woman who is admired for her discipline, artistic temperament, and decorating skills but whom Arthur seeks to divorce for his more vivacious and gregarious new companion. Arthur's decision to finally leave the distant and inward-looking Eve is met with the disapproval of his three grown daughters, who fear that their already fragile mother will be devastated by the news. Yet all three are also ambivalent, for despite their professional accomplishments, the poet, photographer, and actress daughters feel like failures in the face of their mother's "high standards of taste and achievement."[12] The only person brave enough to pursue his last chance at happiness is their aging father, who finally has found an escape from the oppressive perfectionism of his mentally unstable wife.

As film critic Pauline Kael aptly observes, this genteel home with its soft, muted grays and beiges, artfully placed vases, and uncomfortable silences makes up the pristine world of "gentile" society, and when Pearl, the crude, seemingly Jewish other, "bursts into the scene wearing her mink, reds, and floral prints," she threatens to expose the tissue of lies, unfulfilled longings, and seething resentments on which the refined world of goyim propriety is based.[13] In this stunningly shot film with its sullen, Bergmanesque characters and mise-en-scène, the undignified Jewish mother with her loud voice, magic tricks, and drinking uncouthly celebrates the pleasures of bodily, primal urges, while the life-abnegating gentile mother, as Kael writes, "represents the death of instinct" and triumph of the "sterile emptiness of art and cultivation."[14]

What is most poignant about how this tragic story ends is that it is Pearl, the "Jewish" stepmother, brimming with "too much" vitality, who rescues Joey (Mary Beth Hurt), her stepdaughter, as she fruitlessly tries to stop her mother from committing suicide by drowning in the ocean. Given the obsessive concern with death by Allen's characters, either in his serious or comical films, both before and after the Mia Farrow/Soon-Yi Previn scandal, and his overall predilection for stifling Jewish mothers, it is striking that in *Interiors* it is the life-affirming Jewish mother who is privileged, and the will to live is almost as important as, if not more important than, all the highbrow pretentions of beauty and art. In this rare instance, Allen chooses the simple comfort of the Jewish mother over the cool detachment of the gentile mother, who, devoted as she is to artistry and talent, is devoid of life. In the end, he rescues the Jewish mother not only from his own usual ridicule but also from the scornful gaze of the goyim. Two caveats still apply, however: first, Pearl's Jewishness is coded rather than openly affirmed; and second, the threat the Jewish mother figure might have otherwise posed to Arthur's family is mitigated by Pearl's entering the domestic scene when her husband's children are fully grown adults with careers and Pearl herself is beyond childbearing age.

Another ethnically ambiguous or "double-coded" female character who is treated more sympathetically than Allen's garden-variety Jewish women is Fielding Mellish's love interest from *Bananas*, Nancy (Louise Lasser). In

Acting Jewish, Henry Bial explores how Jewish performers from the Yiddish theater to *Seinfeld* (1990–98) manage their ethnic identity by using a set of aural and visual cues that can be read as Jewish or non-Jewish, depending on the audience. Here, Jewishness is not a question of ethnic background or religious affiliation but a set of behaviors, attitudes, gestures, and mannerisms that are acted out for viewers who can attend to or ignore messages expressing insider or outsider knowledge.[15] For Bial, double-coded performance can communicate one set of meanings to Jews, while simultaneously communicating another, often contradictory set, to gentiles.

In *Bananas*, Nancy is a young, idealistic political activist who leaves her boyfriend Fielding because he lacks the qualities of a leader and goes to fight the revolution in a fictional South American country called San Marcos. In an effort to win back his girlfriend, Fielding leaves for San Marcos to topple the military regime and, through a series of misadventures, becomes the rebel commander of a corrupt Banana Republic. When Nancy meets the imposter who is standing in for the real Fidel Castro–like leader who has gone mad, she doesn't realize who is behind the disguise. After a night of sexual intimacy, Fielding reveals his true identity, and Nancy now understands why the night with the celebrated hero fell short of her expectations. Still basking in the fame, romance, and bravery of El Presidente, Nancy marries Fielding. His newfound confidence, however, is put to the test when a camera crew barges into the newlyweds' bedroom to televise the event, with live play-by-play commentary by Howard Cosell. In the post-"bout" interview, Nancy matter-of-factly assesses her husband's performance: "It wasn't the best I've had, but not the worst." Here, not only is Nancy given privileged access to the Jewish stand-up's arsenal of comic put-downs, but she also assumes the mentor relationship vis-à-vis the Jewish schlemiel — reversing the position that Allen's characters would hold in relation to their shiksa lovers in films such as *Annie Hall* and *Manhattan* (1979).[16]

Besides her command of borscht belt shtick, Nancy's Jewish coding can be deciphered in a variety of ways. Nancy is played by the Jewish actor Louise Lasser, Allen's second ex-wife and a former student of Brandeis University.[17] She is portrayed as the type of well-educated, assimilated, second- or third-generation immigrant Jew who grew up in one of the non-Jewish suburbs of New York, where it was prudent to conceal one's ethnicity. Having enjoyed the privileges of her parent's upward mobility, but all too aware of the struggles that minorities face in American society, Nancy identifies with the long tradition of lefty Jewish radicals who stood alongside the proletariat in the class struggle. As a feisty, intelligent Jewish woman with a social conscience, Nancy speaks her mind even if it means ridiculing her husband's manhood. Although Fielding does get the girl at the end, it is unclear how much longer Nancy can tolerate his harebrained schemes and clumsy manner in and out of bed. At the end of the day, the intellectually forceful personality of a Jewish woman may be too threatening and overpowering for her physically weak and sexually inadequate Jewish husband, who falls short of muscular WASP standards of masculinity.[18] For Jewish women, as Stora-Sander further suggests, the schlemiel's sexual ineptness in *Bananas*, traditionally used as an anti-Semitic slur against Jewish men, also inverts Allen's, and others', standard put-downs of the frigid Jewish American princess.[19] Nancy veers from this stereotype in other ways as well: she exhibits none of the JAP's telltale vanity or emotional coldness and is too busy fighting the revolution on the ground to indulge the JAP's status-seeking materialism.

Absent Presence

Even when Jewish women are not even implicitly present in Allen's narratives, they are always lurking in the background, providing the unstated context against which all other sets of possible relationships are defined, Jewish and non-Jewish, and male and female. In *Husbands and Wives*, Allen's most systematic exploration of the predicaments of human relationships, his character, Gabe, finds himself sad and alone despite having taken the higher moral ground. If Allen's project in the film is to examine the contradictions that he feels make happiness and morality mutually incompatible, the ever-mystifying nature of long-term monogamy is inescapably shaped by gender and ethnicity, and the "excription" of Jewish women from the hoary quest for unproblematic, timeless love is deeply revealing for Allen's broader social vision.

In *Husbands and Wives*, Allen essentially maintains that human beings possess fundamentally conflicting desires: on the one hand, they want passionate sex; on the other hand, they want a warm home life, companionship, and intellectual stimulation. For Allen these needs are inherently contradictory. Only unstable, often unintelligent nymphomaniacs or prostitutes seem capable of fulfilling one's desire for sex, but they make for bad companions. Likewise, persons who are suitably matched with their mates and initially make for good sexual partners eventually become boring over time and erotically stale. The four main characters in *Husbands and Wives* all confront this predicament, and to Allen's credit, it applies as much to women as to men, as both sexes seem fated to lead lonely, unsatisfying lives. Unfortunately, Allen's comparative handling of the male and female characters, and his treatment of their responses to the sex-love dilemma, ultimately serves to recapitulate traditional gender roles.

Jack (Sydney Pollack) has the most straightforward response to the paradox at the heart of the film. Bored with his wife Sally (Judy Davis), Jack has sex with prostitutes but eventually goes off with a young, frivolous, blond aerobics instructor; they have spectacular sex, until her shallowness becomes unbearable. He becomes physically abusive when she embarrasses him around his posh friends and eventually returns to his former wife. Before Jack even takes up with his athletic girlfriend, Sally had already parted with her husband. At first she pretends to be happy to be free of her tedious marriage, but later in the film we discover that she left Jack because she suspected him of cheating. While she showed a casual interest in dating during their time apart, she expressed no real sexual drive, was unable to have an orgasm or develop any closeness with the one man she did bed down, and after finding no comfort in life as a single woman, she goes back to her now ex-husband. At the end of the film, both Jack and Sally make clear that their new marriage has no sexual spark and conclude that they would rather settle for mundane companionship than seek a passionate, but ultimately fleeting, sexually gratifying relationship.

Likewise, Gabe, a writer teaching at Columbia, confronts the same predicament as does his friend Jack. The object of his desire is a student in his writing class named Rain (Juliette Lewis), and he flirts with her throughout the film. In one of the last scenes, he kisses Rain at her birthday party, even bringing her a music box as a gift, but then decides that the affair would end badly and does not pursue it.[20] His high-minded behavior does not pay off, however, as his wife Judy (Mia Farrow) leaves him for another man, and he is bereft and alone, writing a novel that is more "political" (i.e., less concerned with what Allen sees as the fundamental, personal dilemmas of life) than his earlier work. The flashbacks and interviews in the film further establish that Judy is a passive-aggressive, manipulative woman and that Gabe was her second husband.

Leaving aside the ironic dimensions of the narrative for lead actors Allen and Farrow — namely, that Allen's affair with Soon-Yi Previn was in full swing and Farrow became aware of it during the film's production (see Brook's chapter for more on this aspect) — *Husbands and Wives* is clearly a meditation on people's differing approaches to the predicament of sexuality and love. In Jack's case, the pursuit of sex for sex's sake is revealed to be unfulfilling, but for both Jack and Sally, settling for a companionable marriage is merely the lesser of two evils. For Gabe, taking the high road and avoiding an illicit affair with a much younger woman simply leads to deeper loneliness. The only character who gains some satisfaction is Judy, but she does so through guile, attracting partners and then discarding them when her interest wanes. Thus, though Allen suggests that both men and women confront the sex-love predicament, he treats their manner of doing so quite differently. Only Jack and Gabe have clearly pronounced sexual drives. Sally performs a bit of sexual braggadocio, but her desire to be single is ultimately revealed as a sham, and she is unable to have an orgasm or enjoy sex.

As for Judy, beyond establishing her as a passive-aggressive who dresses in bulky sweaters and skirts, often wearing no makeup and shot in an unflattering light, Allen doesn't develop her character at all. Moreover, her sexuality is largely absent from the film, except as Gabe's nostalgic memories of their early relationship or when Gabe succumbs to her insistent demands for a child. Where Jack and Gabe lust after traditionally good-looking women (the prostitute, the aerobics instructor, the student, or a "crazy" nymphomaniac Allen dated in his youth), there are no handsome young men for Sally or Judy to seduce. Their sexuality is merely an afterthought. Jack and Gabe still want passionate sex but cannot have it: their options are loneliness or a quasi-platonic relationship. While she tries to put up a brave face, Sally makes off the worst: she no longer has any interest in sex but settles for the weak tea of a romantically dead marriage. The less embittered but deceitful Judy resorts to her feminine wiles to get what she wants, a relationship that she can control with her new, easily dominated husband Michael (Liam Neeson).

Gender difference is not the only variable in *Husbands and Wives*' sex-love predicament, however. Ethnicity, deeply inflected by gender and class, is a powerful subtext as well. In a pivotal scene, Gabe goes to the house of a working-class, Italian American cabdriver to retrieve a novel manuscript of Gabe's that Rain had lost. At the cabdriver's home, domestic bliss is in full flower, suggesting — somewhat patronizingly — that the confrontation of mind and body is less pronounced for the working class, whose purportedly limited intellectual development makes the resolution of mind-body dichotomies less problematic.

On the romantic front, both Jack and Gabe are clearly marked as Jewish, while Sally and Judy are just as clearly non-Jewish, which brings us to Allen's notorious "shiksa complex." Allen of course is far from being alone in having gentile women as the primary object of a Jewish man's desire; this is a classic theme in American popular culture, as it allows the Jewish man to assimilate by rebelling against traditional prohibitions of exogamy and to escape the stereotype of the castrating Jewish wife.[21] As Stora-Sander summarizes the underlying dynamic, for second- and third-generation Jewish men who long for full acceptance from the dominant culture, the capacity to seduce the all-American shiksa is proof of success, an amorous conquest of the forbidden foreigner that represents a triumph almost greater than any fortune or fame.[22] On a more pragmatic level, for the Jewish comic, interethnic romance allows for enhanced humor and conflict stemming from the couple's differential identity.[23] For Allen specifically, were he to make the eponymous Annie Hall, Tracy in *Manhattan,* or his other filmic paramours up through *Hollywood Ending* (2002) Jewish, he would have to share his otherness with a Jewish woman and in so doing wouldn't be able to play up his identity as the consummate Jewish cultural outsider. Of course, less sympathetic rationalizations for Allen's treatment of women, Jewish and gentile alike, have been proposed — some, indirectly, by Allen himself.

Earlier in the cabdriver scene, Rain critiques Gabe's adolescent vision of women in general, reflexively echoing criticism in the media of Allen's misogyny. As in the later *Deconstructing Harry, Husbands and Wives* thus can be seen as Allen's attempt to advance his past handling of the sex-love conundrum by adding a splash of self-deprecation to a universal condition, but his patriarchal vision of gender and sexuality hamstrings the effort. The perceived existential dilemmas that he explores end up recapitulating traditional gender roles, projected onto what is represented as the timeless human predicament. The perfect woman always eludes his Jewish male protagonist. An added problematic in *Husbands and Wives* is that Allen sets his own character up as the moral man done in by his high-minded resolve and Farrow's Judy as a manipulator. During the period that this film was made, just the opposite was the case: Allen was becoming surreptitiously involved with Soon-Yi Previn, Farrow's de jure and Allen's de facto adopted daughter. Unlike Gabe, Allen himself did not choose the high road: "The heart wants what it wants," he told a reporter.[24] Not that his behavior hurt the aging actor/writer/director's career, which weathered the controversy and, after minor setbacks, has rebounded, most recently with box-office and critical success. As for the eerily autobiographical quality of *Husbands and Wives*, one could argue that Allen was prospectively defending himself against his critics by depicting Farrow's character, and by association Farrow herself, as the true villain. Another interpretation is that, unlike Gabe, the aging Allen had the strength to leave a passionless relationship for the highly risky, unconventional if not taboo relationship with a Rain-like younger woman: a university student still in her teens and thirty years his junior.

The inability for Allen to imagine a long-term relationship with a Jewish woman (and, to a lesser extent, all women) is inextricably linked to his pessimistic views of romantic love and desire. It is not that Allen pines for a wholesome, Molly Goldberg–style Jewish family that he feels he is incapable of achieving but rather that marriage to a Jewish woman, in particular, is doomed to fail. All the situations in Allen's films where Jewish men are involved with Jewish women — even the warm, smart, and attractive Allison Porchnik or the intelligent and sexy Nancy — don't last or seem fated to crumble, as the male protagonist, Alvy or Fielding, is inevitably threatened by them and either runs from the relationship or makes a mess of it. By the same token, when a Jewish man (generally not played by Allen) is shown in a long-term relationship with a Jewish woman, there remains a stigma or fatal flaw, as with *Deconstructing Harry*'s (real and fictive) Jewish wives who become or marry Jewish zealots, or the out-of-focus Mel, whose identity is literally subsumed by his family.

Moreover, while Allen's characters (especially those played by himself) usually leave their Jewish romantic interests, as Richard Freadman rightly points out, the gentile ones usually leave him.[25] Reinforcing the double standard, while Allen's characters' extrication from their Jewish marriages (and they're almost always marriages rather than affairs) leaves them embittered or relieved, after Annie leaves Alvy for a record producer in LA, Alvy is jealous but mostly sad, wistful, and nostalgic about their relationship, and the two still feel affection for one another. In fact, when Annie moves back to New York, they spend a wonderful time at a coffee shop catching up, and Alvy is gladdened to hear that she is taking her date to see *The Sorrow and the Pity*, the classic Shoah documentary to which he had introduced her. Allen's character's parting from the teenaged WASP love interest Tracy (Mariel Hemingway) in *Manhattan* is similarly bittersweet and touching.

In *Husbands and Wives*, Gabe remains on good terms with Rain, and even though his relationship with Judy ends badly, it is not for lack of trying. On the night he decides not to have an affair with Rain, Gabe vows to save their relationship and with a renewed sense of hope rushes home only to discover that Judy has left him. It is clear that Gabe is devastated by the dissolution of his marriage and feels betrayed by his wife, but the viewer is not privy to any violent recriminations between the two, and the breakup, compared to those with Jewish women, is remarkably sedate. By contrast, the sheer vitriol Harry reserves for his Jewish ex-wife Joan in *Deconstructing Harry* is only matched by the warmth and generosity he expresses for Fay (Elisabeth Shue), his non-Jewish mistress from the same film, who, having outgrown her Lolitaesque relationship with Harry, dumps him for his best friend Larry (Billy Crystal).

Although Allen's characters, in their breakups with Jewish women, don't explicitly pine for the stable home with wife, children, Jewish food, and Jewish holidays they left behind, the image of Jewish domesticity nevertheless undergirds the romantic pessimism that is so important to his films. Yet if this is the case, then why are there no prominent Jewish women's roles, no space for Jewish women to inhabit, in *Husbands and Wives*, a film that systematically explores different dimensions of identity: moral versus immoral Jewish male (Gabe versus Jack); and cold and abrasive versus passive-aggressive non-Jewish women (Sally versus Judy)? While Allen, as we've seen, is not averse to constructing intellectual and aggressive Jewish female characters, Sally could not be Jewish because, despite possessing the qualities of a Jewish American princess — well educated yet frigid — she is in a long-term relationship with Jack, a Jewish man. Likewise, while Judy's manipulative passive-aggressiveness might also qualify as derisively "JAP-y," the timid, self-effacing manner in which it is expressed most certainly is not. Ultimately, even when Jewish women are not even implicitly present in Allen's narratives, they are always lurking in the background.

Jewish Domesticity Overcome?

There are two major exceptions to Allen's less-than-flattering treatment of explicitly marked Jewish women: the "Oedipus Wrecks" segment from the three-part anthology film *New York Stories* (also Francis Ford Coppola and Martin Scorsese, 1989); and another farcical comedy from his most recent, European phase, *Scoop*. With the exception of *Radio Days* (1987), in which neither Allen nor an ersatz schlemiel appears, "Oedipus Wrecks" is by far the most hopeful, albeit comically absurd portrayal, of Jewish women and Jewish domesticity in Allen's oeuvre. The film's blissfully happy ending is all the more astounding given that it emerges from a premise in which the Jewish male protagonist desperately disavows much of his Jewish identity, including his name (Millstein, changed to Mills).[26] We are introduced to Sheldon Mills (Allen), a successful, mild-mannered lawyer, complaining to his therapist about his loud, meddlesome, über-Jewish mother, Sadie (Mae Questel), who embarrasses him at every turn, to the point that he wishes that this annoying *balabusta* (bossy woman) would simply disappear from his life. One night at a magic show, this is exactly what happens: chosen as a volunteer for a magic-box trick, Sadie vanishes into thin air. Feeling a weight lifted, Sheldon experiences a noticeable improvement in his sexual performance with his fiancée, Lisa (Mia Farrow), a non-Jewish divorcee with children of whom Sadie of course disapproved. A few days later, however, Sheldon's mother literally returns from the repressed, appearing as a giant, godlike, disembodied head floating above the New York skyline, dispensing nagging advice and telling embarrassing stories about him as before, though now for the whole city, if not the world (via media reports), to hear.

Sadie's running public commentary about Sheldon's relationship with his fiancée finally causes Lisa to leave. Guilt stricken and desperate, Sheldon visits a psychic, Treva (Julie Kavner), for help in bringing his mother back to normal. None of Treva's rituals, voodoo dolls, and other quack remedies succeed, but a warm, romantic relationship forms between Sheldon and

Treva — who beneath the psychic trappings turns out to be a nice Jewish girl who knows how to cook. Realizing that Treva is the woman he's been searching for all along, Sheldon proposes, and when he tells his mother the news, Sadie miraculously resumes her normal size, shape, and place.

In the end, Sheldon's lifelong desire to extricate himself from his mother's grasp is dashed. Indeed, he ultimately succumbs to a young, maternal Jewish woman who seduces him with wholesome food and the promise of a loving Jewish home. The *haimischness* decried in *Annie Hall* and skewered in *Deconstructing Harry* here is liberating. Thus, Sheldon's mother both wrecks and saves her son. Her larger-than-life apparition in the sky sends her son into a tailspin, but the psychological crisis also enables him to see his life with greater clarity and ultimately to realize that his happiness does indeed lie with the nice Jewish girl that Sadie's been nudging him to marry all along. If, according to Freud, the joke performs the same role as the dream, Allen, in "Oedipus Wrecks," has his fantasy and eats it too. He turns the role of the Jewish mother — hilariously performed by Mae Questel, who voiced Betty Boop and Olive Oyl early in her career and bears a striking resemblance to Allen's own mother — into an overblown cartoonish figure, but one whose power dissipates once her son finds the love of his life.[27] Here the Jewish mother joke is not only rendered even more absurd and irrepressible but also inverted: despite her flaws, in the end (Jewish) Mother Knows Best.

Scoop does "Oedipus Wrecks" one better, from a Jewish woman's perspective. The film's protagonist here also defies the pessimistic outcome that besets most of the Jewish characters in Allen's films. The Freudian twist, this time, is that the romantic hero in *Scoop* is a Jewish woman, while Allen's character, the Great Splendini, aka Sidney Waterman, is a two-bit magician who tragically dies in the end. Thus, once again, the Jewish man is predestined to lose, if not in his quest for timeless love, then in his attempt to save a young woman who, as it turns out, can save herself. But in this screwball mystery-comedy, Sondra Pransky (Scarlett Johansson), a Jewish journalism student looking for a career break in London, uniquely triumphs. After being placed in Sidney's magic-trick box during a performance (more shades of "Oedipus Wrecks"), Sondra receives the scoop of a lifetime from the ghost of deceased investigative reporter Joe Strombel (Ian McShane), who reveals the true identity of the tarot card serial killer: high-society nabob Peter Lyman (Hugh Jackman). Sondra enlists the help of the skeptical

Sidney in tracking down the killer, and the two humorously pass themselves off as a blue-blooded father-and-daughter team while doubling as Holmes and Watson to crack the case. After being temporarily swayed by Peter's aristocratic good looks and deceitful pose, Sondra's innate intelligence and physical prowess prevail. She tricks Peter, who has taken her out on a lake to kill her, into believing that she has drowned, only to use her excellent swimming skills to make it back to shore and alert the police. In the end, not only does the Jewish girl outsmart her wealthy antagonist, but also she is hired for Strombel's vacant reporter's position.

At first blush, it appears that Allen's wish for the perfect woman, who is equal parts beauty and intellect, might actually be realized in the spunky, shapely, blonde-haired Sondra. However, this assertion must be qualified. For in the lone situation in which Allen does write an explicitly Jewish female lead, he doesn't place her in a straight drama or a comedy with serious elements but in a broadly comic thriller where all the existential dilemmas of love and desire (at least for Allen's character) are absent. Both the generic shift and removal of the romantic context are essential: it is only by excising the threat of Jewish domesticity that Allen is able to place the focus on a Jewish woman and present her in a positive light. In *Scoop*, for the first and, thus far, only time in his filmmaking career, Allen has imagined a kind of female version of himself, providing what amounts to a controlled experiment in which a socially uncomfortable but young, attractive, and ambitious Jewish woman overcomes her insecurities and wins the day through wit and strength.

We can best understand this transformation by a double comparison, one that keeps ethnicity constant but accounts for both gender and age: likening Sondra, on the one hand, to Fielding Mellish (the young Woody Allen character of *Bananas*) and, on the other hand, to Sidney Waterman (the elderly Allen variant of *Scoop*). Like Fielding, Sondra has a Jewish craftiness and tenacity, and both ultimately triumph over the obstacles that confront them. But because Sondra is a beautiful young woman rather than an awkward young man, she has far fewer nebbishe ticks, far less insecurity, and her triumph comes through a combination of brains and brawn, rather than Fielding's Jewish trickster-fool combination of cunning and luck. Like Sidney, Sondra displays her fear in the face of danger and goes through a character arc of personal development. However, Sidney's and Sondra's arcs have very different trajectories. Where Sondra conquers her nerves early on and resolutely pursues her goal, Sidney is terrified throughout and has to be dragged kicking and screaming to participate in the dangerous adventure. Sidney only overcomes his trepidation at the very end but is unable to complete his quest: wracked by nerves, this old dog isn't able to learn new tricks, and he dies in a car accident rushing to save Sondra.

By resurrecting himself in female form, however, Allen, through Sondra, channels both the strength of youth and the gendered form of beauty that he sees women as possessing, without sacrificing the Jewishness. Sondra's winning figure lays claim to Allenish one-liners in her interaction with Peter's wealthy, aristocratic Brits, but unlike the male schlemiel, she isn't wracked by sexual anxieties and her character is thus able to grow with relative ease and emerge the hero. Her only residual weakness is her susceptibility to Peter's WASPY, leisure-class allure, a seduction that she ultimately overcomes with a Jewish persistence and guile. With the issues of domesticity put out of play by generic conventions and the aging Allen's inability to plausibly pull off the lothario role, Allen can conceive of "himself" as bestowed with youth and beauty, and as a Jewish hero who carries the day — without sexual humiliation as the punch line. In other words, "Sondra Allen" may retain a certain social-class anxiety based on her Jewish identity, but her gendered beauty frees her from the dilemmas of love and a crippling sexual inadequacy, enabling her to develop into a more complex person. While Sondra from *Scoop* ultimately presents Jewish women in a manner quite different from Allen's previous depictions, constituting a less regressive vision of gender and Jewish ethnicity, it is not anything like a full-fledged feminist consciousness that would erase his earlier, more patriarchal treatments.

Conclusion

Despite their sympathetic portrayals, Sondra and Treva, and to a lesser extent Nancy and Pearl, are exceptions that prove the rule in Allen's treatment of Jewish women. They do not explain away the fact that Allen has not once cast a richly developed Jewish love interest for himself or another Jewish male character in a drama or serious romantic comedy, but more often than not relegates them to the sidelines. As I have argued, the marginalization of Jewish women in Allen's films is less a function of Allen's interest in exploring the humor of cultural difference than of what he perceives to be the Jewish male protagonist's unresolved psychological fears of Jewish domesticity and all of its trappings: a sexually disinterested wife, the burden of children and religion, and a placid home life that inexorably leads to the erosion of male identity and the stifling of creativity and overall joy in life. For Allen's Jewish male characters, the sexually exciting, adoring shiksa is the antithesis of the scolding, status-obsessed Jewish princess or overbearing Jewish mother. However, what the Jewish men that Allen plays fail to realize is that the rejection of Jewish women — a symbol of Jewish domesticity and of the men's own otherness — may not necessarily make them feel any less insecure or less aware of their difference. Indeed, as Eric Goldstein's work on Jewish identity reveals, no matter how assimilated or how much white social and economic privilege the Jewish man is allowed to enjoy, he will never "feel the kind of freedom whiteness is *supposed* to offer — the freedom to be utterly unselfconscious about [his] cultural background."[28]

This, however, is not to suggest that Allen is or has ever been a nonprofessing Jew. He is certainly critical of religious Jews but also of his own painful shortcomings, both in life and, most pointedly in *Husbands and Wives* and *Deconstructing Harry*, in his films. As for accusations that Allen's fascination with non-Jewish women is merely a repudiation of his Jewish identity, the opposite is the case: Alvy, for example, snubs his nose at the shallowness of the tanned couple he comes across in *Annie Hall*, whose self-satisfied, all-American goyish visions of happiness he finds contemptible. For Allen, life is inherently broken, and his Jewish pessimism is a kind of principled joylessness to which he clings and that ultimately acts as a reminder that we need to work that much harder to make life meaningful, satisfying, and beautiful — even if it is only achievable through Alvy's overactive imagination in *Annie Hall*, Mickey Sach's inspiration from the Marx Brothers in *Hannah and Her Sisters* (1986), or the not-so-moral alchemy of art produced by Allen's alter ego in *Deconstructing Harry*.

Allen's pessimistic view of the human condition, his brutally honest reflection of his own vices, and the power of his art partially to redeem them, provide a measure of serenity in the midst of the chaos. However, none of this wins him any favors with Jewish women. Only one of Allen's Jewish male characters, Sheldon in "Oedipus Wrecks," manages to overcome his fear of Jewish domesticity and is free to pursue a promising, long-term romantic relationship with a Jewish woman. In *Scoop*, the only Allen film featuring a Jewish female lead, Jewish domesticity is made irrelevant by narrative constraints and by Allen's aging schlemiel's ebbing libido. In *Interiors*, Allen's only serious film that presents a sympathetic depiction of a Jewish mother, the character's Jewishness is diluted by its being presented in a double-coded fashion. Further, the qualities that Allen ascribes to Jewish mothers are rendered moot here because of the character's age and her union to a gentile man with grown children from a previous marriage. As for *Husbands and Wives*, which foregrounds Jewish male characters while erasing any trace of Jewish women, the spectral presence of sarcastic professionals, social activists, and doting, sexless homebodies can still be felt. Indeed, these suppressed Jewish female voices haunt the proceedings as a kind of unredeemed ghost of Hanukkah to come, an expression of the anxieties and ambivalence that Allen, and many Jewish men of his generation, have about gender, domesticity, and ethnic identity.

Notes

1. Joyce Antler, "Epilogue: Jewish Women in Television; Too Jewish or not Jewish Enough," in *Talking Back: Images of Jewish Women in American Popular Culture*, ed. Joyce Antler, 242–52 (Hanover, NH: Brandeis University Press, 1997).

2. As Judith Stora-Sander observes, shtetl wives developed strong personalities and sharp business skills that were at odds with the idealized, middle-class gender roles of post–WWII America, which featured attractive mothers who devoted themselves to their children without thwarting their independence. By contrast, the all-American father is a virile, authoritarian figure who commands the respect of the community ("From Eve to the Jewish American Princess: The Comic Representation of Women in Jewish Literature," in *Semites and Stereotypes: Characteristics of Jewish Humor*, ed. Avner Ziv and Anat Zajdman, 131–42 [Westport, CT: Greenwood, 1993]). While these images of the all-American family inaccurately represent the complexities of social life for men and women during this period, they nevertheless made a lasting impression on third-generation Jewish male writers who conceived of comical representations of the Jews in opposition to this idyllic, *goyishe* vision of domestic happiness (see Joanne Meyerwitz, *Not June Cleaver: Women and Gender in Postwar America, 1945–1960* [Philadelphia: Temple University Press, 1994]).

3. Joyce Antler, *You Never Call! You Never Write! A History of the Jewish Mother* (New York: Oxford University Press, 2007), 9.

4. Jeffrey Rubin-Dorsky, "Woody Allen after the Fall: Literary Gold from Amoral Alchemy," *Shofar* 22 (2003): 5–28; 21.

5. Stora-Sander, "From Eve."

6. Alan Dundes, "The J.A.P. and the J.A.M.," *Journal of American Folklore* 98, no. 390 (1985): 456–75.

7. For jokes about the undesirability of the Jewish mother, again see Dundes, "J.A.P. and the J.A.M."

8. See *Woody Allen: A Documentary* (directed by Robert B. Weide, 2011).

9. Jessica Prinz, "Jewish Mothers: Types, Stereotypes, and Countertypes," in *Mommy Angst: Motherhood in American Popular Culture*, ed. Ann C. Hall and Mardia J. Bishop, 197–226 (Santa Barbara, CA: ABC-CLIO, 2009).

10. Dan Greenburg, *How to Be a Jewish Mother, a Very Lovely Training Manual* (New York: Pocket Books, 1964).

11. Martha A. Ravits, "The Jewish Mother: Comedy and Controversy in American Popular Culture," *Meleus* 25, no. 1 (2000): 3–29.

12. Pauline Kael, "Genteel or Gentile?" *This Recording*, 2000, http://thisrecording.com.

13. Ibid.

14. Ibid.

15. Henry Bial, *Acting Jewish: Negotiating Ethnicity on the American Stage and Screen* (Ann Arbor: University of Michigan Press, 2005).

16. This Pygmalion theme is aptly described in Richard Freadman, "Love among the Stereotypes, or Why Woody's Women Leave," in Ziv and Zajdman, *Semites and Stereotypes*, 107–20.

17. Alvy (Allen) lists Brandeis University, named after Jewish Supreme Court Justice Louis Brandeis, among the litany of stereotypical Jewish characteristics he humorously ascribes to Allison Porchnik when he first meets her backstage.

18. See Joshua Moss's chapter in this volume for more on Allen's and his alter egos' countering of dominant American masculine ideals.

19. Stora-Sander, "From Eve"; Dundes, "J.A.P. and the J.A.M."

20. This present is one that Mia Farrow describes Frank Sinatra giving her at the beginning of their romance, in her biography *What Falls Away* (New York: Nan A. Talese, 1997).

21. Ravits, "Jewish Mother"; J. P. Steed, "The Subversion of the Jews: Post–World War II Anxiety, Humor, and Identity in Woody Allen and Philip Roth," *Philip Roth Studies* 2 (2005): 145–62.

22. Stora-Sander, "From Eve."

23. Richard Bauman, "Differential Identity and the Social Base of Folklore," in *Toward New Perspectives in Folklore*, ed. Americo Paredes and Richard Bauman, 33–41 (Austin: University of Texas Press, 1972).

24. Quoted from an Allen interview in Walter Isaacson, "The Heart Wants What It Wants," *Time*, August 31, 1992, 61.

25. Freadman, "Love among the Stereotypes."

26. Several Jewish characters of the semiautobiographical family in *Radio Days*, including the Jewish mother (Julie Kavner) and the Jewish Woman in Search of Marriage, Aunt Bea (Dianne Wiest), are presented sympathetically. For more on Aunt Bea's type, see Riv-Ellen Prell, *Fighting to Become Americans: Jews, Gender, and the Anxiety of Assimilation* (Boston: Beacon, 1999).

27. Antler, "Epilogue."

28. Eric Goldstein, *The Price of Whiteness: Jews, Race, and American Identity* (Princeton, NJ: Princeton University Press, 2006), 236. For more on the issue of whiteness, see Giovanna Del Negro, "Bad Girls of Jewish Comedy: Gender, Class, Assimilation, and Whiteness in Post–WWII America," in *A Jewish Feminine Mystique? Jewish Women in Postwar America*, ed. Hasia R. Diner, Shira M. Kohn, and Rachel Kranson, 144–59 (New Brunswick, NJ: Rutgers University Press, 2010).

SHAINA HAMMERMAN

Reconstructing Woody &~ Representations of Religious Jewish Women in *Deconstructing Harry*

In 2007, two billboards advertising the clothing company American Apparel — one in Manhattan and one in Los Angeles — featured the iconic image of Woody Allen dressed as a Hasidic Jew.[1] They were taken down after less than a week when Allen complained that American Apparel had failed to obtain his permission. He later sued American Apparel for ten million dollars. Showcasing a screenshot from one of Allen's most celebrated films, 1977's *Annie Hall*, the billboard depicted the face of Allen playing the character Alvy Singer, who, at Easter dinner with his girlfriend Annie's family, briefly transforms into a Hasidic Jew. The billboard contained several assumptions about the countless passersby in New York City and Los Angeles who would view it: first, that Allen would be recognizable despite his Hasidic disguise; second, that the disguise would be identifiable as that of a Hasid; and third, that the image came from his film *Annie Hall*. Above the company's logo, a Yiddish text read *"der heyliker rebbe"* (the holy rebbe), a moniker usually reserved for the late Lubavitcher leader Menachem Mendel Schneerson.

This text demanded a kind of insider knowledge, even though many viewers might be able to decipher the Hebrew letters without knowing what they spelled. Finally, the viewer was expected to know, as the company's Jewish CEO, Dov Charney, later explained on his website, that the image and text were meant as an allusion to some of the legal challenges, including charges of sexual harassment, that American Apparel was facing at the time.[2] Thus, the multiple demands for familiarity with Woody Allen's persona — with the signifiers of Hasidism, with a brief scene from *Annie Hall*, with Yiddish, and with the internal politics of American Apparel — necessarily limited the target audience of this billboard and thereby its apparent function: to deflect the controversy surrounding the company's brand and to promote its sales. However, I contend that the signifiers of the Hasidic garb alone make for a powerful image — a power that lies in its ability to signify Jewishness instantly while also yielding dynamic, ambivalent messages about what Jewishness means. These messages multiply when we consider the complex role that gender and sexuality play in this equation.

If the Hasidic man is used to signal Jewishness in general, what does that mean for Jewish women? What might the Easter scene from *Annie Hall* look like if Alvy Singer was a woman? How do images of religious Jewish women signify differently from images of religious Jewish men? What are the implications of these differences? Woody Allen affords some possible answers to these questions in his critically acclaimed *Deconstructing Harry* (1997), a film about a writer whose fiction complicates his life when it too closely mirrors his real relationships. Engaging with feminist film theory grounded in Freudian psychoanalysis, I demonstrate how and why, in *Annie Hall* and other Allen films, the dynamic image of the Hasidic man functions to signify Jewishness both humorously and ambivalently (the ambivalence not incidental to the humor). I then argue that Allen's use of religious Jewish women in *Deconstructing Harry* serves to complicate this dynamic, opening the way for fresh readings of women and religious Jewishness on screen. The questions I pose here uncover gender's role at the center of how viewers approach religious Jewish representations in the films discussed here, in the American Apparel billboards, in relation to Allen's persona, and perhaps even in general.

The Hard-Core Jew

The crisis of representation surrounding religious Jews on-screen ironically recalls the analysis film scholar Linda Williams famously provided about representations of the female orgasm in hard-core pornography. While other filmic forms fetishize the female body by playing "so many games of peekaboo around this body ... hard core tries *not* to play peekaboo with either its male or female bodies." While the stakes for women in hardcore porn are incomparable to those at play when considering popular comedies, the representational possibilities are analogous. Hard core's extreme will to show "everything" has a parallel in representations of the "hard-core" religious Jew, a man whose Jewishness, rather than flesh, is entirely on display. This is in contrast to those representations of hidden, less visible Jews, whose ability to pass as gentile is its own "game of peekaboo." Williams goes on to locate the insufficiency of hard core to accomplish its show-everything goal: "The irony . . . is that, while it is possible, in a certain limited and reductive way, to 'represent' the physical pleasure of the male by showing erection and ejaculation, this maximum visibility proves elusive in the parallel confession of female sexual pleasure. Anatomically, female orgasm takes places . . . in an 'invisible place' that cannot be easily seen. . . . The history of hard-core film could thus be summarized in part as the history of the various strategies devised to overcome this problem of invisibility."[3]

The "maximum visibility" of Hasidic Jewish attire is likewise limited to men. A woman's Jewishness is often restricted to its demonstration by other means, through her alignment with a visibly religious man or through the means Allen uses in *Deconstructing Harry*: he first desexualizes the Jewish woman and then has her verbalize her commitment to Judaism. Not only does male Jewishness not demand such measures, but also, like male physical pleasure, mere seconds are all that is required to demonstrate what is elusive to the representational world of Jewish women. This chapter explores the ways in which the immediacy of male Jewish garb may be understood (again, like the male orgasm) as "limited and reductive." It also suggests that the inverse may be true for representations of Jewish women. Because they demand complex measures to signify their Jewishness, they may automatically evade the reductive nature of the male Hasidic garb.

The garb's signifying immediacy synthesizes with its erotic potential at the moment of the billboard controversy. When Allen sued American Apparel for ten million dollars, CEO Charney made an official statement on the company's website (see endnote 2) attempting to defend his use of the *Annie Hall* image:

> This was intended as a satirical spoof and not to be taken literally. Posed as a riddle, the purpose of the text was to create a parallel between the

sentiment of that moment in the film and what my company and I were experiencing at the time ... the media fallout resulting from a few sexual harassment lawsuits. There were false allegations ... that were sensationalized and exaggerated to the point where my entire persona was vilified.... Some writers characterized me as a rapist and abuser of women, others asserted that I was a bad Jew, and some even stated that I was not fit to run my company. There are no words to express the frustration caused by these gross misperceptions, but this billboard was an attempt to at least make a joke about it.

Charney claimed he used Allen's image on the billboards because he identified with Alvy's predicament. He had been accused of being a "bad Jew" and a perpetrator of sex crimes — two accusations famously shared by Allen though not by his fictional counterpart, Alvy. Charney alludes to Allen's charges of sexual impropriety during the Farrow/Previn scandal while relating to the character Allen plays in *Annie Hall*. The Jewish image becomes at once a testimony of Charney's (and Allen's?) innocence and a signifier of his and Allen's alleged sexual misdeeds and Jewish self-hatred. The Hasidic image thus opens the way toward sexual hypocrisy — it gives the illusion of piety while perversion lurks beneath the beard and hat.

The lawsuit is replete with its own hypocrisies: the clothing company implicitly assumed Allen's image was valuable enough to sell their product, but their legal defense was based on the notion that Allen's image was worthless (certainly not worth the ten million dollars Allen was demanding). Charney identified with Allen's sexual predicament by alluding to the Farrow/Previn scandal on his website, but he also used that scandal against Allen as a way to devalue his image in court. Ultimately, the company's threats to denigrate Allen publicly at trial — including bringing Mia Farrow to the stand as a character witness — resulted in a settlement that awarded five million dollars to Allen. The billboards are provocative not only for their legal repercussions but also for the underlying sexualization of the religious image that arose with the legal discourse. The Hasidic man's sexuality was called into question when Charney used the imagery in connection with his alleged sexual misdeeds and when he raised the issue of Allen's own dubious sexual ethics. Whether the image alone is erotic is debatable, but

Allen's use of it followed by Charney's appropriation accentuates the erotic potential of the Hasidic man.

Distinctive religious markers like beards, broad-brimmed hats, and *peyos* (side curls) are useful visual shorthands for representing Jewishness, a highly contingent and internally diverse category. But the image of the religious Jew on screen has a Janus-faced function. First, the religious garb forcefully and efficiently affirms the authenticity of this type of Jew, and the garb's instant and universally recognizable status points to the intensity and depth of the image. But at the same time, the image undermines the authenticity of the garb by depicting it at the level of signifier only, depriving it of deeper meaning. In other words, a character's ability to don and remove the garb in the manner of a mask points to its superficial, surface quality and its stereotypical utility in conveying humor. This double function — the image is both full and empty, deep and superficial — contributes to the image's dynamic complexity and thereby its power. It is the inherent power of the Hasidic fantasy, its openness to a multiplicity of often-conflicting meanings, that undoubtedly served as partial motivation for Allen when he chose it as a way to signify Alvy's self-conscious Jewishness in *Annie Hall* and for American Apparel's Dov Charney when he designed his company's controversial billboard as a means to assert how conspicuous he felt during his and his company's legal troubles.

Jewish Drag

Annie Hall was not the first or the only time Allen has used the Hasidic figure in his work. In his early slapstick comedy *Take the Money and Run* (1969), the crook protagonist (Allen) samples an experimental drug only to experience the bizarre side effect of being "turned into a rabbi" for several hours — that is, appearing in full Hasidic garb, including a long beard. *Zelig* (1983) contains a sight gag similar to the one from *Annie Hall*. Driving home the performative quality of Hasidic attire, a group of "rabbis" (all bearded Hasidim) stand on a cabaret stage as the chameleonlike Leonard Zelig (Allen) transforms into one of them — beard and all — before a delighted audience. Allen's most recent 2011 one-act play, *Honeymoon Motel*, featured a rabbi who dons Hasidic garb; and in a film set for a 2013 release, Allen will costar with writer-director Jon Turturro in *Fading Gigolo*, about two men in

Hasidic Williamsburg who start a gigolo business, further demonstrating both the ongoing saliency of the Hasidic image, its implicit sexualization, and its continued relationship to Allen's comedic persona.[4]

Allen's Hasidic image in *Annie Hall*, as the American Apparel billboard presumed, remains his most iconic. At Easter dinner with Annie's family, Alvy imagines himself as a Hasidic Jew at a moment when he feels his Jewishness to be exposed. As Alvy awkwardly praises Grammy Hall's "dynamite ham," the camera jumps from face to face: from Alvy to Annie, Grammy, and the other Halls. When the camera points back to Alvy, he appears in full Hasidic garb. Although the image is on-screen for no more than two seconds, Alvy's long beard, *peyos*, black hat, and caftan are projections of his fears of what the Hall family sees when they look at him.

When Alvy imagines himself in Hasidic attire, he sees himself as he believes the gentile Halls see him. From this perspective, his attempt to "fit in" with the WASPY Halls is betrayed by the Jew beneath the sports coat — the Hasidic garb reveals the "real Jew" behind the mask of assimilation. On the other hand, the Hasidic garb is an intense exaggeration of Alvy's Jewishness and therefore equally artificial. Surely the beard and hat form the mask and the "real" Alvy is the man in the sports coat. Hasidic costume play thus presents a dialectic in which Alvy belongs in the garb as much as he does not belong in it.

Anthropologist Esther Newton describes what she calls the "double inversion" of drag performances by composing a formula that exposes the incoherence of the gender binary. "Drag says, 'My "outside" appearance is feminine, but my essence "inside" [the body] is masculine.' At the same time it symbolizes the opposite inversion: 'my appearance "outside" [my body, my gender] is masculine but my essence "inside" [myself] is feminine.'"[5] The message sent by Alvy when he experiments with Hasidic "drag" is the same: My "outside" appearance (the Hasidic garb) is Jewish, but my essence "inside" (my authentic self) is secular, unmarked, and American. My appearance "outside" (my civilized manner, my voice) is American, but my essence "inside" (my authentic self) is Jewish. Allen and Alvy, in performing Jewishness, expose it as a performative category; the simplicity with which Jewishness may be signified through the garb is destabilized by the complex and dynamic possibilities it introduces.

The larger implication here is that in order to act Jewish, one must act like a certain type of Jew, a visible, Hasidic Jew, just as imitating womanness requires the elaborate production of dress, speech, and gesture. But if drag reveals that all women are performing their womanness, then *Annie Hall* brings to light the notion that Jewishness, on stage or off, is performative. But where do these performances of Jewishness leave the Jewish woman (both as image and audience member)? Jewish women viewers, like Jewish men, are invited to identify with this ethnoreligious imagery, forcing them into a double estrangement from what they see on screen. According to the myth of Jewish authenticity communicated by the garb, not only do non-Hasidic Jewish women fail to affiliate with or practice "authentic" Judaism, but also as women, the possibility for them to be authentic Jews does not exist in the easily identifiable realm of what a "real Jew" looks like. Just as the veracity or authenticity of the female orgasm may be called into question even in the most revealing, hard-core performances of pleasure, so too is a woman's Jewish authenticity called into question — in everyday life or on screen — as she lacks the signifying immediacy of the Hasidic man's garb.

At its origins in the 1970s and 80s, feminist film criticism challenged the ways women characters are traditionally objects on screen while men characters are "actors."[6] Women are "looked at" while men do the looking or, to use John Berger's formulation, "men act and women appear."[7] During the Easter scene in *Annie Hall*, however, the Hasidic Jewish man and not the woman is the object of the gaze. Yet, by objectifying his character (one closely identified with himself) and subverting the paradigm of the male-directed gaze, Allen also opened the door for the image's further objectification on the billboards thirty years later.[8] The billboards and the legal grievances surrounding them further confirm the objectification of the Jewish man, in part by sexualizing or eroticizing the image. Even if Allen does not appear on the billboard as an object of sexual desire, his image is sexualized by the billboard's context, a context that reminds the viewer of Allen's alleged sexual perversion. This process of reobjectifying the Jewish man in turn unleashes a new kind of potential for how Jewish women may be represented on-screen, a potential Allen explores at length in *Deconstructing Harry*.

Theories of deconstruction, to which the title of the film alludes, are always aimed at challenging discourses of authenticity. Allen's film is about the blurred boundaries between the "real life" and fictional fantasies of its title character. But in deconstructing Harry and his relationships, the film also deconstructs Jewishness. To explore a complex variety of Jewishness that lent itself to internal conflict as well as religious content, Allen created religious Jewish characters who do not immediately signify Jewishness. Because the religious Jewish male (namely, the Hasidic man) signifies Jewishness instantaneously, these characters had to be women — deeroticized and thereby nonobjectified women. While objectification and eroticization need not always go hand in hand, eliminating sexual desirability from depictions of Jewish women eliminates one possibility for objectification. By reconfiguring Jewishness in this manner, *Deconstructing Harry* paved the way for new readings of women, but this does not make Allen a feminist filmmaker or the film in question a feminist film. Instead, the new paradigm points to the similarities between how women and Jews are signified onscreen and how employing religious Jewish women characters helped Allen to escape Grammy's gaze.

Religious Jewish Women in Harry's World

Deconstructing Harry tells the story of a writer, Harry Block (Allen) whose fictional portrayals of his already troubled relationships lead to disastrous consequences in his real life. Harry struggles to contend with three ex-wives, a self-professed sex obsession, and a near constant feeling of failure and disjointedness. Despite the success of his most recent book, Block has fallen deeper into depression and a bad case of writer's block, as his name suggests. Throughout the film, Harry's literary fiction is illustrated in vignettes, dispersed among related, often parallel, scenes from his real life. Harry narrates these fictional scenes, which include crisp lighting and conventional edits. The actors who portray Harry's creations look polished and sexy, including Harry's neurotic alter egos. The "real-life" scenes, on the other hand, are choppy and halting. Harry's fragmented existence is conveyed through jump cuts that often cut him off midsentence, show an action replayed several times, or leap incongruously between nonconsecutive moments. While many of the actors in these scenes are beautiful women, they appear more disheveled and awkward than their fictional counterparts.

Two scenes in the film, one from Harry's "real life" and one from a fictional vignette, feature religious Jewish women. The film spotlights many other Jewish characters as well, whose names and activities mark them as unmistakably Jewish. Indeed, we might consider *Harry* to be Allen's most Jewish film for its array of Jewish personalities and references. The film's vulgarity — near constant sex jokes and gratuitous use of four-letter words — invited criticism from some, but Allen (not for the first time) got into the most trouble for skewering Jewishness.[9]

Allen reportedly wanted to cast actor Elliott Gould (among others) in the role of Harry, but Gould had to step down due to scheduling conflicts, so he ended up casting himself in the starring role.[10] During production, Allen described the film to the *New Yorker*: "It's about a nasty, shallow, superficial, sexually obsessed guy. I'm sure everyone will think — I know this going in — they'll think it's me."[11] This is not quite a denial that the film is autobiographical, and the film, which constantly calls into question how fiction and "real life" may or may not collide, does little to negate a biographical reading. In Allen's own words, "I'm always fighting against reality."[12] Whether or not we understand his relationship with Soon-Yi Previn and the scandal surrounding it as informing the ultimate meaning of the film, audiences and critics detected an equivalence between Allen and the characters he plays, making his private (or rather, public) affairs an important star in the constellation that makes up any reading of the film.

The film prefigures this perceived equivalence between Allen and Harry since the main conflict hinges on the equivalence the characters detect between Harry and his fictional creations. As he negotiates the troubled waters of family and lovers, Harry's fiction is so successful that the college that once kicked him out (as Allen was from NYU) now wishes to celebrate him with an honorary degree. Accompanied by a friend and hiring a prostitute named Cookie (Hazelle Goodman) to be his date, Harry kidnaps Hilly (Eric Lloyd), his son from a previous marriage, to make the trip to the college. Along the way, Harry stops at his estranged sister's house for a visit, evidence of the way he is reassessing his relationships after the publication of his latest novel. He sits down to talk with his wary sister, Doris (Caroline Aaron), who, like the other women in his life, is enraged by her image as portrayed in his writing.

We learn — through dialogue between Harry and Doris — that Doris became a religious Jew upon marrying her husband, Burt (Eric Bogosian), whom Harry refers to as a "fanatic" and "zealot." Burt sports a knit yarmulke and trimmed beard; he is far from Allen's Hasid in *Annie Hall*. Nevertheless, the beard and yarmulke are alternative signifiers that help establish his religiosity: at the very least, he is proudly, visibly Jewish and a different Jewish type from Harry. The viewer "in the know" about Jewish politics and denominational variations will understand that Burt's particular look generally signals modern Orthodox Judaism with Zionist sensibilities (the modern clothes and trimmed beard for modern Orthodoxy, the knit yarmulke for right-leaning Zionism). Also notable about Burt is that this minor supporting player who has very few lines in the scene is able to convey various messages about his Jewishness via his garb alone.

Doris's Jewishness, on the other hand, is not as immediately, visually obvious. With a simple short haircut, minimal makeup, a long, flowing skirt, and a long-sleeved blouse, Doris appears at first glance as an average-looking, markedly unsexy (especially when compared with the other women in Harry's life), middle-aged woman. Through their conversation, the viewer learns of Doris's turn toward Jewish observance as an adult. In the scene transcribed below, Harry sits down with his sister for a chat while his son Hilly, his friend Richard, and his "companion" Cookie chat outside with Burt. With eyebrows raised in a smug, defensive sneer, Doris aggressively folds napkins.

> DORIS: I know what you think of me.
> HARRY: Oh, please Doris, don't start in.
> DORIS: Am I wrong? It's all over your book. "Jewish." "Too Jewish." "Professionally Jewish." Of course, you attributed it all to your ex-wife, Joan, but you used the details of my life because you wanted to depict her with contempt.
> HARRY: Oh, I don't know what you're talking about.
> DORIS: You don't know what I'm talking about? You made a picture of your ex as a horror. And in order to make that picture unsympathetic and unappetizing, yes, you used some of her, but mostly, mostly you caricatured my religious dedication. Because it has always enraged you that I returned to my roots.

Although Doris appears to be defending herself against the negative portrayal of one of Harry's fictional Jews, she suggests here that her variety of observant Judaism is somehow "unsympathetic and unappetizing." She believes that Harry uses religious Jewishness as a negative trait to portray an unlikeable character, indicating that such Jewishness alone might be cause for disdain from readers. Doris, the "unappetizing" quality that goes along with being Jewish — religious or not — demands no explanation. She assumes Harry already knows why she believes non-Jews see her that way. At the same time, Doris's deliberate gestures and strong, poised tone convey her confidence and pride in her choice to "return" to observant Judaism. Doris resigns herself to the "unappetizing" quality of observant Judaism as a means to assert her pride in her return to her religious roots. The character's self-contradictory position toward her Jewishness underscores the dynamic quality of the religious fantasy on screen.

Annie Hall and *Deconstructing Harry* are two different films, with different comic rhythms and different uses of sight gags, created during vastly different times in the director's career. But significantly, it is difficult to imagine how Allen could have used visual cues to signify Doris's Jewishness the way he was able to do with Alvy. Harry's blend of fascination and disgust with Doris's religious life reflects a complex internal debate between secular and religious Jewishness, a debate absent from the scene in *Annie Hall*. Likewise, it is difficult to imagine Harry visiting an estranged, newly religious brother instead of a sister. The male Hasidic garb creates a signifying wall that blocks the kind of reflective dialogue featured in this scene. In both films, the characters "become" Jewish: Alvy, in a fleeting imaginary flash, and Doris, in the manner of a *ba'al tshuvah*, the tradition of the Jewish "returnee" who comes to religious Judaism as an adult. These two ways of becoming further reinforce the immediacy of Alvy's transformation versus the discursive process of Doris's.

Doris continues, "I'm a Jew. I was born a Jew. What, do you hate me because of that?" Harry responds with a series of reductionist hypotheticals, asking how she would feel "if our parents converted to Catholicism" or "if a gentile gets hurt." "You know what?" Doris responds, looking Harry directly in the eyes. "Burt is right about you. You're a self-hating Jew." Harry replies with one of Allen's great one-liners: "Hey, I may hate myself but not because I'm Jewish." The joke works because Harry's denial is undermined by its telling. The statement functions as a "Jewish joke," one about a Jew who hates himself, even while maintaining that his Jewishness is irrelevant to his insecurity. The denial reinforces the truth of the accusation, although the accusation and the admission have different implications.[13]

Despite Harry's denial about being a self-hating Jew, the viewer knows that Harry's Jewishness is by no means incidental to his or his characters' insecurities or abhorrent qualities. Nearly every one of Harry's short-story vignettes includes identifiably Jewish names: Harvey Stern, Mendel Birnbaum, Reuven, Epstein, Max Pincus, and so forth. One vignette — one that particularly enrages Burt and Doris — is even set at a *Star Wars*–themed bar-mitzvah celebration. Playing on Harry's hypersexual, neurotic persona, his fictional characters tend to do despicable things (a married man "borrows" a comatose friend's apartment in order to hire a prostitute; a man having an affair with his wife's sister performs a sex act in the presence of her blind grandmother; and, most despicably, a Jewish man eats his wife and children). Such actions are clearly meant to be comically deplorable — Harry wrote them that way — and they are deplorable whether or not the characters are Jewish. But as in *Annie Hall*, the religious Jew is brought into the cinematic conversation in order to explore how the non-Jewish gaze affects secular Jewish characters. Doris's religiosity provides a moral compass for the film, even as the viewer is asked to sympathize and identify with Harry, and even as Doris herself ultimately does.

Most of Doris's anger is directed at a specific story, which stars Stanley Tucci as Epstein. In this vignette, Epstein is a sexually depraved neurotic who is strongly attracted to his psychiatrist. Helen, played by the leggy Demi Moore, attributes his feelings to transference until, one day, she terminates his treatment in order to see him socially. They fall in love and eventually marry. Everything is wonderful until their son, Hilly (also the name of Harry's "real-life" son), is born. Then, Helen becomes "what Epstein referred to angrily as 'Jewish with a vengeance.'"

Helen's appearance becomes progressively dowdier throughout the vignette. In the psychiatrist's office, her bare legs feature prominently in the shot; her long black hair drapes provocatively over her shoulders. At home, during the early phase of their relationship, Helen wears a sexy tank top curled up on the couch by Epstein. After the birth of their son, her legs and shoulders all but disappear from view. Helen marches aggressively, angrily, around the kitchen in a long, loose black skirt; a conservative, gray, collared blouse; and a shapeless black cardigan, although Moore's famous curves remain visible and her top blouse button is suggestively open. She wears her hair partly tied back. As she plays out the main gag of the vignette — reciting the Hebrew blessings over wine, challah, candles, and finally, oral sex — Helen maintains her covered-up appearance and conservative hairstyle. In bed for the punch line, she wears a loose, long-sleeved nightshirt. Even the sex act itself loses its eroticism when Helen, whose fully covered body is awkwardly perched over Epstein in their dark bedroom, recites *"borey p'ri ha-blow job."*

The scene then cuts to Helen back in her office working with a new patient. The shot's composition is identical to the initial shot of Epstein as Helen's patient, except that now, Helen shows no skin at all. In stark contrast to the first scene of the vignette, her hair is completely tied back into a low bun. She wears a thick, black turtleneck and a large, heavy shawl across her shoulders, masking her shape completely. In place of bare legs, she wears a long, shapeless black skirt. In the vignette's final joke, Helen uses exactly the same language with her new patient — "an Israeli" — as she used with Epstein. She suggests they terminate treatment in order to pursue a social relationship. Like Doris, Helen's Jewish visibility requires verbalization, more screen time, and subtler costume cues than Alvy Singer's Hasidic moment in *Annie Hall*. With the hypersexualized Moore in the role of Helen, the exaggerated comedy in the vignette amplifies how religious Jewish women's garb works to undercut (albeit unsuccessfully) the eroticism of a woman's body.

When Alvy dons the beard and hat, there is no explicit comment on his sex appeal (although the Hasid's appearance, like most religious figurations, carries with it the implicit sexual pietism of its wearer). Later, in light of the Farrow/Previn scandal and Charney's use of the screen shot on the billboards, the image takes on an erotic, perverse status — carrying with it dueling notions of sexual aggressor and victim of "false allegations" of a sexual nature, thereby playing on the perceived piety of the Hasid. Similarly, in Allen's 1983 mockumentary, *Zelig*, when Allen's character transforms into a Hasidic rabbi, he does so onstage, surrounded by scantily clad cabaret dancers, pointing to the potential (if incongruous) erotic quality of the Hasidic male. Although Alvy and Zelig gain beards and *peyos* in these scenes, their transformations are not about skin and hair as much as they are about costume and disguise. Doris's outfit and especially Helen's costume changes are clearly about the act of covering up skin and shape, and minimizing the sexiness of a hairstyle. In order to have a full voice and complex character, these women are forced to shed their potential erotic natures. Even the famously seductive Moore, who starred a year earlier in *Striptease* (Andrew Bergman, 1996), is stripped of her eroticism in the most erotic moments — oral sex with her husband and subsequent cheating on him with a new patient.

As in the scene with Doris, Helen's transformation from secular to religious must be verbalized and defended. She is presented, like Doris, as angry and even irrationally proud of her tradition, but her arguments about why she maintains this pride take on a rational tone, as if Harry/Allen is arguing with himself about the value of tradition.

EPSTEIN: God, you're like a born again Christian, except you're a Jew.
HELEN: I see my father's face in Hillel.
EPSTEIN: Hilliard. His name is Hilliard. We didn't name him Hillel. We didn't name him after some rabbi. It's Hilliard Epstein.
HELEN: I'm sick of your smug cynicism. There's value in tradition. . . . I see not only meaning in Judaism but true beauty.
EPSTEIN: Helen, you're a scientist.
HELEN: Einstein was a scientist *and* he was a Jew *and* he was religious!

Helen and Epstein, and Harry and Doris, present two extremes of an essentially futile debate about traditional Judaism versus secularism. Like Doris, Helen "becomes" Jewish in the manner of a *ba'al tshuvah*. Harry/Allen recognizes the attraction to this kind of "return" even if he fights it. By providing Doris and Helen with rational voices in the debate, Allen allows religious Judaism to be about more than the fear of the anti-Semitic gaze and a visual one-liner, to which his Hasidic men had been consigned in his earlier comic films. Instead, religious Judaism is the axis around which characters' familial, collegial, and sexual relationships revolve in *Deconstructing Harry*; religious Judaism is at the core of these characters' moral, ethical, and psychological struggles, without losing the characters' potential for humor.

Contrary to feminist criticism on the silenced woman's voice in literature or film, *Deconstructing Harry*'s Jewish women have voices — complicated, full voices that enable them to seem reasonable, irrational, or both at once. Alvy Singer does not have that option. Just as the erotic female body might silence her literary or cinematic voice, the Hasidic man's garb restricts his voice. Through the women in *Deconstructing Harry*, Allen attempts to get beneath how he's seen: to *be* instead of just *being seen*. These religious Jewish women whose lifestyles as depicted by Harry/Allen seem restrictive nevertheless invite the viewer to consider the complex, multiple options that Jewishness presents. These women who are deeroticized by virtue of their clothing, hair, and mannerisms expose the attractiveness of Judaism by articulating its virtues as *ba'alei tshuvah*.[14]

Engendering a Masquerade

According to influential feminist film theorists Laura Mulvey and Mary Ann Doane, women viewers of mainstream narrative films, to receive pleasure from their objectified images on-screen, have basically two options: to identify masochistically with the objectified woman or to make a "transsexual" or "transvestite" identification with the male performer who "controls the look."[15] Doane proceeds to build on these ideas for the spectator, introducing her take on Joan Riviere's idea of the masquerade. "Masquerade" refers to the notion that "womanliness is a mask which can be worn or removed."[16] The religious transformation that Moore's character undergoes in *Deconstructing Harry* exemplifies the womanly masquerade via its removal (reversing the more common trajectory in film where, through a "makeover," a frumpy woman becomes more feminine). Helen's transformation also suggests that Jewishness, like womanliness, is a mask that may be assumed or rejected at will.

Likewise, Allen's male Hasidim who don and remove the Jewish "mask" leave the spectator wondering which face constitutes the mask and which, the "real Jew." One answer to that conundrum — as with the fiction of the womanly masquerade — is that both the womanly and the less womanly, the assimilated Jew's clothing and the Hasid's attire, are masks. Or alternatively, neither are masks. The audience's ability to laugh at (or in dramatic instances, be moved by) such garb switching owes in part to the confusion of the masquerade's powerful dynamics or, as I described earlier, the way in which Alvy belongs, as much as he does not belong, in the garb.

Doane characterizes the masquerade in terms of proximity. Hasidic garb, to adopt Doane's language, "doubles representation" and "effects a defamiliarisation" of Jewish iconography by inventing a distance between the Jew and himself, as it does between the woman and herself. She begins by referring to one of Freud's lectures in which he compared women to hieroglyphic language, explaining that "the relationship between signifier and signified is understood as less arbitrary in imagistic systems of representation than in language 'proper.'"[17] For Freud, women, like hieroglyphics, lack the Saussurian gap between signifier and signified present in phonetic language. "Too close to herself, entangled in her own enigma . . . she could not achieve the necessary distance of a second look."[18] Because the masculine, according to this formulation, contains this distance, it can examine itself, return for a second look, and represent itself. The feminine, on the other hand, "cannot describe itself . . . in formal terms, except by . . . losing itself."[19]

Based on their claims, it appears that Freud and possibly even Doane are making a case for a transcendental condition of womanhood or femininity — a case that the arguments made here about Jewishness and ethnicity must logically reject. There exist, however, standards and expectations for the representation of women that Freud and Doane's metaphors help to explicate. We can thus draw an analogy between Doane's description of Freud's "feminine" and the Hasidic or religious Jewish fantasy. The facility with which a Jewish man can be signified — a facility demonstrated in the screen shot from *Annie Hall* and its reappropriation on American Apparel billboards — indicates that the masculine Hasidic fantasy maintains the necessary distance for a second look. The religious Jewish woman, however, is so close to herself, so enigmatic, that she cannot be described or represented in "formal terms." This is why in *Deconstructing Harry* there is no quick way to visualize Doris's and Helen's Jewishness; in both cases, it must be verbalized.

But the analogy only takes us so far; since the inverse *also* appears to be true. If we reimagine Doane's theory with the gender roles reversed, it is the Hasidic man, like hieroglyphic language, whose signifying garb lacks the arbitrariness of phonetic language. Hasidic male signifiers (the hat, beard, *peyos*, and caftan) are so closely intertwined with their signified — Jewishness — that the image becomes enigmatic and objectified. As Doane claims of the feminine, "The iconic system of representation is inherently deficient — it cannot disengage itself from the 'real,' from the concrete."[20] Such is the case for the Hasidic man, an iconic image so entangled with ideas about Jewishness that an equivalency is created for spectators between "real" Jews and Hasidic men. Here, I use the term "real" in both its senses to mean "real-life" Jews (as opposed to players on screen) and "authentic" Jews (their perceived piety lending them an air of religious authority).

Doane explains, "While the hieroglyphic is an indecipherable or at least enigmatic language, it is also and at the same time potentially the most universally understandable, comprehensible, appropriable of signs."[21] Like hieroglyphics and Doane's claims about representations of the erotic feminine, the powerful dynamism of Hasidic male iconography lies in its contradictory status. The Hasidic man is indecipherable, enigmatic, *and* universally understood by spectators. This is why his image is open to use on billboards while the multifaceted meaning of the billboards remains obscure.

Understood in these theoretical terms, the religious Jewish woman onscreen, as we see in *Deconstructing Harry*, does not suffer from the problem of proximity. Although they must be deeroticized, Allen's Helen and Doris are represented in such a way that they invite the "second look" that Doane claimed only men on screen summon. Lacking iconic (or hieroglyphic) signifiers like the black hat or beard, these religious Jewish women are presented as complex, complete characters. They are at once rational and irrational, angry and affectionate, prudent and irresponsible.

A dialectic surfaces: imagery of the Hasidic Jewish man projects Jewish authenticity, restricting Jewishness to a single type. Doubly estranged from the image on screen, the Jewish woman spectator is oppressed by this image because the potential for Jewish authenticity is limited to men. However, these limitations ultimately liberate the Jewish woman, at least at the level of representation. Not confined to the immediately recognizable Hasidic garb, the religious Jewish woman on screen is unfettered by iconography and can be represented in any number of complex — and I would argue, interesting — ways.

Feminist and Jewish critics have attacked Allen from every angle, particularly after the Farrow/Previn scandal. I have suggested, however, that the religious Jewish women from *Deconstructing Harry* enable Allen to play out debates about Judaism that are foreclosed by his emblematic image as a Hasid. In the years following the scandal, not just women but also Judaism acquires new complex characteristics in Allen's comic oeuvre. Moving away from questions about misogyny or Jewish self-hatred, I have located an opening for a liberating reading of Jewish women on screen, an opening made possible, ironically, by the iconic status of the Hasidic Jewish man. When Linda Williams boldly contends that the history of hard-core pornography may be summarized as a "history of the various strategies devised to overcome [the] problem of invisibility," she may just as well have been writing about the history of Jews in film. The "problem of invisibility" that the Jewish man's Hasidic attire resolves unravels when the lens is directed toward observant Jewish women.

Notes

1. On the billboards and subsequent lawsuit, see Bloomberg News, "Woody Allen Sues Clothing Maker," *New York Times*, April 1, 2008; "Woody Allen Sues Company over Rabbi Billboard," *Huffington Post*, April 9, 2008; Ed Pilkington, "Woody Allen v American Apparel trial opens tomorrow," *Guardian*, May 17, 2009, http://www.guardian.co.uk; Larry Neumeister, "Woody Allen's Sex Life SLAMMED by American Apparel," *Huffington Post*, April 16, 2009; C. J. Hughes, "For $5 Million, Woody Allen Agrees to Drop Lawsuit," *New York Times*, May 18, 2009; U.S. District Court, Southern District of New York, Complaint, "Woody Allen against American Apparel, Inc.," 08 CV 3179.

2. Dov Charney, "Statement from Dov Charney, Founder and CEO of American Apparel," http://www.americanapparel.net, May 18, 2009. Accessed January 8, 2013 (no longer available). An extended version of the statement also appeared under the same title and on the same date in *The Guardian*. http://www.guardian.co.uk/film/2009/may/18/american-apparel-woody-allen. Accessed June 14, 2013.

3. Linda Williams, *Hard Core: Power, Pleasure, and the "Frenzy of the Visible"* (Berkeley: University of California Press, 1989), 49.

4. Jeff Sneider, "Woody Allen Turns Out 'Gigolo' role," *Variety*, March 6, 2012.

5. Esther Newton, *Mother Camp: Female Impersonators in America* (Chicago: University of Chicago Press, 1972), 103. Cf. Judith Butler who clarifies Newton's formulation by introducing the bracketed material. Butler, *Gender Trouble* (New York: Routledge, 1999), 174.

6. Influential contributions to feminist film theory include Laura Mulvey, "Visual Pleasure and Narrative Cinema," *Screen* 16, no. 3 (1975): 6–18; Mary Ann Doane, "Film and the Masquerade: Theorising the Female Spectator," *Screen* 23, nos. 3–4 (September/October 1982): 74–87; Luce Irigaray, "Women's Exile," *Ideology and Consciousness* 1 (May 1977): 62–76.

7. John Berger, *Ways of Seeing* (London: Penguin, 1972), 47.

8. Further complicating the dynamic of male-female images of Jews is the historic feminization of the Jewish man, particularly the religious Jewish man. See Daniel Boyarin, *Unheroic Conduct: The Rise of Heterosexuality and the Invention of the Jewish Man* (Berkeley: University of California Press, 1997).

9. For an example of a Jewish critique of *Harry*, see Elliot B. Gertel, *Over the Top Judaism: Precedents and Trends in the Depiction of Jewish Beliefs and Observances in Film and Television* (Lanham, MD: University Press of America, 2003), 92–94. For an

interesting example of a feminist critique of Allen, see Elayne Rapping, "A Feminist's Love/Hate Relationship with Woody," Cineaste 23, no. 3 (1998): 37–38. *Harry* was received with particular outrage from journalist Maureen Dowd who, in a clear reference to the Farrow/Previn scandal, saw the film as an assertion that "ordinary ethical standards do not apply to people who produce extraordinary art." In her piercing critique, Dowd could not resist reading Allen's film in light of his personal life. Maureen Dowd, "Liberties: Grow Up, Harry," *New York Times*, January 11, 1998.

10. Peter Bailey, *The Reluctant Film Art of Woody Allen* (Lexington: University Press of Kentucky, 2001), 244. According to Eric Lax, in *Conversations with Woody Allen: His Films, the Movies, and Moviemaking* (New York: Knopf, 2007), 147, Robert De Niro and Albert Brooks were also considered for the Harry role.

11. John Lahr, "The Imperfectionist," *New Yorker*, December 9, 1996, 82. See also Vincent Brook's chapter in this volume, "The Gospel according to Woody," which discusses the parallels between Harry's and Allen's life and work.

12. Lahr, "The Imperfectionist," 70.

13. On the phenomenon of self-hatred, see Sander L. Gilman, *Jewish Self-Hatred: Anti-Semitism and the Hidden Language of the Jews* (Baltimore: Johns Hopkins University Press, 1990) and Paul Reitter, *On the Origins of Jewish Self-Hatred* (Princeton: Princeton University Press, 2012).

14. Muslim dress presents an interesting challenge to these readings of the implications behind Jewish women's comparative dearth of immediately visible signification. By virtue of the hijab (a wide variety of headdress including the full burqa), Muslim women hold the reigns of religious visibility while Muslim men may not bear any immediate signifiers of their religious dedication.

15. Doane cites Mulvey's "Afterthoughts . . . Inspired by *Duel in the Sun*," *Framework* (Summer 1981): 13. In her work *The Desire to Desire*, Doane addresses the "excessive" (if imagined) desire and pleasure inherent to women's spectatorship with reference to Allen's film *The Purple Rose of Cairo* (1985), about a woman spectator and male actor who cross the boundaries of reality/fantasy and looking/being looked at. Mary Ann Doane, *The Desire to Desire: The Woman's Film of the 1940s* (Bloomington: Indiana University Press, 1987), 1–2.

16. Quoted in Doane, "Film and the Masquerade," 82.

17. Ibid., 75.

18. Ibid., 75–76.

19. "The masculine can partly look at itself, speculate about itself, represent itself and describe itself for what it is, whilst the feminine can try to speak to itself through a new language, but cannot describe itself from outside or in formal terms, except by identifying itself with the masculine, thus by losing itself." Irigaray, "Women's Exile," 65. Cf. Doane, "Film and the Masquerade," 80.

20. Doane, "Film and the Masquerade," 76.

21. Ibid.

> You've always had problems writing for women.
> —Ellen to David, *Bullets Over Broadway*

ELLIOT SHAPIRO

"Toot, Toot, Tootsie! (Goodbye)" & Disposable Women in the Films of Woody Allen

Alvy Singer might begin this way: "There's an old joke. Women: can't live with them. Can't kill them." That this joke is offensive doesn't mean it hasn't been played for laughs. When we hear, in *Manhattan* (1979), that Isaac (Woody Allen) tried to run over his ex-wife and her girlfriend, or when he shows up at their door and says to his ex-wife (Meryl Streep), "I came here to strangle you," we take these as jokes, in part because the character, like all characters played by Allen, is so thoroughly unthreatening. We know that Isaac — the shrimpy, neurotic, guilt-ridden, and (not incidentally) Jewish comedy writer for TV — could no more go through with it than could any of the other characters Woody Allen has played in his own movies. In later movies, the joke turns. Sometimes you can kill them, and sometimes it's supposed to be funny.

Something not very funny happened on the way from *Manhattan* to *Match Point* (2005). In *Manhattan*, when Yale (Michael Murphy) and Isaac are confronted by an old dilemma — how does a man dispose of one woman when he is involved with two? — Yale and Isaac do the honorable thing: they dump someone. In *Crimes and Misdemeanors* (1989) and *Match Point*, Judah Rosenthal (Martin Landau) and Chris Wilton (Jonathan Rhys Meyers) take more extreme action. Judah contracts out the murder of his mistress. Chris takes care of the job himself, with a shotgun, a solution made more coldhearted by his decision to obscure the motive for the murder by also murdering an elderly widow who lives next door.

For a filmmaker who has been identified for decades with comedy — as a writer, stand-up performer, actor, and director — it is striking how many women Woody Allen has killed in the movies he has directed and (co-) written since 1989. While this cycle begins with *Crimes and Misdemeanors*, one of the last films to feature Mia Farrow (whose character, one must note, is not killed), a narrative preoccupation with women who must be gotten rid of reaches full flower after the last Farrow film, *Husbands and Wives* (1992). At least one woman per movie is murdered in *Manhattan Murder Mystery* (1993), *Bullets Over Broadway* (1994), and *Match Point*. In *Scoop* (2006), the death toll exceeds a dozen, with a failed murder attempt to wrap up the picture. In each case, the women are murdered by men.[1] While no one would confuse *Match Point* with a comedy — no matter who wrote and directed it — the same could not be said of *Manhattan Murder Mystery*, *Bullets Over Broadway*, and *Scoop*.

In the hopes of achieving depth perception, this chapter interchanges two lenses to view the place of Jewishness in Woody Allen's post-1992 films. One lens focuses on film itself, the medium that is foregrounded in so many of Allen's films: film as storytelling; film as made object; and most of all, film as cultural heritage. Although Hollywood was (to invert Neal Gabler's line) invented by Jews, characters identifiable as Jews were largely banished from the screen for much of the period generally identified as classical.[2] Engaging with the film genres of classical Hollywood, as Allen does in highly reflexive ways, means engaging with the question of where the Jews weren't and figuring out where they belong. As Allen makes films in which women die, he seems to try out different genre models: Do Jews belong in whodunit versions of smart, urbane comedies modeled on the *Thin Man* series (W. S. Van Dyke and others, 1934–47)? Do they belong in backstage comedies whose long history in sound pictures can be traced to the intensely Jewish musical melodrama *The Jazz Singer* (Alan Crosland, 1927)? Do they belong in Alfred Hitchcock–style thrillers?

If the view through this first lens requires long shots, intended to trace the lineage of certain generic features of Allen's films, the second lens, which focuses on the place of women's bodies in these same films, moves in for tighter shots. Not only do a surprising number of women in these films turn up dead — but a surprising number of the living women are professional sex workers.

Live women as prostitutes and dead women as plot devices could crudely describe a significant percentage of the filmmaker's output after Allen's very public breakup with Mia Farrow. This chapter focuses on points where the representation of Jewishness — or its notable absence — intersects with the presence of dead women's bodies, thus illuminating a persistent concern in Allen's films with Jewishness as a template for ethical behavior, alongside the even more persistent presence of markers of Jewishness as cultural baggage to be called for when needed and disposed of when the journey requires some other kind of suitcase.

While this chapter and this book focus on Allen's films post-1992, one cannot write about disposable women in recent Woody Allen films without some discussion of *Crimes and Misdemeanors*, the film in which questions of Jewish identity intersect most overtly with the presence of disposable women. For this reason, *Crimes and Misdemeanors* provides a template for post-1992 films that feature "tootsies," living and dead. This chapter's central text is *Bullets Over Broadway*, the film in which Jewish show-business culture, the heritage of Hollywood, and the murder of a woman for comic effect collide. *Bullets Over Broadway* functions as a genre fulcrum between the psychological thriller plots of *Crimes and Misdemeanors* and its English cousin, *Match Point*, and the campier comedy thrillers — *Manhattan Murder Mystery* and *Scoop*. A brief discussion of Woody Allen's genre work helps set the stage for my discussion of his lady-killer movies.

Whether comedies or thrillers, Allen's lady-killer films pick up a question posed by one thriller after another: what kind of man can get away with murder? Not just what are the mechanics of it (although the mechanics matter), but what psychological toll does it exact? Do men exist who — through some combination of foresight and luck — can not only plan a murder for which they will not be held responsible but also be so free of moral compass that they can cash in on the benefits of their actions without the burden of guilt?[3] In Allen's late career thrillers, and his backstage assassination comedy, the answer seems to be, yes, such men exist, but they probably aren't Jewish.

Take the Genre and Run

One striking feature of Allen's long career has been his ability, as a writer and a director, to both produce convincing work in a variety of film genres and to make genres collide for comic effect. In *The Purple Rose of Cairo* (1985), for example, parody and homage coexist. Even as *The Purple Rose of Cairo* parodies urbane comedies that feature New Yorkers whose sophistication is marked by martinis, society parties, and world travel, it also evinces nostalgia for those same films.

Allen can claim to have been present at the creation of several comic genres — notably, the mockumentary (*Take the Money and Run* [1969], *Bananas* [1971], and *Zelig* [1983]). But the genre whose patent he can claim most completely might be best described as the "Woody Allen movie": a story about self-absorbed Manhattanites, usually Jews (if they are men), who listen to classical music and jazz, are conversant in classical Hollywood and European art cinema, and follow New York sports teams. These men and their (often non-Jewish) wives and girlfriends break up and get together between visits to analysts, restaurants, and New York landmarks.[4] While these films reveal their debts to broad ranges of films, the pleasure they take in smart talk reveals ancestry that can be traced to the fast-talking comedies of the 1930 and 40s.

Updating the urbane 1930s comedy and locating it in New York of the 1970s and after means bringing in Jews and their cultural baggage. This represents a significant shift in genre.[5] While coded representations of Jews are evident in certain classical Hollywood genres — notably, comedies derived from vaudeville, another of Allen's cinematic goldmines — the presence of Jewish characters in an urbane comedy from the 1930s would represent a kind of comic collision: Alvy Singer would be as out of place in Cary Grant vehicles like *The Awful Truth* (Leo McCarey, 1937) or *Holiday* (George Cukor, 1938) as Cecilia (Mia Farrow) is in "*The Purple Rose of Cairo*"[6] or Professor Kugelmass is in *Madame Bovary*.[7]

The prominence of thrillers among Woody Allen's filmic output after 1992 coincides with a tendency to feature films in which women die. The connection between these two trends is not incidental. If it's hard to imagine a character played by Woody Allen popping up next to Cary Grant or Katharine Hepburn, it's equally hard to imagine a character played by Woody Allen — or any of the characters who appear in *Annie Hall*, *Manhattan*, or *Hannah and Her Sisters* — in a Hitchcock movie, playing the parts played by Robert Walker in *Strangers on a Train* (1951); Raymond Burr in *Rear Window* (1954); or Tom Helmore in *Vertigo* (1958) — cold-blooded murderers of wives, their own or someone else's.

The centrality of dead women in Allen's films post–Mia Farrow marks the intertextual relationship between three films in particular — *Manhattan Murder Mystery*, *Match Point*, and *Scoop* — and Hollywood's classic thrillers. The obvious antecedents include *Double Indemnity* (Billy Wilder, 1944) and *The Lady from Shanghai* (Orson Welles, 1947) — both excerpted on-screen in *Manhattan Murder Mystery* — and the three Hitchcock films noted above. Several critics, prompted by Allen himself, have noted the relationship between two films that feature detecting couples — *Manhattan Murder Mystery* and *Scoop* — and the six *Thin Man* films released between 1934 and 1947. In the *Thin Man* films, Nick and Nora Charles (William Powell and Myrna Loy) solve crimes while exchanging witty banter and swigging cocktail after cocktail.[8]

Dead women are the lifeblood of thrillers. At the center of the three Hitchcock films noted above is the same question: how does a man get rid of a wife who is troublesome for one reason or another? She might be a nag (*Rear Window*); she might refuse to divorce her husband, thus hindering his desire to marry up (*Strangers on a Train*); or she might just be married to a man who is bored and wants to start over, something he can do more comfortably if he has unfettered access to her money (*Vertigo*). As Allen demonstrates an increasing engagement with the thriller, his films wrestle with the place for Jews within the thriller. Should the film be about the struggle for the soul of a Jewish man? Should the film be a comedy? Should the film concern itself with guilt or the absence of guilt? Can one make a better thriller without Jews and their guilt-ridden tendencies?

Disposable women — whether prostitutes or women destined to die before the final fade — are not particularly rare in Hollywood cinema. Dead and doomed women are as integral to the melodrama as they are to the thriller. Classic thrillers worked around the Production Code's absolute injunction against representing any kind of sex worker by featuring women who are effectively, but not officially, prostitutes: women who trade sex (or, officially, sex appeal) for some combination of money and power. In *Double Indemnity*, Phyllis Dietrichson's backstory includes the murder of her husband's first wife. Having snared Mr. Dietrichson with sex appeal, she turns it on Neff and maneuvers him into murdering her husband so they can collect the insurance money. In *Vertigo*, Judy (Kim Novak) plays Madeline to help her lover, Gavin Elster (Tom Helmore), murder his wife.

Afterward, when Judy meets Scotty (James Stewart) as herself, she admits she's been "picked up before." In Hitchcock's *North by Northwest* (1959), after Eve Kendall (Eva Marie Saint) falls in love with Vandamm (James Mason), she is hired by the CIA to continue to be his lover while collecting information. Then she makes love to Roger Thornhill (Cary Grant) on orders from Vandamm in order to set him up to be murdered.

Prostitutes did not suddenly appear in Allen's films after he parted ways with Farrow. In *The Purple Rose of Cairo*, 1930s film character Tom Baxter is perplexed by a houseful of warmhearted professionals, women he would not meet in a 1930s movie. In *Hannah and Her Sisters*, Mickey's (Allen) assistant Gail (Julie Kavner) suggests he take his mind off an existential crisis by visiting a "whorehouse." But prostitutes do feature more prominently in the Allen films of the 1990s and 2000s.[9] Among the minor characters interviewed during *Husbands and Wives* is a call girl who represents one of Jack's (Sydney Pollack) early experiments with sex outside of marriage. In *Bullets Over Broadway*, Olive Neal (Jennifer Tilly) is a former stripper turned chorus girl who appears in a serious play bankrolled by her mobster boyfriend. Not technically a prostitute, she is a kept gangster's girl, a tootsie, which any moviegoer knows is virtually the same thing. *Mighty Aphrodite* (1995) replays one of Hollywood's most durable clichés: the hooker (played by Mira Sorvino) with a heart of gold. We meet another gold-hearted hustler (Hazelle Goodman) in *Deconstructing Harry* (1997), along with one short story that features an orientalist fantasy of a prostitute and another short story about a man who murdered his wife, stepchildren, and mistress with an ax and then ate them all. *Scoop* brings the two threads together: one dead woman is named and identified and even appears on-screen after her death. She was murdered because she suspected that her boss — a wealthy, young aristocrat long on charm but short on morals — was a modern-day Jack the Ripper, responsible for the serial murder of a dozen or more London streetwalkers. She turned out to be partly right.[10]

In the Allen films from the 1990s and 2000s, the dead women and the prostitutes are largely segregated by genre. The dead women appear mostly in the thrillers, which become progressively less concerned with Jewish ethics or Jewish guilt. The prostitutes take as their primary residence comedies that feature male Jewish characters played by Woody Allen.

Crimes and Misdemeanors

Among Woody Allen's films, *Crimes and Misdemeanors* is noteworthy for its obsessive interest in Jewish culture. It also stands out, even among Woody Allen films, for the degree to which it foregrounds film itself: as genre, as cultural heritage, and as made object. Generically unstable — the film moves back and forth from comedy to melodrama to thriller — *Crimes and Misdemeanors* establishes a template for several post-1992 films, most of which will inhabit a single genre in a cleaner way than does this one.

The melodramatic plotline in *Crimes and Misdemeanors* dramatizes a struggle for the soul of a well-traveled, adulterous, Jewish, golfing ophthalmologist. Judah Rosenthal's decision to murder his mistress, Dolores Paley (Anjelica Huston) is presented as an exploration of his own conscience and his own religious identity. Judah's decision is presented dramatically and dialectically: Judah argues with his conscience, represented by the imaginary presence of his rabbi, who happens to be a patient and a friend. During their imagined conversation, Rabbi Ben (Sam Waterston) presents conventional arguments for moral behavior in a universe ruled by forgiveness and an all-seeing God. Judah responds, "God is a luxury I can't afford." After the murder is committed, his guilty conscience almost convinces him that God exists, as it existed for his father and exists for his rabbi. The fact that he gets away with murder convinces him otherwise.

Continuing the film's dialectical mode, *Crimes and Misdemeanors* stages the "thriller question" — what kind of man can get away with murder? — as dialogue. The possibility that some men are psychologically equipped to "push the guilt under the rug," as Chris Wilton will later put it, is framed dialectically at the film's conclusion. Two Jewish men in tuxedos "plot the perfect murder." Because both men's lines were written by Woody Allen, one could read them as the author's argument with himself and as a template for the thriller films to follow. If a man murders someone, can he live with the guilt or can he rationalize it away? If a man can live with the crime, is that proof of a godless universe? Men untroubled by guilt appear in Allen's subsequent thrillers, but unlike Judah Rosenthal, they aren't Jewish.

Crimes and Misdemeanors also differs from the later films in that it actually shows a dead woman's body — not just a hand or an arm (as in *Manhattan Murder Mystery* and *Match Point*) or the sound of a splash, outside the frame, when the corpse hits the river (as in *Bullets Over Broadway*) — but a whole dead woman, her unseeing eyes part of the heavy-handed symbolic system of blindness and sight that also incorporates Judah's profession (ophthalmologist); his father's religious beliefs ("The eyes of God are on us always"); the rabbi's affliction (blindness); and the closing song ("I'll be seeing you"). In showing us the body, the film confronts us with the consequences of murder, in ways the later films do not.

Crimes and Misdemeanors foregrounds, in multiple ways, films made and in production. The film quotes several films visually and one aurally. Clips of Hollywood films such as *Mr. and Mrs. Smith* (Alfred Hitchcock, 1941) and *Happy Go Lucky* (Connie Rasinski, 1947) appear on-screen when Cliff (Allen) and his niece Jenny (Jenny Nichols) watch them at the Bleeker Street Cinema. When Cliff and Halley watch *Singin' in the Rain* (Gene Kelly and Stanley Donen, 1952) in Cliff's studio, we see the light of the film on their faces as we hear "All I Do Is Dream of You." (The song also plays over the trailer.) Documentary filmmaker Cliff films TV producer Lester (Alan Alda) as he talks about his craft and meets with staff and crew. We see Cliff surrounded by film stock in his studio. We view his tapes of a documentary subject. When we see Cliff's rough cut of the footage he has shot of Lester, we see that film can tell the truth, distort the truth, create fictional truths, and serve the narrative agenda of a particular filmmaker.

The whole movie moves toward the moment at the film's conclusion when the two male protagonists, whose stories have been running in parallel, meet for the first time. When they get together they discuss the aesthetization of murder. Plotting the perfect murder, Cliff starts with a murder he'd like to commit. Judah tells the story of a murder he actually committed. Cliff then edits the script for an imaginary film project. Both call our attention to the almost concluded film we are watching and its reflexive engagement with a broad range of film genres: thriller, psychological drama, comedy, documentary, and musical.

Manhattan Murder Mystery

Allen has described the murder films of Hitchcock as "delightful, but completely insignificant."[11] While this might not be a fair description of Hitchcock's *Psycho* (1960) or *Vertigo*, it seems a more plausible assessment of *Rear*

Window, the film to which *Manhattan Murder Mystery* is most transparently indebted. As in *Rear Window*, one member of a couple, shut up at home (in this case, because her career was stalled by motherhood), tries to convince the other member that a murder has happened right outside their door. A wedding ring provides a critical clue. An attempt to catch the murderer turns a lark into a real threat, which is defused after the elapse of very little movie time. Haunting both films is a grim view of marriage: *Rear Window* features one couple contemplating the barriers to marriage (Jeff/James Stewart and Carol/Grace Kelly); another recently married couple whose marriage turns sour in the space of a few days (the newlyweds through the window on the left); and a middle-aged couple comprised of a cheating husband and a wife whose days are numbered (this describes both the Thorwalds in *Rear Window* and the Houses in *Manhattan Murder Mystery*). The starring couple in *Manhattan Murder Mystery*, Larry and Carol Lipton, are played by our old friends Woody Allen and Diane Keaton. (We are left to wonder whether they would be a comfortable middle-aged couple if they had stayed together instead of breaking up back in *Annie Hall*.) Boredom threatens this marriage, but we see no trace of the exhausting toxicity characteristic of the late Woody/Mia movies. Detective work livens things up, just as it livened up the marriage of Nick and Nora Charles in the *Thin Man* series, and just as it livens up the relationship between Jeff and Carol in *Rear Window*.

Rear Window has long been recognized as a film that thematizes the voyeuristic character of moviegoing.[12] Where *Rear Window* thematizes spectatorship, *Manhattan Murder Mystery* quotes old movies. When characters see *Double Indemnity*, Allen's favorite thriller, we see it too.[13] The climactic gunfight takes place in an old movie house while *The Lady from Shanghai* provides aural and visual commentary. As in *Double Indemnity* and *Vertigo*, a living person takes the place of a dead one in order to make a murder look like an accident or suicide. (As in both of those movies, the living person who plays dead ends up dead.) In order to explain plot twists to the audience, *Manhattan Murder Mystery* combines two of the thriller's most durable storytelling strategies: the voice-over that describes a crime (as in *Double Indemnity*) and the visual replay of the murder, edited to show what really happened, rather than what seemed to happen (as in *Vertigo*).

While the debts to classic Hollywood, as sources both of plot and of narrative technique, are to be expected in a Woody Allen film, somewhat less expected is the fact that the film seems to be scrubbed clean of references to Jewish life or culture. Few Allen films are as overtly about Jewishness as is *Crimes and Misdemeanors*. But in Allen films where Jewishness does not figure prominently, incidental references are often sprinkled throughout. In *Manhattan*, Isaac tells Yale that his parents won't get good seats at the synagogue if he doesn't make a substantial contribution. In *Husbands and Wives*, Jack says to Gabe, "Don't give me some moralizing discourse. You're not my rabbi." *Manhattan Murder Mystery* contains cultural markers that, if they point anywhere, seem to point toward WASP culture. Larry Lipton is in publishing, not show business. Larry and Carol's son goes to Brown. The family eats celebratory dinners at 21. Lipton buys his son a cashmere sweater at Brooks Brothers and cooks tuna casserole for his wife, who happens to be a gourmet chef. Although Lillian House is played by Lynn Cohen, and Paul House is played by Jerry Adler — whose most visible performance may have been his later role as a Jewish mobster on *The Sopranos* (1999–2007) — their names, apartment, and conversation display no cultural markers that suggest Jewishness.

The film's last joke calls attention to the ambiguity inherent in reading cultural markers when the characters have only the history and psychology provided for them by a script and an audience's frames of reference. Within the diegesis, the film's final lines compare two men competing for attention from the same woman. For viewers, the following exchange might read as a comparison of the most iconic Jewish actor from the 1970s and another 1970s icon who always seems Jewish but is not: Woody Allen and Alan Alda. As the movie closes, the Liptons discuss Ted, their friend and partner in crime solving, played by Alan Alda:

> LARRY/WOODY: Take away his elevator shoes and his fake suntan and his capped teeth and what do you have?
> CAROL/DIANE: You.

Alda's character in *Manhattan Murder Mystery* is no more marked as Jewish than is Allen's, despite their public personae, despite the fact that, before this film, the actors last appeared together at the wedding of Alda/Lester's niece, the rabbi's daughter, in the final scene of *Crimes and Misdemeanors*. That fiction ended with Woody, jealous over Lester's conquest of his would-be wife

(Farrow), plotting Lester's murder. At the conclusion of *Manhattan Murder Mystery*, the Lipton marriage — livened up by a few murders — seems secure in ways that couples played by Allen and Farrow rarely did.

Even in a Woody Allen film, the absence of Jewishness can be as hard to pin down as its presence. We may all know Jews send their children to Brown, work in publishing, eat at 21, shop at Brooks Brothers, and cook tuna casserole. But the comparison to *Crimes and Misdemeanors* is instructive. When Judah Rosenthal wants to kill his mistress, we get a psychological thriller about a man's conscience. Perhaps if he's not Jewish, like Paul House, it's easier to make him a man with no conscience — unburdened by guilt — and to make the movie a comedy, a lark, a "trivial picture," to quote Woody Allen, in which two women die and a third is a middle-aged jealous lover with glasses, a limp, a cane, and a gun, all to combat the boredom of a couple of Upper East Siders.[14]

Bullets Over Broadway

While *Bullets Over Broadway* is, on its surface, one of Allen's campiest comedies — a sharp shift from astringent narratives of marital discord like *Crimes and Misdemeanors* and *Husbands and Wives* — on the same surface it is an argument, performed dialectically, about aesthetics, with life-and-death stakes.[15] Its aesthetics are unabashedly nostalgic: for Greenwich Village coffeehouse culture; for the music, fashion, and art of the 1920s; for Hollywood's backstage comedies; for Hollywood's gangsters; and for Hollywood's nostalgia films about the 1920s that feature gangsters and backstage comedy, sometimes (as in *Singin' in the Rain* and *Some Like It Hot* [Billy Wilder, 1959]) in the same movies.

In *Bullets Over Broadway*'s first line of dialogue — after we hear Al Jolson sing "Toot, Toot, Tootsie! (Goodbye)" over the opening credits and after we see a retro shot of Times Square — playwright David Shayne (John Cusack) yells, "I'm an artist. And I won't change a word of my play to pander to some commercial Broadway audience." *Bullets Over Broadway* is a story about a playwright who finds an uncompromising artistic voice: the voice just happens to belong to someone else. The artist unwilling to compromise makes so many compromises that he realizes he is not an artist at all, not only because of the compromises, and not only because he discovers his artistic vision is so much less visionary than is his collaborator's, but also because the price is just too high. Being a great artist seems to require being a failed human being.[16] The movie poses and leaves hanging questions about the responsibility of artists to art and to their audiences. Should art educate, should it entertain, and should it make money? Who should benefit?

One can read in this dialectic the kind of internal critique of Woody Allen movies often evident *in* Woody Allen movies. Ellen (Mary-Louise Parker), David's girlfriend, tells David, "You've always had problems writing for women." The tone may be milder than is Rain's (Juliette Lewis) critique of Gabriel Roth's (Allen) manuscript in *Husbands and Wives* ("The way your lead character views women, it's so retrograde. It's so shallow"), but both comments could stand in for some of the most persistent criticisms of Allen's films: misogyny (or at least sexism) stands on a podium next to accusations of Jewish self-hatred, comments on the general absence of people of color, and the near universal assumption that Allen's movies are either thinly disguised autobiographical narratives or obsessive recapitulations of the filmmaker's own neuroses and anxieties (or both).[17] One could also read a response to the tabloid scandal that dominated public discussions of Allen and his work as the script for *Bullets Over Broadway* was being written. Even if the filmmaker were unwilling to say that "an artist creates his own moral universe," as David's friend Sheldon Flender (Rob Reiner) does, he might be inclined to assert that what the artist does in his private life has no bearing on how one should read his work.

Early in the movie, Flender, a playwright even less successful than David, and a fellow habitué of Greenwich Village coffeehouses, poses the kind of hypothetical moral dilemma that Allen's characters are wont to make. In the opening scene of *Manhattan*, set at Elaine's, Isaac diverts his dinner companions from a conversation about aesthetics by asking whether any of the people at the table would have the courage to dive off a bridge into an icy river to save a drowning person. In a Greenwich Village café, Flender restates the dilemma as follows: "Let's say there was a burning building and you could rush in and save only one thing: either the last known copy of Shakespeare's plays or some anonymous human being. What would you do?" Flender and David agree, wholeheartedly, that the plays merit saving more than the person.

David is not faced with this exact dilemma. When faced with a parallel dilemma, he does not murder Olive (Jennifer Tilly), the girlfriend of gangster Nick Valenti (Joe Viterelli) and the actress foisted upon him as a condition of Valenti's financial backing. David also does not write the version of his play that opens on Broadway. But he receives the benefit of Olive's death — she is no longer there to ruin his play — and he receives full credit — "the find of the decade" — for a play written in collaboration with an uncredited ghostwriter.

The man who rewrote David's play, killed the problematic actress, and is then conveniently murdered himself, is Cheech (Chazz Palminteri), Valenti's hit man and a man for whom art, like his day job, is a life-and-death business. When David discovers that Olive has been killed to save his (their) play, he says to Cheech, "I'm an artist, too. I'm not a great artist like you, but I'm an artist. But... first I'm a human being." While we would undoubtedly agree with David's assertion that a human life is, in fact, more valuable than a work of art, we are nevertheless led to conclude that the murderer is a greater artist than is the mensch and that his single-minded commitment to the work has something to do with his greatness.

In *Crimes and Misdemeanors*, Allen demonstrated that he could stage and shoot a set piece of thriller suspense as skillfully as Hitchcock. As the prospective killer tracks Dolores, we enjoy the voyeuristic pleasures of the thriller; we then share Judah's shock, horror, and guilt when we learn, at the same moment he does, that his mistress is dead. Shock, horror, and guilt play little role in *Bullets Over Broadway*, for killer or audience. Right before he shoots her, Cheech tells Olive, "You're a horrible actress." Cheech's next line silences any doubts an audience might have about whether this murder is played for laughs: "Thank God I don't have to hear her voice anymore."

Not hearing the grating voice of an actress from the 1920s figures prominently in *Singin' in the Rain*, one of the films to which *Bullets Over Broadway* is obviously indebted. In *Singin' in the Rain*, Cosmo Brown (Donald O'Connor) figures out how Monumental Pictures can continue to make money from Lina Lamont's face (Jean Hagen) without losing money with her voice. Once a successor is found whose voice is as audiogenic as her face is photogenic, Lina becomes expendable. The murder is symbolic: her career is dead, but she will live. Olive Neal is not so lucky.

As Carol Clover and Steven Cohan have pointed out, *Singin' in the Rain* presents itself as a morality play about receiving credit where credit is due but is actually a film haunted by uncredited labor, particularly in its focus on voices that substitute for other voices.[18] *Bullets Over Broadway* is also centrally concerned with giving and taking credit. Olive is sacrificed so the play can succeed. Cheech gives both his work and his life to the play, and David gets all the credit. This complicated credit swap could stand in for the complex transactions through which the voices of Jews — embodied in dialogue and music — come out of the mouths of non-Jewish characters in one Hollywood movie after another, and the even more complex transaction characteristic of blackface musicals.

Neither *Singin' in the Rain* nor *Bullets Over Broadway* hides its debts to the first movie musical, the backstage melodrama that is credited with killing silent cinema. In *Singin' in the Rain*, the fictional studio bets all its chips on sound cinema after the success of *The Jazz Singer*. The opening credits to *Bullets Over Broadway* are accompanied by Al Jolson in *The Jazz Singer* singing "Toot, Toot, Tootsie! (Goodbye)," the song that follows the first recorded words spoken by Jolson, or anyone else, in a feature film: "You ain't heard nothing yet."[19] No film has more fully dramatized the competing claims of silence and voice and the competing claims on Jews of tradition and assimilation than does *The Jazz Singer* when Cantor Rabinowitz (Warner Oland) silences his jazz-singing son (Al Jolson), only to fall ill and die of a broken heart.

During the brief moments when *The Jazz Singer* is a talking picture, Robin/Jolson serenades his adoring mother with a rendition of "Blue Skies," the popular (in every sense) song written by Irving Berlin (formerly Israel Isidore Baline). Berlin, like Jolson himself, represents a model for success through assimilation. Berlin's assimilationist contributions to American music can be shorthanded by listing the holy trinity of "God Bless America," "Easter Parade," and "White Christmas." The lesson of *The Jazz Singer* is clear: Jewish men can succeed in show business if they are willing to leave their Jewishness behind, to murder versions of themselves.

Woody Allen represents a later generation of Jewish entertainers. Although he changed his name — as did Jolson and Berlin and countless other show-business Jews — he ranks first among the comedians who successfully brought the borscht belt to the mainstream, who made broadly popular film comedy from Jewish cultural identity. His arrival as director/writer/actor coincided with an ethnic moment in the 1960s and 70s — a moment Allen helped create — when characters explicitly identified as Jews reappeared in American cinema (alongside other hyphenated Americans), after being virtually banished in 1934 under the twin threats of the Production Code and rising anti-Semitism, not just in Europe (an important market for Hollywood films) but also in the United States. When Jews resurfaced in the 1940s, they appeared primarily in war films and postwar problem films, only to go undercover again during the McCarthyist 1950s. In films about show business made between the 1930s and the 1960s, characters recognizable as Jews made infrequent appearances.

In *The Jazz Singer*, the cultural gap between Jewish culture and show-business culture is particularly evident in two moments. In one, Moisha Yudelson (Otto Lederer) goes backstage looking for Jack Robin (Jolson). His ethnically inflected pronunciation of the word "actor" — spelled "ector" in the intertitles — marks him as a Yiddish speaker and an outsider when he walks through a Broadway stage door. In the film's melodramatic climax, Robin's girlfriend and costar, Mary Dale (May McAvoy), along with the producer of *April Follies* visit Robin at his parents' apartment. When they hear Robin chanting *Kol Nidre* at the synagogue next door, they listen at the window as if to an exotic tribal ritual. *Singin' in the Rain*, a product of Arthur Freed's celebrated MGM production unit, was conceived as a showcase for Tin Pan Alley–inflected songs written by Freed and Herb Nacio Brown, all but two recycled from earlier films, plus one plagiarized for the occasion.[20] Despite the cultural roots of the music, and the film's period setting at a moment when it can refer to the 1927 release of *The Jazz Singer* as a contemporary event, Jews appear in *Singin' in the Rain* only in repressed form, in blackface that echoes Jolson's blackface performance in *The Jazz Singer*. Cosmo sings a few words about Mammy, not as an African American singer, but as Jolson in blackface. Cosmo and Don Lockwood (Gene Kelly) have brief conversations with two actors, one named Maxie, one with a Bronx accent; both are costumed as grotesque African cannibals, and both are (arguably) Jews.[21]

In *Bullets Over Broadway*, the repressed Jewish presence in show business returns. Julian Marx (Jack Warden), the producer of David Shayne's play in *Bullets Over Broadway*, would not find the *Kol Nidre* melody quite so exotic. Not only does Marx's name play on Groucho's given name (Julius), but also he is described by Helen Sinclair (Dianne Wiest) as a "Yiddish pants salesman turned producer." (That pretty much describes the career of the original Hollywood Jews.) The cast is populated by actors like Warden, Reiner, and Harvey Fierstein, all of whom read as Jewish and all of whom have histories as actors playing Jews. *Bullets Over Broadway* is not particularly concerned with Jewish religion or ethical practices (as in *Crimes and Misdemeanors*), with the visibility of Jewish public figures (as in *Annie Hall* and *Deconstructing Harry*), or with Jews trying to pass as non-Jews (as in "Oedipus Wrecks" [1989]). Like *Broadway Danny Rose* (1984), however, *Bullets Over Broadway* seems marinated in show-business cultures, past and present, that are intensely Jewish. If the young playwright—the Woody Allen part that Allen was too old to play—projects Jewish angst without obvious markers of Jewish identity, it may be because he is played by John Cusack instead of Woody Allen. However, in glasses, politics, career path, and underwear, David Shayne resembles politically committed playwright Barton Fink, the title character of the Coen brothers' anti-nostalgic parody of Broadway and Hollywood that appeared three years before *Bullets Over Broadway*. Barton Fink is undeniably Jewish, as is the Hollywood mogul who hires him and bosses him around. David Shayne almost doesn't have to be Jewish: we know that the playwrights on whom he and Fink are modeled—from Clifford Odets to Arthur Miller—were Jewish.

So true is *Bullets Over Broadway* to the aesthetics of classical Hollywood that the cast includes Venus (Annie Joe Edwards), a comic African American servant and a stereotypical Mammy. (Rogin describes this particular embodiment of the stereotype "grotesque."[22]) Edwards played virtually the same part, in virtually the same costume, as Delilah in "*The Purple Rose of Cairo.*"[23]

If the racial politics of *Bullets Over Broadway* echo the Jewish performance of blackface apotheosized in *The Jazz Singer* and repressed in *Singin' in the Rain*, the ethnic politics—a Jewish-Italian criminal alliance, sealed over a woman's dead body—evoke another unsavory set of representations. David's uncredited collaborator is an Italian gangster. Although the character shares his name with a Mexican American stoner comic, Cheech is identified as Italian when we learn that his father loved the opera and, in Palermo, once killed a singer whose performance was subpar. The alliance of an Italian hit man with a Jewish playwright recaps another hoary Hollywood narrative. From *The Godfather, Part II* (Francis Ford Coppola, 1974) to *The Sopranos*—the myth implicitly (and inaccurately) goes—when Jews and Italians worked together, the Jews provided the brains but never the muscle. Part of the comedy in *Bullets Over Broadway* emerges from the fact that, in this case, the Italian muscle also brings the brains.[24]

The presence of comic gangsters represents one crucial element of the film's nostalgia, not just for classical Hollywood, but also for classical Hollywood's nostalgia for its own past. Although pre-Code crime films like *Little Caesar* (Mervyn LeRoy, 1931) and *Scarface* (Howard Hawks, 1932) dramatized genuine anxiety about the power and reach of organized crime,[25] comic gangsters appeared on-screen and parodied their film representations at almost the same moment, in films like the Marx Brothers' *Monkey Business* (Norman Z. McLeod, 1931) and the first *Thin Man* (Willard Van Dyke, 1934). In nostalgia pieces about the 1920s like *Singin' in the Rain* and *Some Like It Hot*, the presence of gangsters on the fringes of show business is both a convention and a source of comedy.[26] One doesn't have to be terribly conversant in classical Hollywood to recognize that the craps-shooting, wise-cracking, gun-toting hood named Cheech is a movie type, updated by his hidden talent.

A gangster in a comedy who actually kills people need not disrupt comedy. In *Some Like It Hot*, a garage-full of gangsters are gunned down in Chicago. Spats Colombo is the victim of a banquet murder, followed immediately by the climactic chase scene that features multiple costume changes, a wheelchair, a bicycle, and a speedboat. But one would expect more comic disruption when one of the film's featured comic characters is murdered. In *Bullets Over Broadway*, Olive's murder provokes an argument between David and Cheech about whether terrible acting is de facto reason enough to kill someone, but her murder does not slow the comedy in any significant way — nor does the death of Cheech, who is chased all over the theater by Valenti's hoods, murdered backstage, and dies with a final rewrite and a laugh line on his lips.

In the midst of an astute reading about the relationship between Jolson's song and Allen's movie, Peter Bailey can't resist making, or revealing, a joke about the murder of the woman Cheech calls a tramp. "'You think it's right,' [Cheech] asks Shayne, 'some Tootsie walks in and messes up a beautiful thing . . . ?' At which point it's — to cite the title of the Al Jolson song opening the film — 'Toot, Toot, Tootsie, goodbye.'"[27]

This, ultimately, is what distinguishes Olive's murder from the murder of Dolores in *Crimes and Misdemeanors* or the murder of Nola Rice (Scarlett

Johansson) in *Match Point*. The pleasures of the thriller may be guilty, but they do at least pose to the audience questions of complicity. In *Bullets Over Broadway*, the murdered woman is a tootsie, no more than one step closer to respectability than is a prostitute. Olive's death is a splash — out of the frame — and silence where a voice once grated. Her murder is, in every sense, bloodless. Her murder will be avenged, but we laugh over her watery grave.

Match Point and *Scoop*

When Woody Allen's filmmaking operation moved to London, the films become almost as *Judenrein* as is London generally in the movies (its current rank as the world's fifteenth-largest Jewish metropolis notwithstanding).[28] The only Jews in either *Match Point* or *Scoop* are expat Americans. The Hewett family in *Match Point* and the Lyman family in *Scoop* represent a fantasy of the British upper class: good looking, well spoken, conversant in conventional markers of high culture, successful in business, and possessed of multiple immaculate houses in town and country (no dissolute eccentrics or dilapidated estates in these films). Both families include beautiful, young upper-class men who pick up women when it strikes them and drop them when it's desirable. Each young man picks up an American woman played by Scarlett Johansson and drops her, figuratively in the first film, into a lake in the second. Tom Hewett (Matthew Goode) has the charm, confidence, and taste in wine of a young man from a good family. He dabbles with an interloping American before tying the knot with a woman of his own class. Coasting through life on wheels greased with family wealth and connections, he is thoroughly overmatched by the Irish climber who marries his sister, sleeps with his fiancée, and apparently leapfrogs ahead of him in the family business. (In one of the film's last lines, we learn that Chris Wilton has moved into the office of the man under whom he first worked, apparently ahead of Tom). Playing for higher stakes, with a great deal more to lose, Wilton plays every game more seriously than does Hewett. Not satisfied with just dumping Nola Rice, he shoots her.

Match Point owes almost as much to Hitchcock's *Strangers on a Train* as *Manhattan Murder Mystery* does to *Rear Window*. A rich, young man and a tennis pro meet by chance. A murder solves one man's entanglement with a lower-class woman who stands in the way of social advancement through marriage. As in *Rear Window* and *Manhattan Murder Mystery*, a wedding ring provides the critical clue, but in a surprisingly lucky twist, the ring absolves the killer. Is it a coincidence that Tom Hewett resembles Farley Granger, the better tennis player and the better man in *Strangers on a Train*?[29]

According to the view of life attributed to Wilton, articulated starkly in his voice-over that begins the film (and again at a dinner-table conversation with his future brother-in-law, his future wife, and his future mistress), luck matters more than hard work or talent. His is a world without faith. Told that "despair is the path of least resistance," he counters that "faith [is] the path of least resistance." Despite his nihilistic worldview, Chris Wilton struggles with his conscience. Confronted by the ghosts of the women he killed, one of them pregnant with his child, he quotes Sophocles: "To never have been born, may be the greatest boon of all." He asserts that his capture would represent evidence of justice in the universe. But he remains convinced that there is none, that it is better to be "lucky than good." A world without faith, in an indifferent universe, is not so different from the view of life Allen himself has espoused. Allen speaks about the sustaining power of religious faith, then says, "The universe is banal . . . because it's banal, it's evil. . . . Its indifference is evil."[30]

In an earlier era, in another country, the ruthless social climber might be the role played by a Jewish character of Sammy Glick's ilk. Set in a milieu where a working-class Irish kid is the interloper, Allen need not confront the possibility he confronted in *Crimes and Misdemeanors*, that a Jewish man might be ruthless enough to murder and then go through life guilt free. *Match Point*, a film without Jews and without faith, articulates an exceptionally bleak view of life and death. A man who murders faces no consequence more severe than a few sleepless nights. He can escape detection, and consequences, because a wedding ring takes a lucky bounce on a fence by the Thames.

In *Scoop*, Peter Lyman (Hugh Jackman) combines the roles of Hewett and Wilton. Before saving Sondra Pransky/Jade Spence (Johansson) from drowning (or so he thinks), he carries on a long relationship with a prostitute who made two mistakes: she started blackmailing the young aristocrat, and she cut her hair short and dyed it brown. Because of her short, dark hair, she resembled the victims of a serial killer, whose multiple murders allowed Lyman to cover his one successful attempt. When Lyman is done with a woman, he doesn't just dump her; he kills her (or tries to). Unlike Judah and Wilton, who suffer pangs of conscience, Lyman resembles Paul House and Cheech in that his character shows no evidence that he has a conscience.

Recognizing, perhaps, that his presence would turn a London-based psychological thriller into something else, Allen absents himself from *Match Point*, as he absented himself from the thriller half of *Crimes and Misdemeanors*. A comic thriller set in London, on the other hand, can contain both Woody Allen and a young Jewish would-be journalist. In *Scoop*, Allen plays Sid Waterman, a small-time entertainer who is stuck in London for unexplained reasons. Allen casts himself as sidekick to Sondra Pransky (Scarlett Johansson), a Jewish journalism student from Brooklyn whose "small-timeyness" is signaled by her matriculation at Adair, the fictional upstate college from which Allen's character Harry Block (of *Deconstructing Harry*) did not graduate.

In *Scoop*, Allen demonstrates once again that he can make comedy over the dead bodies of tootsies. But this time, he lets Pransky swim to safety while, for a change, he kills his own character. As with the other characters killed in the movie, death presents only limited obstacles to his career: Waterman continues to do card tricks on the boat across the River Styx.

In *Deconstructing Harry*, Harry Block asks his sister whether it matters to her more when a Jew is murdered than when a non-Jew is murdered. She says, "Yes it does. I can't help it. It's my people." Despite his evident ambivalence about his own Jewish identity, and his ruthless parody of Jews and Jewishness in films early and late, perhaps for Allen it also matters, not just who kills but also who is killed. Is it a coincidence that the woman who survives in *Scoop* is one of a rare breed among the protagonists in Woody Allen's forty-plus films, a Jewish woman?

Notes

1. *Manhattan Murder Mystery* is the only one of these films in which a woman is permitted to return the favor: Mrs. Dalton shoots Paul House, her two- (or three-) timing lover.

2. In their catalogs of Hollywood films that feature Jewish characters, even in minor roles, Patricia Erens and Lester Friedman describe the social and political circumstances that more or less erased Jews from the screen for most of the 1930s and much of the 1950s. See Patricia Erens, *The Jew in American Cinema* (Bloomington: Indiana University Press, 1984), 135–36; and Lester Friedman, *Hollywood's Image of the Jew* (New York: Frederick Ungar Publishing, 1982), 57, 135. Tom Doherty describes a direct relationship between the enforcement of the Production Code under Joseph Breen and the disappearance of Jews from the screen: "Turning away from racial and ethnic diversity, the Breen Office smoothed out the multicolored rawness of pre-Code Hollywood.... In *Gentlemen's Agreement* (1947) ... gentile reporter Gregory Peck ... blurts out a word barely whispered in a Hollywood film since 1934. 'I'll be a Jew!'" Tom Doherty, *Pre-Code Hollywood: Sex, Immorality, and Insurrection in American Cinema 1930–1934* (New York: Columbia University Press, 1999), 339–40. Michael Rogin provides a broader cultural and political framework for the whitening of the movies: "Responding to the Nazi seizure of power, and to the fascist sympathies of the Hays/Breen Production Code Administration ... the Jewish moguls evaded anti-Semitism by simply eliminating Jews from the screen." Michael Rogin, *Blackface, White Noise: Jewish Immigrants in the Hollywood Melting Pot* (Berkeley: University of California Press, 1998), 209. Gabler writes, "The Jews became the phantoms of the film history they had created, haunting it but never really able to inhabit it." Neal Gabler, *An Empire of Their Own: How the Jews Invented Hollywood* (New York: Anchor, 1988), 2.

3. While man-killing women play crucial roles in many classic thrillers, especially noir thrillers, my use of "men" in this context is gender specific.

4. The most obvious example of a "Woody Allen film" produced by someone other than Woody Allen is *When Harry Met Sally* (1989), written by Nora Ephron and directed by Rob Reiner.

5. The almost complete erasure of characters identifiable as Jews during the 1930s, noted above, coincides with the classic period of urbane comedy.

6. In order to distinguish the Woody Allen film from the RKO film within the film, the latter title appears in quotes.

7. In Allen's short story, a Professor Kugelmass tries to avoid the complications of an affair with a real woman by getting himself "imported" into *Madame Bovary*, where he carries on a torrid affair with Emma Bovary herself. "The Kugelmass Episode," *New Yorker*, May 2, 1977, 34–39.

8. A discussion about Nick and Nora in relation to *Manhattan Murder Mystery* appears in Mary P. Nichols, *Reconstructing Woody: Art, Love, and Life in the Films of Woody Allen* (Lanham, MD: Rowman & Littlefield, 1998), 165–67. The title of Manohla Dargis's *New York Times* review makes clear the connection she sees between *The Thin Man* and *Scoop*: Manohla Dargis, "'Scoop': Shades of Nick and

Nora, with Woody Allen's Shtick," *New York Times*, July 28, 2006, http://movies.nytimes.com.

9. Allen is not alone in finding room for prostitutes in films post-1990 that are neither thrillers nor melodramas. The astonishing success of *Pretty Woman* (Garry Marshall, 1990) opened up new territory for sex workers in romantic comedies.

10. The presence of prostitutes in Allen films does not end with *Scoop*. In *To Rome with Love* (2012), Penelope Cruz plays another working woman.

11. Woody Allen, *Woody Allen on Woody Allen: In Conversation with Stig Björkman* (New York: Grove, 2004), 256.

12. Laura Mulvey writes, "Jeffries is the audience, the events in the apartment block opposite correspond to the screen. As he watches, an erotic dimension is added to his look." Laura Mulvey, "Visual Pleasure and Narrative Cinema," in *Feminism and Film Theory*, ed. Constance Penley (New York: Routledge, 1988), 66.

13. "*Double Indemnity* is the top. You just don't get anything better than that." Allen, *Woody Allen*, 256.

14. Allen, *Woody Allen*, 225. Peter Bailey compares *Manhattan Murder Mystery*'s conclusion unfavorably with the "silly cheerfulness" of Nick and Nora movies; he describes the closing image as "smug." Peter Bailey, *The Reluctant Film Art of Woody Allen* (Lexington: University Press of Kentucky, 2001), 208.

15. See also Bailey, *Reluctant Film Art*, 169–70.

16. Bailey points out that "the farther the Woody Allen protagonist is from being an artist, the more likely is his narrative to result in a happy ending." Bailey, *Reluctant Film Art*, 9.

17. Pauline Kael's review of *Stardust Memories* (1980) can stand in for some of these persistent criticisms: "The Jewish self-hatred that spills out in this movie could be a great subject, but all it does is spill out." Pauline Kael, "The Frog Who Turned into a Prince, the Prince Who Turned into a Frog," *New Yorker*, October 27, 1980, 186. Maureen Dowd's article about *Deconstructing Harry* covers the rest of the territory: "Mr. Allen at long last introduces a black character to his cloistered Gotham world. This exercise in the social extension of his imagination has produced an African-American hooker in pink vinyl hot pants. . . . Mr. Allen's arrested adolescence . . . is best exemplified by his disgusting attitude towards women." Maureen Dowd, "Grow Up Harry," *New York Times*, January 11, 1998, http://www.nytimes.com.

18. Carol Clover, "Dancin' in the Rain," *Critical Inquiry* 21 (1995): 722–47; Steven Cohan, *Incongruous Entertainment: Camp, Cultural Value, and the MGM Musical* (Durham, NC: Duke University Press, 2005), 220–45.

19. *The Purple Rose of Cairo* anticipates Allen's tribute to Jolson in *Bullets Over Broadway*. During an impromptu sing-along, Gil Shepherd (Jeff Daniels) and Cecilia (Farrow) sing Ray Henderson and Buddy DeSylva's "Alabamy Bound." One

of Jolson's hits, "Alabamy Bound" exemplifies the manufactured nostalgia for Dixie that runs through Tin Pan Alley songs, many written by immigrant Jews.

20. "Make 'em Laugh" is a transparent rip-off of Cole Porter's "Be a Clown," sung by Kelly and Judy Garland at the conclusion of *The Pirate* (Vincente Minelli, 1948).

21. For a more highly articulated reading of the blackface presence of Jews in *Singin' in the Rain*, see Rogin, *Blackface, White Noise*, 206.

22. Rogin, *Blackface, White Noise*, 115n.

23. The one redeeming feature of these parts as written is the fact that Delilah and Venus get to engage in "backtalk," a comic reversal unimaginable in period films like *Holiday Inn* (Mark Sandrich, 1942).

24. Rich Cohen writes about intergenerational nostalgia for tough Jews as models of masculinity. Men who grew up in Brooklyn in the 1930s and 40s — like Cohen's father and Woody Allen — knew or knew about Jewish gangsters and boxers, role models who counteracted the stereotypical image of the bookish, passive Jew. Rich Cohen, *Tough Jews: Fathers, Sons, and Gangster Dreams* (New York: Vintage, 1999), 258.

25. Doherty delineates the relationship between newsreel gangsters and movie gangsters in *Pre-Code Hollywood*, 137–70.

26. In *Singin' in the Rain* gangsters make brief, silent appearances in the "Broadway Melody" production number.

27. Bailey, *Reluctant Film Art*, 167.

28. Sergio DellaPergola, *World Jewish Population, 2010* (Storrs, CT: Center for Judaic Studies and Contemporary Jewish Life, 2010), 21.

29. We are reminded that we are watching a thriller when Wilton and Chloe Hewett (Emily Mortimer) while away an afternoon watching Jules Dassin's *Rififi* (1955), a French thriller celebrated for its intricately plotted jewel heist. The eros of thriller viewing is such that Wilton and Chloe's next scene is in bed.

30. Allen, *Woody Allen*, 223, 225.

CULTURAL
STUDIES

"I'm a Jew. We don't believe in Heaven."
"So where do you want to go?"
"A Chinese restaurant."
~*Deconstructing Harry* (1997)

NATHAN ABRAMS

Digesting Woody is Food and Foodways in the Movies of Woody Allen

Woody Allen has made inordinate use of the nature and function of food, drink, and dining in his movies. Indeed, although post–Mia Farrow, Allen has deviated from his representational routine in a number of ways — increasingly eschewing himself as protagonist and frequently abandoning Jew York City for what he sees as the cosmopolitan Old World sophistication of Europe's top cities (London, Paris, Barcelona, and Rome) — his fascination with food and foodways has continued unabated. Food or some allusion to food, especially, links the movies across his oeuvre. Surprisingly, however, this is not an area that has received much scholarly attention beyond a few chapters.[1] This chapter addresses the analytical gap by exploring the nature and function of Allen's gastronomic representations. I will show how obsessive concern with food and foodways, while encouraged by the Jewish scriptural and religious tradition, has been exacerbated by the conflicts of Jewish assimilation in the post-Emancipation European and American periods. Through examples from Allen's films in particular, I will demonstrate how the writer-director employs these bodily functions to use humor to make deeply serious points about the Jewish American condition, as he sees it, in the contemporary world.

The importance of food to Allen's oeuvre was indicated early on in his film career. In the epigraph above from the post–Mia Farrow period, we find an encapsulation of Allen's (and of much of Jewish humor's) comedic formula. In equating (the Christian) heaven and God with Chinese food, Allen deflates lofty ideas and conflates them with the quotidian, blurring and demystifying the line between the profane and the divine. David Desser and Lester Friedman suggest that Allen's philosophy repeatedly "thrusts downward from the sacred to the mundane."[2] Like Mel Brooks, to whom he has been compared, Allen holds the mirror not up to life but "a little behind and below."[3] As I will further argue, Allen manages to mingle high and low, kosher and *treyf* (explicitly nonkosher), in tune with his professed (if often contradicted) existentialist philosophy to both hilarious and profound effect. Extrapolating from Ronald LeBlanc, I would even say that food and foodways are used in Allen's movies "as effective metaphors for posing ultimate questions about humans, life, and the universe."[4]

Restauration Comedies

Jews and food have long been linked in the American audiovisual imagination, at least as far back as Gertrude Berg's *Goldbergs* radio and TV show (1929–50, 1949–56), which itself built on the archetype of the emotionally and gastronomically nurturing *Yiddische mama*. Phil Rosenthal, cocreator of *Everyone Loves Raymond* (1996–2005), for example, quipped about the strong cultural affinities of Jews and Italians: "All problems are solved with food, and the mother won't leave you alone."[5] In this vein, Allen's pre-1990 movies already abound with memorable Jewish moments and food allusions: The central conceit of his first directorial effort, *What's Up, Tiger Lily?* (1966), involves trying to find the secret recipe for egg salad (that Jewish delicatessen staple). Other examples include the surreal staging, with WASP-ish goys playing Jews, of a childhood memory of a Seder in *Sleeper* (1973) reenacted while Miles (Allen) is an hypnotic state; the plates of kosher meat at the Carnegie Deli that provides the main setting for *Broadway Danny Rose* (1984); the juxtaposition of fasting and *treyf* (unkosher) food during Yom Kippur in *Radio Days* (1987); the serious ethical discussion at another childhood-memory Seder in *Crimes and Misdemeanors* (1989); and, most iconic, the split-screen WASP-Jewish families and their contrasting foods and foodways in *Annie Hall* (1977) — to be discussed in greater detail below. Allen himself, while raised in a nominally observant family that respected kashrut (kosher food laws), has since veered from formal religious practices and religious faith altogether, as his body of work underscores. However, his use of food and drink in his movies intrinsically connects them to Yiddishkeit ("Jewishness" or "Jewish culture") as well as to Yiddishkeit's relation to the larger, often anti-Semitic, society.

As LeBlanc, extrapolating from Freud's *Jokes and Their Relation to the Unconscious*, avers, "Allen uses food jokes not just for laughs, but also for serious commentary about life."[6] *Annie Hall* once again set the pattern in this regard, in two jokes Alvy Singer (Allen) relates, one to his gentile love interest Annie Hall (Diane Keaton), the other in direct address to the audience. In the first, "Two elderly women are at a Catskills mountain resort, and one of 'em says: 'Boy, the food at this place is really terrible.' The other one says, 'Yeah, I know, and such small portions.' Well, that's essentially how I feel about life. Full of loneliness and misery and suffering and unhappiness, and it's all over much too quickly." In the second, "This guy goes to a psychiatrist and says, 'Doc, uh, my brother's crazy. He thinks he's a chicken.' And, the doctor says, 'Well, why don't you turn him in?' And the guy says, 'I would, but I need the eggs.' Well, I guess that's pretty much how I feel about relationships. You know, they're totally irrational and crazy and absurd... but, I guess we keep going through it because, most of us need the eggs."

Douglas Brode argues that all of the food imagery in Allen's movies is subsumed under a restaurant metaphor, asserting that emotional and psychological hunger motivates Allen's characters.[7] LeBlanc goes further: "One of the primary roles that food imagery plays in [Allen's] movies is to remind us — amid all the lofty philosophical speculation engendered by abstractions such as 'love' and 'death,' 'war' and 'peace,' 'crime' and 'punishment' — of immediate physical sensations and instinctual urges. The act of eating, by returning us to our bodies, helps to affirm the élan vital of human life.... [It] debunks the sterile and futile philosophizing of intellectuals and reaffirms instead life's essential vitality by satisfying one of man's most basic appetites."[8] Both Allen's philosophy and his foibles are communicated through food and foodways-related situations and similes. J. Hoberman has commented on *Melinda and Melinda* (2004; and this comment is applicable to several of Allen's films), "Drinking serves as a narrative lubricant throughout."[9]

To this can be added eating, cooking, and dining. These elements provide the meat of Allen's mise-en-scène, which rarely strays far from domestic or restaurant-based foodways. Furthermore, maybe because he believes they bring added gusto to his movies or because he equates their cuisine with high gastronomic sophistication, Allen's films are often set in exotic eateries. This is particularly the case with his more recent continental European films: *Vicky Cristina Barcelona* (2008), *Midnight in Paris* (2011), and *To Rome with Love* (2012). But even in his beloved Jew York, Allen frequently locates the action in French restaurants and bistros, deliberately contrasting fine Parisian-style dining with the more down-to-earth edibles of Jew Yorkers such as Chinese food and Jewish deli, which also play prominent roles in his films. *Melinda and Melinda*, for example, opens with exterior shots of a Greenwich Village bistro. Inside, its cozy interior is the setting for an amiable philosophical discussion among writers, over dinner, on which is harder to write: comedy or tragedy. One of them gets things started by relating a story about a young woman whose unannounced appearance disrupts another sophisticated Manhattan dinner party consisting of gourmet French-style food (coquilles Saint Jacques, Chilean sea bass with an herb crust, and so on). Two other writers then exchange comic and tragic versions of the story. Thus, no less than three sophisticated dining occasions provide the narrative catalyst for the parallel-universe adventures of Melinda and Melinda. Later on, however, we'll see how Chinese, not French, food wins the day.

Ordeal, or Meal, of Civility

It is not just the foods that Jews eat but also their foodways — how they behave while eating them — that are key signifiers of their difference from the gentile world. The struggle of Eastern European Jews in Western society can be characterized as what Norbert Elias and John Murray Cuddihy called the "civilizing process" and "the ordeal of civility," respectively.[10] The "ordeal of civility" is the Jew's attempt to mold his or her behavior, speech, and even thoughts into more "civil" (Christian and WASP) behavior. As Cuddihy explains,

> Jewish Emancipation involved Jews in collisions with the differentiations of Western society. The differentiations most foreign to the *shtetl* subculture of Yiddishkeit were those of public from private behavior and of manners from morals. Jews were being asked, in effect, to become bourgeois, and to become bourgeois quickly. The problem of behavior, then, became strategic to the whole problematic of "assimilation." The

modernization process, the civilizational process, and the assimilation process were experienced as one — as the "price of admission" to the bourgeois civil society of the West.[11]

Gentile etiquette, Jon Stratton elaborates, are "those expressive and situational norms ubiquitously if informally institutionalized in the social interaction ritual of our modern Western societies," or "the conventionalised system in which civility is practiced."[12] One of the markers of such civility is dining. Eating in a public or familial setting involves table manners, namely, how to behave in a civilized manner, including knowing how to use the correct cutlery, not to eat noisily, and not to speak with a full mouth.[13] Of course, this discourse on table manners is by no means uniquely Jewish as, in the American context at least, it has come to apply to all ethnic minorities.

However, the "association of Jewishness with vulgarity and lack of cultivation" is a fairly widespread belief "and not least among Jews."[14] The dinner table, therefore, is a test of Jewish civility, and nowhere is this more so than the public dinner table and the locus of fine dining: the restaurant. An eighteenth-century Parisian invention that, although following the French Revolution, also became a place to promote social equality, the restaurant developed, on the middle- and upper-middle-class plane, into "a civilized place normally associated with elegant dining."[15] As Peter Melville explains, "At the social dinner tasting is policed by a taste of a higher kind. The party becomes an aesthetic procession, a performance through which the individual's relation to and consumption of the other is regulated according to aesthetic norms of sociality and table etiquette. The individual learns to present itself tastefully to the other by practising the protocols of 'civilized' conduct."[16] Public eating thus becomes a performance test of Jewish civility. By performing well at the dining table, the Jew demonstrates good taste, as well as consciousness of the aesthetic that defines social class and status. Similarly, performing indecorously at the dining table is an indication either of ignorance of proper decorum or — more damning and dangerous — of inability or unwillingness to abide by genteel (read, gentile) standards.[17]

However, cinematic Jews rarely pass the "civility" test. They interrupt each other continually and argue heatedly, often with food in their mouths. Even ordinary conversations are conducted in loud voices, and their body language does not convey the expected reserve. This is most clearly articulated in *Annie Hall*'s "Grammy Hall" sequence, especially when compared in split screen with Alvy Singer's Jewish family meal, setting a trend that is often replicated in contemporary cinema. Alvy is invited to the house of Annie's WASP parents for an Easter meal. Everything there conspires to remind him that he is a Jew of low status, both in the Halls' and in *his own* eyes, and both as Alvy the protagonist and as Allen the director. The establishing exterior shot shows a largish suburban house surrounded by greenery. Inside, the table is laid with all kinds of gentile delights, including a clearly visible, red Jell-O desert. Jell-O symbolizes *treyf* because it contains the ingredient gelatin, which is derived from the skin and bones of non-kosher animals, in particular pigs; hence, it is a prohibited substance.[18] As comedian Lenny Bruce put it, in his legendary taxonomy of the differences between Jews and gentiles: "Jell-O is goyish."

Desperate to fit in, to pass, Alvy has mimicked what he believes to be the correct attire of WASP gentiles: a sports jacket and plaid shirt (combining the garments of Annie's dad and brother respectively). The opening line spoken by Annie's mother (Colleen Dewhurst) to Grammy Hall (Helen Ludlam) captures the milieu and values of the Halls' all-American suburban home and the family's latent social, class, ethnic, and psychological discomfort over Alvy's Jewishness: "It's a nice ham, this year, Mom." Feeling like a fish out of water and desperate to fit in, Alvy compliments Grammy Hall on her "dynamite ham," which of course, as the quintessential *treyf* meat dish, he has probably never sampled. The utter failure of this gesture, as well as of his sartorial mimicry, is underlined when Allen imagines Alvy imagining Grammy (whom he describes as "a classic Jewish hater") imagining Alvy dressed in the long black coat and hat of a *haredi* (Hasidic) Jew, complete with beard and *peyos* (side curls). (See Shaina Hammerman's chapter in this book for extensive treatment of Alvy's *haredi* image.) He then attempts to make a joke in response to Mom's reference to his fifteen years in psychoanalysis: "Yes, I'm making excellent progress. Pretty soon when I lie down on his couch, I won't have to wear the lobster bib." The (similarly *treyf*) joke falls flat, compounding Alvy's ambivalent feelings of alienation from, yet envy of, Annie's über-WASP Midwestern family, which he sees as stereotypically solid and wholesome but also as bland as "white bread."[19] Alvy's direct address to the camera to describe the family whom he perceives as healthy and American — "not like my family" — not only violates Hollywood convention but also conveys his distance from this hostile and gentile social setting.

The subsequent use of split screen serves to emphasize the differences. The Singers literally dominate the screen as they squeeze the Halls into one-third of the cinematic space. The lower-middle-class Singer family home is remembered as warm, affectionate, loving, exuberant, animated, verbose, and indelicate — in other words, a house full of *menschlekhayt* (simple humanity) — in contrast to the "reticent, tight-lipped, slightly inebriated, sterile" decorum of the all-American Halls.[20] As Desser and Friedman point out, "When the Singers and another couple (presumably an aunt and uncle) are seen at the dinner table — the mother standing and everyone talking at once — the behavioral differences between them and the sedate, polite Halls are obvious. While the Halls speak of swapmeets and boating, the Singers discuss failure and disease. The ordeal of civility indeed!"[21]

Allen's Seders

Jewish "incivility" and its other stereotypically indecorous traits (the focus on failure and disease, the nagging Jewish mother, the tawdry materialism, and the excesses of religiosity) have also been skewered by Allen, to be sure. But when it comes to food and foodways, his own kind tends to win out. This applies especially to the Seder meal, the centerpiece of the celebration of Passover. An ur-religious holiday commemorating the ancient Hebrews' deliverance from Egyptian bondage and their bestowal of the Ten Commandments, the Passover ritual is a family repast revolving entirely around food, much of which is given symbolic significance: matzo standing for the flatbread Jews were forced to bake during their hasty flight to freedom; a pungent herb such as horseradish standing for the bitterness of slavery; the dipping of the finger into a glass of red wine standing for the ten plagues; and so on. An added irony is that the Last Supper was itself a Seder (Jesus and the disciples were, after all, *frum* [pious] Jews), and the sacred wafer and wine that transmute Christ's body and blood stem from the book of Exodus's matzo and wine. Note even here, however, how the Seder foods, which combined religious content with family communion, in the Christian appropriation have been rendered "purely" religious, with the *menshlikayt* bleached out.

Allen's use of the Seder in his films, unlike most other of his Judaic references, tends to defer to its foundational religious and familial significance. This is particularly evident in *Crimes and Misdemeanors* (and briefly in *Hollywood Ending* [2002]) where a fondly remembered Passover Seder provides a safe space for Allen to explore the interior psychological condition of its protagonist Judah Rosenthal (Martin Landau). Judah, an outwardly successful ophthalmologist, whom we meet being feted at the beginning of the movie at a, no less significantly, gala dinner in his honor, has not only conducted a secret extramarital affair but also had his lover murdered when she threatens to reveal the relationship to his wife and family. Torn (significantly, the word *treyf* derives from the Hebrew for "torn") by what he has done, Judah returns to his boyhood home in Brooklyn. Wandering around the old house he peers through the dining-room door, Bergman-style, into his childhood, where a Passover Seder with the extended family is in full flow and a heated debate ensues between his father and his aunt over faith, morality, power, and the "eyes of God."

Besides its relevance to the film's plot (Judah, who has committed murder, engages his father in a discussion about crime, punishment, and guilt), the Seder scene is also important because the family is gathered around the dinner table, united in its observation of the traditional ritual. Even though they are arguing over complex moral issues and cannot reconcile their views, disputation, building on the Talmud, is presented as a staple of the Jewish diet. It is also significant that Allen uses this fondly remember Seder as the scene for "the external dramatization of an internal psychic debate over conscience," in contrast to the gentile meal in *Annie Hall*, which revolves around superficial trifles and where Allen deliberately removes Alvy by having him directly address the camera.[22] In *Crimes and Misdemeanors*, in comparison, Judah does not address the audience but interpolates himself directly into a childhood memory, and it is the characters in his memory that respond to his ethical/moral dilemmas.

Woody on Rye and Other Breads

As mentioned earlier, there is a long-standing linkage between Jews and food. Thus, in Allen's movies a corned beef or pastrami sandwich on rye bread, bagels, and other stereotypical Jewish foodstuffs tend to code the

Jewish world in semiotic terms, even if many of these products have long been assimilated into mainstream U.S. and other cultures. In contrast, white bread, in particular Wonder Bread, stands for whiteness not only because of its color but even more so in relation to its comparative blandness, tastelessness, and lack of nutritional value. As Lenny Bruce observed, expanding on his shtick regarding the differences between Jews and goyim, "Pumpernickel is Jewish and, as you know, white bread is very goyish."[23] White bread also signifies the competitive world of *goyim naches* (pleasure for the goyim, or the games that non-Jews play), especially its class divisions, distinguishing "those who ate white bread," symbolizing an "unattainable style of life," from those who did not.[24] Similarly, presumably also for its unnaturally white color, Nora Ephron commented on the socioethnic construction of mayonnaise, in particular Hellman's, as *goyische*.[25] This mirrors the view of Mel Brooks of a non-Jewish Midwesterner as someone who "drives a white Ford station wagon, eats white bread, vanilla milkshakes, and mayonnaise."[26] A savvy audience watching an Allen film will pick up on what Stratton calls "Jewish moments," those incidents or bits of behavior that "those in the know" will decode as ethnically specific markers and general audiences will disregard or take as universal.[27] Thus when Mickey (Allen) converts to Catholicism in *Hannah and Her Sisters* (1986) and returns to his apartment carrying a brown paper bag from which he is shown removing a series of items — a crucifix, a prayer book, a framed picture of Jesus, a loaf of Wonder Bread, and a jar of Hellman's mayonnaise — "insiders" understand that Mickey's newly found faith will not last. He "will not be able to abandon his heritage for a culture of white bread and mayo."[28]

The use of foods as tropes for the clash of ethnic cultures is illustrated again in *Annie Hall*. In a reversal of the Easter dinner to come, Annie clearly feels out of place in a Jewish delicatessen. With no idea of how to order "properly" in such an establishment, she requests pastrami on white bread "with mayonnaise, tomatoes, and lettuce." The joke works on two levels. While pastrami (despite its Turkish origins) is coded as (New York) Jewish, by asking to have it with mayonnaise on white bread Annie has violated New York Jewish tradition, which "prescribes" that pastrami must be eaten on rye bread with mustard. As comic Milton Berle quipped, "Anytime a person goes to a delicatessen and orders a pastrami on white bread, somewhere a Jew dies." Alvy visibly winces as she orders, and Annie's sandwich becomes emblematic of the cultural rift between them, hinting at the problems that their relationship will face in attempting to merge "oil and water."

Allen also deploys the Reuben sandwich, as a semiotic device, to code Jewish difference. Although *halachically treyf* (nonkosher according to normative rabbinic Judaism) on multiple levels, the Reuben sandwich — a grilled combination of corned beef, Swiss cheese, and sauerkraut (or coleslaw) on sourdough pumpernickel bread — is a clear signifier of Jewish ethnicity. Its specific origins may be unclear, but it is associated inextricably with New York Jewish delicatessens, as well as its name, which, from its Old Testament origins, also implies Jewishness.[29] In *Scoop* (2006), Sidney Waterman (Allen) finds himself playing poker at an exclusive elitist gentlemen's club in London among a group of upper-class Brits. Doubly defined by his difference (a lower-class Jew from Brooklyn), Sidney feels out of place but asserts his Jewish alterity by reference to the Reuben sandwich.

> SIDNEY: Actually I bought my first Reubens with poker winnings.
> INTERLOCUTOR: You bought a Rubens painting?
> SIDNEY: Not a painting. A sandwich.

Of course, Waterman's Jewishness here is defined by not only the food reference but also, as in many of the previous and subsequent examples, his use of humor to express it.

Finally, bagels, being a Jewish tradition imported into the United States and other Western countries, stand as perhaps the quintessential culinary signifier of Jewishness to the public at large, but also often mark the Jew as a subject of humorous difference in the world of the goyim. Allen uses this device in a variety of movies. A bagel on Val Waxman's (Allen) desk in *Hollywood Ending* marks him thus, as does his proclamation: "I'm gonna order a corned beef sandwich as she's talking to her lover on the phone." In *Celebrity* (1998), Rabbi Kaufman (Kenneth Edelson), a guest on a talk show, asks "Where are the bagels? Did the skinheads eat all the bagels already?"

Safe *Treyf*

A distinctly non-Jewish food that has become closely associated with Jews is Chinese food. The consumption of Chinese food amongst New York Ashkenazi Jews has grown in such popularity since the 1950s that Gaye

Tuchman and Harry Levine remark, "Cantonese Chinese restaurants had become a New York Jewish family tradition." Indeed, Chinese food has even earned the name "safe *treyf*." The main reason for this is that Chinese food generally excludes dairy and is thus closer to kashrut, and when there is *treyf* in the dishes it is in such small quantities as to be of no account. In Tuchman and Levine's study, one woman reminisced how her aunt had three sets of dishes at that time: the traditional dairy and meat sets as required by kashrut for the separation of dairy and meat products and a disposable set exclusively for takeout Chinese meals. Another Jewish interviewee recalled that in his small town outside Seattle, eating Chinese food was regarded as sophisticated in the same way as was going to an art house movie, precisely the sort of theater in which Allen's movies play.[30]

Allen makes use of Chinese food and restaurants in many of his films, firmly locating him in the New York Jewish milieu. Yet, Chinese food signifies more than simply Jewish urban geography for Allen; paraphrasing Shakespeare, if Chinese food be the food of love, eat on, says Allen. For him it has a certain frisson, a sexual dimension, which plays on the various meanings of the phrase "fresh meat." Certainly, Allen connects the consumption of animal flesh with sex as in *Husbands and Wives* (1992), when Gabe (Allen) fondly sketches a portrait of a former lover as a "sexually carnivorous" woman. Allen's proclivity for such Asian "food" was shown as early as *What's Up, Tiger Lily?* when an underworld flunky boasts that the gangsters have just received another shipment of women, "loin, flank, sirloin: why this is the best shipment of meat we had this year." And when two "delicious" sisters are introduced, their names reflect this intertwining — Teri Yaki (Mie Hama) and Suki Yaki (Akiko Wakabayashi) — they are "dishes" in both senses of the term.[31] The movie has an ending unrelated to the plot, in which China Lee, the Asian American Playboy Playmate and then wife of Allen's comic idol Mort Sahl, and who does not appear elsewhere in the film, performs a striptease while Allen, who is eating an apple, explains that he promised he would put her in the film somewhere.

Richard Feldstein has commented on this sequence: "There is again introduced a term-by-term reconversion exemplifying a gastronomical equation between food and sexuality. Interestingly, it is such oral needs coupled with sexual aggression that drives various gangland factions in an overriding compulsion to find their fetishized object of desire, the great egg-salad recipe: 'one so good you could plotz.'"[32] Of course, one can't help but note that Allen's equation between Chinese food and sexual desire would bear fruit on the personal level in his own subsequent romantic and marital proclivities. As for his movies, in *Love and Death* (1975), when Sonja (Diane Keaton) suggests having sex with Boris (Allen), he agrees with the words, "Nice idea! I'll bring the soy sauce." In *Whatever Works* (2009), against the backdrop of Chinese restaurants and stores, Boris Yellnikoff (Larry David), a Jewish misanthropic physicist, in a direct address to the audience, informs us that he has fallen for the much younger Melody St. Ann Celestine (Evan Rachel Wood), a fresh-faced innocent from a town in the South, who still believes in the world she conquered in beauty pageants. Later, in front of the same Chinese restaurants, Boris describes the sexual liberation, by a Jewish friend, of Melody's mother (Patricia Clarkson). Here Allen slyly equates Chinese food not only with sexual desire but also with Jewish sexual potency.

At the same time, Chinese food for Allen is a source of consolation and reassurance. Thus Chinese food appears in an uplifting scene in *Manhattan* (1979), as well as in the opening sequence of *Husbands and Wives* when Jack (Sydney Pollack) and Sally (Judy Davis) announce their separation to a shocked Gabe (Allen) and hurt Judy (Mia Farrow). Confused, they go out for comfort food: dinner at a Chinese restaurant. In *Deconstructing Harry*, as indicated in the opening epigram, Allen even idealizes the afterlife as a Chinese eatery. Harry makes a deal with the Devil (Billy Crystal) and gains his Jewish father's release from hell. But his father states that as a Jew he does not believe in Heaven. When asked "So where do you want to go?" he replies, "A Chinese restaurant."

In this fashion, Chinese food is particularly key to Allen's comic heist-cum-social-climbing caper *Small Time Crooks* (2000). A key planning sequence for the bank robbery at the beginning of the film takes place in a Chinese restaurant. A cookie (although not a fortune one) shop becomes the cover for the robbery, which is disastrous. Yet, having failed to rob the bank, Ray Winkler (Allen) and his wife Frenchy (Tracey Ullman) make it big in the cookie business. Now fabulously nouveau riche, Frenchy attempts to translate that wealth into social standing and cultivation. No doubt in a pun on her name, Frenchy's idea of Old World sophistication reaches a level of vulgarity that only serves to emphasize her and Ray's parvenu status.

This also means a regime of such fancy French foods as frogs legs, snails, and truffles, all of which Ray detests.[33] One night he cheats on Frenchy's French diet and goes out for Chinese food with her cousin May (Elaine May). Ray waxes lyrical about the meal's virtues: "Dinner was so great... the MSG and the grease... what a treat. I'm so sick of continental food every night." Chinese food, along with baseball, pizza, poker, and turkey meatballs, represents Ray's nostalgic yearning for the earlier, simpler life before he was rich.

Similarly, in the comic narrative strand of *Melinda and Melinda*, when nebbisher out-of-work husband Hobie (Will Ferrell), who is reduced to playing second fiddle to his much more successful wife (Amanda Peet), burns the Chilean sea bass with lime crust at a sophisticated Manhattan dinner party, it is Chinese takeout that is ordered as a replacement. That the dish of "Ants Climb a Tree" (*mayi shang shu*, an informal spicy Szechwanese combination of cellophane noodles and chopped meat) provides a substitute for the Michelin-style dish Hobie had ruined, suggests that this earthier peasant food, whose mundane image of tree-climbing ants contrasts with the metaphors of phoenix and dragon tails of Chinese haute cuisine, is what they really wanted to be eating in the first place. They don't even dispense with the disposable boxes, eating straight out of them with their chopsticks. By having the figuratively castrated (and later actually cuckolded) Hobie trash the French cuisine seems also to suggest that while it may be okay (even a step up) for a Jew (Hobie is clearly an Allenish surrogate) to eat such high-class fare, preparing it is another matter entirely.

Sondra Pransky (Scarlett Johansson) in *Scoop*, while playing private detective, masquerades as Jade Julliard Spence to hide her Jewishness. Yet, her ethnic self cannot be fully contained behind her disguise. Because she likes Chinese food, she asks for a Chinese restaurant recommendation in London. It is a moment of slippage but, for the informed audience, a "Jewish moment," hinting at her hidden ethnic identity.

Perhaps most profoundly, in *Alice* (1990), Dr. Yang (Keye Luke), an immigrant Chinese healer in New York, sends the eponymous protagonist (Mia Farrow) on an Alice in Wonderland journey of self-discovery via a series of magic herbs and potions that eventually lead her to abandon her upscale but shallow existence for one of social service.

Finally, Allen has even compared his filmmaking craft to Chinese food:

I've been around a long time, and some people may just get tired of me, which I can understand. I've tried to keep my films different over the years, but it's like they complain, "We've eaten Chinese food every day this week." I want to say, "Well, yes, but you had a shrimp meal and you had a pork meal and you had a chicken meal." They say, "Yes, yes, but it's all Chinese food." That's the way I feel about myself. I have a certain amount of obsessive themes and a certain amount of things I'm interested in and no matter how different the film is, whether it's *Small Time Crooks* here or *Zelig* there, you find in the end that it's Chinese food.[34]

Food, Sex, and Shellfish

As we have already seen, Allen's oeuvre is shot through with the comingling of food and sex, and there's more to come. "Food and sex are always good for a laugh," he once said.[35] In *Love and Death* when Countess Alexandrovna (Olga Georges-Picot) invites Boris to tea, he proceeds to "run a quick check" of her erogenous zones.[36] In *Annie Hall*, Alvy says, "We'll kiss now... then go eat." When Allen arrives at Keaton's apartment in *Manhattan*, hoping to have sex, he asks, "Have you got anything to eat here?" Lunch, in particular, has sexual connotations: in *Manhattan* he tells his young date, "You'll have lunch — and attachments form," while in *The Purple Rose of Cairo* (1985) he suggests buying lunch as a prelude to sex.

Deconstructing Harry includes one of the most unusual scenes linking food and sex in Allen's post–Mia Farrow menu. Harry (Allen), a famous writer whose work intersects uncomfortably with his life, recounts one of his short stories in which Helen (Demi Moore), patterned after his sister Doris (Caroline Aaron), is a *ba'alat teshuvah* ("she who has returned," referring to a formerly nonreligious Jewess who adopts more Orthodox ways), whom he caricatures as "Jewish with a vengeance," "like a born again Christian but a Jew." In one especially humorous (or blasphemous, depending on your point of view) sequence, Harry explains how "Jews, of course, fearing a wrathful and vengeful God" recite blessings over everything: wine, challah, and candles. Manifesting the zeal of the newly converted *ba'alat teshuvah*, Helen obsessively and compulsively blesses *everything*, including her husband's penis before performing fellatio, using the Hebrew words "*borey p'ri ha*-blow job" (literally translating as "He who creates the fruit of the blow job"), mixing prayer, profanity, pornography, and perversity, but also ridiculing Judaism and its penchant for benedictions.[37]

Along similarly blasphemous lines, Allen occasionally links sex with kashrut (kosher food laws), but only for those able to decode the signs. Rarely does Allen allude explicitly to kashrut, and most of his characters do not observe the dietary laws. A rare exception occurs in *Radio Days* when, on Yom Kippur, the Jewish family (broadly based on Allen's own) is upset because their communist Jewish neighbors are playing the radio loudly and ignoring the fast. Abe (Josh Mostel) goes next door to complain, but he does not return for an hour. When Abe does, at last, come back, he has rejected Judaism and is spouting the communist line and has broken the fast by eating, of all things, pork chops, clams, French fries, and chocolate pudding. When his wife tells him that God will punish him, Abe begins to have chest pains, but it turns out to be indigestion.

Probably the classic articulation of the food-sex conjunction in Allen's oeuvre comes in what many consider to be the most outrageous and offensive sketch in *Everything You Always Wanted to Know About Sex* (*But Were Afraid to Ask)* (1972). In answer to the question "What are sex perverts?" Allen produces a parody of the game show *What's My Line?* called "What's My Perversion?" in which panelists like Regis Philbin must guess the odd behaviors of contestants instead of their professions. At the end of the show an elderly contestant from the Midwest, Rabbi Chaim Baumel (Baruch Lumet), who corrects host Jack Barry on how to pronounce his given name, is allowed to live out his sadomasochistic humiliation fantasy by being tied up and spanked, while his wife sits at his feet and is made to violate a kashrut taboo by being forced to eat pork ribs. The juxtaposition of forbidden sexual pleasure and prohibited foods in this sequence suggests that "the Jew lusts after all that has been denied him — sexual pleasure and pork."[38]

Since, according to Leviticus, fish is only kosher if it has fins and scales, those without and, by extension, all shellfish (indeed anything with a shell) is forbidden (they are also outlawed because anything that creeps and crawls is verboten). A symbolic or allegorical interpretation of these kashrut laws suggests that because fins and scales on a fish are signs of endurance and self-control, the lack of them on any sea-based creature can be construed to mean wild, impetuous abandon, as well as both literal and symbolic transgression.[39] This is further borne out by the fact that the epithet "shiksa" (or "shikse"), employed widely in modern Yiddish and English to refer to a non-Jewish woman, etymologically derives from the biblical Hebrew *sheketz* and is translated into English as "'unclean creature,' reptile; abomination, detestation, uncleanliness."[40] In the biblical dietary laws, *sheketz* denotes a dirty, unpleasant creature, unfit for consumption, such as shellfish and insects. The threat posed by shellfish and snails is the same as that posed by a non-Jewish woman.

Perhaps this is another reason paranoid Jewish gun nut of *Anything Else* (2003), David Dobel (Allen), who sees anti-Semitism everywhere, "make[s] it a practice never to ingest bivalves," so he can stay 100 percent pure and alert, focused on the dangers around him.[41] In the same film, in a reworking of an earlier gag from *Everything You Always Wanted to Know About Sex*, the non-Jewish Amanda (Christina Ricci) asks, "Shall we order caviar?" as an amuse-bouche before making love to her Jewish boyfriend, fledgling comic writer Jerry Falk (Jason Biggs) — another Allen surrogate, or in this film, his character's protégé — in a hotel room. Not heeding the warning in *Vicky Cristina Barcelona* the titular Cristina (Scarlett Johansson) eats shellfish for supper, which gives her food poisoning, thus preventing Juan Antonio (Javier Bardem) from seducing her. This allows him to seduce her friend Vicky (Rebecca Hall) instead, setting up the love triangle plot of the film.

Shellfish, in particular the king of shellfish, lobster, stands as a code for wanton excess in the symbolic interpretation of kashrut. In this vein, for Allen, lobsters are the symbol of insatiable sexual attraction and sexual liberation. They symbolize love affairs, as opposed to the more humdrum foods of marriage. In *A Midsummer Night's Sex Comedy* (1982), when his wife interrogates him about a previous relationship, Allen's character nervously replies, "I went out with her *once* . . . and had a couple of *lobsters* . . . that's *it*!" In *Whatever Works*, against the backdrop of two large signs advertising lobster, Boris informs us that he has fallen for Melody. And in *Annie Hall*, Alvy and Annie spontaneously laugh at crawling crustaceans on the kitchen floor as they awkwardly prepare a lobster dinner at a beach house in the Hamptons: "Maybe we should just call the police. Dial 911. It's the lobster squad." Alvy is fearful of the creatures, and when he realizes that one big lobster has crawled behind the refrigerator, he jokes, "It'll turn up in our bed at night. Talk to him. You speak shellfish. . . . Annie, there's a big lobster behind the refrigerator. I can't get it out. . . . Maybe if I put a little dish of butter sauce here with a nutcracker, it will run out the other side? . . . We should have gotten steaks, 'cause they don't have legs. They don't run around." The exuberance and vitality of the scene conveys the strength of his feelings for Annie but also just how out of his depth Alvy feels in the *goyische* Hamptons with the *treyf* lobsters. Thereafter, he attempts to capture lost love with a woman who will not laugh over wandering lobsters. Later on in the film, he proves more adept, albeit only slightly more so, at killing other crawly creatures: two spiders that are in Annie's bathroom.

Allen's ambivalence toward lobsters in *Annie Hall* is even greater toward land-based invertebrates. His more recent characters show a particular disgust for snails. This may, in part, be attributable to his New York Jewish upbringing in which snails probably did not feature that often on the family menu. It may also, in part, be a humorous dig at the culinary pretensions of social climbing parvenus or the nouveau riche, or a nod and wink to the omnivorous cosmopolitanism of the French, enthusiastic imbibers of his movies, which not only often open and regularly play to packed houses in France but also often reference or are set in Paris (*Everyone Says I Love You* [1996], *Hollywood Ending*, and *Midnight in Paris*). In *Hollywood Ending*, Val describes his ex-wife's (Téa Leoni) love affair with Hal (Treat Williams) thus: "You had the escargot that afternoon. So disgusting. Sex and snails with that roast beef from Beverly Hills."[42] Allen's use of snails and oysters here hints at Hal's narcissistic, libertine, all-consuming but entirely self-directed, passions, warped sexuality, and licentiousness. Hal's turpitude, as expressed through his sybaritic and *treyf* tastes, is designed to invoke repugnance in the audience and to censure the man who stole his wife away from him. Of course, the attribution of sexual depravity to Hal rather than Val is highly ironic in light of the Farrow/Previn scandal (a strategy in some of Allen's postscandal films that Vincent Brook's chapter further explores).

In *Small Time Crooks*, Ray refuses to eat snails because "a snail leaves a little trail of scum in the yard when it walks." It is also surely not coincidental that the comment occurs in a seafood restaurant specializing in oysters. Showing his class- and ethnically inflected ignorance, Ray confuses truffles with oysters believing that pigs sniff out the pearls in oysters. Elsewhere oysters stand as a female sexual metaphor: as Helen Sinclair (Dianne Wiest) tells David Shayne (John Cusack) in *Bullets Over Broadway* (1994), "You stand on the brink of greatness, the world will open to you like an oyster. No, not like an oyster. The world will open to you like a magnificent vagina."

The final word on food and foodways in Allen's films must be left to a scene in *Deconstructing Harry*. One of Harry's stories aptly summarizes the ironic, grotesque, satirical, subversive, even absurdist meanings that Allen's culinary-based humor, at its best, conveys. The story, which Harry's sister Doris recounts as a classic example of Harry's Jewish self-hatred (of which Allen himself has often been accused), describes an elderly Jewish couple, Max (Hy Anzell) and Dolly (Shifra Lerer) Pincus, who are thinly disguised versions of Harry and Doris's parents. The short vignette culminates with Dolly discovering, at the end of forty years of marriage, not only that Max had previously been married but also that he had killed and eaten his first wife and their children. When Dolly confronts him over his horrid misdeeds — naturally, at the dinner table — he matter-of-factly explains, "Some bury, some burn, I ate!"

Notes

1. See Douglas Brode, *Woody Allen: His Films and Career* (Secaucus, NJ: Citadel, 1992); Ronald D. LeBlanc, "*Love and Death* and Food: Woody Allen's Comic Use of Gastronomy," in *The Movies of Woody Allen: Critical Essays*, ed. Charles L. P. Silet, 100–111 (Lanham, MD: Scarecrow, 2006); Nathan Abrams, "'I'll Have Whatever She's Having': Jewish Food on Film," in *Reel Food: Essays on Food and Film*, ed. Anne Bowers, 87–100 (New York: Routledge, 2004); Nathan Abrams, *The New Jew in Film: Exploring Jewishness and Judaism in Contemporary Cinema* (New Brunswick, NJ: Rutgers University Press, 2012).

2. David Desser and Lester D. Friedman, *American-Jewish Filmmakers: Traditions and Trends* (Urbana: University of Illinois Press, 1993), 85.

3. Quoted in Desser and Friedman, *American-Jewish Filmmakers*, 124.

4. LeBlanc, "*Love and Death*," 106.

5. Quoted in Danielle Barrin, "The Elusive Essence of Jew-ness," *Hollywood Jew: A Blog by Danielle Barrin,*" March 2, 2012, http://www.jewishjournal.com/hollywoodjew.

6. Sigmund Freud, *Jokes and Their Relation to the Unconscious* (Harmondsworth, UK: Penguin, 1994); LeBlanc, "*Love and Death*," 106.

7. Brode, *Woody Allen*, 69, and throughout Brode's book wherever food is discussed in relation to each individual film.

8. LeBlanc "*Love and Death*," 103, 106.

9. J. Hoberman, "Double Negative: Woody's Latest a Tricksy Soap Opera," *Village Voice*, March 8, 2005.

10. John Murray Cuddihy, *The Ordeal of Civility: Freud, Marx, Lévi-Strauss, and the Jewish Struggle with Modernity* (Boston: Beacon, 1978); Norbert Elias, *The Civilizing Process: The History of Manners*, vol. 1, trans. Edmund Jephcott (New York: Urizen, 1968).

11. Cuddihy, *Ordeal of Civility*, 12–13.

12. Jon Stratton, *Coming Out Jewish: Constructing Ambivalent Identities* (London: Routledge, 2000), 285, 308.

13. David Bell and Gill Valentine, *Consuming Geographies: We Are Where We Eat* (London: Routledge, 1997), 64.

14. Norman Podhoretz, *Making It* (New York: Random House, 1967), 161.

15. LeBlanc, "Love and Death," 106.

16. Peter Melville, "A 'Friendship of Taste': The Aesthetics of Eating Well in Kant's *Anthropology from a Pragmatic Point of View*," in *Cultures of Taste/Theories of Appetite: Eating Romanticism*, ed. Timothy Morton, 203–16 (New York: Palgrave Macmillan, 2004), 209.

17. Gerwyn Owen, "Taste of Film: Food and Drink in the Movies of Max Ophuls" (unpublished master's thesis, Bangor University, 2009), 31.

18. See Nathan Abrams, "'More Than One Million Mothers Know It's the REAL Thing': The Rosenbergs, Jell-O, Old-Fashioned Gefilte Fish, and 1950s America," in *Edible Ideologies: Representing Food and Meaning*, ed. Katie LeBesco and Peter Naccarato, 79–103 (Ithaca: State University of New York Press, 2008).

19. Desser and Friedman, *American-Jewish Filmmakers*, 81.

20. Sam B. Girgus, *The Films of Woody Allen*, 2nd ed. (Cambridge: Cambridge University Press, 2002), 58.

21. Desser and Friedman, *American-Jewish Filmmakers*, 81.

22. Girgus, *Films of Woody Allen*, 142.

23. Quoted in William Novak and Moshe Waldoks, eds., *The Big Book of Jewish Humor* (New York: Harper & Row, 1981), 60.

24. Andrew R. Heinze, *Adapting to Abundance: Jewish Immigrants, Mass Consumption and the Search for American Identity* (New York: Columbia University Press, 1990), 34–35. In *Glengarry Glen Ross* (directed by David Mamet, 1992), for example, a Jew insults a gentile colleague with the words "you're *scum*, you're fucking white-bread."

25. See Deborah Tannen, *Talking Voices: Repetition, Dialogue, and Imagery in Conversational Discourse* (Cambridge: Cambridge University Press, 1989), 156.

26. Quoted in Desser and Friedman, *American-Jewish Filmmakers*, 128.

27. Stratton, *Coming Out Jewish*, 300.

28. Sander H. Lee, *Eighteen Woody Allen Films Analyzed: Anguish, God and Existentialism* (Jefferson, NC: McFarland, 2002), 111.

29. Reuben was the eldest son of Jacob and Leah, from whom one of the twelve tribes of Israel took its name.

30. Gaye Tuchman and Harry Levine, "Safe Treyf," *Brandeis Review* (1996): 28–30.

31. Brode, *Woody Allen*, 49.

32. Richard Feldstein, "Displaced Feminine Representation in Woody Allen's Cinema," in *Discontented Discourses: Feminism/Textual Intervention/Psychoanalysis*, ed. Marleen S. Barr and Richard Feldstein, 69–86 (Urbana: University of Illinois Press, 1989), 71.

33. Another way Allen shows his comic contempt for the foods of high-class society is when the extremely straight Jewish doctor Doug Ross (Gene Wilder) orders it as a prelude to having sex with a sheep in *Everything You Always Wanted to Know About Sex* (*But Were Afraid to Ask)*. Since Doug has fallen in love with the sheep, he may, absurdly, be trying to impress her with this gastronomic symbol of high society. By combining caviar with sheep sex, Allen achieves a grotesque effect. At the same time, since caviar is, in general, *treyf*, deriving as it does from nonkosher fish, it may be read as an oblique "Jewish moment" that is commenting on the *treyf*-ness of Doug's actions.

34. Allen, quoted in "Biography for Woody Allen," IMDb, accessed December 2011, http://www.imdb.com.

35. Brode, *Woody Allen*, 48.

36. LeBlanc "*Love and Death*," 103.

37. Girgus, *Films of Woody Allen*, 162.

38. Patricia Erens, *The Jew in American Cinema* (Bloomington: Indiana University Press, 1984), 316.

39. I have drawn this discussion on the symbolic or allegorical interpretation of the kashrut laws from Isaac Rosenfeld, "Adam and Eve on Delancey Street," *Commentary* 8, no. 4 (1949): 385–87; and Jean Soler, "The Dietary Prohibitions of the Hebrews," *New York Review of Books*, June 14, 1979, http://www.columbia.edu.

40. Reuben Alcalay, *The Complete Hebrew-English Dictionary* (Bridgeport, CT: Prayerbook Press/Hartmore House, 1974), 2711. I am grateful to Josh Lambert for pointing this out.

41. Echoing Alvy Singer's famous paranoid mishearing of "did you eat?" as "Jew eat?" in *Annie Hall*, the ultraparanoid Dobel mishears a man in a restaurant allegedly tell his companions, "Jews start all wars."

42. The close juxtaposition of sex and snails here can be read as an homage to the infamous and censored scene in *Spartacus* (Stanley Kubrick, 1960) when Roman Marcus Licinius Crassus (Laurence Olivier) attempts to seduce his newly acquired Greek slave boy Antoninus (Tony Curtis).

JAMES FISHER

Schlemiel on Broadway
Woody Allen's Jewish Identity in His Stage Plays from *Don't Drink the Water* to *Honeymoon Motel*

Woody Allen's enduring screen persona as an urban schlemiel has remained fundamentally the same across the years, whether in comic or dramatic works, and whether or not Allen himself played the role. Rife with neuroses and skepticism, caught between the orthodox traditions of his Jewish heritage and secular modern America, Allen's character is also a romantic and, more often than not, surrenders a certain amount of his skepticism to a guardedly optimistic view of romance and human nature even when surrounded by evidence to the contrary. In his most romantic and comic films and plays, love usually conquers all obstacles (the heart wants what it wants, as he famously stated at the height of the Farrow/Previn scandal), including his outsider status as a Jewish American. His persona as a Jew — and those aspects of his ethnicity that have evolved as popular cultural stereotypes — has been exploited by Allen throughout his career and proven to be a significant boon but also a challenge to the endurance of his achievement.

Allen's use of Jewish humor is founded, to a great extent, within a long tradition reaching back to the mid-nineteenth century. In that period in America, Yiddish theater established itself, both in dramatic and comic forms, as a rich resource of traditions that have proven enduring. Yiddish theater in its purest state essentially died away by the 1930s, but it had provided characters (stereotypical and otherwise), a uniquely Jewish brand of irony, and the absurd view of life's vicissitudes central to Allen's work and found in subsequent forms often dominated by Jewish performers and writers: late nineteenth- and early twentieth-century vaudeville and burlesque, Broadway musicals and comedies, and manifestations of these seen in the developing movie and broadcast media. Allen, whose work as a stand-up comic, playwright, short-story writer, and filmmaker is part of a continuum of comic traditions born in Yiddish theater, self-identifies as a Jew. Yet he also sees the comic persona of the Jew as something of an American Everyman, as a reflection of a culture made up of outsiders from a range of ethnic origins seeking to be part of a still young nation that is forming an identity while retaining skepticism about the values articled as quintessentially American. Allen's indebtedness to the traditions of Jewish comedy dating back to Yiddish theater (though he was only a child when the golden age of Yiddish theater in America ended) reflects a complex intersection of the rigidities of Old World tradition with the rapid pace of American life in the twentieth century. This dynamic has been deeply worked into the cultural DNA of Jewish writers and performers, and Allen is no exception, though he is unique in the ways in which he reveals comic tensions in the American melting pot where, as another Jewish American writer, Tony Kushner, has posited, "nothing melted."[1]

In the first four decades of Allen's career, he took the role of protagonist in his comic plays and films, but in the years during and following the Farrow/Previn scandal, Allen increasingly deferred to younger actors. Most (John Cusack, Kenneth Branagh, Jason Biggs, Will Ferrell, Owen Wilson) have been non-Jewish, and few have exhibited culturally defined Jewish aspects of character as obviously as has Allen. But this did not deter him from continuing to feature Jewish humor and to imbue the comic protagonists with aspects of the schlemiel. A sizable portion of the large Jewish audience in New York theater seems to appreciate the sort of Jewish comedy often (and increasingly) considered stereotypical by many Jews and non-Jews. This intriguing paradox is revealing in regard to the ways Jews see themselves in modern America. The history of Yiddish theater offers a clue to this Jewish self-identification, as this tradition sprang up for a Jewish audience, and its creation of characters and jokes now often viewed as stereotypical explains, to some extent, that Jews of Allen's generation view this type of humor as solely their own.

The Plays: An Introduction

Allen's earliest Broadway comedies, *Don't Drink the Water* (1966) and *Play It Again, Sam* (1969), are formative in regard to his depictions of Jewish American life and, especially so with *Play It Again, Sam*, in the creation of his schlemiel persona. He subsequently has made only periodic returns to playwriting, but Allen's work on the stage presents a consistency in regard to Jewish humor demonstrated in his most recent return to Broadway with *Honeymoon Motel* (2011). His theater work generally seems to hold firmly to the early roots of his comedy even as ethnic humor has increasingly become controversial for audiences, as critical reaction to *Honeymoon Motel* makes all too evident.

Offered on a bill of one-act plays with works by Elaine May and Ethan Coen, *Honeymoon Motel* is a broad farce centered on a typical Allenesque schlemiel, Jerry Spector (played in the Broadway premiere by Steve Guttenberg), a middle-aged Long Island Jew who finds himself in a cheesy motel love nest with his stepson's bride, Nina Roth (Ari Graynor), with whom he has fled in the midst of the wedding ceremony. Nina, still wearing her wedding dress, and Jerry, in a tux, are trailed to the motel by the shocked wedding party, including Jerry's wife, the beleaguered stepson groom, Nina's stunned parents, family friends, and, most outrageously, the presiding rabbi. As a fever pitch of recriminations and "kvetching" ensue, as *New York Times* critic Charles Isherwood describes it, Allen "grabs at anything and everything — waterboarding! Netflix! pogroms! — if it will serve for a good joke."[2] And why not? Unavoidable associations to the Farrow/Previn scandal aside, farcical tradition, dating to the dawn of time, suggests that a farce need be only one thing — funny — and that nothing is sacred and no taboo too sensitive to be overlooked. Some critics applauded Allen's play as the best of the trio of one acts with the overarching title *Relatively Speaking*, with Isherwood finding Allen at his "most firecracker funny" in what several of Isherwood's peers referred to as a "Borscht Belt farce."[3] Others, like Scott Brown, writing in *New York Magazine*, found Allen's comedy "petrified shtick that smells of a writer's sock drawer," yet despite mixed reviews, *Relatively Speaking* racked up 109 performances by its closing on January 29, 2012.[4] More to the point, opposing viewpoints of critics underscore the dilemma for writers of farce, particularly those employing ethnic humor. In short, is Jewish humor funny and, as such, beyond content criticism? Or is it passé, a regressive remnant of the past? And why has Allen continued to mine Jewish humor in his theater work, not to mention even his most recent films, when it risks creating offense?

In a delightfully silly interview for the *New York Times* published a week before *Relatively Speaking* opened, Allen seems to reveal a clue. Elaine May serves as interviewer and Allen, with his tongue firmly planted in his cheek, states that his play has "no redeeming social value" and, in fact, "no entertainment value. I wrote this sprightly little one-acter only to test out my new paper shredder."[5] Allen's joking implies an important point — farcical comedy depicting the absurdity of existence is just that, no more and no less. Most farces — and this is certainly true of *Honeymoon Motel* — laugh in the face of life's absurdity. Typically set in ordinary circumstances where, through the actions of one or another character, extraordinary things happen and the "normal" world spins deliriously out of control. From such chaos emerges commentary on moral values, satire of cultural norms, and revelations of human caprice and the inherent corruption of the species. Allen's recognition of these key aspects of farce means that *Honeymoon Motel* is a farce in the enduring sense that it questions morality and whatever is considered normal. Such issues pervade the play, while humor about Jewish life and social expectations is also rampant. Characters, largely one dimensional, represent aspects of human frailties; instead of stereotypes (in the negative sense), these figures become archetypes.

The play reveals Allen continuing a career-long exploration of the comic form and reaching back to the roots of Jewish humor in the full range of its ironic and absurd perspective, as well as exploring his own autobiography, at least in regard to his heritage. In creating *Honeymoon Motel*, he also mines elements of his own work, in this case including a 1980 story, "Retribution," in which the Jewish protagonist has an affair with the daughter of the woman he intends to marry — and gives in to the girl's advances on his wedding day. The resemblance to *Honeymoon Motel* and, in broad outlines, to the Farrow/Previn scandal, is of course uncanny if also unintentional; the confusions of human behavior, as revealed by farce, are not. At the conclusion of *Honeymoon Motel*, as the aggrieved characters exhaust expression of their frustrations, a pizza delivery man offers what in light of the Farrow/Previn scandal may be the bluntest statement of Allen's aesthetic philosophy (at least in the comic form): "Life is short, and there are no rules."[6]

Farce, in Allen's hands, has strict laws in construction and presentation but depicts a world (a predominantly Jewish world) in which characters violate accepted norms and traditions of mainstream life with the result that not only does the world spin into chaos but also human desires, contradictions, and weaknesses are proven as unresolvable, ending only with the descent of the stage curtain. In this it is possible to understand why Allen, at this late juncture in his distinguished screen career, returns to the stage, and these reasons extend beyond simply testing his new paper shredder. Allen's films have demonstrated a recurrent, if fluctuating, tendency toward a more serious thematic arc, even as he retains his deep-seated romanticism. His return to the absurd madness of farce — and the freedoms inherent in it and in live stage work in general — enables him to tap into a place where the contradictions and absurdities of life, including his own, reign supreme. In addition, his conflicted response to his Jewish American background, which seems ultimately unavoidable in regard to his image as the schlemiel adrift among the conundrums of postmodern American life, remains central.

Although *Honeymoon Motel* marks a blatant return to farce and broadly conceived Jewish humor for Allen, it also begs to be read as a veiled response to the Farrow/Previn scandal — or at least (in accordance with Allen's defense of his actions during the scandal) as a depiction of the inexplicable desires of the heart.[7] Critic John Del Signore gave Allen the benefit of the doubt, writing of the "breezy, almost old-fashioned" *Honeymoon Motel* that "taboos were made to be gleefully broken."[8] Whether Allen broke them gleefully in his own life only he knows, but more than one reviewer pointed to the play's catalytic plot point of Jerry's largely shameless (if somewhat tortured) running away with his stepson's intended bride. Some critics stressed that the situation reflected "uncomfortable similarities" with Allen's personal life, while others analyzed the play's strengths and weaknesses in light of Allen's "earlier, funnier" movies (an attitude Allen had joked about in his 1980 film *Stardust Memories*).[9] Critics mostly (and rather oddly) overlooked connections to Allen's prior stage plays, which in fact may be most informative in understanding *Honeymoon Motel* within Allen's romantic philosophy and his employment of Jewish humor.

Certainly reviewers of *Honeymoon Motel* pointed out the use of Jewish humor and the long stage history from whence it came in their responses to the play. Marilyn Stasio, writing in *Variety*, found *Honeymoon Motel* "a fond salute to the old jokes."[10] And David Sheward, in a review in *Backstage*, called it "intellectual" comedy in which the characters, members of an extended family, "dredge up old grudges," while a rabbi and an analyst "debate the existence of God," who, they posit, exists but "he just has attention deficit disorder."[11]

Surely, however, *Honeymoon Motel* is more than a victory lap for old ethnic jokes; Jewish elements in Allen's work are more complex and varied than this viewpoint would suggest. Critics and audiences, sharply divided over the appropriateness of ethnic humor, express this division in surprising ways. A few reviewers scoffed at what they considered antiquated or offensive Jewish jokes in *Honeymoon Motel*, while, somewhat ironically, the *Jewish Week* critic Ted Merwin called it "riotously funny" and "priceless" in its use of Jewish stereotypes.[12] As Merwin writes, the best lines of the evening are reserved for the stereotypical rabbi character who, "in typical Allen fashion, is the worst hypocrite of all" and does not mind devouring a pepperoni pizza, as long as he eats it out of view, in the bathroom.[13] It should be pointed out, of course, that Allen has at times depicted rabbi characters, such as Rabbi Ben (Sam Waterston) in *Crimes and Misdemeanors* (1989), admittedly a more serious film, with far greater sympathy. On the other hand, the farcical portrayal of the rabbi in *Honeymoon Motel* (as in films such as *Take the Money and Run* [1969]), are quite in keeping with a post-Haskalah (Jewish enlightenment) tradition of modern, urbanized Jews poking fun at the "backwater" Orthodox rabbis of Eastern Europe.[14] Of paramount interest here, however, is the seeming contradiction of the *Jewish Week* reviewer's positive response to Jewish humor in *Honeymoon Motel* versus non-Jewish reviewers' negative responses — a paradox central to understanding Allen's brand of Jewish American humor, the nature of comedy itself, and the ancient traditions of the farcical form.

Jewish Humor: An Introduction

To fully appreciate *Honeymoon Motel* in relation to Allen's use of Jewish humor, and to help explain why, at this late moment in his career, he chose to write again for the stage with such an emphasis, requires a back-to-the-future approach. Tracking this solely through Allen's estimable cinematic output is an incomplete study; indeed, his stage plays are an invaluable aid in understanding his relationship to his Jewish heritage and the evolution of his comic works on both stage and screen. Allen has been generally less attentive to theater, in terms of the quantity of his creative output, which may explain why scholars and biographers have paid comparatively scant attention to his stage achievements. This slight is regrettable from a cinematic standpoint as well, not only because his two most successful full-length plays, *Don't Drink the Water* and *Play It Again, Sam*, which date from the 1960s, are now most known for their subsequent film versions. More significantly, the filmed *Play It Again, Sam* (Herbert Ross, 1972), rather than its literary source, is now regarded as the Ur-text for Allen's iconic schlemiel character.

Allen's other stage writing presented on Broadway thus far include *From A to Z* (1960), a revue for which Allen contributed sketches; *The Floating Light Bulb* (1981), a semiautobiographical comedy-drama set in 1945 that ran at Lincoln Center; and the aforementioned *Honeymoon Motel*. A few Allen one acts have been presented Off-Broadway, including *Central Park West* (1995), offered on a triple bill with David Mamet's *An Interview* and Elaine May's *Hotline*. The bill, with the overarching title *Death Defying Acts*, won Linda Lavin Obie and Lucille Lortel awards and ran for 417 performances. On an Atlantic Theatre Company bill called *Writer's Block* (2003), Allen's one acts *Old Saybrook* (written 1995) and *Riverside Drive* (2003) featured only minimal evidence of Jewish American life in any significant way. The Atlantic also staged a full-length Allen drama, *A Second Hand Memory* (2004), which met with perhaps the most negative critical commentary of Allen's career, dismissed by Isherwood as "unrelentingly glum" in its depiction of emotional detachment within a Brooklyn family in the 1960s.[15] The Wolfe family members depicted in the play are clearly Jews, but there is little humor, as Allen (as with his serious films, to similar critical response) pursued a desire to write in a tragic vein. Allen's prose writings contain short comic plays, including most notably *God* and *Death*, both from 1975, and an Allen story has been adapted as a play, by Ron Krikac and others, called *Death Knocks* (1971, written 1968). *God*, *Death*, and *Death Knocks* feature Allen ruminating on questions of life and death, but in a broadly comic tone, mocking popular culture concepts of death and ideas of an afterlife. The Jewish element is evident in all three of these, most particularly in *Death Knocks*, wherein an elderly Jewish man persuades the schleppy embodiment of Death, who has arrived clumsily to claim him, in a lifesaving game of pinochle.

In regard to Allen himself, his work in the theater, and Jewish humor, the importance of *Don't Drink the Water* is central; and *Play It Again, Sam*, as indicated, provides the first and most defining presentation of the romantic schlemiel persona Allen capitalized on and developed further in films such as *Annie Hall* (1977) and *Manhattan* (1979). It should be noted that theater often figures in Allen's films as well: for example, Alvy Singer, the Allen character in *Annie Hall*, is writing a play; the eponymous *Broadway Danny Rose* (1984) is a theatrical agent (of a decidedly low-brow variety); and *Bullets Over Broadway* (1994) is set in the rarefied theatrical world of 1920s Broadway. But it is in Allen's romantic protagonists that the influence of theater, and especially Yiddish theater tradition, is most keenly felt. Across Allen's decades of playwriting and filmmaking, his schlemiel character retains the profound romanticism of Allan Felix, the neurotic film critic and misadventurer in matters of love, in *Play It Again, Sam*. Whether depicted lightly or seriously, explicitly Jewish or not, the Allen protagonist longs for romance and acceptance in the mostly non-Jewish world around him, usually the contemporary urban landscape of New York City. Both full-length comedies and both commercial hits, *Don't Drink the Water* (598 performances) and *Play It Again, Sam* (453 performances), were instrumental successes for Allen and opened doors to filmmaking and screen stardom for him. They also display to an inordinate degree Allen's inspiration in the Jewish-inspired American popular culture of the first half of the twentieth century, with roots extending back to the nineteenth century.

Allen's prior plays and his screen persona set the stage for *Honeymoon Motel*, in its emphasis on the confrontation of Orthodox Jewish tradition with the imperatives and confusions of contemporary urban life. Critics also referred to the recurrence of "borscht belt" humor in *Honeymoon Motel*, a term too often applied generically (sometimes dismissively or derisively) to virtually any Jewish American comic performer, character, or work. Serving as a kind of shorthand for stereotypical parodies of Jewish characters and rife with self-deprecating humor, smothering mothers, and Yiddish American malapropisms, the borscht belt label originated in the vast summer resorts of the Catskills where Jewish performers and writers honed their craft entertaining vacationers in the decades before and after

World War II. Allen is one of a generation of Jewish comic writers and performers — including Neil Simon, Mel Brooks, Jackie Mason, Elaine May, Wendy Wasserstein, and others — who have had their work dismissed as extensions of borscht belt comedy when, in fact, diverse influences are present. That said, so much Jewish humor in American culture flows from the same fundamental sources — especially life in Kushner's unmelted melting pot where old ways meet the new and in the long traditions of Jewish comedy reaching back to Yiddish theater.

The "Jewishness" of the comedy, at first glance, consists of merely pointing out particular foibles and cultural collisions. Jews are not alone in this; in America, virtually every racial and ethnic group has wrung humor from similar circumstances: the problems of assimilating, of retaining the defining characteristics of ethnicity, of matching old ways with new ideas, and of stressing uniquely identifying traits of their particular ethnicity within the societal whole. Among these groups, Jews seem, for complicated reasons related to their historic status as outsiders, to view with humor themselves and their experience, except when most catastrophic and tragic (and sometimes even then). In Allen's case, he self-identifies not only as a Jew but also as an eternal outsider, at once longing for the safety of assimilation while resisting acceptance in the guise of a non-Jew. At the same time, he acknowledges that denial of his ethnicity is ultimately an impossibility. Allen sees the comic persona of the Jew as enduring, as in a figure like Charlie Chaplin's "Little Tramp" (and the clowns and fools of ancient and Renaissance theater or the existential clowns of Absurdist theater), whose eternal struggle to survive a hostile universe includes transforming outsider status from a liability to a strength, with humor as a potent tool to achieve that desired end.

Yiddish theater, like the borscht belt, tends to be used as an all-encompassing label for a type of ethnic theater of an antiquated variety. In fact, it represents an era far more complex, in which Jews maintained a firm grip on Eastern European orthodoxies while acclimating to American life. Yiddish theater posited that complete assimilation may not be possible or even desirable for the Jew and that retaining valued aspects of Eastern European life and Jewish traditions is essential — the past must not be lost entirely in an American society as yet not fully formed. Everything about Allen's works, despite his equivocations on the subject, seems to reflect this view. *Honeymoon Motel* is but the latest evidence that Allen is inexorably drawn back to his Jewish roots, which are firmly planted in the era in which European Jews came to America in great numbers — and the rise of the Yiddish theater on New York's Second Avenue was a major cultural manifestation of that exodus to America.

Yiddish theater's influence on the astonishingly diverse culture of New York City is profound, much in the way New York is essential, even something like a character, in Allen's work and, apparently, in his life. It would be an exaggeration to suggest that New York is a Jewish city, but for generations its large Jewish population supported the city's arts and culture to a phenomenal degree, and for Allen, this unique urban environment is an essential crucible for his work. There would be no Woody Allen without New York (even if he and his characters occasionally, and more often recently, find themselves in other cities); and, it might also be said, there is no New York culture without Jews. Jewish influence on New York theater, in particular, is perhaps the most profound of all and can be seen most vividly and in its purest form in the rich and diverse history of Yiddish theater.

Yiddish Theater: An Introduction

Taking it back to the Old World, Yiddish theater emerged in the eighteenth century and flourished in European capitals. Avrom Goldfadn, generally regarded as the founder of the first professional Yiddish theater troupe in Romania, established his theater in Bucharest and ultimately performed in New York. Initially an all-male company, Goldfadn's troupe eventually included women, sometimes playing male roles, but the Russian ban on Yiddish theater of 1883 finally pushed the entire industry to Western Europe and the United States. Remarkably, in the years between 1890 and 1940, over two hundred Yiddish theaters or touring troupes were operating in the United States. As many as a dozen companies functioned in New York at any given time and, in 1903, the Grand Theatre, situated on Second Avenue, became the first edifice constructed with the specific purpose of presenting Yiddish theater in America, inaugurating a golden age for Yiddish theater. From this point, its influence was profound and pervasive.[16]

Focused on plays by Jews about Jewish life, written and usually performed in Yiddish (the language of the Eastern European Ashkenazic community), Yiddish theater was diverse in content and form, including works in every stage genre: drama, comedy, operetta, musicals, revues, and variety entertainments. A Jewish actor or writer was required to be proficient in multiple forms, and it should be stressed, Allen's plays and films demonstrate his experimentation with many forms, not only comedy and drama, but also musicals and mysteries, period pieces, techniques, and content inspired by international cinema (Fellini and Bergman especially); a range of literary and philosophical thought; and much that he finds in American popular culture. In essence, Allen is a true product of the Yiddish stage in all its variety and exploration even if he may not have been aware of this fact at the outset or have known much about Yiddish theater history (though it should be noted, he makes a joke about Yiddish theater in *Zelig* [1983], in which the narrator explains that the main character's father had received a tepid response playing Puck in an Orthodox version of *A Midsummer Night's Dream*). As his more immediate forebears in Jewish American comedy were direct by-products of the Yiddish theater world, the influence of Yiddish theater — particularly in the comic vein, and as a resident of New York — would have infused his "shtick" by osmosis.

Most informative in regard to Allen's comic persona are the stock characters that emerged from Yiddish theater (and found their way into mainstream American entertainment forms), most specifically the aforementioned schlemiel character. A traditional figure whose specific roots are obscure (and may well date back to ancient theater), the modern schlemiel type seems to come into full focus in the Yiddish theater of the mid-nineteenth century in the character Schmendrick, who starred in Goldfadn's 1877 comedy *Schmendrick, or The Comical Wedding*. Schmendrick is a fool in the tradition of the trickster of ancient theater but one who is also a "Mama's boy" with an overprotective, but also warm and nurturing, *Yiddishe momme* blind to his faults.[17] Curiously, for decades the Schmendrick role was occasionally played by women, most notably in America by legendary Yiddish theater star Molly Picon, who, with ironic coincidence any Jewish humorist would appreciate, also made a career playing the quintessentially overbearing Jewish American mother, although as an atypically benign version of the character (see, for example, the 1963 film version of Neil Simon's first play, *Come Blow Your Horn* [1961]).

Although he didn't invent the smothering Jewish American mother (Philip Roth offered stiff competition, and certainly domineering mothers in other cultures were prevalent as well), Allen was instrumental in popularizing this postwar U.S. variant of the stock persona. Drawing on his own life, Allen seemed to find the Jewish mother a particularly oppressive figure. Nettie Cherrie Konigsberg, Allen's mother, is often found in Allen's version of the Jewish mother as unloving and a figure related to the rigidities of Jewish orthodoxies. Unlike Schmendrick, Allen's schlemiel had a mother who was not blind to his faults but focused like a laser beam on them. As such, his humor about this figure tends to be a kind of retaliation. In *Manhattan*, for example, Allen makes a joke about writing a novel based on his mother entitled "The Castrating Zionist," while in his "Oedipus Wrecks" segment of *New York Stories* (1989), the mother character, as memorably portrayed by Mae Questel in a far more oppressive version of Picon's lovable Jewish mother, is a giant figure (a la James Thurber's all-devouring cartoon wives), scolding him as she floats in the sky above New York City. The character, Allen explained, vanishes but reappears in the sky. In his original version, he stressed that everyone in New York was bothered by her oppressiveness. Ultimately, however, "they realized what I've been up against for all those years, when they had to take it."[18] Confirming the inspiration, Allen said that Questel, once the voice of cartoon flapper Betty Boop and a frequent portrayer of a range of stereotypical Jewish mothers, "even looks like my mother."[19]

Nowhere in evidence in Allen's work is the (generally immigrant) Jewish mother of the Molly Picon or "Molly Goldberg" variety, or those seen on Broadway in the years Allen began his career, as in Leonard Spigelgass's *A Majority of One* (1959). In this play by Spigelgass, a typical Brooklynese Jewish mother forms an unlikely emotional relationship with a Japanese man; while the character clings to her traditions, she is open to experiencing new ways of thinking. This role was first played on Broadway by Gertrude Berg, an actress and writer who gained fame on radio (and later television) as Molly Goldberg, a warm, nurturing, family-centered, *Yiddishe momme* type whose meddlesomeness was mild and more than made up for by a deeply loving nature.

Despite the differences in his approach to the Jewish mother character, Allen's schlemiel, with or without a mother, is similar to the model found in Yiddish theater comedy. The schlemiel is typically a rather lamebrained, awkward, or unlucky character or, as most often seen within the Jewish American tradition (and in Allen's version of the character), a bungler, an outsider, and a failure at romance. It would take much more space than permitted here to list and describe varied examples of this character type over the decades since Goldfadn's Schmendrick was born. But even in 2012 — and after decades of resistance to such stereotypes — a present-day variation on this character can be occasionally found in films and on television, as, for example, in the persona of Howard Wolowitz (played by Jewish American actor Simon Helberg) on the hit TV comedy *The Big Bang Theory* (2007–), or on big screens in Judd Apatow's so-called Jew Tang Clan: Seth Rogen, Jonah Hill, Michael Cera, Jason Segel, and Paul Rudd. Allen, who preceded them, has otherwise been nearly the sole "A-list" purveyor of the schlemiel persona on stage and screen (although in literature writers like Philip Roth also explored such a character). Allen, while still playing such roles in his plays and films, expanded on this figure as a bumbling romantic whose assimilation might come, in part, if he can succeed in love with a gentile girl.

The schlemiel as Allen envisions him, and as appears fully formed in *Play It Again, Sam*, is a classically self-deprecating figure. The use of self-deprecation in Jewish humor, and especially in Allen's work, is a topic thoroughly examined by Mark Bleiweiss in his essay "Self-Deprecation and the Jewish Humor of Woody Allen."[20] Self-deprecation has long been a feature of much Jewish-based stage and screen comedy; show-business Jews recognized early on that winning over mainstream audiences, in an anti-Semitic environment, required self-deprecation as a character trait. Both Jewish and non-Jewish audiences could laugh at the stereotypes, and since the Jewish performer was making the joke first, it could be seen as something other than a negative presentation or an attack. Yiddish theater writers and performers recognized the effectiveness of owning the joke from the start.

Fanny Brice, for example, left Yiddish theater burlesque to achieve stardom (and become one of the great legends of American show business) in the *Ziegfeld Follies*, where she appeared in musical numbers and sketches as a rare female schlemiel, playing a broadly klutzy (but often touching) Jewish girl thrust into incongruous settings ("Becky Is Back in the Ballet"); a bratty Jewish child (Baby Snooks, her radio persona); or a Jewish mother ("Mrs. Cohen at the Beach"). Brice pointedly explained that she "wasn't standing apart making fun"; when she amused with a Jewish joke, the audience identified with her, "which made it all right to get a laugh, because they were laughing at me as much as at themselves."[21] Allen certainly won over his stand-up audiences through this sort of "identification" with his audience, and he used self-deprecation in the emergence of his stage persona in the seminal *Play It Again, Sam*. As with Brice, and other Yiddish theater performers and writers, self-deprecation proved to be a powerful tool for Allen not only in the formative phase of his career but also in the wake of the Farrow/Previn scandal, helping him win back his audience in the wake of a torrent of negative publicity.

In the contemporary period, audience resistance to stereotypical devices such as self-deprecation and the inevitable smothering-mother jokes seems to have hindered Allen less than some of his cohorts.[22] Certainly his stand-up act and earliest plays, like *Don't Drink the Water*, depend on use of these well-worn clichés. Some other Jewish American comedians — notably Jackie Mason and Mel Brooks — have in recent years revived their old Jewish comedy gambits for spectacularly successful returns to mainstream success, offering to new generations a sampling of humor appreciated and sometimes rejected by their forebears. Mason and Brooks, and to some extent Allen, belong to an earlier generation whose entertainments were steeped in all manner of ethnic and racial humor when it was accepted as the norm. Allen is able to draw from this deep well, though the result inspires a divided critical response, as suggested by criticisms of *Honeymoon Motel*. Throughout his long career, Allen has fallen in and out of favor several times, due to the Jewish American humor he presents, the Farrow/Previn controversy, and generational changes of taste. However, as demonstrated by the success of the Apatow stock company, old wine can be transferred to new bottles and, in the 2000s, the Allen vintage is once again prized. Now in his seventies, Allen is experiencing something like the renaissance Mason and Brooks achieved a decade or so ago due, in part, to the critical acclaim and box-office success of *Midnight in Paris* (2011) but also to what seems a growing affection (nostalgia?) for Jewish American humor and its purveyors.

Jewish American dramatists of the post–World War II era, whether in serious or comic plays, exhibit a need to reckon with their Jewish heritage. David Mamet, for example, perhaps the best-known Jewish dramatist at work today, states, "For my generation, Jewish culture consisted of Jewish food and Jewish jokes, neither of which, probably, were very good for us."[23] Mamet and Allen otherwise have little in common, either as Jews or as playwrights, though both are part of the same generation and share decidedly ambivalent feelings about their religious background. Within his comic repertory, *The Floating Light Bulb* exhibits one of the darker portraits of Allen's Jewish American past. The play features significant autobiographical elements and, similar to Eugene O'Neill's *Long Day's Journey into Night* (1956) and especially Tennessee Williams's *The Glass Menagerie* (1944), if in a more comic vein, is drawn from unhappy adolescent memories. Set in 1945 Canarsie, Brooklyn, the play seems to center on the usual Allen schlemiel, here a lonely teenager, Paul, who escapes family conflict through an interest in magic and show business. The element of fantasy (as in the memory play device employed in *The Glass Menagerie*) and the theatrical world to which Paul aspires simultaneously underscore and liberate the play from its otherwise somber mood. There are Jewish jokes and stereotypes in this play, but these are not played for full *comic* value; instead, they are seen as handicaps to Paul in his desires to achieve his show-business dreams and escape an unhappy family life. Paul's mother, Enid (played in the original production by Beatrice Arthur), is actually the troubled center of the play and the stumbling block for Paul's dream. A frustrated aspiring performer herself, Enid, like Amanda Wingfield of *The Glass Menagerie*, coincidentally first produced on Broadway in 1945, lives in an imaginary past and imagines a fantasy future to avoid the stifling realities of her present. Critics of *The Floating Light Bulb* pointed to the Williams influence on Allen, including *New York Times* reviewer Frank Rich, who wrote that the play's "milieu is pure 'Glass Menagerie.'"[24]

Comic elements are comparatively sparse in *The Floating Light Bulb*, but the characters are Jewish American archetypes (domineering mother and schlemiel son), though drawn more poignantly, and somewhat sympathetically, with most humor centering on the show-business milieu (rife with borscht belt elements) around the play's edges. When Paul is given an opportunity to audition for a theatrical agent, Enid's dreams crowd out her unhappy child, and finally, there is no escape from the treadmill of dashed hopes for Paul or Enid in this glimpse of a Jewish American past with striking resonances to Allen's own past. Despite its commercial failure and what Rich described as the play's "modest attainments," *The Floating Light Bulb* is a forerunner of the more serious films Allen began exploring during the late 1970s and 1980s, such as *Interiors* (1978), *Hannah and Her Sisters* (1986), *September* (1987), *Another Woman* (1988), and *Crimes and Misdemeanors* (1989).[25] Allen's oft-expressed (if overly defensive) dismissive attitude about his theater work surfaces in his recollections of *The Floating Light Bulb*. When asked if he might revisit the play or adapt it for the screen, he replied, no, stressing that "it was a little idea I had, and I never did anything with it. I just let it be."[26] Personal disclaimers notwithstanding, *The Floating Light Bulb* may be, in its way, the most revealing of Allen's plays in explaining his relationship to his Jewish past. Earlier plays, especially *Don't Drink the Water* and *Play It Again, Sam*, emphasize a humorous approach; *The Floating Light Bulb* takes a more serious tack on the Jewish American world of his youth. But all reflect Allen's ambivalence about his heritage and his rejection of organized religion and its rigidities, and all demonstrate his debt to the long traditions of Jewish comedy. Here Allen may be something of a forerunner of such Jewish American playwrights as Wendy Wasserstein, whose *The Heidi Chronicles* (1988) and *The Sisters Rosensweig* (1992) feature considerable amounts of Jewish humor and characters seemingly inspired by stereotypical images, yet move beyond the clichés through more full-dimensional characters and a pathos resulting from more complex conceptions of familiar tropes.

Allen's Jewish-themed work is also revealing in comparison to borscht belt contemporaries such as Mel Brooks and Neil Simon. Brooks, for example, shamelessly assaults and mocks any and all racial, ethnic, and gender stereotypes (and, some might suggest, strengthens them while also debunking them) in wild, parodistic farces. Simon, by contrast, has taken an increasingly gentle, more dramatic, and character-driven approach to depictions of Jewish American life, often masking stereotypical Jewish characteristics in generic archetypes, avoiding in most cases specific reference to ethnic identity. Simon is at his most Jewish in depictions of himself coming of age between the Great Depression and the 1950s in a trio of autobiographical plays, *Brighton Beach Memoirs* (1983), *Biloxi Blues* (1985), and *Broadway Bound* (1986), each of which contains rich snapshots of mid-twentieth-century Jewish American life. Allen's uniqueness stems partly from his making use of elements in the works of both Brooks and Simon, often mixing Brooksian farcical lunacy (as in *Honeymoon Motel*) with the lightly absurd realism of Simon's oeuvre (*Play It Again, Sam* and *The Floating Light Bulb*). Ostensibly appearing as himself or, more accurately, as an exaggeration of himself in his plays and films, Allen's persona grapples with neuroses tied to his roots as the child of immigrant Eastern European Jews while attempting to belong to a more diverse contemporary culture as represented by New York City, a dynamic also present in Simon's plays and, however farcically, in the varied work of Brooks. Allen's plays (like Simon's) are also akin to the theatrical comedy of manners, stressing moral hypocrisy, but his unique variation on this classical form is the deep ambivalence the works display about his ethnicity and the tenets of organized religion that, despite attempts to escape them, remain central to his identity.

Schlemiel: Revisited

Allen's schlemiel, much like Goldfadn's Schmendrick, appears as effectively in broadly farcical works (*Don't Drink the Water* and *Honeymoon Motel*), romantic comedies (*Play It Again, Sam*), and near dramas (*The Floating Light Bulb*); the resilience and longevity of this figure in Allen's work (not to mention its sources) is impressive, and the character can also transcend its foundation in overt ethnicity. Specific evidence of this transcendence is to be found in Allen's plays. In the stage version of *Play It Again, Sam* (and in the film as well), Allen, as schlemiel Allan Felix, ruminates on his persistent failure in relationships with the women he meets in the urban landscape. A comic dynamic inherent in the firmly established schlemiel persona is the core of the play. Frustrated by his failures in love, Allan calls up a ghostly hallucination of the cinematic icon of romanticism, Humphrey Bogart (in his iconic persona as Rick Blaine, the romantically wounded, disaffected, and ultimately quietly heroic figure from the screen classic *Casablanca*). Clearly lacking Bogart's memorable physical attributes, Allen recognized that his physical being — slight and balding, with thick horn-rimmed glasses — not only presented the perfect foil to Bogart's persona but also perfectly positioned him to play the schlemiel.

As Allen has aged and turned the schlemiel role over to younger stars, it is curious that he has often chosen more traditional (and less obviously ethnic) leading men as his alter ego. Cusack, Branagh, Ferrell, and the like, may not exactly be Bogart-style tough guys, but these choices suggest that perhaps for Allen physical image is less important than psychic or spiritual scars. Allen's schlemiel, nerdy or handsome, derives his comic potency from his romantic wounds, his losses, and his confused view of the absurdities of the world around him. He is trapped in the image of a schlemiel, but in the core of his being he is also a spiritual heir of Bogartian romanticism. In this case, Allen's (and Allan's) Jewishness seems implied by his being a confirmed New Yorker. Separating Jewish humor from New York humor is nearly impossible. Linguistic rhythms and social attitudes that are recognizably New York suggest an immersion in the life of a city of multiple ethnic and racial characteristics blended into a point of view about life and its vicissitudes found in much of Allen's work. Even in his most recent films and plays, his characters may live either in New York or in European cities, but they are New York urban types born out of Kushner's unmelted melting pot of multiple ethnic traditions, most particularly those of the Jewish persuasion.

Young or old, the essential aspects of Allan Felix are ever present in Allen's schlemiel throughout the years. However, for his prior and first full-length play, *Don't Drink the Water*, Allen had yet to fully define his schlemiel (there is no obvious Allen character in this play), even though aspects of the persona were certainly present in his stand-up comedy. In *Don't Drink the Water*, Allen seems focused more on his parents' generation than his own, even though secondary (and rather generic) younger characters are included to add conventional romantic elements. Written boldly in the Jewish idiom, *Don't Drink the Water* features an archetypal mid-twentieth-century New York Jewish American family as the ugly Americans abroad. The play's central conceit places the broadly stereotypical Walter and Marion Hollander, and their children, in the American embassy in the imaginary Communist bloc country, Vulgaria. They are seeking sanctuary after an incident in which Walter innocently snapped a photograph of a top-secret military site. Once unwillingly established in the embassy, the bickering and complaining of the Hollanders makes life a veritable hell for embassy employees, capped by Walter's insults directed at a visiting sultan, which sets off a diplomatic disaster. The Jewish American family members are thus the true "Vulgarians," kvetching excessively about the local cuisine and their accommodations in a farcical culture clash. The Jewishness of the characters is the wellspring of the play's broad humor, as are the grotesque exaggerations of their stereotypical traits, which, a la Mel Brooks, turn all the characters — Jewish or otherwise — into broad caricatures.

An anecdote from the original production of *Don't Drink the Water* illustrates the trickiest aspects of Jewish American humor in performance. When producer David Merrick hired television personality Vivian Vance to play Marion, the quintessential Jewish American mother, Allen thought her a poor choice since, in his view, she lacked a plausible Jewish dialect or the necessary Brooklynese vocal cadences. During rehearsals, Vance was replaced by Kay Medford who, though not a Jew, often played such characters (including a critically acclaimed performance as Fanny Brice's mother in the musical *Funny Girl*) and evoked the necessary vocal and comic attributes typical of the quintessential Jewish American mother of popular culture. In Allen's estimation, once Medford took over the role, the play's comedy worked. This points to a major reason for the rise and decline of Jewish comedy: it is nearly impossible to fake Jewish American personas and the humor arising from the comic perspective and experience of a Jewish American, especially that of a veteran Jew Yorker. The font of Jewish humor springs from more than a mere dialect or stereotypical jokes; Jewish Americans possess a unique sense of the world and their place in it, and the humor grows proportionately from that singular knowledge.

At the time of its Broadway premiere, however, critics described *Don't Drink the Water* as a guilty pleasure, funny but "the story and staging format suggest pre–World War II farce"; most ironically, they regarded the Jewish humor and boldly drawn characters as stereotypes in parallel with critical responses to *Honeymoon Motel* forty-five years later.[27] Despite a mixed critical response, *Don't Drink the Water* had a long, successful run, and the film rights were sold to Hollywood. There, the filmmakers repeated Merrick's casting misjudgment by employing Jackie Gleason and Estelle Parsons to play the Hollanders. As with Vance, Gleason especially, despite his estimable comic gifts, did not possess the Jewish American characteristics essential for the role, and the film (released in 1969) failed to impress critics or audiences — although Gleason was not the only problem. When a second film version of *Don't Drink the Water* was made for television in 1994, Allen himself played Hollander, supported by Julie Kavner as Marion, and this time the Jewish American aspects were boldly evident. However, the use of these elements in such a broadly conceived farce was then viewed, in the post-Soviet era, as overemphasizing the play's clichéd qualities, and critics were merciless. Allen had chosen not to revise the material in any way, and thus humor considered passé in 1966 seemed hopelessly dated in 1994 and, in the case of stereotypical portrayals of Jews (and Arabs), offensive. In the same period, similar dismissive responses met a made-for-TV film of Neil Simon's, *The Sunshine Boys*, starring Allen as an aging Jewish vaudevillian.

Bringing It All Back Home

The harsh critical response to *Don't Drink the Water* may explain why Allen's more recent theater works, prior to *Honeymoon Motel* and after *The Floating Light Bulb*, avoided overtly Jewish humor. That said, it should be noted that these "in-between" plays retain the rapid-fire, New York-infused language and rhythms typical of Allen's work on stage and screen. It is thus not necessarily the case that Allen's more recent plays are lacking in Jewish humor. For example, though his set of three one acts, *Riverside Drive*, *Old Saybrook*, and *Central Park West*, eschew overt Jewishness in the onstage characters, nonetheless, characters' speech patterns and their status as New Yorkers and urban sophisticates provides them with a Jewish "coating" (and coding), a Jewishness by association. The thematic emphasis of these plays centers on Allen's more general philosophical probing of self-delusion and the dialectical rationalization of behaviors outside accepted mainstream norms (seen, in these cases, through a range of sexual deceptions and romantic disillusionments). Some of the characters, however, such as Jim Swain in *Riverside Drive*, exhibit a muted version of the patented Allen schlemiel persona; meanwhile in *Old Saybrook*, Allen uses Jewish names to generate a little humor from the audience's imagining unseen characters (Howard Nadelman and Doctor Fineglass), presumably to remind his audience of the world from which these characters emerge.

The emphasis in these pre–*Honeymoon Motel* one acts, as well as in the darker family drama *A Second Hand Memory*, written in a disillusioned tone similar to *The Floating Light Bulb*, is on romantic dysfunction and moral confusion among those of the New York smart set, in a manner akin to the most sophisticated of Allen's romantic films. The Jewishness of the play is also present — if in sublimated form — in the anxieties and neuroses of his characters more than in any broader Jewish jokes or stereotypes. In that sense, all of these "in-between" Allen plays seem somewhat tempered or chastened in their Jewishness, as though Allen had consciously chosen to keep clear of the farcical Jewish world of *Don't Drink the Water* or the stifling constraints of a dysfunctional Jewish family life and the outsider status of the Jewish American characters in *The Floating Light Bulb*. In *A Second Hand Memory*, the family strife, although emanating from a show-business world (in this case, Hollywood) with clear Jewish overtones, registers as a work more in the vein of Tennessee Williams and Arthur Miller. Much as his serious films aspired to the Strindbergian heights of Ingmar Bergman, this "unrelentingly glum" play examines profound moral questions typical of the first rank of American dramatists.

While not denying the ecumenical impact of Williams and Miller (nor of Bergman, on his films), Allen has discussed more explicitly Jewish influences on his stage work, such as S. J. Perelman, Groucho Marx, and Robert Benchley. Ethnicity aside, these latter writers were all keen cultural observers and humorists whose own personas, especially in the case of performers Marx and Benchley, were variations on the schlemiel type. *Don't Drink the Water*, specifically, Allen explained, was written "under the influence of George S. Kaufman and Moss Hart. They wrote those kind of plays, although they were much better at it."[28] Usually the Kaufman and Hart comedies depend on Jewish humor, though almost never in overt ways. Such cultural identification was viewed in those more prejudiced, pre–World War II times as counterproductive to Broadway success. Despite being Jews themselves (and writing for a Broadway audience made up of a significant number of Jews), Kaufman's and Hart's characters rarely had Jewish names or otherwise self-identified as Jews; instead, the authors applied, as Allen later would as well, the comic rhythms of New York Jewish speech and comic attitudes drawn from the Jewish American tradition. Presumably, Kaufman and Hart aimed to depict their characters as universally generic and kept their Jewish heritage in the closet. Although Allen was able to "come out" Jewish, he did, for more personal reasons, as we have seen, occasionally cloak his characters' Jewishness in the trappings of New Yorkness.

Conclusion

Although the ambivalence Allen projects about his Jewish heritage, and that creates the essential tension in his work, does not often express itself in religious terms, this aspect must be viewed as a contributing factor. It was Allen's mother who, through her love for her highly religious father, pressed Allen's Jewish education. He attended Hebrew school as he was told to and accompanied his grandfather to the synagogue. They were an Orthodox family, meaning that Allen prayed every morning "with phylacteries bound to his arms and forehead, attended temple in a yarmulke, fasted on the high holidays," and attended Hebrew school throughout his childhood, all of which, as John Baxter writes, "merely accentuated his resentment of religion."[29] Consequently, Allen developed, as Eric Lax notes, "an ecumenical view of religion. That is, he found all organized faiths equally useless."[30] He increasingly came to view all religious strictures as absurd, later stating, "All of these religions' do's and don'ts ranged for me from the laughable to the offensive."[31] Surely the root of his Jewish ambivalence (simplistically judged as self-hatred by some) springs partly from this strict religious upbringing and his rejection of it. By the same token, however, though Allen's family were religiously observant, they were not secluded from the secular world around them; for most Jews of their class and time, the struggle over assimilating had mostly played out. Thus, for Allen, enmeshment in Orthodox Judaism and the "double life" it engendered further enhanced (or exacerbated) his sense of being an alien in the non-Jewish world.

As it did for many borscht belt comics of his generation, the philosophical underpinning of Allen's Jewish comedy is a response to the strictures of an increasingly outmoded Old World way of life, combined with a striving for acceptance in the secular world of American popular culture the comics themselves helped to construct. What seems to set Allen most apart not only from his fellow Jewish comics but also from the Yiddish comedy tradition is an intellectual hunger and creative aspiration that, while not denying its Jewish roots, aspires for something more universal and all encompassing. The dual strains come out in Allen's yes-but claims of not seeing himself as a distinctly Jewish artist, of finding ideas in whatever interests him. The Jewish element is only one among many, in his estimation, but "certain subjects, like Jewishness, are unusually vivid; they have a disproportionate resonance."[32] Or as he further muddied the issue on another occasion, he was depicting "the reality as I experienced it, my own authenticity."[33] He only attempted to depict that reality honestly as he saw it, whether it was a positive or a negative view, even as he accepted the fact that Jewish groups and others might be critical. For Allen, all that mattered, finally, was the "authenticity of the scene."[34] As his stage work from *Don't Drink the Water* through *Honeymoon Motel* goes to show, that authenticity never leaves Allen's Jewishness far behind.

Notes

1. Tony Kushner, *Angels in America: A Gay Fantasia on National Themes; Part One: Millennium Approaches* (New York: Theatre Communications Group, 1993), 10.
2. Charles Isherwood, "Each Family, Tortured in Its Own Way," *New York Times*, October 20, 2011, C1.
3. Isherwood, "Each Family"; Joe Dziemianowicz, "'Relatively Speaking' Review: Ethan Coen, Elaine May and Woody Allen Spin Unfunny Trio of Plays," *New York Daily News*, October 28, 2011, http://articles.nydailynews.com.
4. Scott Brown, "O Brother," *New York Magazine*, October 21, 2011, http://nymag.com.
5. Quoted in Elaine May, "Allen, Coen and May: 3 Wits, One Show," *New York Times*, October 13, 2011, AR1.
6. Isherwood, "Each Family."
7. Allen's exact words, quoting Pascal, were "The heart wants what it wants." Walter Isaacson and Wood Allen, "The Heart Wants What It Wants," *Time*, August 31, 1992, http://www.time.com.
8. John Del Signore, "Review: *Relatively Speaking*," *Gothamist*, October 23, 2011, http://gothamist.com.
9. David Rooney, "*Relatively Speaking*: Theater Review," *Hollywood Reporter*, October 20, 2011, http://www.hollywoodreporter.com.
10. Marilyn Stasio, "Relatively Speaking," *Variety*, October 20, 2011, http://www.variety.com.
11. David Sheward, "*Relatively Speaking* at the Brooks Atkinson Theatre," *Backstage*, October 20, 2011, http://www.backstage.com.
12. Ted Merwin, "Woody's 'Honeymoon' Home Run," *Jewish Week*, October 23, 2011, http://www.thejewishweek.com.
13. Ibid.
14. See William Novak and Moshe Waldoks, eds., *The Big Book of Jewish Humor* (New York: Harper & Row, 1981).
15. Charles Isherwood, "Woody Allen's Hearts of Darkness, Stuck in Brooklyn," *New York Times*, November 23, 2004, http://theater.nytimes.com.
16. For more on Yiddish theater, see Joel Berkowitz, ed., *The Yiddish Theatre: New Approaches* (New York: Littman Library of Jewish Civilization, 2008); Joel Berkowitz and Barbara Henry, eds., *Inventing the Modern Yiddish Stage: Essays in Drama, Performance, and Show Business* (Detroit: Wayne State University Press, 2012); Nahma Sandrow, *Vagabond Stars: A World History of Yiddish Theatre* (Syracuse, NY: Syracuse University Press, 1995); Joel Schecter, *Messiahs of 1933: How American Yiddish Theatre Survived Adversity through Satire* (Philadelphia: Temple University Press, 2008).

17. Aspects of the schlemiel are also closely related to such European archetypes as Arlecchino of Italian *commedia dell'arte*, Pierrot of French theater, the buffoons of Elizabethan comedy, and the farcical personas of a host of music hall and vaudeville legends from various ethnic backgrounds, not to mention from silent film comedians led by Chaplin, Buster Keaton, Harold Lloyd, and others.

18. Quoted in Woody Allen, *Woody Allen on Woody Allen: In Conversation with Stig Björkman* (New York: Grove, 1993), 203.

19. Ibid., 205.

20. Mark E. Bleiweiss, "Self-Deprecation and the Jewish Humor of Woody Allen," in *The Films of Woody Allen: Critical Essays*, ed. Charles L. P. Silet, 58–77 (Lanham, MD: Scarecrow, 2006).

21. Quoted in Barbara W. Grossman, *Funny Woman: The Life and Times of Fanny Brice* (Bloomington: Indiana University Press, 1991), 102.

22. Less resilient Jewish-themed playwrights include Carl Reiner, George Axelrod, Herb Gardner, Larry Gelbart, Israel Horovitz, Ira Levin, Craig Lucas, Donald Margulies, Martin Sherman, and Alfred Uhry, all of whom experienced a gradual loss of interest in their theater work and either decamped for movies and television or disappeared from the scene altogether by the 1980s. See James Fisher, *The Theatre of Yesterday and Tomorrow: Commedia dell'arte on the Modern Stage* (Lewiston, NY: Edwin Mellen, 1992).

23. Quoted in John Baxter, *Woody Allen: A Biography* (New York: Carroll & Graf, 1998), 10.

24. Frank Rich, "Stage: 'Light Bulb,' by Woody Allen," *New York Times*, April 28, 1981, http://www.nytimes.com.

25. Ibid.

26. Quoted in Allen, *Woody Allen*, 361.

27. Marion Meade, *The Unruly Life of Woody Allen: A Biography* (New York: Cooper Square Press, 2000), 71.

28. Allen, *Woody Allen*, 304.

29. Baxter, *Woody Allen*, 27.

30. Eric Lax, *Woody Allen: A Biography* (New York: Knopf, 1991), 40.

31. Quoted in Allen, *Woody Allen*, 204.

32. Quoted in Robert F. Moss, "Creators on Creating: Woody Allen," in *Woody Allen: Interviews*, ed. Robert E. Kapsis and Kathie Coblentz, 49–57 (Jackson: University Press of Mississippi, 2006), 56–57.

33. Quoted in Allen, *Woody Allen*, 47.

34. Ibid.

WOODY ALLEN: FILMOGRAPHY

Unless otherwise specified, Allen was director/writer/actor.

1965	What's New Pussycat? (writer/actor)	1983	Zelig
1966	What's Up, Tiger Lily?	1984	Broadway Danny Rose
1967	Casino Royale (writer/actor)	1985	The Purple Rose of Cairo (director/writer)
1969	Don't Drink the Water (writer) (TV movie)	1986	Hannah and Her Sisters
1969	Take the Money and Run	1986	Meetin' WA (as himself in documentary)
1971	Bananas	1987	King Lear (actor)
1971	Men of Crisis: The Harvey Wallinger Story (twenty-five-minute short)	1987	Radio Days (director/writer/voice-over narrator)
1972	Everything You Always Wanted to Know About Sex* (*But Were Afraid to Ask)	1987	September (director/writer)
		1988	Another Woman (director/writer)
1972	Play It Again, Sam (writer/actor)	1989	Crimes and Misdemeanors
		1989	"Oedipus Wrecks" (one of three New York Stories)
1973	Sleeper	1990	Alice (director/writer)
1975	Love and Death	1991	Scenes from a Mall (actor)
1976	The Front (actor)	1992	Husbands and Wives
1977	Annie Hall	1991	Shadows and Fog
1978	Interiors (director/writer)	1993	Manhattan Murder Mystery
1979	Manhattan	1994	Bullets Over Broadway (director/writer)
1980	Stardust Memories		
1980	To Woody Allen, From Europe with Love (as himself in documentary)	1994	Don't Drink the Water
		1995	Mighty Aphrodite
		1996	The Sunshine Boys (actor) (TV movie)
1982	A Midsummer Night's Sex Comedy	1996	Everyone Says I Love You

1997 *Deconstructing Harry*
1997 *Wild Man Blues* (as himself in documentary)
1998 *Antz* (animated character's voice)
1998 *Celebrity* (director/writer)
1998 *The Impostors* (actor)
1999 *Sweet and Lowdown* (director/writer)
2000 *Company Man* (actor)
2000 *Picking Up the Pieces* (actor)
2000 *Small Time Crooks*
2001 *The Curse of the Jade Scorpion*
2001 *Sounds from a Town I Love* (director/writer; three-minute short)
2002 *Hollywood Ending*
2002 *Woody Allen: A Life in Film* (himself in documentary)
2003 *Anything Else*
2004 *Melinda and Melinda* (director/writer)
2005 *The Ballad of Greenwich Village* (himself in documentary)
2005 *Match Point* (director/writer)
2005 *The Outsider* (himself in documentary)
2006 *Scoop*
2007 *Cassandra's Dream* (director/writer)
2008 *Vicky Cristina Barcelona* (director/writer)
2009 *Whatever Works* (director/writer)
2010 *You Will Meet a Tall Dark Stranger* (director/writer)
2011 *Midnight in Paris* (director/writer)
2011 *Woody Allen: A Documentary* (himself)
2012 *To Rome with Love*
2013 *Fading Gigolo* (actor)
2013 *Blue Jasmine* (director/writer)

WOODY ALLEN: PLAY LIST

1960   *From A to Z*, full length (Allen contributed only sketches to this musical revue)
Opened April 20, 1960; Plymouth Theatre, New York.

1966   *Don't Drink the Water*, full length
Opened November 17, 1966; Morosco Theatre, New York.

1968   *Death Knocks*, one act
Published in the *New Yorker*, July 27, 1968.

1969   *Play It Again, Sam*, full length
Opened February 12, 1969; Broadhurst Theatre, New York.

1975   *Death*, one act
Published in *Without Feathers* (New York: Random House, 1975).

1975   *God*, one act
Published in *Without Feathers*.

1981   *The Floating Light Bulb*, full length
Opened April 27, 1981; Vivian Beaumont Theatre, New York.

1995   *Central Park West*, one act (part of three-play bill titled *Death Defying Acts*, together with David Mamet's *An Interview* and Elaine May's *Hotline*)
Opened March 6, 1995; Atlantic Theater Company, New York.

2003   *Old Saybrook* (written 1995), one act (part of bill titled *Writer's Block*)
Opened May 15, 2003; Atlantic Theater Company, New York.

2003   *Riverside Drive*, one act (part of *Writer's Block* bill)
Opened May 15, 2003; Atlantic Theater Company, New York.

2004   *A Second Hand Memory*, full length
Opened November 22, 2004; Atlantic Theater Company, New York.

2011   *Honeymoon Motel*, one act (part of three-play bill titled *Relatively Speaking*, together with Ethan Coen's *Talking Cure* and Elaine May's *George Is Dead*)
Opened October 20, 2011; Brooks Atkinson Theatre, New York.

LIST OF CONTRIBUTORS

NATHAN ABRAMS is a senior lecturer in film studies at Bangor University in Wales. He has published extensively on Jewish film and new media, including most recently *The New Jew in Film: Exploring Jewishness and Judaism in Contemporary Cinema* (Rutgers University Press, 2012). He is also the founding co-editor of *Jewish Film and New Media: An International Journal*. He is currently working on two book-length projects: the first explores the ethnicity in the films of Stanley Kubrick, while the second is titled *The Hidden Presence of Jews in British Film and Television* (contracted to Northwestern University Press).

PETER J. BAILEY is the author of *Reading Stanley Elkin* (1985), *The Reluctant Film Art of Woody Allen* (2003), and *Rabbit (Un)Redeemed: The Drama of Belief in John Updike's Fiction* (2006). With Sam B. Girgus, he co-edited *Companion to Woody Allen* (Wiley-Blackwell, 2013). He teaches American literature, film, and creative writing at St. Lawrence University in Canton, NY.

VINCENT BROOK teaches media and cultural studies at UCLA, USC, Cal-State LA, and Pierce College. He has edited the anthology *You Should See Yourself: Jewish Identity in Postmodern American Culture* (2006); and authored three books: *Something Ain't Kosher Here: The Rise of the "Jewish" Sitcom* (2003), *Driven to Darkness: Jewish Émigré Directors and the Rise of Film Noir* (2009), and *Land of Smoke and Mirrors: A Cultural History of Los Angeles* (2013).

GIOVANNA DEL NEGRO is an Associate Professor of English at Texas A&M University. Her books include *Looking Through My Mother's Eyes: Life Stories of Nine Italian Immigrant Women in Canada* (1997, 2003) and *The Passeggiata and Popular Culture in an Italian Town: Folklore and the Performance of Modernity* (2005), which was awarded the Elli Köngäs-Maranda Prize. She is co-author of *Identity and Everyday Life* (2005) and for five years co-edited the *Journal of American Folklore*. Her recent work on the bestselling party records of bawdy Jewish women comics of the 1950s has been widely published.

MENACHEM FEUER teaches in the Jewish Studies Department at the University of Waterloo. Besides essays in forthcoming book collections, he has published essays and book reviews in *Modern Fiction Studies, Shofar,* MELUS, *German Studies Review, International Studies in Philosophy, Comparative Literature and Culture, Ctheory,* and *Cinemaction*. He is also the author of the blog Schlemiel-in-Theory (www.schlemielintheory.com) where he posts daily on the schlemiel and hosts guest posts by various scholars, writers, and comedians. He is currently working on a book-length treatment of the schlemiel, and was himself the subject of a documentary titled *Shlemiel* (2011), directed by Chad Derrick.

JAMES FISHER is Head of the Department of Theatre at the University of North Carolina at Greensboro. He is the author of a dozen books, including the two-volume *Historical Dictionary of Contemporary American Theater: 1930 to 2010* (2011) and *Understanding Tony Kushner* (2008), and has edited several books, including *To Have or Have Not: Essays on Commerce and Capital in Modernist Theatre* (2011). Fisher is also a director and received the 2007 Betty Jean Jones Award for Excellence in the Teaching of American Theatre from the American Theatre and Drama Society.

MARAT GRINBERG is an Associate Professor of Russian and Humanities at Reed College in Portland, Oregon. He is the author of *"I Am to Be Read not from Left to Right, but in Jewish: From Right to Left": The Poetics of Boris Slutsky* (Academic Studies Press, 2011, 2013) and has published widely on literature, film, and modern Jewish culture and politics. His current book-length project is tentatively titled *Meaningful Silences/Hidden Sources: Six Case Studies of Adaptation and Jewish Cinema*.

SHAINA HAMMERMAN currently serves as Visiting Assistant Professor at Mills College in Oakland and at the Graduate Theological Union in Berkeley. Her research and teaching explore how Jewishness is negotiated through film, television, and literature.

CURTIS MALOLEY teaches sociology in the Spanning the Gaps program at Ryerson University, and sociology and film studies at Humber College in Toronto. His essay "American Idol'atry: The Practice of Democracy in the Age of Reality Television" appears in the sixth and seventh editions of *Popping Culture* (2010, 2012).

JOSHUA LOUIS MOSS is currently a visiting assistant professor in the Department of Film and Media at the University of California, Santa Barbara. Moss holds a Ph.D. in Critical Studies from the University of Southern California's School of Cinematic Arts.

ELLIOT H. SHAPIRO teaches at Cornell University, where he directs the Writing in the Majors program and is Director of Instruction for the University Courses program. His essays on *Modern Times*, *His Girl Friday*, *Singin' in the Rain*, and *Chinatown* appeared in *50 Key U.S. Films* (Haenni and White 2009). He is currently working on a project about Jews on film in classical Hollywood.

INDEX

Adorno, Theodor, xxvi, 80, 82, 87, 96, 97
Alice (1990), 14, 71, 129, 131; and food, 227; magic, 71, 131, 132; schlemiel, 14
Allen, Woody: and children of, xxxiiin84, 12, 13, 26, 30; comedy/serious film conflict, 4, 5, 10, 11, 14, 60; existentialism, xix, xviii, 39, 40, 216; family background, 9, 124, 125, 164, 246, 255, 256; French reputation, 18, 21, 24; name change, xiv; religious upbringing, 124, 125, 255, 256; social conscience, xxi, xxv, xxvi, 61, 65, 67–69, 74. *See also* Allen's persona; art, cinema; Borscht Belt; death; Farrow, Mia; Farrow/Previn scandal; gentile women; Jewish mother; Jewish women; Jewishness; Judaism, religion; love relationships; New York City; Previn, Soon-Yi; schlemiel; *individual films, plays, prose*
Allen's persona, xix, xxiv, 3, 4, 13, 16, 17, 19, 122–38, 143, 144, 148, 179, 220, 230; and aging, xxvvii, 25, 26, 29, 166, 205, 251; in Allen's plays, 235, 236, 243, 245–47, 250; Christian-Jewish dialectic, 100–118; European phase, xxiii, xxv, 60, 74; New York Jew, xii, xiv, xv, xxviii, 29, 59, 151, 182, 235, 236. *See also* schlemiel; *individual films, plays, prose*
Annie Hall (1977), ix, xiv, xx, xxiv, 9, 55, 79, 106, 193, 205; and Allen's persona, 3, 26; anti-Semitism, 148, 152; box office, 4; critical reaction, 4, 60; food, 153, 216, 217, 220, 222, 223, 228, 230; gentiles, 144, 152, 160, 164, 177; gentile women, 3, 26, 148, 149, 152, 156, 217; Holocaust, 162; Jewish humor, 148, 175; Jewish mother, 152–54; Judaism, religion, xv, xxvii, 171–77, 180–83, 186, 220; love relationships, 43, 79, 143, 198, 217; other Allen film references to, 27, 28, 30; schlemiel, 79, 81, 95, 98, 242; self-hatred, 174; Yiddish, 154, 172
Another Woman (1988), 31n10; and box office, 11, 60; critical reaction, 11, 60; serious films, 5, 11, 59, 60, 112, 249; "WASP women" trilogy, 11, 59
anti-Semitism: and Hollywood, xiv, 104, 210n2; paranoia about, 27, 103, 115, 184, 234n41; practice of, 7, 120n21, 157, 204, 217, 247. *See also individual films*
Anything Else (2003), x, 24–28, 30, 31n24, 66, 123, 230; and anti-Semitism, 230; death, 140n24; food, 230; gentile women, 26, 66; Holocaust, 162; Jewish humor, 28; Judaism, religion, 26–28; schlemiel, 66
Arendt, Hannah, xxvi, 82, 84–86, 88–90, 92, 93, 96, 97
art, cinema, xv, xvi, 3, 4, 43, 54, 71, 167; and Farrow/Previn scandal, xxiii; Holocaust, xxvi, 79–98; morality, 20, 22, 23. *See also individual films, plays*

Bananas (1971), xiv, 165, 193; and food, 151; Jewish mother, 150, 151; Jewish

268 Index

women, 151, 152, 155, 156, 157; parody, 143; schlemiel, 81, 89, 101, 156, 157
Bellow, Saul, xii, xvii, xviii, 40, 44, 55n7
Bergman, Ingmar, 7, 32n40, 61, 112, 211, 245, 255; and Fellini, 3, 6, 8, 19, 26, 32–33n50
Borscht Belt (Catskills), xii, xiv, 32n40, 151, 154, 156, 203, 217. *See also individual films, plays*
Broadway Danny Rose (1984): and art, cinema, xix, 4, 123, 127, 128; Borscht Belt, xix, 4, 5, 9, 123, 125, 126, 138, 205; comedy film, 5, 112; food, 216; Jewish humor, 126; Jewishness, 39, 64, 126, 134; Judaism, religion, 9, 124, 127, 128; love relationships, 126, 135, 136; magic, 127; schlemiel, 9; Yiddish, 9, 39, 124
Brooks, Mel, xxii, 216, 223, 243, 248, 250–52
Bullets Over Broadway (1994): and Allen surrogates, 114, 116; art, cinema, 23, 114, 202; blackface, 205; death, 200, 202, 206, 207; Farrow/Previn scandal, 22, 201, 202; food, 231; gangsters, 206; Judaism, religion, 205; show business, 200, 202, 204, 205, 211, 242; women, 191, 192, 195, 197, 207; Yiddish, 204

Casino Royale (Val Guest and Ken Hughes, 1967), 106, 107
"Cassandra's Dream" (poem, Edouard Roditi), 53, 54
Cassandra's Dream (2007): and art, cinema, 49; death, 57n37; Dostoevsky, xxv; European phase, xxv, 24, 37, 58, 73, 74, 116; existentialism, 69, 70; Farrow/Previn scandal, 20; Judaism, religion, 37, 47–51; Greek drama, myth, xxiv, xxv, 38, 46, 47, 49, 51, 52, 54, 67–70; morality, xxiv, 20, 37, 38, 65, 70; social class, 59, 61, 65, 67, 69, 70, 74
Celebrity (1998), 21, 29, 114, 115, 214; and art, cinema 22; and Judaism, religion, 224; love relationships, 22
Central Park West (play, on *Death Defying Acts* bill, 1995), 241, 254
Chaplin, Charlie, xiii, 88, 89, 125, 243, 258n17
Charney, Dov, 171, 173–75, 183; and American Apparel billboard, 171–73, 176, 186
Christianity, xviii, 135, 218; and Christonormativity, 102, 105–6, 107, 108, 110, 111, 113, 115–17, 118–19n11, 119n12; food, xxviii, 217–22, 233n24; gentile (goy, WASP), xiv, xvi, xvii, xxvi, xxviii, 138, 150, 151, 156, 157, 168, 173, 176, 181, 199, 210n2; Jewish interplay with, 10, 11, 39, 100–118, 118n1, 119n12, 156, 216; Judaism, religion, xxvi, 39–42, 46, 62, 65, 92, 105–6, 121n31, 184, 215, 221, 228; WASP drama, 10, 11, 59, 113, 116. *See also* gentile women; masculinity
Crimes and Misdemeanors (1989), xviii, 4, 28, 31n10, 38–40, 122, 205, 216, 222; and art, cinema, 11, 12; critical reaction, 11; death, 40; Dostoevsky, 41, 45, 61–63; European phase relation, 58, 73, 112, 114; food, 216, 222; gentile women, 12, 112, 113; Greek drama, myth, 38, 42, 44–51, 69; Holocaust, 12, 40, 64; Jewish women, xxvii, 190–92, 196, 200, 206; Judaism, religion, 9, 12, 37–44, 51, 62–65, 196, 197, 240; love relationships, 11, 12, 38, 40, 42, 64, 67, 73; morality, xxi, xxiv, 12, 20, 37, 64, 65, 68, 208; Nazis, 10;

schlemiel, 38, 44, 45; seriocomedy, 5, 9, 11, 14, 60, 197, 202, 209, 240, 249
critical reaction (to Allen's work), xxi–xxiii, 9, 12, 161; and European phase, 21, 161; Farrow/Previn scandal, 13, 16, 17, 20, 161, 187; lack of originality, 6, 7, 194; self-hatred, xiii, 4, 18; serious films, 11, 60; women, xxi, xxii, 187, 188–89n9. *See also individual films, plays, prose*
Curse of the Jade Scorpion, The (2001), 23, 116, 122, 123, 133; and gentile women, 21; magic, 133

death: in Allen's plays, 241, 242; and Dostoevsky, 40–42; Freud, xvii; Jewish view of, xviii; Edouard Roditi, 53, 57n37. *See also individual films, plays*
Death (play, 1975), 241
Death Knocks (play, 1968), 241
Deconstructing Harry (1997), ix, xviii, 17, 115, 122, 129, 205, 209, 211; and anti–Semitism, 148; art, cinema, 167; box office, 20; critical reaction, xiii, xxiii, 20, 60, 172; food, 215, 224, 226, 228, 232; gentile women, 17, 149; Holocaust, 19; Jewish humor, 19, 148, 172, 184, 232; Jewish women, xxvii, 143, 145, 148, 149, 160, 162, 164, 167; Judaism, religion, 18, 147, 172, 173, 177, 178, 181, 183–87, 195, 215, 222, 228; love relationships, 149, 160, 172, 178, 179, 184; Philip Roth, xx, 17, 115; self-hatred, 5, 15, 17, 18, 181, 182, 232
Desser, David, x, xv, xxii, xiii, 5, 6, 10, 11, 71, 105, 110, 113, 216, 221
Doane, Marry Ann, 185–87, 189n15
Don't Drink the Water (Howard Morris, 1969), 16, 253

Don't Drink the Water (play, 1966), 16, 241, 251; and Allen's persona, 252; critical reaction, 253; influences on, 255; Jewish humor, 242, 252, 254; Jewish mother, 248, 250; Jewishness, 237, 256; New York City, 252; schlemiel, 252
Don't Drink the Water (TV movie, 1994), 16, 253
Dostoevsky, Fyodor, x, xxv, 11, 41, 42, 44, 45, 61–63, 65

Everyone Says I love You (1996), 231; and gentile women, 17
Everything You Always Wanted to Know About Sex* (*But Were Afraid to Ask) (1972), 114, 230, 234n33; and food, 229; Judaism, religion, 229

Fading Giggolo (John Turturro, 2013), 139n4; and Judaism, religion, 175–76
Farrow, Mia: and *Alice*, 14, 131, 227; *Broadway Danny Rose*, 9, 39, 125; *Crimes and Misdemeanors*, 12, 112, 191, 200; family of, 12, 13, 14, 21, 30; *Hannah and Her Sisters*, 9–10; *Husbands and Wives*, 12, 158, 159, 161, 191, 226; "Oedipus Wrecks," 163; *Purple Rose of Cairo*, 193, 195, 211n19; *Rosemary's Baby*, 13; *Shadows and Fog*, 16, 131. *See also* Farrow/Previn scandal
Farrow/Previn scandal, ix, xxi, xxiv, xxvi, xxviii, 16, 19, 20, 114, 155, 159, 174, 183, 187, 188–89n9, 215, 231, 235–39, 248; and Farrow's relation to, 12–14, 16, 21, 29, 30, 113, 169n20, 174, 192, 194, 228; Previn's relation to, 12, 14, 29, 161, 179. *See also individual films, plays*
Fellini, Federico, 3, 4, 6, 8, 19, 26, 32–33n50, 245. *See also* Bergman, Ingmar

feminism, xxi, xxiii, 105, 151, 152, 166, 172, 177, 178, 184, 185, 187
Floating Light Bulb, The (play, 1982), 241, 251, 254; and Jewish humor, 254; Jewish mother, 249; Judaism, religion, 250; magic, 130, 136, 249; New York City, 249; schlemiel, 249; Tennessee Williams influence, 130, 249
Friedman, Lester, xv, 5, 6, 10, 11, 71, 113, 210n2, 216, 221
Freud, Sigmund, xiii, xix, xvii, 8, 29, 79, 102, 103, 107, 164, 172, 186, 217
Front, The (Martin Ritt, 1976), xix, 3, 20, 106, 119n19

gentile women (shiksas), xi, xii, xviii, xix, xxiv, 4, 25, 143, 144, 148, 150, 160, 167; and gentile mother, 155; "WASP women" trilogy, 5, 11, 59. *See also individual films, plays*
Girgus, Sam B., xix, xx, xxii, xiii, 7, 11, 17
God (play, 1975), 241
Greek drama, myth, x, xii, xix, 84, 169n16; and Judaism, religion, 11, 37–54, 56n29. *See also individual films*

Hannah and Her Sisters (1986), 4, 193; and art, cinema, 10; critical reaction, 58, 60; death, 112; Holocaust, 19; Judaism, religion, 9, 10, 19, 39, 64, 71, 112, 223; seriocomedy, 5, 9, 11, 14, 22, 60, 71, 73, 112, 167, 249; women, 195
"Hasidic Tales, with a Guide to Their Interpretation by the Noted Scholar" (short story, 2007), 86, 87
Hebrew: and food, 221, 22, 228, 230; Greek drama, myth relation, xxiv, 37–54, 55n14, 56n29, 68, 70; language, 55n3, 83, 171; prophets, 53; school, 255, 256. *See also* Judaism, religion

Heine, Heinrich, xvi, xvii, 8, 84, 85, 88, 89
Hemingway, Ernest, xviii, 21, 94, 100, 102
Hirsch, Foster, ix–xiii, xvi
Hollywood: and films/film business, xx, xxviii, 21, 24, 26, 28, 49, 191, 193, 194, 197, 198, 203–206, 221, 253; Jews, 191, 205, 210n2, 254; masculinity, 103, 105, 108
Hollywood Ending (2000), 21, 23, 31n24, 123, 129; and food, 222, 224, 231; gentile women, 23; Jewish humor, 23; Jewish women, 160; love relationships, 93; schlemiel, xxvi, 81, 90, 92, 93, 95–98, 108, 116
Holocaust (Final Solution, Shoah), ix, x, xv, xvii, xviii, xxvi, 53, 84; and "After Auschwitz," xxvi, 82, 96–98
Honeymoon Motel (play, on *Relatively Speaking* bill, 2012), 241, 250, 251, 254; and Allen's persona, 242; Borscht Belt, xxviii, 242; critical reaction, 237, 239–40, 248, 253; Farrow/Previn scandal, 20, 238; Jewish humor, 237–40, 254; Jewishness, 256; Judaism, religion, 175, 237, 240, 242; New York City, 243–44; schlemiel, 237
Husbands and Wives (1992): and art, cinema, 132; Farrow/Previn scandal, 12, 14; food, 225, 226; gentile women, 12, 148, 160; Jewish identity, 114, 119; Jewish women, 42, 116, 143, 157–62, 167, 168, 191, 195, 200, 201; Judaism, religion, 9, 199; love relationships, 157–59

Interiors (1979): and art, cinema, 155; box office, 60; critical reaction, 4, 60; death, 155; Jewish mother, 154, 155, 168; Jewish women, xxii, xxvii, 5, 144;

magic, 155; serious films, xxii, 3–5, 59, 60, 112, 168, 249; "WASP women" trilogy, 5, 11, 59

Jewish humor (comedy), ix, x, xiii, 3, 8, 10, 79–82, 98, 115, 160, 167; and American literary influences on, xvi, xix, xx, xxi, 150, 255; Arendt's theory on, 84, 88, 97; Christian drama contrasted with, 10, 11, 112, 113, 117; Heine's influence on, xvi; New York City, 193, 252–54; New York phase, 58, 59. *See also* Borscht Belt; Holocaust; schlemiel; Yiddish: humor; *individual films, plays, prose*
Jewish mother, xviii, xix, 129, 143, 153, 154, 163, 164, 167, 168, 221, 246, 247; and Yiddishe mama/*Yiddishe momme*, xviii, 150, 216, 245, 246. *See also individual films, plays*
Jewishness: and chameleon complex, xvii, xxiv, 4, 6–8; diaspora, xiii, xv, xvi, 79; emancipation period, 7, 215, 218; Eastern European/Ashkenazi: xv, xvii, 4, 8, 84, 85, 148, 153, 168n2, 218, 224, 240, 243, 244, 250; food, xxviii, 162, 215–32, 224, 229, 248; Israel, xiii, xv, 18, 23, 28, 46, 146, 83, 234n29; Jewish New Wave, 105, 112, 114; *Menschlichkeit*, xvii, 9, 221. *See also* anti-Semitism; Borsht Belt; Christianity; gentile women; Holocaust; Jewish humor; Jewish mother; Jewish women; Judaism, religion; masculinity; New York City; pariah; schlemiel; self-hatred; Yiddish; *individual films, plays, prose*
Jewish women, xi, xii, xvii, 5, 143–68, 172–88, 190–209; and Jewish American princess (JAP), x, xi, 149, 152, 157, 162, 167. *See also* Jewish mother; women; *individual films, plays*
Johansson, Scarlett, xxvii, 24, 25, 59, 66, 116, 134, 164, 207–9, 227, 230
Judaism, religion, viii, xiii, xv, xvi, 6–8, 51, 56n25, 65, 71, 83, 87, 98, 119n12, 124, 143, 167, 177; in Allen's plays, 250, 251; and God, 9, 10, 12, 18, 26, 38–43, 47–50, 55n14, 62, 112, 127, 128, 184, 196, 197, 215, 222, 228, 229, 240; Hasidim, xviii, 86, 172, 173, 175–76, 178, 181, 183–88; Hebrew Bible, xv, 9, 11, 45, 46, 48, 50, 54, 55n6, 56n25, 68–70, 83, 230; Jewish religious women, 172, 173, 177, 178, 181, 184, 185–87, 195; Orthodox, xvii, 33, 156, 180, 228, 235, 240, 242, 245, 255, 256; rabbis, xiii, 12, 38, 40, 44, 56n25, 64, 87, 175, 184, 196, 199, 224, 229, 237, 240. *See also individual films, plays, prose*

Kafka, Franz, x, xiii, xvi, xvii, xix, xxxn30, 5, 6, 8, 14, 17, 18, 29, 46, 88
Keaton, Diane, 3, 30, 25, 26, 108, 109, 135, 198, 217, 226, 228
Kinne, Thomas, x, xv–xvii, xx, xxi
"Kugelmass Episode, The" (short story, 1977), 193, 210n7

Lax, Eric, 60, 122, 129, 135, 137, 256
Lee, Sander, 37, 42, 64, 65
London, England: and *Cassandra's Dream*, 67; Jack the Ripper, 15, 295; *Match Point*, 47, 60, 65, 207, 209; *Scoop*, 24, 59, 123, 134, 138, 164, 195, 209, 224, 227; setting for Allen films, xxv, 24, 58, 65, 67, 107, 215; *You Will Meet a Tall Dark Stranger*, 70; *What's New Pussycat?*, 107

Los Angeles, xx, 27, 30, 171
Love and Death (1975), xiv, xvi, xvii, 81, 101; and food, 226, 228
love relationships, xi, xxv, xxviii, 43, 134, 143, 160. *See also individual films, plays, prose*

magic, xxvi, 133, 137; Allen's practice of, 32n40, 127, 129, 137. *See also individual films, plays*
Mandelstam, Osip, 46, 51, 52, 56n30
Manhattan (1979), 3, 22, 193, 199; and art, cinema, 71; box office, 4; critical reaction, 4; food, 218, 226–28; gentile women, 13, 156, 162; Jewish humor, 4, 60; Jewish women, xxvii, 9, 22, 156, 160, 190, 246; love relationships, 43, 71, 73, 116, 242; morality, 37, 64, 201; schlemiel, 242
Manhattan Murder Mystery (1993), 59, 136, 191, 192, 194, 196–200, 207, 208, 209n1; and gentile women, 25; Jewish women, 25
Marx, Groucho, 79, 115, 116, 121n35, 204, 255
Marx, Karl, 8, 39, 111, 114
Marx Brothers, xiv, 10, 22, 71, 121n35, 167, 206
masculinity, 12, 100, 102, 117, 144, 176, 189n19; and Christian norms, xxvi, 101, 103, 105–12, 114, 116, 157, 169n18; Jewish norms, xxvii, 105–7, 110–13, 149, 186, 188n8
Match Point: and *Cassandra's Dream*, 59, 65, 69, 70, 73, 74; *Crimes and Misdemeanors*, 37–46, 62, 63, 69, 190, 191, 208, 209; critical reaction, 60; death, 57n37, 190, 191, 196, 208; Dostoevsky, 45, 61, 63; European phase, xxv, 24, 47, 58, 65, 67, 116;
existentialism, 61; Greek drama, myth, 38, 45, 46; Judaism, religion, 27; morality, xxiv, 20, 38, 68; schlemiel, 65; *Scoop*, 209; serious films, xxiv, 60; thriller, 194, 207
Melinda and Melinda (2004), 114, 115, 133; and food, 217, 218, 227; magic, 133
Midnight in Paris (2011), xviii, 129; and art, cinema, xviii, 108, 117; box office, 101, 248; critical reaction, xxiii, 20, 29, 33n54, 101, 248; death, 100, 101; European phase, 58, 218, 231, 248; food, 218; Farrow/Previn scandal, 21, 29; Jewish humor, 100, 102, 115, 117; love relationships, 60, 67; schlemiel, xxvi, 21, 81, 90, 94–98, 100, 108, 114, 116, 117
Midsummer Night's Sex Comedy, A (1982), 4, 5, 129, 131; and food, 230; magic, 131
Mighty Aphrodite (1995), 17, 21, 22, 123, 195; and gentile women, 17; Greek drama, myth, 22
Miller, Arthur, xxi, 205, 255

New York City, xx, xxiv, 3, 26–28, 54, 147, 156, 162, 163, 193; and the Bronx, 204; Brooklyn, 9, 44, 130, 134, 152, 209, 212n24, 222, 224, 241, 249; Carnegie Deli, 125–27, 129, 138, 216; film phase, xxii, xxiii, xxv, xxviii, 23, 24, 58, 59, 61; food, 223–25, 227, 231; Greenwich Village, 109, 200, 201, 218; Jewishness, 58, 74, 223–25, 231, 236, 244, 252, 255; Jew York (City), xii, xiv, xix, 6, 9, 215, 218, 253; Long Island, 237; Manhattan, xi, 9, 22, 24, 92, 93, 125, 131, 136, 171, 193, 218, 227; schlemiel, xxv, 3, 4, 25, 29, 60, 66, 90, 92. *See also individual films, plays*

"Oedipus Wrecks" (part of *New York Stories*, 1989), xi, 5, 129, 136, 167, 205, 206; and food, 164; Jewish mother, 9, 163, 164, 246; Jewish women, 163, 164, 167–68; love relationships, 136; magic, 136, 163; schlemiel, 163

Old Saybrook (play, 1995, on *Writer's Block* bill, 2003), 16, 241, 254

pariah (outsider), 8, 61, 65, 106, 156, 160, 204, 235, 236, 243, 247, 254; and Arendt, 82, 84, 88–90, 92, 93–96, 98; and parvenu/arriviste, xix, 7, 84, 88, 89, 226

Perelman, S. J., xvi, xx, xxi, 255

Picking Up the Pieces (Alfonso Arau, 2000), 16, 24

Play It Again, Sam (film, Herbert Ross, 1972), 3, 10, 30, 108, 117; and art, cinema, 108, 117; schlemiel, 108, 237

Play It Again, Sam (play, 1971), 241, 250; and Allen's persona, 237, 242, 248, 251; critical reaction, 242; Jewish humor, 250; schlemiel, 108, 237, 242, 247, 251

Portnoy's Complaint (film, Ernest Lehman, 1972), 115

Portnoy's Complaint (novel, Philip Roth, 1969), xx, xii, xviii–xx, 115, 118–19n11

Previn, Soon-Yi: and children of, xxxiiin84, 26, 30. *See also* Farrow/Previn scandal

Production Code Administration, 204, 206, 210n2

Purple Rose of Cairo, The (1985), 5, 43, 112, 189n15, 192, 193, 195, 205, 211n19; and food, 228

Questel, Mae, 163, 164, 246

Radio Days: 5, 9, 163; and food, 216, 229; Jewish mother, 170n26; Judaism, religion, 216, 229

"Retribution" (short story, 1980), 138; and critical reaction, 13

Riverside Drive (play, on *Writer's Block* bill, 2003), 241; and Allen's persona, 254; schlemiel, 254

Roditi, Edouard, xxv, 46, 51–54, 68

Roth, Philip, x, xii, xviii–xx, 17, 115, 118–19n11, 150, 245, 247. *See also Portnoy's Complaint*

Ruben-Dorsky, Jeffrey, ix, xxi–xxiv, 9, 11, 19, 22, 39, 121n32, 128, 147

Schiller, Friederich, 80, 85

schlemiel, xii, xxi, xxiv, 3, 10, 79–98, 100–118, 122–38, 143, 150, 239, 258n17; Charlie Chaplin as, 88, 89; Eastern European–Yiddish tradition of, xxv, 84, 85, 245, 246, 258n17; Hannah Arendt's theory of, 82, 84–86, 89, 90; "Hassidic Tales," 86, 87; Heinrich Heine's development of, 85, 89; New York City version of, xxv, xii, 3, 66; Philip Roth's version of, 118n11, 247; Ruth Wisse's theory of, xii, 83, 84, 86. *See also* Jewish humor; *individual films, plays, prose*

Schmendrick, or the Comical Wedding (play, Avrom Goldfafn, 1877), 245–47, 251

Scoop (2006), 8, 31n24, 116, 123, 138; and anti-Semitism, 134; death, 59, 60, 61, 136, 195, 209; European film phase, xxv, 24, 59–61, 65, 207; food, 224, 227; Jewish humor, 224; Judaism, religion, 24, 123, 134, 135; love relationships, 25, 64, 165, 166; magic, xxvi, 24, 25, 124, 127, 128, 134–37, 164; schlemiel, xxvi,

24, 59, 166; women, xxvii, xxviii, 24, 25, 28, 144, 163–66, 168, 191, 192, 194, 195, 208, 209, 210–11n8
"Scrolls, The" (short story, 2007), 87
Second Hand Memory, A (play, 2004), 241, 254
self-hatred, xiii, 7, 10, 105, 115, 187, 201, 256; and Kafka, xiii, 14, 18. *See also individual films, plays*
September (1987): and box office, 11, 60; critical reaction to, 11, 60; serious films, 5, 11, 112, 60, 112, 249; "WASP women" trilogy," 11, 59
Shadows and Fog (1992), ix, 5, 14; and art, 132; expressionist, 14, 15; Farrow/Previn scandal, 14, 16; Holocaust, 15; Jack the Ripper, 15; Kafka, xvii, 5, 14; magic, 33n61, 71, 74, 131, 132, 138; Nazis, 15; schlemiel, 81; self-hatred, 15
shiksas. *See gentile women*
Simon, Neil, 16, 243, 245, 250, 251
Singer, I. B., xii, 86
Sleeper (1973): and anti-Semitism, 109; food, 216; gentile women, 9, 111; Jewishness, xiv; Judaism, religion, 110; masculinity, xxvi, 109–11, 114; schlemiel, 101, 111; Yiddish, 109
Small Time Crooks (2000), 20, 21, 23, 88, 116, 123, 226, 228, 231; and food, 216, 226, 228
Stardust Memories (1980), xvi, xviii, 4; and art, cinema, 129, 130; and comedy/tragedy conflict, 5, 6, 10, 28, 239; *Deconstructing Harry*, 17, 18, 211n17; gentile women, xviii; magic, 124, 129; schlemiel, 71; self-hatred, 4, 211n17; self-reflexivity, 3, 4
Stora-Sander, Judith, 148, 157, 160, 168
Sunshine Boys, The (TV movie, John Erman, 1996), 16, 253

Sweet and Lowdown (1999), 21–23, 121n37, 129; and art, cinema, 22; and love relationships, 22

Take the Money and Run (1969), xiv, 4, 9, 21, 32n31, 81, 101, 193, 240; and Judaism, religion, 175
To Rome with Love (2012), xxvi, 13, 29, 30, 31n24, 43, 58, 116, 121n37, 123, 211n10, 218; and box office, 29; critical reaction, 29; food, 218; schlemiel, xxvii

Vicky Cristina Barcelona (2008), 33n54, 58, 121n33; and food, 218, 230
"Vodka Ad" joke: and schlemiel, 83–86, 96, 97

Whatever Works: and food, 226, 230; gentile women, 24; Jewish humor, 98; love relationships, 24, 43, 73, 93; magic, 136; New York City, 24, 59; schlemiel, xxvi, 81, 90, 92, 95–98, 116
What's New Pussycat? (Clive Donner, 1965): and parody, 106–7; schlemiel, xxvi, 106–7; self-reflexivity, 106–7
What's Up, Tiger Lily? (1966), 136; and food, xxii, 216, 225–26; Jewish mother, 150; parody, 143, 150; women, xxii, 13, 143, 225; Yiddish, 150
Wild Man Blues (Barbara Kopple, 1997), 16
Williams, Linda, 172, 173, 188
Williams, Tennessee, 110, 130, 249, 255
Wilson, Owen, x, xvi, 21, 94, 95, 100–102, 114, 117, 118n1, 236
Wisse, Ruth, xii, 83–86
women, xix, xxi, xxii, xxvii, xxviii, 13, 22, 29, 42, 79, 103, 105, 108, 190–209, 211n17, 225, 251. *See also* gentile

women; Jewish mother; Jewish women; *individual films, plays, prose*

Writer's Block (playbill for two Allen one–acts, 2003), 241

Yiddish, xviii, xix; and Borscht Belt, 242; cinema, 4; Dov Charney, 171; food, 216, 230; humor, xiv, 80, 83, 85–87, 150, 151, 236, 243, 245, 246, 256; literature, 87; schlemiel, xxv, 3, 80, 85, 86; theater, xxix, 51, 156, 235, 236, 241–48, 256; Yiddishisms, 110, 124, 151; Yiddishkeit, xxviii, 218. *See also individual films, plays*

You Will Meet a Tall Dark Stranger (2010), xxv, 33n55, 59, 65, 70, 71, 73, 74, 114; and art, cinema, 72; magic, 71

Zelig (1983), x, xvii, xxi, 4–6, 8, 81, 193, 228, 245; and anti-Semitism, 6; food, 228; Judaism, religion, 175, 183, 229; love relationships, 70–72, 74; and Nazis, xvii, 6